THE LAW
— OF —
EMPLOYEES' PROVIDENT FUNDS

Disclaimer

While every effort has been made to avoid any mistake or omission, this publication is being sold on the condition and understanding that neither the author nor the publishers would be liable in any manner to any person by reason of any mistake or omission in this publication or for any action taken or omitted to be taken on advice rendered or accepted based on this work. The information in the book is for general application only. It does not offer legal advice for any specific cases, and specific legitimate questions should be referred to an advocate/counsel for help. The author wrote this book in his personal capacity and the views expressed are the opinion of the author and does not necessarily represent the views or practices of the organisation he belongs to.

THE LAW OF EMPLOYEES' PROVIDENT FUNDS

A Case-Law Perspective

CHIDAMBARAM RAMESH

ISBN-13: 978-1983893346
ISBN-10: 198389334X

This book has been published with all reasonable efforts taken to make the material error-free after the consent of the author. No part of this book shall be used, reproduced in any manner whatsoever without written permission from the author, except in the case of brief quotations embodied in critical articles and reviews.

The Author of this book is solely responsible and liable for its content including but not limited to the views, representations, descriptions, statements, information, opinions and references ["Content"]. The Content of this book shall not constitute or be construed or deemed to reflect the opinion or expression of the Publisher or Editor. Neither the Publisher nor Editor endorse or approve the Content of this book or guarantee the reliability, accuracy or completeness of the Content published herein and do not make any representations or warranties of any kind, express or implied, including but not limited to the implied warranties of merchantability, fitness for a particular purpose. The Publisher and Editor shall not be liable whatsoever for any errors, omissions, whether such errors or omissions result from negligence, accident, or any other cause or claims for loss or damages of any kind, including without limitation, indirect or consequential loss or damage arising out of use, inability to use, or about the reliability, accuracy or sufficiency of the information contained in this book.

To the members of the judicial fraternity who have expanded the social welfare legislations by liberal interpretation and espoused the cause of working class.

Contents

Preface		*ix*
Abbreviations		*xi*
References to Other Acts		*xv*
Chapter I	Introduction	1
Chapter II	Interpretation of Statutes	10
Chapter III	Application of the Act	18
Chapter IV	Definitions	30
Chapter V	Departments/Branches and Composite Establishments	66
Chapter VI	Employee-Employer Relationship	75
Chapter VII	Liability to Contribute	86
Chapter VIII	Central Board of Trustees	91
Chapter IX	Determination of Dues	94
Chapter X	EPF Appellate Tribunal	117
Chapter XI	Levy of Penal Damages and Interest	122
Chapter XII	Protection Against Attachment	149
Chapter XIII	Priority of Payment over other Debts	157
Chapter XIV	Recovery of Arrears	165
Chapter XV	Inspectors	210
Chapter XVI	Penal Provisions	214
Chapter XVII	Exemption	240
Chapter XVIII	Transferor-Transferee Liabilities	252
Chapter XIX	Public Servants and their Protection	258
Chapter XX	Schedule Head Entries	263
Chapter XXI	Nature and Scope of Writ Jurisdiction	274
Chapter XXII	Schemes Framed under the Act	280
Appendix	*Controlled Industry*	*291*
References		*295*
Index		*297*

Preface

A statute is an edict of the legislature, and interpreting the laws is confined to courts of law. In the course of time, courts have evolved an enormous storehouse of judicial explanations and theories to shed light in construing or interpreting the law. If the words of the statute are in themselves precise and unambiguous, there can be no problem in understanding those words in their natural and ordinary sense. In other occasions, we need the light which the judicial lantern sheds on the issues for a proper understanding of the concepts and topics. Courts follow the doctrine of precedent (*stare decisis*) to ensure uniformity in the application of law. Thus, judicial decisions make up one of the most important sources of legal authority.

The saying of former Chief Minister of Tamilnadu C.N. Annadurai that law is a dark room where the lawyer's argument is a lamp, is sure and worthy of full acceptance. However, those who represent the employers or other parties before the quasi-judicial authorities and tribunals need not be lawyers. It is therefore essential that there should be a legal treatise which will serve as a guide to those who have had no legal training. This need has been supplied by the author's industry and research. This title has been written with a straightforward aim in mind—to document critical judicial interpretations relating to the Employees' Provident Funds and Miscellaneous Provisions Act, 1952 in a wide variety of situations.

The book annotates the statute section by section from the legal standpoint and offers a systematic exposition of the Act in the form of a narrative, arranged under relevant chapters and topical headings. It traces the legislative history of the Act and fulfils the long-felt need for an introductory study of the Act. The analytical sub-headings of the chapters, marginal notes and index at the end of the book will serve as excellent aids for easy reference. A case citation describes the identity of the parties concerned, the legal reporter in which the case can be found, the volume, page number and the year in which the case was decided. Citations will be useful to those who wish to conduct further study on the matter.

I have collected as much material as has been accessible intending to publishing such content in one volume. This work which provides within a reasonable compass the relevant legal information should be of great help to all who have to deal with the Employees' Provident Funds and Miscellaneous Provisions Act, 1952. The busy legal practitioners and the Provident Fund Commissioners should find it useful as it would relieve them of their hours of work.

Preface

Finally, a word of caution here. Relying on a short report instead of getting a fuller description is a poor use of case law. The drawing up of the extracts by a right selection of relevant passages from judgments covering thousands of pages inevitably involves subjective choices, and my work here is limited to them. Hence, I recommend the readers to go through the entire contents of the relevant judgments for a better and brighter understanding.

I record my thanks to the officers and colleagues in the Employees' Provident Fund Organisation (EPFO) who encouraged my scholarly interest and provided much of knowledge by way of many hours of frank conversations and discussions. In preparing the final manuscript for publication, my wife Bhuvana Narayanan did the proofreading and final touches.

Comments and suggestions for amendments and corrections are gratefully received.

Chidambaram Ramesh
Email: c.ramesh@yahoo.com
Vellore
2nd October 2017

Abbreviations

The following are the abbreviations used for the legislations and legal journals cited in this book.

A.C.	(Appeal Cases)
A.D.(S.C.)	Apex Decisions (Supreme Court)
AIR (N.O.C)	All India Reporter (Notes of Cases)
AIR (N.S.C)	All India Reporter (Notes of Supreme Court Cases)
AIR (S.C.W)	All India Reporter (Supreme Court Weekly)
All.C.J.	Allahabad Civil Journal
All.Cr.C	Allahabad Criminal Cases
All.Cr.R.	Allahabad Criminal Reports
All.L.J.	Allahabad Law Journal
All.L.R	Allahabad Law Reports
All.L.T.	Allahabad Law Times.
All.Ren.Cas.	Allahabad Rent Cases
Andh.L.T.	Andhra Law Times
Andh.W.R.	Andhra Weekly Reporter
Art.	Article
Bank C.	Bank Cases
Bank C.L.R	Banking Commercial Law Reporter
Bank J.	Banker's Journal
Bank L.J.	Banking Law Judgment
Bank L.R	Banking Law Reporter
BLJR	Bihar Law Journal Reports
C.L.C.	Corporate Law Cases
Cal.Cri.L.R.	Calcutta Criminal Law Reports
Cal L.J.	Calcutta Law Journal

Abbreviations

Cal.L.T.	Calcutta Law Times
Cal.W.N.(D.R.)	Calcutta Weekly Notes
CLR	Calcutta Law Reporter
Com.Cas.	Company Cases
Cri.C.J.	Criminal Court Judgment
Cri.L.C.	Criminal Law Cases
Cri.L.J.	Criminal Law Journal
D.B	Division Bench
D.L.T.	Delhi Law Times
EPF Act	Employees' Provident Funds and Miscellaneous Provisions Act, 1952
E.P.W	Economic and Political Weekly
F.B	Full Bench
FJR	Indian Factories Journal
FLR	Indian Factories & Labour Reports
Guj.L.R.	Gujarat Law Reporter
JT.	Judgment Today
Kar.L.J	Karnataka Law Journal
Ker.L.J.(Tax)	Kerala Law Journal
Ker.L.R.	Kerala Law Reports
Lab.A.C.	Labour Appeal Cases
Lab IC	Labour and Industrial Cases
Lab.I.C.(N.O.C.)	Labour and Industrial Cases (Notes of Cases)
L.L.J.	Labour Law Journal
L.L.N	Labour Law Notes
L.L.R	Labour Law Reporter
Lab.I.C.	Labour and Industrial Cases
Mah.L.J.	Maharashtra Law Journal
M.P.L.J	Madhya Pradesh Law Journal
P.& H.	Punjab and Haryana
P.	Page

Abbreviations

P.C.	Privy Council
P.F.	Provident Fund
PLJR	Patna Law Journal Reports
R.P.F.C	Regional Provident Fund Commissioner
R.A.J.	Recent Apex Judgments
S.C.	Supreme Court
S.C.J.	Supreme Court Journal
S.C.R.	Supreme Court Reports
S.L.T.	Supreme Laws Today
S.R.J.	Supreme Reported Judgments
S.C.C.(Cri.)	Supreme Court Cases (Criminal)
S.	Section
Tax L.D.	Tax Law Decisions.
W.L.R.	Weekly Law Reporter
Writ L.R	Writ Law Reporter

References to Other Acts

- Advocates Act, 1961
- Agricultural Refinance Corporation Act, 1963 (10 of 1963)
- Apprentices Act, 1961
- Banking Companies (Acquisition and Transfer of Undertaking) Act, 1970 (5 of 1970)
- Chartered Accountants Act 1949
- Cine Workers and Cinema Theatre Workers (Regulation and Employment) Act (50 of 1981)
- Code of Civil Procedure, 1908
- Code of Criminal Procedure, 1898 (5 of 1898)
- Code of Criminal Procedure, 1973 (2 of 1974)
- Companies Act, 1956 (1 of 1956)
- Cooperative Societies Act, 1912 (2 of 1912)
- Costs and Works Accountants Act 1959
- Factories Act 1948
- Guardians and Wards Act, 1890 (8 of 1890)
- Income Tax Act, 1961 (43 of 1961)
- Indian Income Tax Act, 1922 (11 of 1922)
- Indian Lunacy Act, 1912 (4 of 1912)
- Indian Penal Code, 1860 (45 of 1860)
- Indian Trusts Act, 1882 (11 of 1882)
- Industrial Development Bank of India Act, 1964 (18 of 1964)
- Industrial Disputes Act, 1947 (14 of 1947)
- Industrial Finance Corporation Act, 1948
- Information Technology Act, 2000 (21 of 2000)
- Life Insurance Corporation Act, 1956 (31 of 1956)
- National Trust for Welfare of Persons with Autism, Cerebral Palsy, Mental Retardation and Multiple Disabilities Act, 1999
- Persons with Disabilities (Equal Opportunities, Protection of Right and Full Participation) Act, 1995
- Pondicherry (Laws) Regulation, 1963 (7 of 1963)

References to Other Acts

- Presidency Towns Insolvency Act, 1909 (3 of 1909)
- Provincial Insolvency Act, 1920 (5 of 1920)
- Public Debts Act, 1944 (18 of 1944)
- State Bank of India Act, 1955 (23 of 1955)
- Sick Industrial Companies (Special Provisions) Act, 1985 (1 of 1986)
- Unit Trust of India Act, 1963 (52 of 1963)
- Working Journalists (Conditions of Service) and Miscellaneous Provisions Act, 1955

EMPLOYEES' PROVIDENT FUNDS AND MISCELLANEOUS PROVISIONS ACT, 1952

Chapter I
INTRODUCTION

AN INTRODUCTION TO THE ACT

Historical Background – The Iron Road to Social Security

The underlying philosophy of social security is that the State shall make itself responsible for ensuring a minimum standard of material welfare to all its citizens to cover all the contingencies of life. In other sense, social security is primarily an instrument of social and economic justice. In India, the concept of 'social security' has been an ancient one, though the framing of laws and institutionalisation of social security may be of recent origin. There is evidence to show that provident fund scheme was in vogue during the Chandragupta period. Specific references have been made in Kautilya's *Arthasasthra* and *Nitisara* about this.[1]

G.C. Hallen[2] stressed upon the historical evolution of social security in India from joint family system model to the present day institutionalised structure. According to him, the joint family, as a cohesive unit, enfolded in its lap several relations, no one of which was to feel insecure at any stage of life.[3] The breaking down of the joint family system created the demand for social security in the industrial and urban sectors.

Provident Funds under the Colonial regime

During the colonial regime, little had been done for the working class in the sphere of social security, although there were ample opportunity and resources to provide for any scheme to that effect. Before the legislative measures were taken to introduce a Provident Fund scheme in factories, some large-scale private undertakings had established their Provident Fund schemes. For instance, the Tata Iron and Steel Company had its Provident Fund scheme as early as in 1920. Empress Mills at Nagpur, besides a contributory Provident Fund, also had a pension scheme under which their old employees were given a pension. During 1947–48, 5,493 workers were members of the Provident Fund in the mill, and 993 former employees drew the pension. The Buckingham and Carnatic Mills in Madras had a contributory

---

[1] *Savings in a Welfare State* by VR. Mutalik Desai (1966) P.C. Manaktalas & Sons Pvt. Ltd., Bombay
[2] The Editor of *Indian Journal of Social Research*
[3] *Dynamic of Social Security*, C.G. Hallen (1967) p.84

Provident Fund scheme for its employees. In other sectors also, some Provident Fund schemes were in vogue. The revised s.41 of the Bombay Cooperative Societies Act, 1925 provided for the establishment of a Provident Fund, not only for its staff but also for members of the Society. The Bombay Secondary School Teachers' Provident Fund was organised by the Government of Bombay, and almost all aided schools were required to join it. The subscriptions were received at certain rates from the teachers, and the school management was required to contribute half as much. The Bombay Government contributed one-third of the sum standing to the teachers' credit, which was paid at the time of the final payment when the teachers retired.[4] In the local government, Provident Fund schemes were in existent in almost all municipalities to which only permanent workers were eligible. Sometimes there was a condition of a lower income limit of Rs.20/- per month for contribution to the provident fund. In the engineering industry, several large firms had undertaken several labour welfare activities which had been standardised after an award of the Engineering Tribunal in West Bengal in April 1948. All engineering firms employing 100 or more workers, those who were members of the Engineering Association of India had adopted a scheme of a mandatory Provident Fund (R.C. Saxena, 1952). For seamen, the Sindhia Steam Navigation Company had instituted a Provident Fund scheme for the benefit of its staff afloat. The Indian Merchant Shipping (Amendment) Act, 1939 allowed deductions from wages of the seamen by way of Provident Fund contributions with effect from 17th February 1939 (Das, 1941).

Legislative Developments

But in a majority of cases, labour had not got the benefit and that for various reasons. Employers had been generally found to be unwilling to take the initiative in starting such Funds. Under the Montague-Chelmsford Reforms in 1919, the Central Legislature was given definite legislative authority to enact industrial laws. For the first time, the Labour Commission of 1921 recommended that the rules regarding the Provident Fund should be changed and those who get Rs.20 and over and put in at least one year's service should be made to subscribe to Provident Fund. The first legislative measure relating to Provident Funds was undertaken by the Government of India with the enactment of the Provident Funds Act in 1925. The Act was restricted in scope and dealt with Provident Funds relating to government undertakings, railway administrations, etc. When the Indian Income Tax Act of 1922 was amended by the Indian Income Tax (Provident Fund Relief) Act, 1929, it laid down rules for protection of compulsory Provident Fund deposits made by the employees. There was no legislation relating to Provident Funds in private industries

---

[4] *Provident Fund for Workers*, D.G. Damle is Labour Officer, East India Cotton Association, Bombay

until 1929, incorporating a new chapter containing special provisions relating to certain classes of Provident Funds. (S.K. Wadhawan, 1968)

As the 1925 Act did not cover the factory and industrial workers, the workers demanded a Provident Fund scheme. On 4th July 1929, the Royal Commission on Labour (also called the *Whitely Commission*) was appointed by George Fifth of Great Britain to inquire into the labour-related problems in India. N.M. Joshi and Diwan Chaman Lall, two stalwarts of the Indian labour movement, were members of the Royal Commission on Labour, and they put forth the labour's case for a Provident Fund right in 1929. Though the Royal Commission recognised the justice of the workers' claim, N.M. Joshi and Diwan Chaman Lall were of the opinion that a suitable recommendation about Provident Fund should be made in the report. The result was that though a strong case was made out, the Royal Commission only recommended that the Government should encourage employers to inaugurate a scheme of this nature for their employees. That was in 1931. Though the Royal Commission recommended that the Government should promote it, and though the Government in the then Labour Department did all possible to encourage the employers, the response from the employers was most disappointing.[5]

'Labour' under the Government of India Act, 1935 became a concurrent subject, i.e., it came within the spheres both of the Central and Provincial Governments. The provincial autonomy further sped up the pace of labour legislation. The dual responsibility created the need for joint consultation between the Centre and the Provinces. This led to the institution of the machinery known as the Labour Ministers' Conference,' wherein Labour Ministers or their representatives from the Central and Provincial Governments had taken part to discuss urgent labour problems and to plan a coordinated labour policy.

In the meantime, there were some remarkable developments in the provinces. The Cawnpore[6] Labour Enquiry Committee in 1937 suggested the establishment of a general Provident Fund to provide for sickness, unemployment and old age. The Sind Workers' Provident Fund Bill, 1939 was introduced on 28th January 1939, making it obligatory for the permanent employees in factories, tramways and motor services with wages of Rs.20 and above per month to contribute to Provident Fund. But a worker should be 15 years in the service of the employer to become entitled to the employer's share of contribution. (Das, 1941)

The role of the International Labour Organisation, since its inception in 1919, in the promotion of social security, has been significant. Through its Conventions

---

[5] *Parliamentary Debates*, Official Report, Volume 41, Issue 1–10
[6] Present, Kanpur

and Recommendations, the ILO has exerted its influence to extend the range and the classes of persons protected and the contingencies covered and to improve the efficacy of the benefits assured. In the meantime, the Beveridge Report had been published in England and Social Security Act, 1935, the Marsh Plan (Report on Social Security) in Canada and the Wagner-Murray-Dingell Bill in the USA. These international developments compelled the colonial Indian Government to come out with some meaningful legislative measures for social security.

Thus, the question of the mandatory Provident Fund came up for discussion in the 3rd Labour Ministers' Conference held on 19th April 1942, and it was agreed to prepare a set of model Provident Fund rules for circulation among the employers. The Central Labour Ministry was required to prepare a detailed scheme within about six months. Model Provident Fund rules were framed and placed before the 5th Labour Ministers' Conference held in 1943 and then submitted to the Standing Committee on Labour in 1944.

In the meantime, the Tripartite Labour Conference at its meeting in September 1943 recommended the setting up of machinery to investigate conditions of labour, intending to plan a policy of social security for the workers. In pursuance of that resolution, the Labour Investigation Committee was appointed by the Government of India Resolution No. L 4012 dated 12th February 1944 under the chairmanship of D.V. Rege (known as *Rege Committee*) to carry out the investigations. The *Rege Committee* submitted its report on 5th March 1946 stating that the absence of social security measures like Provident Funds, gratuities and pensions in most concerns had contributed to the migratory character of Indian labour. The Committee recommended that all Provident Funds, wherever they exist, should be compulsorily registered and treated as '*trust*.' It further recommended that workers' contribution to the Provident Fund made by private employers and certified by Government for the purpose should be safeguarded against attachment.[7]

A few months after India achieved independence, the ILO organised its first Asian Regional Conference in New Delhi in 1947. The question of providing social security benefits in the form of Provident Fund and pension benefits was discussed in the Conference. It was decided that given the financial and administrative conditions in India, a contributory provident fund scheme was preferable to a scheme of pension or gratuity payments. Following the recommendation of the Asian Regional Conference, the matter was discussed at the 10th session of the Indian Labour Conference held in 1948. It was agreed that introducing a statutory provident fund scheme for industrial workers might be undertaken.[8]

---

[7] *Labour Investigation Report*, 1946 published by the Manager, Publication Dept., Govt. of India.

[8] *Annual Report on the working of the EPF Scheme*, 1952 for period 1953–54

Following the Preparatory Asian Regional Conference, the first Pakistan Labour Conference had also decided that the Model Provident Fund Rules which had been drawn up in pre-partition India should be circulated again for the opinion of employers and employees and a scheme should be submitted at the first meeting of the Standing Committee.

The Board of Conciliation (Colliery Disputes) appointed by the Government of India in February 1947, for coal mines in Bengal and Bihar had recommended the institution of a compulsory provident fund scheme. The Fact Finding Committee appointed in May 1947 also approved the same. These recommendations were accepted by the Government and discussed at the first meeting of the Tripartite Industrial Committee on Coal Mining held in January 1948. As a result, first, an ordinance was passed which was later replaced by the Coal Mines Provident Fund and Bonus Schemes Act of 1948. The Coal Mines Provident Fund Scheme framed under the Coal Mines Provident Fund and Bonus Schemes Act, 1948, came into force for all coal mines in West Bengal and Bihar from 12 May 1947.

Following this, the desirability of constituting mandatory provident funds was high in the country for all industrial workers. In several cases, the awards given by the Industrial Tribunals had been like determining policies which in the ordinary course laid in the domain of the Central Government. The Bihar and Bengal Colliery Awards and the Madras Textile Mills Award had recommended the institution of compulsory provident fund schemes (B.S. Narula, 1963). These recommendations were to a large extent responsible for the Central Government's proposal for starting a plan of a mandatory provident fund in all industrial undertakings. The question was also discussed in January 1951 at the Labour Ministers' Conference at Patna, in which there was unanimous agreement on the need for legislation for a mandatory provident fund for industrial workers. (R.C. Saxena, 1952).

On 11th February 1948, a private member's bill was introduced in the Constituent Assembly of India by R.K. Sidhwa to provide for the establishment of provident fund benefits to certain classes of workers by their employers. The motion for the circulation of the Bill was adopted on 11th February 1949. The Bill came up again for discussion before the Constituent Assembly towards the middle of December. The then Labour Minister Jagjivan Ram suggested that while there was universal support for the principle underlying the Bill, it could not be undertaken at that junction as the Government and others were preoccupied with problems likely to arise out of retrenchment and consequent unemployment. The Labour Minister, however, assured the House that comprehensive labour legislation including provision for the grant of provident fund for all categories of workers in various industries and commercial establishments would be placed before the House by the Government next year. On that assurance, the Bill was withdrawn by S.K. Sidhwa.

The subject was further discussed at the 12th meeting of the Standing Labour Committee in November 1950 which unanimously recommended for the introduction of a provident fund scheme for industrial workers. In 1951, the Labour Ministers' Conference held at Patna emphasised the urgency for enacting legislation for the purpose. As the Parliament was not in session, the Employees' Provident Funds Ordinance (8 of 1951) was promulgated and received the assent of the President of India (Dr. Rajendra Prasad) on November 15th, 1951. The ordinance which came to force at once was to extend to the whole of India except the State of Jammu and Kashmir. The Ordinance promulgated on the 15th November 1951 was replaced by the EPF Act, which was laid before the Parliament on February 13th, 1952 and enacted on March 4th, 1952. The Scheme framed under s.5 of the Act was brought into force by stages and was enforced in its entirety by the 1st November 1952.

The Employees' Provident Fund Act was followed by the enactment of the Assam Tea Plantations Provident Fund Act, 1955, the Seamen's Provident Fund Act, 1966, Jammu & Kashmir Employees' Provident Fund Act, 1961. The schemes framed under these Acts are Assam Tea Plantation Provident Fund Scheme (1955), Jammu & Kashmir State Provident Fund Scheme (1961) and Seamen Provident Fund Scheme (1966). All these funds offer benefits similar to the Employees' Provident Fund with minor variations.

Preamble

The preamble is the Act in a nutshell and an essential aid in interpreting an ambiguous Act. It expresses the scope and object of the Act more comprehensively than the title of the Act. The preamble to the Employees Provident Fund and Miscellaneous Provisions Act, 1952, shows it is an Act to provide for the institution of Provident Fund, family pension fund and deposit linked insurance fund for employees. This objective should not be allowed to be scuttled by mere devices.[9]

The preamble of a statute which is often described as a key to the understanding of it may legitimately be consulted to solve an ambiguity or to ascertain and fix the meaning of words in their context which otherwise bear more meanings than one.[10]

Statement of Objects and Reasons

A statement of Objects and Reasons is included in the Bill by which an enactment is introduced in Parliament.

---

[9] *S.K. Nasurruddin Bidi Merchant v Regional P.F. Commissioner* 1990 (1) BLJR 348
[10] *A.C. Sharma v Delhi Administration*, (1973) 1 SCC 726: AIR 1973 SC 913

The question of making some provision for the future of the industrial worker after he retires or for his dependents in case of his early death, has been under consideration for some years. The ideal way would have been provisions through old-age and survivors' pensions as has been done in the industrially advanced countries. But in the prevailing conditions of India, the institution of a pension scheme cannot be visualised in the near future. Another alternative may be for provision of gratuities after a prescribed period of service. The main defect of a gratuity scheme, however, is that the amount paid to a worker or his dependents would be small, as the worker would not himself be making any contribution to the fund. Taking into account the various difficulties, financial and administrative, the most appropriate course appears to be the institution compulsorily of contributory provident funds in which both the worker and the employer contribute. Apart from other advantages, there is the obvious one of cultivating among the workers a spirit of saving something regularly. The institution of a provident fund of this type would also encourage the stabilisation of a steady labour force in industrial centres.

The subject of legislation for compulsory institution of contributory provident funds in industrial undertakings was discussed several times at tripartite meetings in which representatives of the Central and State Governments and of employers and workers took part. A large measure of agreement was reached that there should be such legislation. Further, a non-official Bill on this subject was introduced in the Central Legislature in 1948 and was withdrawn only on an assurance given that Government itself would soon consider the introduction of a comprehensive Bill. The view that the proposed legislation should be undertaken was lastly endorsed by the Conference of Provincial Labour Ministers held in January 1951. It may be added that a statutory Contributory Provident Fund already exists for workers in coal mines, covering about 3,00,000 persons. This has been in operation for about five years and is working very satisfactorily.

The Bill provides for institution, in the first instance, of contributory provident funds in the six major organised industries named in Schedule I; except undertakings owned by the Central or a State Government or by a local authority. There is also a provision empowering the Central Government, by notification, to add other industries to the Schedule or to apply the Act to industrial undertakings employing less than fifty persons.

To avoid any hardship to the new establishment, a provision has been made for exempting them for a period of three years and similar exemptions are given to other establishments which are less than three years old till they have been in operation for a period of three years in all. The rate of contribution will be in operation for a period of three years in all. The rate of contribution will be 6 ¼ per cent of the total emoluments of the worker, the worker and the employer each contributing these amounts. Further, the scheme could empower payment of a higher subscription by the workers at their option.

Where provident funds exist in private industry, contributions are usually a percentage of the basic wage. Unlike government departments, wages in private industry have not, however, been rationalised and there are very great variations in the level of basic wages in private industry, even in different units in the same industry. If contributions are reckoned on the basis of basic wage only, there will, therefore, be wide changes in the degree of benefit received. This will be unfair to the workers and may also penalize those employers who have brought the level of basic wages more in accord with current requirements. Government appreciates that dearness allowance is a variable factor depending on the cost of living. Nevertheless, for the reasons explained, Government is satisfied that contributions to the provident fund should be on the basis of basic pay plus dearness allowance on the existing rates are to be recognised as a permanent measure.

Most of the details relating to the Fund will be settled in accordance with a scheme which, in the interest of uniformity, will be framed by the Central Government. The administration will, to a large extent, be decentralised in regard to undertakings falling within the sphere of State Governments.

Where provident funds offering equal or more advantageous terms are operating efficiently, provision has been made for them to continue subject to certain safeguards in the interest of the workers.

This Bill when enacted will repeal and re-enact an Ordinance promulgated on the same lines on the 15th November 1951.[11]

Statement of Objects and Reasons—Significance of

The Statement of Objects and Reasons though not relevant to interpret the sections of the Act, will throw light upon the object of the legislature from the historical viewpoint.[12] In *Committee for Protection of Rights of ONGC Employees v Oil & Natural Gas Commission*[13] the Supreme Court observed: "The Statement of Objects and Reasons shows that the scheme of Contributory Provident Fund, by way of retiral benefit, envisaged by the Provident Fund Act, is in the nature of a substitute for old-age pension because it was felt that in the prevailing conditions in India, the institution of a pension scheme could not be visualised in the near future."

---

[11] *Gazette of India*, 1952 Pt.II, s.2, pp.67–69
[12] *Kelara State Electricity Board v Indian Aluminum Co.* 976 AIR 1031, 1976 SCR (1) 552
[13] AIR 1990 SC 1167: 1990(2) SCC 472: 1990 (60) FLR 747: 1990 Lab IC 922: 1990(2) SCR 156: 1991(2) LLJ 271 (SC)

In *Balbir Kaur v Steel Authority of India Ltd.*,[14] the Supreme Court explained the object of the EPF Act in the following terms: "It is significant to note that the Employees' Provident Fund & Miscellaneous Provisions Act of 1952 is a beneficial piece of legislation and can amply be described as a social security statute, the object of which is to ensure better future of the employee concerned on his retirement and for the benefit of the dependants in case of his earlier death." The phrases used in the Statement of Objects and Reasons cannot curtail the scope of the words 'any other establishment' in s.1 (3)(b) of the Act.[15] The Act is intended to instil a sense of compulsory savings by the employees to help them in their later period of life.[16] It is a unique substantive law with a social welfare goal and provides within itself the means and procedures for its enforcement and to penalise those who violate its provisions.[17]

---

[14] (2000) 6 SCC 493
[15] *Cosmopolitan Club, Madras v Regional P.F. Commissioner*, (1973) 44 FJR 229(Mad.) (1974) 1 MLJ 83: (1974) Lab.IC 385.
[16] *Battula veeraswamy v The Regional P.F. Commissioner and others*, 2010(3) LLJ 420(AP.HC)
[17] *Bank of India v The Assistant P.F. Commissioner and another*, 2009 (122)FLR 746: 2006(2) KLT 553 (Ker.HC)

Chapter II
INTERPRETATION OF STATUTES

BASIC RULES OF INTERPRETATION

Statutory interpretation is the process by which the courts interpret and apply legislation enacted by the Parliament. Over the years, courts of law have used many methods, referred to as cannons of construction, to aid in the discovery of the meaning of legislation.

First in 1584 came the *Mischief Rule*, which required the judges 'to make such constructions as shall suppress the mischief and advance the remedy.' In 1844 came the *Literal Rule*, which said, they alone do, in such a case, best declare the intention of the lawgiver. Then in 1877 came the *Golden Rule*, later called the *Absurdity Rule*. Take the whole statute together—giving the words their ordinary meaning, unless when so applied they produce an inconsistency, or absurdity or an inconvenience so high as to convince the court that the intention of the Parliament could not have been to use their ordinary meaning and to justify the court in putting on them some other significance, which the court thinks the words will bear. But now the judges apply the *Purpose Rule* by which statutes are liberally interpreted to promote the general legislative purpose underlying the provision. (Renton 1990)

GENERAL PRINCIPLES OF INTERPRETATION

In *Poppatlal Shah v State of Madras*,[18] the Supreme Court observed that it is a settled rule of construction that to find out the legislative intent, all the constituent parts of a statute are to be taken together, and each word, phrase, or sentence is to be considered in the light of the general purpose of the Act itself. In *State of Jharkhand v Ambay Cements and another*,[19] the Supreme Court held that it is the cardinal rule of interpretation that where a statute provides that a particular thing should be done, it should be done in the manner prescribed and not in any other way. The following points need to be kept in mind while interpreting the statutes.

1. An Act must be read as a whole. Therefore, the language of one section may affect the construction of another. 2. An Act may be interpreted by reference to other Acts dealing with the same or a similar subject. 3. Special provision will control general provisions. 4. Where particular words are followed by general words that the generality

---

[18] AIR 1953 SC 274
[19] 2005(I) SCC 368

of the latter will be limited by reference to the former (*Ejusdem Generis* rule). 5. The general rule, subject to important exceptions, is that a guilty mind (*mens rea*) is an essential element in a breach of a criminal or penal law. It should, therefore, be considered whether the words 'willfully' or 'knowingly' should be inserted, and whether, if not inserted, they would be implied, unless expressly negated. 6. The presumption that the legislature intends no alteration in the rules or principles of common law beyond what it expressly declares.7. The presumption against an intention to oust or limit the jurisdiction of the superior courts.8. The presumption that an Act of Parliament will not have extra-territorial application. 9. The presumption against any intention to contravene a rule of international law. 10. The rule that a power conferred on a public authority may be construed as duty cast on that authority ('may = shall').

INTERNAL AND EXTERNAL AIDS IN INTERPRETATION

Internal aids are those which are found in the statute. These are (i) Title of the Statute (ii) Preamble (iii) Chapter or Section Headings (iv) Marginal notes (v) Punctuations (vi) Illustrations (vii) Definitions (viii) Proviso (ix) Explanation (x) Saving Clauses and (xi) Non-obstante clauses.

External aids for interpretation are those which are not contained in the statute but are found elsewhere. They may be (i) Historical background (ii) Statement of Objects and Reasons (iii) The original bill (iv) Parliamentary debates[20] (v) Statements of the Ministers (vi) Judicial construction (vii) Legal dictionaries and (viii) Commonsense.

RULES OF CONSTRUCTION

The primary and foremost task of a court in interpreting a statute is to ascertain the intention of the legislature, actual or implied. The words of the statute are to be construed to find out the mind of the legislature from the natural and grammatical meaning of the words which it has used – 'The *essence of the Law*,' according to Salmond.[21] Over the years, the judiciary has evolved the following principles of interpretation of statutes.

Strict and Liberal Construction

In *Regional Provident Fund Commissioner v The Hooghly Mills Co Ltd. and others*,[22] the Supreme Court pointed out the difference in interpreting the social welfare

---

[20] Lord Scarman in *Davis v Johnson (1979)AC 264 at 350* stated that parliamentary debates were an unreliable guide and promoted confusion, not clarity.
[21] *Jurisprudence*, 11th Edition, p 152
[22] 2012(2) S.C.T. 145: 2012 AIR (SCW) 902: 2012(1) CLR 380: 2012 LIC 1083: 2012(2) LLJ 1: 2012(2) SCC 489: 2012(2) PLJR 31: 2012(2) SLR 481: 2012(4) Mah.LJ 52

legislation and penal statutes. The Court observed that the typical canon of interpretation is that a remedial statute or social welfare law if there is any doubt, the same is resolved in favour of the class of persons for whose benefit the statute is enacted. But in case of penal laws, if there is any doubt, the same is resolved in favour of the alleged offender.

A penal statute must be construed strictly. But welfare legislation is to be liberally interpreted so that its benefits go to the weaker section.[23] The principles applicable to taxing statutes should not be applied to a piece of welfare legislation. Legislation dealing with human rights of exploited and the backward clan of people should be interpreted in the light of constitutional protection available to them.[24]

Purposive Construction

In *International Ore and Fertilizer (P) Ltd. v ESI Corporation*,[25] the Supreme Court held that welfare legislation should be liberally construed so that the purpose thereof may be allowed to be achieved rather than frustrated or stultified. In *Maharashtra State Coop Bank Ltd. v Provident Fund Commissioner*,[26] the Supreme Court described the philosophy of the Act very eloquently. Since the Act is a social welfare legislation intended to protect the interest of a weaker section of the society, i.e., the workers employed in factories and other establishments, it is imperative for the courts to give a purposive interpretation to the provisions contained therein keeping in view the Directive Principles of State Policy embodied in Articles 38 and 43 of the Constitution. In *State v Giridhari Lal Bajaj*,[27] the Bombay Court observed that when there is doubt about their meaning, it is to be understood in the sense in which it best harmonises with the subject of the enactment and the object which the legislature has in view. Where a liberal construction of a rule may lead to a consequence not envisaged by the Act, the rule must be construed strictly.[28]

Harmonious Construction

The doctrine of harmonious construction aims to make the enactment a consistent whole, and it seeks to avoid inconsistency or repugnance between various sections or parts of the statute. It has already been seen that a statute must be read as a whole and

---

[23] *Sudhakar Pani v Assistant Provident Fund Commissioner* ILR 2005 KAR 2792, 2005 (4) KarLJ 18, (2005) III LLJ 239 Kant
[24] *Comptroller and Auditor General of India v Jagnnathan* (1986) 2 SC 679; 1986 SCC (L & S) 345; (1986) 1 ATC 1; (1986) 2 LLN 1
[25] (1987) 4 SCC 203; 1987 SCC (L & S) 391; (1987) 2 LLN 911
[26] (2009)10SCC 123
[27] *1962 II LLJ46(Bom. DB)*,
[28] *A.K. Roy v State of Punjab*, (1986) 4 SCC 326: AIR 1986 SC 2160

one provision of the Act should be construed with reference to other provisions of the same Act to make a consistent enactment of the whole statute. Such a construction has the merit of avoiding any inconsistency or repugnancy either within a section or between a section and other parts of the statute. For instance, in *Gowri Shankar Theatre v The Assistant Provident Fund Commissioner, Vellore*,[29] the petitioner contended that the provisions of s.1(5) of the Act were applicable only in such cases where the employment strength fell below 20, and this requirement will not govern the theatres employing 5 or fewer persons. The Madras High Court adopted a harmonious construction and held, "once the applicability of the Employees' Provident Funds and Miscellaneous Provisions Act, 1952 has been extended to Cine Workers as per Section 24 of the Cine-Workers and Cinema Theatre Workers (Regulation and Employment) Act 1981, necessarily all provisions of the Employees' Provident Funds and Miscellaneous Provisions Act, 1952 are to be applied by harmonious construction of Section 1(5) of the Act in respect of Cine Theatre. Therefore, it should be taken as five instead of 20 since under the Cine-Workers and Cinema Theatre Workers (Regulation and Employment) Act 1981, the minimum requirement is 5."

INTERPRETATION OF THE EPF ACT

In *J.G. Vakharia v Regional Provident Fund Commissioner*,[30] the Bombay High Court held that 'the court must not countenance any subterfuge which would defeat the provisions of a social legislation and the court must even if necessary strain the language of the Act in order to achieve the purpose which the legislature had in placing this legislation on the statute book. Therefore, not only the court must disapprove all subterfuges to defeat a social legislation but must actively try to prevent such subterfuges succeeding in their object. In *Organo Chemical Industries and another v Union of India and others*,[31] the Supreme Court observed: "A policy-oriented interpretation, when a welfare legislation falls for determination, especially in the context of a developing country, is sanctioned by principle and precedent and is implicit in Article 37 of the Constitution since the judicial branch is, in a sense, part of the State. So it is reasonable to assign to 'damages' a larger, fulfilling meaning." In *Otis Elevator Employees' Union and others v Union of India and others*,[32] the Supreme Court, while upholding the constitutional validity of the EPF & MP Act, 1952 and the Employees' Pension Scheme 1995, observed that the Act is a social welfare legislation to provide "for the institution of Provident Fund,

---

[29] Mad HC 1195
[30] 1957 (1) LLJ 448
[31] 1979(4) SCC 573
[32] 2003(99) FLR 1179: 2004(1)LLJ 217: 2004(1) LLN 450: 2004 LLR 63: AIR 2004 SC 3264 (SC – 2M)

Pension Fund and Deposit-Linked Insurance Fund for employees in factories and other establishments." If the legislation is not patently arbitrary, the Court will not monitor implementation of such a policy unless the same is discriminatory or arbitrary. The Court declared that since the Scheme is for the welfare of the employees, the same cannot be held to be violative of the Constitution.

In *Regional Provident Fund Commissioner v Madras Pencil Factory*,[33] the Madras High Court declined to agree with the argument of the Petitioner's counsel that because the Act is intended to confer some benefit on the workmen employed in factories, a facile interpretation can be relied upon to extend the operation of the Act. In *Regional Director, ESI Corporation v Ramanuia Match Industries*,[34] the Supreme Court held that beneficial legislation should have liberal construction to implement the legislative intent but where such beneficial legislation has a scheme of its own, there is no warrant for the Court to travel beyond the scheme and extend the scope of the statute on the pretext of extending the statutory benefit to those who are not covered by the scheme.

In *Central India Excise Traders v Regional Provident Fund Commissioner*,[35] the Madhya Pradesh High Court held that the notification which requires an establishment to comply with certain provisions of an enactment and non-compliance thereof resulting in penal consequences must be given strict and literal construction. The Court further observed, 'it is true that the Act is a piece of social welfare legislation conferring provident fund benefits on the employees, but in the matter of construing its provisions regarding applicability of the said Act to specified establishments, the notification must be strictly construed because the Act confers some benefits to the employees but adversely affects rights of the employers and exposes them to penal consequences in the case of non-compliance.' In *Turabuddin Haji Niaz Ahmed v Commissioner*,[36] the Supreme Court held that an interpretation which renders any provision of the statute nugatory should be avoided. Interpretation of the Act is to be in consonance with the uplift and betterment of the working condition of the employees.[37]

It is imperative to construe the provisions in the Act and the schemes framed there under to as wide an interpretation, as it would enhance and advance the objectives behind the Act and the schemes framed thereunder.[38] The Courts should

---

[33] (1961) 2 LLJ 783 (Mad).
[34] AIR 1985 SC 278; 1985 Lab.I.C. 544
[35] 1990 (0) MPLJ 611
[36] AIR 1972 All 146.
[37] *Bhaskara Ceramic Industries v Regional P.F. Commissioner*, 1991 Lab.I.C. 1138(AP)
[38] *Battula Veeraswamy v Regional P.F. Commissioner and others* 2009(6)ALT464 (AP)

not, in the guise of extending the benefits of social legislation, strain the language of the enactment beyond reasonable limits."[39]

When two interpretations are equally possible

In *Varjivandas Hirji & Co. v Regional Provident Fund Commissioner*,[40] the Bombay High Court accepted the contention of the Respondent's counsel that the Act is a beneficent piece of legislation and where more than one interpretation of a provision is possible, it should be so construed as to benefit a large number of persons. The construction which advances the object of the legislation must be preferred to one which may retard or frustrate that object.[41] The interpretation which would be taking a retrograde step, putting back the clock of social reform, should not be accepted.[42] Any construction which would facilitate evasion of the provisions of the Act should as far as possible be avoided.[43] If two views are reasonably possible, the Courts should prefer the one which helps the achievement of the object though for such purpose straining of the words to an unreasonable degree is not proper.[44] In a welfare legislation, if any provision is capable of two interpretations, the one that is more favourable to the person for whose benefit the legislation has been made should be adopted.[45]

Hardship, inconvenience etc. are not relevant

The statutory provision may cause hardship or inconvenience to a party, but the Court has no choice but to enforce it giving full effect to the same. The legal maxim *dura lex sed lex* (the law is hard, but it is the law), stands attracted in such a situation. It has consistently been held that inconvenience is not a decisive factor to be considered while interpreting a statute.

No external aid in interpretation

Every enactment has its objectives and ends to serve. As Lord Loreburn stated in *Macbeth v Chislett*,[46] 'it would be a new terror in the construction of Acts of Parliament if we were required to limit a word to an unnatural sense because, in some Act which is not incorporated or referred to, such an interpretation was given

---

[39] *Pamadi Subbarama Chetti v Mirza Zawar Ali*, 1959 II LLJ 524 (Mys.HC)
[40] (1968) II LLJ 744 Bom
[41] *Shiveshwar Prasad Narain Singh v Ghurahu*, 1979 (3) SCC 23: 1979
[42] *Gurupad Khandappa Magdum v Hirabai Khandappa Magdum*, AIR 1978 SC 1239 ; [1981] 129 ITR 440
[43] *Sayaji Mills Ltd. v Regional P.F. Commissioner* 1985 SCC (C&S)310: 1985 Supp SCC 610: AIR 1985 SC 373
[44] *Regional P.F. Commissioner v Shibu Metal Works* (1965) 1 LLJ 473: AIR 1965 SC 1076
[45] *Lipton (India) Ltd. v Gokul Chandra Mondal*, 1981 Lab.I.C. 1300: (1982) 1 LLJ 255 (Cal)(FB)
[46] [1910] A.C. 220 (224)

to it for the purposes of that Act alone.' Executive instructions issued by either the Government of India or the State Government can have no binding force on the interpretation of statutory rules. The Court must interpret the statutory rules in accordance with the language used in the statutory rules in the light of well-established rules of interpretation.[47]

Non-obstante clause in a statute

A clause beginning with the expression *'notwithstanding anything contained'* in some particular provision in the Act, is more often than not appended to a section, in the beginning, to give an overriding effect over the provision of the Act mentioned in the *non-obstante* clause. It is equivalent to saying that despite the provision of the Act or any other Act mentioned in the *non-obstante* clause or any contract or document mentioned in the enactment following it will have its full operation or that the provisions embraced in the *non-obstante* clause would not be an impediment to an operation of the enactment.[48] When a provision of any enactment is made 'subject to' some other provision, it conveys the idea that the former shall yield to the latter to which it is made subject. Whereas a *non-obstante* clause is a legislative device to give overriding effect to certain provisions over some contrary provisions that may be found either in the same enactment or some other enactment, that is to say, to avoid the operation and effect of all contrary provisions, to which such *non-obstante* provision has been given over-riding effect.[49]

Proviso—the exception clause

A proviso operates as an exception to the section. The function of a proviso is to limit the main part of the section and carve out something which but for the proviso would have been within the operative part. There may be a case, however, where a proviso is not coextensive with but covers a field wider than the main part and an independent legislative provision. The natural presumption is that, but for the proviso, the enacting part of the section would have included the subject matter of the proviso; but the clear language of the substantive portion, and the proviso, may establish that the proviso is not a qualifying clause of the main provisions, but is in itself a substantive provision.[50]

"Such as"—Meaning of

The expression *'such as'* is intended to indicate that the specification of categories that follows after that, is illustrative and not exhaustive. The expression *'such as'* indicates

---

[47] *Brajnandan Prasad v State of Bihar,* AIR 1956 Pat 353: 1955 BLJR 302 (DB).
[48] *Chandavarkar S.R. Rao v Ashalata S. Guram* 1986 4 SCC 447
[49] *Jawahar Sons Enterprises Pvt. Ltd. v State and others.,* 2002(2)WLN56
[50] *Commissioner of Income Tax v P. Krishna Warriar,* AIR 1965 SC 59: (1964) 8 SCR 36

that the ambit of the words which precede it must be construed contextually with the category or type made up by the words that follow.[51]

Use of Titles

The Supreme Court held that it is permissible to assign the heading or title of a section a limited role to play in the construction of statutes. They may be taken as broad and general indicators of the nature of the subject-matter dealt with thereunder. In case of a conflict between the plain language of the provisions and the meaning of the heading or title, the heading or title would not control the meaning, which is clearly and plainly discernible from the provision thereunder.[52] Notifications issued by the Government on the authority conferred by a statute will form part of the statute itself.[53]

Interpretation of 'shall' and 'may'

The standard rule is that the provision containing *shall* is mandatory and the provision containing *may* is either permissive or discretionary. To construe '*shall*' as '*may*' and '*may*' as '*shall*,' there must be compelling reasons discernible from the context and the statutory aim, object and purpose.[54] Ordinarily, though the word '*shall*' is mandatory, it can be interpreted as directory only if the context and intention demand.[55]

'Save as otherwise provided in this Act'—Meaning of

In legal phraseology, '*save as otherwise provided in this Act*' means this provision might well be surpassed by some other provision of this Act. It is the counterpart of 'notwithstanding anything contained in this Act to the contrary,'

CONCEPT OF LEGAL FICTION

A legal fiction is a statement about some event or occurrence that is not true in the real sense but assumed to be true for the convenience of executing a legal principle. An interesting example is the Explanation to s.405 of IPC which creates a legal fiction to the effect that an employer who had deducted the workers' share of provident fund contributions, but failed to remit it "*shall be deemed to have dishonestly used*" the money. In construing the scope of a legal fiction, it would be proper and even necessary to assume all those facts on which alone the fiction can operate.[56]

---

[51] *Tata Consultancy Services Ltd. v Regional P.F. Commissioner* 2007 (2) LLJ 452 (Bom.)
[52] *Dalgaon Agro Industries Ltd. v Union of India and others* (2006) 1 CALLT 32 HC, 2005 (3) CHN 428, (2005) IIILLJ 356 Cal
[53] *Jacob K.B v Regional .P.F. Commissioner* 1987 LIC 1139; 1986 II LLN 543; 1986 II CLR 475 (Ker.HC)
[54] *Washdev Singh Biji v Union of India*, AIR 1970 Del 85
[55] *Sainik Motors v. State of Rajasthan*, AIR 1961 SC 1480
[56] *The Commissioner of Income Tax v Teja Singh* (1959) 35 ITR 408 at p. 413 = (AIR 1959 SC 352 at p. 355).

Chapter III
APPLICATION OF THE ACT

SHORT TITLE OF THE ACT

The Provident Fund Act was initially known as '*The Employees' Provident Funds Act 1952.*' By Provident Fund Laws Amendment Act 1971, a family pension scheme was added to the existing Act, and the Act was rechristened as '*The Employees' Provident Funds and Family Pension Act 1952.*' The Labour Provident Fund Laws (Amendment) Act 1976 introduced the Employees' Deposit-Linked Insurance Scheme, and the Act was again renamed as '*The Employees' Provident Funds and Miscellaneous Provisions Act 1952*' with effect from August 1st, 1976.

EXTEND

The provisions of the Act apply to the whole of India, except the state of Jammu & Kashmir, which has its Provident Funds Act viz., Jammu and Kashmir Employees' Provident Funds and Miscellaneous Provisions Act, 1961. They were extended to Pondicherry (present Puducherry) with effect from October 1st, 1963 by Pondicherry (Laws) Regulation of 1963, s.3, schedule I, to Dadra and Nagar Haveli with effect from July 1st, 1965 by Regulation 6 of 1963, s.2, Schedule I, to Goa, Daman and Diu with effect from July 1st, 1964 by Regulation 11 of 1963, s.3, schedule I, and to Laccadive, Minicoy and Amindivi Islands (now, Lakshadweep) with effect from October 1st, 1967 by Regulation 8 of 1965, s.3 and schedule 2. In *Regional P.F. Commissioner v Shillong City Bus Syndicate*,[57] the Supreme Court held that the provisions of the EPF Act apply to the area of the Khasi Hills Autonomous District, stating that the EPF Act is not an occupied field assigned to the Autonomous District Council under the VI Schedule to the Constitution of India.

APPLICATION OF THE ACT
Constitutional Validity

The Supreme Court, in the case of *Mohmedalli and others v Union of India and another*,[58] upheld the constitutional validity of the Employees' Provident Funds and Miscellaneous Provisions Act, 1952 (as amended by the Act 46 of 1960), s.1(3), s.16 and 17 thereof.

---

[57] 1996 AIR (SC) 1546: 1996(3) SCR 942: 1996(8) SCC 741: 1992(2) LLJ 753
[58] 1964 AIR 980, 1963 SCR Supl. (1) 993

The provisions of the Act do apply on the fulfilment of two conditions: (i) it must be a factory engaged in an industry specified in Schedule-I or class of establishments notified by the Central Government, and the number of employees should not be less than twenty.[59]

Section 1(3) should be read with Section 2(f)

Clauses (a) and (b) of sub-section (3) of s.1 have to be interpreted in the light of the definition of the term 'employee' as contained in s.2(f) and not in isolation, independent of the definition. That being the real position, the definition brings in contract labour within the scope of s.1(3). s.1(3) is not confined to direct labour, and contract labour has also to be counted for determining the applicability of s.1(3).[60]

Twenty or more persons—Meaning of

The word 'employment' must be construed as employment in the regular course of business of the establishment.[61] The regular employment rests not on the nature of terms of employment but the nature of the business of the establishment and its commercial nexus.[62] Where an establishment employs temporary employees as a part of the regular feature of the establishment, such employees cannot be construed as casual employees.[63] All persons employed in an establishment, whether drawing wages more or less than the statutory ceiling should be taken into account to find out whether the establishment satisfies the test of numerical strength provided under s.1(3).[64]

S.1 (3) (b)—A Residuary Provision

The expression *'any other establishment'* shows that s.1(3)(b) is a residuary provision in the sense that it will take in only establishments which are not covered by sub-section (3)(a). In other words, when once it is found that an establishment comes within the scope of sub-section (3)(a), there can be no question of its being covered by sub-section 3(b), since by reason of its inclusion within the scope of clause (a) the applicability of clause (b) stands automatically excluded.[65] The expression 'any

---

[59] Prior to amendment by Act 94 of 1956, the required number of employees was 50.
[60] *Nazeena Traders (P) Ltd. v Regional PF Com*missioner, AIR 1965 AP 200: (1966) 1 LLJ 334: *Goel Textile Industries v. Union of India*, (1991) 62 FLR 436 (All)(DB)
[61] *Regional P.F. Commissioner v T.S. Hariharan*, (1971) 2 SCC 68: (1971) 1 LLJ 416
[62] *Laksmi Restaurant v. Regional P.F. Commissioner*, 1975 Lab IC 1186 (Del).
[63] *Chatram Agarwalla v Regional Provident Fund Commissioner*, (1972) 1 LLJ 603: 1973 Lab IC 530 (Ori).
[64] *Bankim Chandra Chakravarty v Regional Provident Fund Commissioner*, AIR 1958 Pat 314, 1958 (6) BLJR 239, (1958) IILLJ 444 Pat
[65] *Ernakulam Coop. Milk Supply Union Ltd. v Government of India* 1969 LIC 223: 1968 II LLJ 666 (Ker. HC)

other establishment' in clause (b) is capable of the interpretation that the reference is to any establishment that does not fall under clause (a), whether such establishment is or is not a factory.[66]

By clause (a) of sub-section 3 of s.1 only factories employing twenty or more men engaged in specified industries are brought within the Provident Funds Act. To all other establishments, factory or non-factory, whether engaged in industry or otherwise, the Act may be applied by resorting to notification under clause (b) of sub-section 3 of s.1. Factories engaged in industries other than those mentioned in Schedule 1 may also be brought within the ambit of the Act by a notification under s.4, thus adding to Schedule I.[67] Whether a present perfect tense or a participle be used the meaning is the same. Cl. (b) of sec. 1(3) which uses the participle and Cl. (a) of the same section which employs the present perfect tense both merely describe the establishments and convey no different meanings.[68]

ACT APPLIES ON ITS OWN FORCE

If at least for one day in a year, the establishment employs more than 20 persons, the Act becomes applicable automatically to the establishment from that date.[69] The word 'employ' means employed and actually working, and employment even for one single day would bring the establishment within the purview of the Act.[70]

There is a considerable volume of authority in support of the view that the provisions of the Act to take effect on their own once the statutory requirements are fulfilled, and it does not depend upon the discovery made by the authorities and issue of the notice calling upon the employer to make the contributions under the Act.

In *Sri Andal & Co. v Regional Provident Fund Commissioner*,[71] the Madras High Court held that the Act takes effect at once, and the provisions of the Act become enforceable against the employer or a factory of an establishment

---

[66] *Ojas Corporation v Regional P.F. Commissioner*, 1970 Lab IC 81 (Guj. DB).
[67] *P.F. Inspector, Quilon v Kerala Janatha Printers and Publishers (P) Ltd.*, AIR 1965 Kerala 130.
[68] *R. Ramakrishna Rao Versus State Of Kerala*, AIR 1968 SC 1367: 1968 AIJEL_SC 22127
[69] *Deep Cycle Industries v Union of India* (1971) 39 FJR 407
[70] *G.V.Joshi v State of Mysore*, AIR 1969 Mys.300: 1969 Lab IC 1216: (Mys.DB)
[71] ILR (1965) 2 Mad 302

with effect from the date on which the relevant clause of the Scheme comes intoforce, and that it does not depend upon the discovery made by the authorities of the department and the issue of the notice calling upon the employer to make the contribution according to the Act. Similar view was taken by a Bench of the Punjab High Court in *Kapur Bhimber Union v Regional Provident Fund Commissioner, Punjab*,[72] a Bench of the Andhra Pradesh High Court in *Nazeena Traders (Private) Ltd. v Regional Provident Fund Commissioner*,[73] a Full Bench of the Kerala High Court in *Kokkalai Rice & Oil Mill Foundry v Regional Provident Fund Commissioner*,[74] and the Allahabad High Court in *N.K. Industries (Private) Ltd. v Regional Provident Fund Commissioner, U.P.*[75]

In *Shapoorji Nusserwanji Co.v The Regional P.F. Commissioner*,[76] a Division Bench of the Bombay High Court observed: " There is nothing in the Act or the Scheme to indicate that the Scheme becomes applicable only when the discovery is made and/or an order in that respect is made. This construction if accepted would encourage evasion for an undertaking to whom the Scheme is applicable may remain undiscovered either inadvertently or deliberately." In *Radha Krishnan Narayandas v Regional Provident Fund Commissioner, Indore*,[77] the High Court of Madhya Pradesh held that it would be incorrect to say that the scheme becomes operative only on and from the point of time when the authorities hold that a particular establishment is within the ambit of the Act and makes a consequential demand in terms of the Act. The Act comes into operation by its own vigour, that it applies if the conditions stated in the Act are satisfied, and that its operation is not dependent on any decision being taken by the authorities under the Act. The applicability of the provisions of the Act cannot be made to depend upon the magnitude of business.[78]

Though the Madras High Court in *Subbaier v Regional P.F. Commissioner*,[79] held that the provisions of the Act and Scheme became operative only on and from the point of time when the Commissioner holds that a particular unit is within the ambit of the Act and the Scheme, such proposition was laid down with reference to the liability for damages under s.14-B of the Act. In *Kunhipaly v Regional P.F.*

---

[72] (1966–66) 29 FJR 232 (Punj)
[73] (1965–66) 29 FJR 277 = (AIR 1965 Andh Pra 200)
[74] (1960–61) 19 FJR 362 = (AIR 1961 Ker 57) (FB)
[75] (1958–59) 15 FJR 249 = (AIR 1958 All 474)
[76] 1971 (22) FLR 110, (1968) IILLJ 739 Bom
[77] 1967 – II LLJ 649
[78] *Canbank Financial Services Ltd. v Regional P.F. Commissioner* 1995 (71) FLR 446, ILR 1995 KAR 1064, 1995 (2) KarLJ 395
[79] 1963–1 Lab LJ 23: (AIR 1963 Mad 112)

Commissioner,[80] the Kerala High Court refused to accept the view and observed that the Act comes into operation by its own vigour and it applies if the conditions stated in the Act are satisfied.

In clause 26 of the EPF Scheme, the words used are 'every employee shall be entitled and required to become a member of the Fund.' In *The Regional Provident Fund Commissioner v K.R. Subbaier Tape Factory*,[81] the Madras High Court held that the word 'entitled' means that the employee has got an absolute right to get the benefits of the Act. The word 'required' implies an obligation on the employer to treat all the employees, who are qualified and who are not exempted, as members of the fund, and to pay the contribution to the fund (both the employer's and the employees') from the date of the coming into force of the Scheme without allowing any interval to lapse either for the awaiting of a notice of demand from the Provident Fund Commissioner or for clearing a point of doubt.

Act applies to Factories and not to their Owners

In *Chagganlal Textile Mills Pvt Ltd. v P.A. Bhaskar*, the Bombay High Court observed that the Act is made applicable to factories and not the owners thereof; or, in other words, it applies to factories irrespective of who the owners from time to time may be. The same view was endorsed by the Madras High Court in *Venwood v Regional P.F. Commissioner*.[82] It is well settled that a change in the ownership or location of an establishment does not affect the applicability of the Act to that establishment. It is clear from s.1(3) of the Act that it applies to an establishment and its owner incurs the liability under the Act. It is not concerned who the owner is.[83]

Profit-making: No criterion for application of the Act

The question whether the establishment is a charitable institution or a commercial institution is outside the purview of discussion while deciding the applicability of the Act.[84] Whether the establishment makes a profit or not or whether its objective is earning a profit or not, is quite immaterial.[85] The requirement for application of

---

[80] 1966–1 Lab LJ 642 (Ker)
[81] (1966) 2 MLJ 403
[82] 41 FJR 172: 1972 I LLN 339 (Mad. HC)
[83] *Ernakulam Radio company, Calicut v Regional P.F. Commissioner* 1974 KLT 603
[84] *Venkataramana Dispensary Ayurvedic College v Union of India*, 1986 II LLN 942: 1986 II LLJ 411: 54 FLR 128 (Mad.HC)
[85] *Regional P.F. Commissioner v Osmania University*, 43 FJR 139: 1973 LIc 912: 1973 I LLN 153 153 (AP DB)

the Act is only the manufacture of goods and what happens to the manufactured goods, later on, is not a concern.[86]

Applicability of the Act: Burden of Proof

Mere averments made by an official in the visit-book, unless proved by way of substantive evidence, cannot be relied upon as proved facts to determine the applicability of the Act to the establishment concerned.[87] To ascertain whether an establishment employed more than 19 persons and that thereby attracted the provisions of the Act, the authority concerned can collect material by resorting to powers under various provisions of law. But, his finding must be based on evidence and relevant material on record. The authority cannot decide the case merely on the question of onus of proof.[88] There is no presumption of law that every establishment employs more than twenty persons and that a person making an allegation to the contrary must establish his allegation.[89] S.106 of the Evidence Act provided that when any fact is specifically within the knowledge of any person, the burden of proving that fact is upon him. Whether the establishment at the material time had employed twenty or more persons is certainly within the special knowledge of the employer.[90]

In *Capital Dyeing Company v Regional Provident Fund Commissioner*,[91] a dispute regarding the finding of facts about the number of employees engaged by the petitioner came into consideration before the High Court of Punjab and Haryana. The Court suggested that the EPF Department has to utilize recording of panchanama by video-graphing and insisting for installation of CCTV in and around factory premises, in order to avoid disputes relating to the number of employees employed by the employer and if there is no co-operation from the employer or its agent/manager/any person in such circumstances. Thus in a disputed matter evidence can be taken from video-graphing.

Since the Act automatically applies to an establishment engaged in an industry specified in Schedule I and employing at any time 20 or more persons, a party claiming non-applicability of the Act must prove by cogent evidence that the additional employees above the statutory strength were necessitated not for regular business of the establishment but by some abnormal contingency which was not the regular feature of the business of the establishment.[92]

---

[86] *Standard Dyeing & Finishing Mills v Union of India and othes*, 38 FJR 360 (P& H HC)
[87] *State Provident Fund Inspector v Perinan*, 1973 Lab IC 183 (Mad.)
[88] *Lakshmi Restaurant v Regional Provident Fund Commissioner*, 47 (1975) FJR 186
[89] *Lakshmi Restaurant v Regional Provident Fund Commissioner*, 47 (1975) FJR 186
[90] *State of West Bengal v Board of Revenue, West Bengal*, 1975 LIC 1162 (Cal.DB)
[91] CWP No.17366 of 1998
[92] *Chudasma Engineering Works v Regional P.F. Commissioner*, (1986) 1 LLN 242 (Kant) (DB)

Establishment run by Official Liquidator

In *Mahalaxmi Cotton Mills Ltd. v Regional Provident Fund Commissioner*,[93] the Calcutta High Court held that the expression 'ultimate control' used in the definition of the term 'employer' and 'occupier' in s.2(e) and 2(k) of the Act should be read to include the control exercised by the Official Liquidator appointed by the High Court to run the business of the factory with a view to sell it as a going concern. But if the Official Liquidator is asked to wind up the factory and close it down, he would not be liable because the factory would no longer be 'engaged' in the specified industry. In fact, it will then be disengaged from the industry and closed down.

Act applies to Minority institutions

The fact that the constitution provides in Article 30(1) that all minorities, whether based on religion or language, shall have the right to establish and administer educational institution of their choice, does not mean that the state cannot make laws of any nature with respect to those institutions, like the EPF Act, 1952, which has been enacted for the benefit of the workers in an establishment.[94]

Act cannot be applied retrospectively

It is entirely against the purpose and object of the Act to apply a Scheme under the Act retrospectively to a company for a period within which some employees have already left.[95] Retrospective application of the provisions of the Act and the schemes framed thereunder and demand for contribution from an earlier period is not warranted by the provisions of the Act.[96]

Applicability: Mixed Question of Fact and Law

Whether an establishment is within or outside the Act is a mixed question of fact and law. The work done is a premise is purely a question of fact. But whether it constitutes a 'manufacture' within the meaning of the Act would be a question of law. The number of persons employed is a question of fact. Whether the persons engaged in works in the factory are employed for wages whether their relationship with the employer is that of a servant and a master or whether they are independent contractors is very largely a question of fact.[97] The question whether an establishment is within or outside the Act is not a pure question of law but is a mixed question of

---

[93] (1960) 1 LLJ 468: AIR 1960 Cal 199
[94] *Christian Medical College & Hospital & Brown Memorial Hospital v Regional Provident Fund Commissioner* 1982 Lab IC 952 (P & H)
[95] *Aluminium Corporation of India v Regional P.F. Commissioner*, AIR 1958 Cal 570
[96] *Evershine Metals v Regional P.F. Commissioner*, AIR 1958 Cal 570: (1959) 1 LLJ 249
[97] *T.R. Raghava Iyengar & Co. v Regional P.F. Commissioner*, (1963) 1 LLJ 32 (Mad).

fact, and law and the same cannot be settled without a proper determination of facts forming the cornerstone of the whole statutory edifice.[98] It is certainly not a pure question of law.[99] The question whether the establishment is covered by a particular notification or not is a mixed question of law and fact.[100] Whether an employee is an apprentice under the Standing Orders or not is a question of fact that has to be decided on evidence.[101]

Continuity of Application

Sub-section (5) of s.1 was introduced into the Act only by Amendment Act 46 of 1960. When it was introduced, it contained a proviso which read thus: "Provided that where for a continuous period of not less than one year the number of persons employed therein has been less than 15, the employer in relation to such an establishment may cease to give effect to the provisions of this Act and any scheme framed thereunder with effect from beginning of the month following the expiry of the said period of one year but he shall within one month of the date of such cessation, intimate, by registered post, the fact thereof to such authority as may be specified by the appropriate government in that behalf." The proviso was omitted by Amendment Act 16 of 1971. The Statement of Objects and Reasons for Amendment Act No. 46 of 1960, in so far as it concerned sub-section (5) of s.1, read thus: "In order to ensure that the establishments once covered under the Act do not go out of the purview of the Act merely due to a small reduction in their strength, provision is being made that an establishment once covered under the Act will continue to be so covered despite a reduction in the employment strength, except where the employment strength is reduced to less than 15 and remains so for a period of one year continuously."[102]

S.1(5) of the Act says that even if the employment strength falls below 20, the cessation of coverage will not take place. Even if the employment strength falls below 20, the establishment, whether covered under s.1(3) or 16(1), it cannot go out of coverage.[103] S.1(5) bars exit from the applicability of the Act only on the ground of the number of employees falling below twenty and not on the ground of non-fulfilment of any other condition of the applicability of the Act.[104]

---

[98] *Wadi Stone Marketing Co Pvt Ltd. v Regional P.F. Commissioner* 27 FJR 43: 1965 II LLJ 32 (Mys.DB)
[99] *T.R. Raghava Iyengar & Company v Regional P.F. Commissioner*, 1963 I LLJ 32 (Mad. HC)
[100] *Professional Assistance for Development Action v Presiding Officer, EPFAT (Delhi)*, 2011 LIC 767: 2011 (3) LLJ 119: 2010(168) DLT 555: 2010(115) DRJ 605: 2010(125) FLR 961: 2010(6) S.C.T. 890
[101] *Tirupati Jute Industries Ltd. vRegional P.F. Commissioner* W.P. No. 16954 (W) of 2010 decided on 4-2-2011 (Cal.HC)
[102] *V. Venkatesh v. Union of India and others*, (1987) 89 BOMLR 325, (1988) ILLJ 87 Bom
[103] *Kottahala Handloom Weavers industrial Cooperative Society Ltd., and another v Enforcement Officer* 2008(118) FLR 149:2008(2) LLN 900: 2008 LLR 744 (Ker.HC)
[104] *United Western Bank Ltd. v Central P.F. Commissioner and others* (1985) 1 LLN 202(Bom)(DB)

Cinema Theatres—Harmonious Construction of S.1 (5)

When once the applicability of the Employees' Provident Funds and Miscellaneous Provisions Act, 1952 has been extended to Cine Workers as per s.24 of the Cine-Workers and Cinema Theatre Workers (Regulation and Employment) Act 1981, necessarily all provisions of the Employees' Provident Funds and Miscellaneous Provisions Act, 1952 are to be applied by harmonious construction of s.1(5) of the Act in respect of Cine Theatre. Therefore, it should be taken as five instead of 20 since under the Cine-Workers and Cinema Theatre Workers (Regulation and Employment) Act 1981, the minimum requirement is 5.[105]

Act does not apply on Closure of Establishment

In *Jai Krishna Aggarwal and another v The Regional PF Commissioner and another*,[106] the Allahabad High Court held that once the factory was validly closed down in accordance with the legal provisions and after giving due notices, the Act will not apply. The Court refused to accept the contentions of the Provident Fund Commissioner in holding that s.2(g) defines 'factory' as premises in any part of which a manufacturing process is being carried on or is ordinarily so carried. It is thus apparent that where the manufacturing process is permanently stopped and the factory has been closed down for good, and it cannot be validly contended that the statute will continue to apply to the establishment. Even after the closure of the factory the employers might like to engage some employees in looking after the assets and properties of the establishment. But thereby the statute cannot become applicable to the establishment.

In *Purex Laboratories India (P) Ltd. v Regional Provident Fund Commissioner*,[107] the Karnataka High Court held, "there is no provision of the Act which deals with cessation of its application and though s.1(5) of the Act is normally taken recourse to, to contend that the Act would continue to apply, such continued application would require at least three aspects viz., an establishment, an employer and at least one employee." In *Venkatesh v Union of India and others*,[108] held, there is no provision in the Act which deals with cessation of its application and that, when a statute sets out the requirements for its application but not for the cessation of its application, it must be held that once it applies, it continues to apply.

---

[105] *Gowri Shankar Theatre v The Assistant Provident Fund Commissioner, Vellore* Mad HC 1195
[106] 1987 Lab. IC 10 (All. HC)
[107] 1997 (4) KarLJ 677, (1998) ILLJ 78 Kant
[108] 1988-I-LLJ-87

Partition of the Establishment—Effect of

In *T.A. Zainulabdeen v Regional Provident Fund Commissioner, Kerala*,[109] the Kerala High Court held that sub-section 5 of section 1 does not prevent the disruption of an establishment and breaking up thereof into new and separate establishments either expressly or by implication. The Court observed, 'Where a disruption takes place by a partition and different establishments are created with less than twenty persons employed, the liability under the Act does not continue, and such separate establishments cannot be treated as departments or branches of the original establishment.' If the partition is real and *bona fide* and the integrity of the establishment was disrupted and three separate establishments were created as a result of partition and the separate establishments employed less than 20 persons, the Act will not apply.[110] Where there is no break-up in the homogeneity and integrity of the establishment after partition, the Act will continue to apply.[111] If the disruption, however, effected is a ruse or camouflage to get out of the provisions of the Act/Scheme, then it will be completely ignored. To say that an establishment to which the Act applied shall continue to be governed by the Act, even though the number of persons employed therein subsequently falls below twenty, presupposes the continuation of the establishment as an integral whole. But, when the integrity of the establishment gets split up, and such a splitting up is real and *bona fide*, then the relevant question that has got to be posed for an answer is whether the Act individually governs the split-up establishments.[112]

Act continues to apply notwithstanding Partition or Dissolution of Partnership

In *Pratap Chand Sukhoni v Regional P.F. Commissioner*,[113] the Calcutta High Court held that when the original partnership was dissolved, and the assets were divided among the partners, and subsequently another business was commenced under the same name and at the same place of that of the original partnership, it does not follow that the two establishments are the same or that the latter is a continuation of the earlier. In *Union of India v A.S. Amarnath*,[114] the facts were that the business of the old firm was closed as the managing partner died. All workmen were given closure compensation, and partners of the new firm were entirely different. The Supreme Court held there merely the name of the new firm is identical with the

---

[109] 1975 LIC 412
[110] *Mohammad Kutti v Regional P.F. Commissioner, Trivandrum* (1968) 2 LLJ 466
[111] T.M.VAbdul Rahman & Sons v Regional P.F. Commissioner, Madras
[112] *N. Jagie Gounder v Regional Provident Fund Commissioner* (1983) 1 LLJ 179.
[113] 1980(2) LLJ 296 (Cal.)
[114] 1999(1) LLJ1365: 1999(1)Scale 183: 1999(81) FLR 27

name of old firm and items of machinery utilised by the old firm is availed of by the new concern, it cannot be said that the business had continued. When once the Act governs the firm, it continues to be governed by it till the concerned authorities conclude that such firm no more exists and nobody continued the business of the said firm either separately or collectively. In the absence of specific evidence regarding the winding up of the business of the firm, the employer does continue to have the liability.[115] Where it was found on facts that in spite of the dissolution of the firm, what had really happened was only a transfer of ownership for getting out of the reach of the Act and not the creation of independent concerns unconnected with one another, it was held that the continuity of the old establishment was alive and not extinguished.[116]

Purchase of Machinery *per se* cast no Liability

There is no provision in the Act which mandates that it is the machinery used in the factory that is subject to the liability. A person who purchases machinery from a covered establishment cannot be made to contribute to EPF when the number of employees engaged by him is fewer than the statutory minimum for coverage.[117]

VOLUNTARY COVERAGE

Notification is a *sine qua non*

In *J. Engineering Company v The Assistant Provident Fund Commissioner*,[118] the Madras High Court held that the provisions of the Act could not be enforced till notification in the official gazette is published, in case of voluntary coverage made under s. 1(4) of the Act. 'The respondent has neither the authority nor jurisdiction to enforce the provisions of the Act merely because an agreement has been arrived at between the employer and the employees. Till a notification is issued extending the Act to the petitioner-establishment, the respondent has no authority or jurisdiction to call upon the petitioner to file the returns or remit employer's or employees' contribution as required under the provisions of the Act.'

Option to go out of the Ambit of Act

In *Sampath Kumaran and Co. v Regional Provident Fund Commissioner*,[119] an establishment having only four employees voluntarily got itself covered

---

[115] *Provident Fund Commissioner v Kodali and Sons Transport and others* 2005(2)ALD(Cri)545; [2006(109)FLR380]; (2006)ILLJ558AP
[116] *P. Madhavan Thampi v Regional P.F. Commissioner*, (1987) 2 LLJ 467: 1978(37) FLR 298
[117] *Pamadi Subbarama Chetti v Mirza Zawar Ali*, 1959 II LLJ 524 (Mys.HC)
[118] WP No.16040/1995, order dated 17.8.2001
[119] (1974) 1 MLJ 153

under the Employees' Provident Funds Act, 1952, by an application under s.1(4), subsequently, when the employer was reconstituted as a partnership firm, the employer along with the employees sought release from the liability under the Act. On a refusal, the employer filed a writ petition to quash the order of the authorities. The Madras High Court held that, notwithstanding the constitution of the employer from a proprietary one to a partnership one, since a majority of the employees together with the employer wish to withdraw from the liability under the Act the authorities are bound to release them. Under s.21 of the General Clauses Act, 1897, if a person or a body of persons can do an act for their benefit, but contemporaneously burdened with obligations, they would be in order at any time thereafter to seek for a relief of such obligations created by their voluntary act of commission by once again expressing in unequivocal terms their desire not to be burdened any more with such liabilities or obligations. The Court held that notwithstanding the reconstitution of the firm from a proprietary one to a partnership one, the majority of the employees together with the employer could seek for a withdrawal of their original application which bound them under the provisions of the Employees' Provident Funds Act, 1952.

In *Kidathirukkai Primary Agri. Cooperative Bank v Regional Provident Fund Commissioner*,[120] the Madras High Court, citing s.21 of the General Clauses Act of 1897, held that when the petitioner got voluntary coverage and then prayed to withdraw from the provisions of the Act, then the Respondent is bound to accept the request, and the proceedings initiated against the petitioner establishment after the request for withdrawal were totally without jurisdiction. Pertinently, s.21 of the General Clauses Act reads, 'whereby any Central Act or Regulations a power to issue notifications, orders, rules or bye-laws is conferred, then that power includes a power, exercisable in the like manner and subject to the like sanction and conditions (if any), to add to, amend, vary or rescind any notifications, orders, rules or bye-laws so issued.'

---

[120] 2012(2) LLJ 689: 2011(12) S.C.T. 6

Chapter IV

DEFINITIONS

The Supreme Court, in *S.K. Gupta v K.P. Jain*,[121] made a detailed analysis of the role and significance of the definitions in the statutes. The Court observed that a word used in a provision in a statute must bear the same meaning throughout that statute as set out in the definition section unless the context otherwise requires.

ESTABLISHMENT – MEANING OF

The word *"establishment"* has a broad as well as a narrow meaning. Broadly it means that "something that has been established" that is to say, any organisation, particularly of business or industry. In the narrower sense, it may at times mean a more or less fixed and usually sizable place of 'business or residence together with all the things that are an essential part of it. It is a body of men maintained for a purpose, and is a 'house of business.'[122] It is an organised body of men maintained for a purpose.[123] Employees cannot be synonymous with establishment or part of the establishment. Employees are one among the several components of the establishment. A component cannot be termed as a part of the whole structure.[124] In *Sri Varadarajswarmi Transports Pvt Ltd. v Regional Provident Fund Commissioner*,[125] the Madras High Court observed that "the word 'establishment' has not been defined in the Act, though that word has been used in several provisions of the Act, as also in other terms which have been defined in the definition section. An 'establishment' therefore must be given its ordinary meaning, and it means an organisation which employs persons between whom and the establishment the relationship of employee and employer comes to exist." It only means an organisation which employs a certain number of persons and nothing more.[126] The word "establishment" in s.1(3) (a) would continue to apply to the factory even though the factory may be shifted from place to place.[127] The word 'establishment' is used not only in sub-section (3) but also in some of the other sections of the Act, for example, s.16 and 17 and

---

[121] 1979 AIR 734, 1979 SCR (2)1184
[122] *Regional PF Commissioner v Jagannathadas* (1969) 2 MLJ 118 (Mad HC DB)
[123] Regional P.F. Commissioner v Assam Ayurvedic Bhandar, 1984 LIC 392 (Gau.DB)
[124] *HMT Ex-Servicemen's Association v Union of India* (2001) 2 CLR 529, (2001) 89 FLR 1089: (2001) 99 FJR 244
[125] AIR 1965 Mad 466, (1966) I LLJ 699 Mad
[126] *Cosmopolitan Club v Regional Provident Fund Commissioner* (1967) 1 LLJ 797 (Mad)
[127] *K. Gopalan v Union of India and others* ILR 1972 Delhi 438, 1973 LablC 287

sub-section (4) and (5) of s.1. It appears that the word 'establishment' has been used as a genus of which the factory is a species.

Travelling Establishments

The vast majority of establishments have the fairly fixed location of work, and it is only a few establishments like a circus or travelling dramatic companies or travelling groups of musicians or other performers who are constantly moving from place to place. A travelling establishment is in the same position as a non-travelling establishment and can comply with the Act and the Scheme just as well.[128]

Trust is an establishment

Trust can be treated to be an establishment.[129]

Government Contractor is an 'establishment.'

In *Central India Excise Traders v Regional P.F. Commissioner, Indore*[130] the facts were that the petitioner partnership firm was a contractor undertaking job-work in Government Warehouses and claimed protection as a warehouse established under any Central or State Act. Refuting the claim, a Division Bench of the Madhya Pradesh High Court held that activities of the petitioner as an excise contractor in the Government warehouses were definitely business activities or trading activities which may have been undertaken under the strict control and supervision of the State, but the same is undoubtedly an 'establishment' within the meaning of the word used under the provisions of the Act.

"Unless the context otherwise requires" – Scope of

In *N.K. Jain and others v C.K. Shah and others,*[131] the Supreme Court held that the subject matter and the context in which a particular word is used are of great importance and it is axiomatic that the object underlying the Act must always be kept in view in construing the context in which a particular word is used. The concept which prompted the legislature to enact this welfare law should also be borne in mind in interpreting the provisions. Due weight ought to be given to the words "unless the context otherwise requires" occurring in s.2, which show that restricted meaning in the definitions should not be applied."

---

[128] *K. Gopalan v Union of India and others* ILR 1972 Delhi 438, 1973 LabIC 287
[129] *Jotindra Nath Roy v. Surendra Bikram Singh Agarwal,* 1996 II SCC (L&S(960 (SC)
[130] 1990(2) CLR 605: 1990(2) LLN 852: 1992(1) LLJ 498: 1990 M.P.L.J. 611: 1990 M.P.L.S.R. 115
[131] 1991 AIR 1289, 1991 SCR (1) 938

SECTION 2: CLAUSE (A): APPROPRIATE GOVERNMENT

The Central Government is the appropriate Government in respect of establishments belonging to or under the control of Central Government. By 'controlled industry' is meant any industry the control of which by the Union has been declared by a Central Act to be expedient in the public interest. These are the industries specified in the First Schedule to the Industries (Development & Regulation) Act, 1951. S.2 of the Act above declares that 'it is expedient in the public interest that the Union should take under its control the industries specified in the First Schedule. In that, schedule item (4) is iron and steel and item (31) is hurricane lanterns. The explanation I to that schedule says that item (4) 'iron and steel' shall include any manufactured product of iron and steel. Hence, where the business in which the petitioner company is engaged comes under these items, it is a controlled industry.[132] The state government is the 'appropriate government' in respect of industries other than those specified in the First Schedule to the Industries (Development and Regulation)Act, 1951 and those establishments connected with a railway company, a major port, a mine or an oil field. List of the controlled industries for which the appropriate government is the Central Government is provided in the *Appendix*. There can be only one Government which can be regarded as the appropriate Government for any establishment.[133]

SECTION 2: CLAUSE (AA): AUTHORISED OFFICER

This clause was inserted by s.2(a) of the 33rd Amendment Act of 1988 and given effect to from August 1, 1988.

Section 2: Clause (b) Basic Wages

With effect from August 1, 1988, s.2 (b) of the EPF Act has substituted the words 'on leave or on holidays with wages in either case' for the words 'on leave with wages' occurring in the original clause (b). After this amendment, the definition of the term 'basic wages' includes emoluments earned while on holidays with wages.

Concept of Basic wages

The 'universality test' evolved by the Supreme Court in *Bridge and Roofs Co. Ltd. v Union of India*,[134] is that whatever allowances are payable to all the permanent employees would be included in the definition of basic wages, and those who are

---

[132] *Bankim Chandra v Regional Provident Fund Commissioner, Bihar* AIR 1958 Pat 314, 1958 (6) BLJR 239, (1958) IILLJ 444 Pat
[133] *J. and J. Dechane Distributors v State of Kerala and others*, (1974) IILLJ 9 Ker
[134] AIR 1963 SC 1474

not paid/payable to all the employees are excluded therefrom. In *Kichha Sugar Company Ltd. v Tarai Chini Mill Majdoor Union,*[135] the Supreme Court had an occasion (though in a different context) to discuss the meaning of 'basic wages' as defined under s.2(b) of the EPF Act. The Supreme Court observed that those wages which are universally, necessarily and ordinarily paid to all the employees across the board are basic wages. Where the payment is available to those who avail the opportunity more than others, the amount paid for that cannot be included in the basic wages. In *Manipal Academy of Higher Education v Provident Fund Commissioner,*[136] the Supreme Court summed up the basic principles of 'basic wages' as laid down in *Bridge & Roof* case, on a combined reading of s.2(b) and s.6 of the Act, as follows: (a) where the wage is universally, necessarily and ordinarily paid to all across the board such emoluments are basic wages (b) where the payment is available to be specially paid to those who avail of the opportunity is not basic wages (By way of example, it was held that overtime allowance, though it is generally in force in all concerns is not earned by all employees of a concern. It is also earned in accordance with the terms of the contract of employment, but because it may not be earned by all employees of a concern, it is excluded from basic wages.) (c) Conversely, any payment by way of special incentive or work is not basic wages.

Basic Wages – Comprehensive enough to include other allowances

In *Gujarat Gypromet Ltd. v Assistant Provident Fund Commissioner,*[137] the Gujarat High Court held that the term basic wages under s.2(b) of the said Act does not permit any ambiguity, and the plain intention of the Legislature appears to be to include all emoluments other than those which are specifically excluded. There is no need to interpret s.2(b) of the said Act to exclude the allowances such as medical allowance, lunch allowance and conveyance allowance from the definition of term "basic wages." Referring to the decision of the Bombay High Court in *Hindustan Lever Employees' Union v Regional P.F. Commissioner and another,*[138] the Gujarat High Court held that in context of the term 'basic wages' as defined under s.2(b), unless the payment falls in any one of the specifically mentioned excepted categories, every emolument which is earned by the employee while on duty or on leave or on holidays with wages in either case in accordance with the terms of the contract of employment and which are paid or payable in cash to him must be included within basic wages.

---

[135] 2014(1)SCR 157: 2014(1)LLJ257:
[136] AIR 2008 SC 1951
[137] 2004 (3) CLR 485
[138] 1995 (II) LLJ 279

No difference between 'salary' and 'wage.'

In *Hindustan Electric Company Ltd. v Regional Provident Fund Commissioner*,[139] the High Court examined the definition of 'employee' in the Act to hold that only a particular type of 'employee' was covered and not all employees. In fact, at that time, there was a conflict as to whether the Act covered salaried employees, and it was held that only persons who were getting wages amount to less than Rs.200 per month were to be counted and persons getting monthly salaries were not to be included. The Supreme Court, in the case of *Mohmedalli and others v Union of India and another*,[140] held that 'the Act makes no distinction between wages and salary. Both may be paid weekly, fortnightly or monthly, though remuneration for day's work is not ordinarily termed 'salary.'

Production Bonus

The Supreme Court explained the nature of production bonus in the cases of *Bridge and Roof Company (India) Limited and others v Union of India and others*[141] and *Jay Engineering Works Limited and others v Union of India and others*.[142] The Supreme Court held that the typical production bonus which is in force in the former company is excluded from the definition of 'basic wages' as given in s.2(b) of the Act and is therefore not liable for provident fund deductions.

A typical production bonus scheme has a base or standard, and the worker is not bound to produce more than the base. Time wages are guaranteed up to that base or standard and any payment for production above that base or standard, whatever the name of this payment, is production bonus. The peculiar feature of the production bonus scheme in Jay Engineering Works is that it has got two bases viz., the quota and the norm – the quota being much lower than the norm. The workmen are expected to give the 'norm' as the minimum production, and if there is any deliberate deviation therefrom they are liable to be charged with misconduct in the shape of go-glow and may be dismissed for such misconduct. It was held that the portion of the payment which is made by the petitioner for production above the 'norm' would be production bonus and would be covered by the judgment in *Bridge and Roof Company* case (supra), holding that the base or standard of the typical production bonus scheme corresponds to the norm of the peculiar production bonus scheme of the *Jay Engineering Works Limited* case (supra). In *Daily Partap v Regional Provident Fund Commissioner, Punjab*,[143] the Supreme Court held that the payment of bonus

---

[139] AIR 1959 P H 27, (1960) ILLJ 640 P H
[140] 1964 AIR 980, 1963 SCR Supl. (1) 993
[141] 963(3) SCR 978.
[142] 1963(3) SCR 995
[143] 1999(1) CLR 2: 1999(1) S.C.T. 216: 1999 AIR (SC) 2015: 1998(8) SCC 90

should vary in proportion to the extra-output beyond the norms of output. This requirement is the very heart of genuine production bonus scheme, which is missing in the present scheme. The scheme in question does not fulfil the criteria laid down for a genuine production bonus scheme by either of the judgments of the Supreme Court in *Bridge and Roof Co. (India) Ltd. v Union of India case*[144] or *Jay Engineering Works Ltd. and others v The Union of India and others* Case.[145] Payment made by way of bonus or compensation for overtime work is not part of basic wages.[146]

Special Allowance

In *Regional P.F. Commissioner v Management of Southern Alloys (P) Ltd*, the Madras High Court quashed the order passed under s.7-A for the simple reason that it was bereft of reasoning for holding special allowance as deemed dearness allowance. The Court held that the Provident Fund Commissioner could not deem something to be something else. Thus, the test evolved by the Supreme Court in *Bridge and Roofs Co. Ltd. v Union of India*[147] is that whatever allowances are payable to all the permanent employees would be included in the definition of basic wages, and those which are not paid/payable to all the employees are excluded therefrom. The reason for exclusion of HRA, overtime allowance, bonus, and commissions or any other similar allowance, i.e. which is similar to commission payable to the employees in respect of his employment, from the definition of 'basic wages' appears to be that the aforesaid allowances could be employee-specific, and would generally not be payable to all the employees across the board. The 'special allowances' paid universally and necessarily to all the employees across the board should be treated as part of the 'basic wages' for the purpose of EPF contributions.

In *The Regional Provident Fund Commissioner-II, West Bengal and another v Vivekananda Vidya Mandir and others*,[148] the High Court of Calcutta went into the question whether a special allowance could be treated as part of the basic wages in terms of s.2(b) of the Act. The Court observed, "Admittedly, the special allowance is not a retaining allowance which is payable when the employee is retained without work. It is not a cash payment for a food concession. Neither is it overtime allowance, nor house rent, nor bonus, nor commission. Neither does it come within clause (iii), i.e., presents by the employer. Therefore, this special allowance is either some other similar allowance or dearness allowance, if it is not, then, it will be part of the basic wages since it is an emolument paid on account of the employment in terms of the contract therefor and

---

[144] 963(3) SCR 978.
[145] 1963(3) SCR 995.
[146] *T.R. Industries v Central Board of Trustees*, (1988) 57 FLR 130(Del).
[147] AIR 1963 SC 1474
[148] 2005-II-LLJ-721

is payable to each employee. The Court held that the special allowance could not be treated one of the other similar allowances which are otherwise exempted under s.6 of the Act, and it is either part of the basic wages or it is the Dearness allowance itself described or called as 'special allowance' or in the garb of special allowance it is the Dearness Allowance, which is being wrongly described.

Leave Encashment – Not Basic wage

In *Thiru Arooran Sugars Ltd. v Assistant Provident Fund Commissioner*,[149] the Madras High Court held that the basic wages as defined under s.2(b) of the Act does not include 'leave encashment.' The Court observed, "if the two decisions of the Supreme Court in *Bridge & Roof Company (India) Ltd.*'s case, as well as *TI Cycles of India*'s case, read together, there will be no difficulty in arriving at the conclusion that the basic wage was never intended to include the leave with wages for which encashment is allowed. The term basic wage which includes all emoluments which are earned by an employee while on duty or leave or holidays with wages. In accordance with the terms of the contract of employment, it cannot mean it can only mean the weekly holidays, national festival holidays. In many cases, the employees do not take leave and encash it only at the time of retirement or as legal heirs at the time of his death, which is an uncertain contingency. Even though the employer made annual provisions for such contingency unless the contingency of encashing of leave takes place, the question of the actual payment to the workmen never takes place. In case, he avails the entire leave, during his tenure, then the question of payment of any contribution may not arise. Any payment of contribution cannot be based upon different contingencies and uncertainties.

In *Hindustan Lever Employees' Union v Regional Provident Fund Commissioner and another*,[150] the Bombay High Court held that the amount payable on account of encashment of leave would form part of the 'basic wages.' The Court reasoned that if an employee who goes on leave, his salary can obviously fall within the terms of 'basic wages,' and there can be no reason to hold that in the event of his not availing the leave but encashing it, the amount which he gets as leave encashment, should be excluded from the 'basic wages.'

"Commission" – Not a part of 'basic wages' nor should it be added

In *Usha Sales Ltd. v Regional P.F. Commissioner*,[151] it was found that the employer was paying various sorts of commissions to different categories of employees in addition to salary, as, shop pool commission, individual transaction commission,

---

[149] 2008(1) LLJ 806
[150] 1995 LLR416 (Bom.)
[151] 1980 Lab IC 546: (1980) 1 LLN 452 (Del.)

hire purchase commission, service and repair commission, aggregate commission, etc. The commission and salary varied with the category of shop where a person was posted, and the employer's case was that it was inherent in a wage structure which is evolved for sales promotion or is efficiency-oriented that the basic wages are far below than what is paid in concerns which have no commission or incentive oriented scheme. The Delhi High Court held that "commission, in any case, stands excluded from the definition of wage, whether one takes the statutory definition or the definition in the petitioner's rules." The Court, however, observed that the plea of subterfuge would have been tenable if it could be demonstrated that the commission payable to the employees was so fixed that a minimum of a specified sum would be payable to each employee irrespective of the work done by him.

Revised pay with retrospective effect should be taken into account

In *P.T. Varghese and others v Regional Provident Fund Commissioner & another*,[152] the Kerala High Court, following the *ratio decidendi* of the Supreme Court in *Prantiya Vidhyut Mandal Mazdoor Federation and others v Rajasthan State Electricity Board and others*[153] held that the quantum of pension should be recomputed on the basis of revised pay, even if the revisions was effected only retrospectively. In this case, the employer had paid the difference in the contribution by retrospective revision of pay, and the Provident Fund Commissioner was directed to recalculate the pension after reckoning the revised quantum of pay.

Adhoc payment under Sec.12(3) Settlement

In *Burmah Shell Oil Storage and Distributing Co Ltd. v Regional Provident Fund Commissioner, Delhi*,[154] the Delhi High Court held, the ad hoc payment may not be a present in the conventional sense of the term and as it is not earned, nor has it any relation to time or period or payable only to those who are in service on a particular date, it is something the nature of a present, though ceasing to be gratuitous on account of the contract of service, and hence cannot be termed as 'basic wages.'

Notice Pay – Not Wages

In *India United Mills Ltd. v Regional Provident Fund Commissioner, Bombay*,[155] Bombay High Court held that the payment in question (notice pay) is not a payment earned for duty done. It is not a payment earned while on duty. It is a payment by way of consideration for terminating the contract of employment of

---

[152] W.P. No.23031 of 2014 order dated 3rd August 2010
[153] (1992) (2) SCC
[154] 1981 (42) FLR 315, ILR 1980 Delhi 841, (1981) IILLJ 86 Del
[155] (1959) 61 BOMLR 1385, (1959) IILLJ 733 Bom

a permanent employee without notice. The payment made cannot in any sense be regarded as representing 'emoluments earned while on duty' and are not and do not constitute 'basic wages' within the meaning of the definition given in the Employees' Provident Funds Act, 1952, and no percentage thereof is payable by way of provident fund contribution. Similarly, in the case of *Dinesh Khare v Industrial Tribunal, Jaipur and others*,[156] the High Court of Rajasthan held that one month's wages paid to a workman under s.33(2) of the Industrial Disputes Act was in the nature of a notice pay and was, therefore, not a basic wages within the meaning of s.2(b) of the Employees' Provident Fund Act and therefore, provident fund was not deductible on this amount.

Settlement allowance is not basic wages

In *Southern Alloy Foundries (P) Ltd. v, Regional Commissioner, EPF*[157] the Madras High Court was considering the question whether the Commissioner could go into the fairness of the wage fixed in the backdrop of fixation of wages under various settlements entered into between the employer and the employees. Similar is the decision in the case of *E.I. Parry (India) Ltd. v Regional Provident Fund Commissioner, Tamilnadu and another*.[158] In the said case, the Court took the view that flat *ad hoc* allowance paid to all employees under a settlement cannot partake the character of basic wages and does not attract liability for contribution under the EPF Act.

Lump sum back wages based on Court order attract EPF Liability

In the *Changdeo Sugar Mills and another v Union of India and another*,[159] the Supreme Court observed that even in a case of lump sum payment of full and final settlement of all the labour claims, the management is required to contribute to the Provident Fund. The provident fund deductions are to be made even when the employee is absent provided he is entitled to wages for that period. The real test is not whether the employee is on duty but whether the employee is entitled to basic wages even during the period of absence from duty.[160]

Illegal Lock-out – Deemed to be on duty

In *Shree Changdeo Sugar Mills and another v Union of India and another*,[161] the Supreme Court observed: "Undoubtedly contribution towards Provident fund

---

[156] (1982) IILLJ 17 Raj, 1981 WLN 678
[157] 56 FJR 46
[158] 1984 (1) LL Notes 527
[159] [(2001)2 SCC 529]
[160] *Gosalia Shipping Pvt Ltd. v Regional P.F. Commissioner*, 1997 II LLJ 38 (Bom.HC)
[161] 2001 (2) SCC 519

can only be on the basic wage. However, it is not at all necessary that the workman must be actually on duty or that the workman should have worked to attract the provisions of the Employees' Provident Fund Act. For example, there may be a lockout in a Company. During the period of the lockout the workmen may not have worked yet for the Employees' Provident Fund Act, they will be deemed to have been on duty and Provident Fund would be deductible on their wages."

A similar view was taken by the Supreme Court, in *Prantiya Vidyut Mandal Mazdoor Federation v Rajasthan State Electricity Board & Ors*[162] where it was held that the EPF contributions would be payable on the arrears of wages given to the employees by an award. The Supreme Court observed, "when the original emoluments earned by an employee were basic wages under the Provident Fund Act, the 'substituted emoluments' as a result of the award are also to be regarded as basic wages. When an award gives revised pay scales, the employees become entitled to the revised emoluments and where the said revision is with retrospective effect, the arrears paid to the employees, as a consequence, are the emoluments earned by them while on duty. The real test is not whether the employee is on duty but whether the employee is entitled to basic wages even during the period of absence from duty. If this test is not accepted then in case of an illegal closure, illegal termination etc., though the employee is kept out of work for no fault of his, the employer can contend that no contributions are due and payable. This is not what the Act contemplates.[163]

Contributions for lock-out period

The High Court of Delhi, in the case of *Regional P.F. Commissioner v United India Periodicals Pvt Ltd.*,[164] held that the liability of the employer to pay wages in case of lock-out would depend upon whether the lock out was legal and justified. If the lock-out is illegal, the employer would be liable to pay full wages to the workman. If the lock-out is legal but is unjustified, the workman is entitled to receive full wages and other benefits. The dispute regarding payment of wages during the lock-out need to be decided by the Tribunal by applying mind to the question of apportionment of the blame on the two parties and to its effect on the amount of wages to be awarded to the workman. If the wages are paid during lock-out, even though not worked they would be deemed to be on duty and provident fund to be deductible on their wages.

---

[162] 1992 LLR 401; 1993(I) LLJ 222 (SC)
[163] *Gosalia Shipping Pvt Ltd. v Regional P.F. Commissioner* 1997 (1)LLJ38 (Bom.HC)
[164] WP No.463 of 1999

Allowances – Whether forms part of 'basic wages'

Judicial pronouncements have held that the expression *"any other similar allowance"* would mean an allowance which is similar to "commission." To construe the words *"any other similar allowance"* generally and widely to include any or all payments that the employer may refer to as an "allowance" would have the effect of narrowing the scope of the expression "basic wages." If "allowance" was construed widely, the employer could split the basic wages into several allowances, including those specifically contained in the exclusionary clauses (i), (ii) and (iii) of s.2(b) of the Act, to reduce its liability towards PF contribution. It is the well-settled rule of interpretation that a proviso of an exclusionary clause could not be given so wide an interpretation as to consume the main provision itself.

In *India United Mills Ltd. v Regional Provident Fund Commissioner, Bombay and others*,[165] the Bombay High Court held that 'the expression 'emoluments which are earned by an employer while on duty' represents the amounts earned by an employee during the period of his employment while he is actually on duty. The payment in question is not a payment earned for duty done. It is not a payment earned while on duty. It is a payment by way of consideration for terminating the contract of employment of a permanent employee without notice. The payments made cannot in any sense be regarded as representing "emoluments earned while on duty" and are not and do not constitute "basic wages" within the meaning of the definition given in the Employees' Provident Funds Act, 1952, and no percentage thereof is payable by way of provident fund contribution." Payment made to transporters towards reimbursement of the cost of feeding and maintaining animals is not 'basic wages' under s.2(b).[166]

Overtime Allowance

Remuneration for additional houses did not form part of basic wages to reckon the employer's contribution to the provident fund under s.6.[167] Extra-leaf price paid in the tea garden to pluckers who pluck more tea than the normal fixed is 'basic wages.' Extra-leaf price was not payment for something which was done beyond the regular working hours, and therefore it could not be overtime. Overtime means work done not on time but after that. Extra-leaf price, therefore, could not be 'overtime allowance' which is excluded from the definition of 'basic wages' by s.2(b)(ii).[168]

---

[165] 1959(2)LLJ 733: AIR 1960 Bom.203
[166] *Mohd. & Sons v. J.M. Pandya,* 1979 Lab IC (NOC) 115 (Raj).
[167] *I.T.C. Ltd. v Regional P.F. Commissioner,* (1987) 2 LLN 932
[168] *Amal Kumar Ghatak v Regional P.F. Commissioner,* (1980) 2 LLJ 308

Canteen Allowance

The employer is liable to pay the provident fund contribution by taking into account the 'canteen allowance' – being paid to the employees in terms of a binding settlement. In *Whirlpool of India v The Regional P.F. Commissioner,*[169] the Delhi High Court held that the liability arises, even if the petitioner's contention that the canteen allowance cannot be construed as 'the cash value of any food concession' is accepted because the canteen allowance is part of the 'basic wages' itself.

In *Tata Power Company Limited and others v Regional P.F. Commissioner,*[170] the Bombay High Court held that in respect of the supply of an amenity, the cash value of the concession could not be deduced. Under the Minimum Wages Act, the cash value of a concession always means the amount by which the value of an essential supply is reduced when supplied. Therefore the term 'cash value of any food concession' allowed to the employee means such value of the component by which the price of the item is reduced. This necessarily postulates the provision of the supply of an amenity such as food grain for, without such supply, it would not be possible to calculate the value of any food concession allowed to the employee. There being no supply of any food by the petitioner, the payment of food allowance cannot be treated as the cash value of food concession allowed to the employee. In *The Regional P.F. Commissioner v Wipro Limited,*[171] the Madras High Court held that the question of considering provident fund on the cash value of any food concession would only rise in an establishment like a catering establishment where providing a canteen is a statutory requirement. Held, canteen facilities are equally applicable to the performance-linked compensation which would not attract provident fund contributions.

Subterfuge of wages

It was held by a Division Bench of the High Court of Karnataka, in the case of *Group 4 Securities Guarding Ltd. v Regional P.F. Commissioner*[172] that House Rent Allowance, Traveling Allowance and commissions other than Dearness Allowance are not part of the basic wages. But if split up of the wages under these heads is only a subterfuge to reduce the PF contribution, then the inquiry authority under s.7-A has jurisdiction to probe into the reality of the fact, and if he finds that this split is only a subterfuge then he can determine the Provident Fund dues after clubbing all these heads of wages as basic wages.

---

[169] W.P.(C.) 7729/1999] dated 22.07.2013. (Delhi HC).
[170] 2008 (III) LLJ 992
[171] (2009) 4 MLJ 972
[172] (2000) LLJ-II (1142) (Karnataka)

SECTION 2: CLAUSE (C): CONTRIBUTION

S.6 read with Chapter V of the Employees' Provident Funds Scheme, 1952 deals with contributions payable in respect of a member under the said Scheme. S.6-A(2) of the EPF Act read with Paragraph 4 of the Employees' Pension Scheme, 1995 deals with contributions payable in respect of the members of the Pension Scheme. Sub-sections (2) and (3) of s.6(C) of the Act, read with paragraphs 7 and 8 of the Employees' Deposit-Linked Insurance Scheme, 1976 deal with contributions payable under the Insurance Scheme.

SECTION 2: CLAUSE (D): CONTROLLED INDUSTRY

S.2 of the Industries (Development and Regulation) Act 1952 has, in the public interest, placed the industries specified in the First Schedule to that Act under the control of the Union. A list of such controlled industries for which the appropriate Government is the Central Government is provided in the *Appendix*.

SECTION 2: CLAUSE (E): EMPLOYER

The definition of the word 'employer' takes within its fold the owner or occupier of the factory inclusive of the agent of such owner or occupier, the legal representative of a deceased owner or occupier as well as the manager so named under s.7(1)(f) of the Factories Act. This definition is concerning an establishment, which is a factory. Concerning any other establishment, the person or the authority exercising ultimate control would be the employer and where such authority or control is entrusted to a manager, managing director or managing agent, such manager, managing director or managing agent.[173]

The expressions 'occupier' and 'owner' are not interchangeable. The question whether the statutory dues under the ESI Act can be recovered either from the owner or the occupier as defined under s.2(e) of the said Act, came for consideration before the Supreme Court in *Employees' State Insurance Corporation v S.K. Aggarwal and others*.[174] The Court held that the words 'owner' and 'occupier' found in s.2(e) of the said Act had been used disjunctively and therefore, in a case where the owner is public limited company, it would not be necessary to refer to the word 'occupier' while construing the word 'owner.'

A perusal of the first part of s.2(e)(i) of the EPF Act would show that the employer can be either owner or occupier. The second part, however, sets out when the person has been named as Manager of the factory, under sub section (1) of

---

[173] *Shri Angappa Spinning Mills v. Regional Commissioner, Employees' Provident Fund*, (1986) 1 MLJ 386
[174] 1998 II CLR 518

s.7 of the Factories Act, 1948 the person so named under the provisions of the Factories Act is the occupier. The occupier under s.2(g) of the Factories Act has been defined to mean a person who is having control over the affairs of the factory. The Provisions of the Factories Act and the EPF Act, therefore, will have to be read together to know who the occupier is. An employer, therefore, can either be the owner or the occupier.[175]

The term 'owner' is not defined in the Act. However, the term 'owner' has been used in the Factories Act, 1948 and 'the owner who was within the contemplation of the legislature, was a person who bore some relationship with the workers who were working on the premises. A person who is merely the owner of a place on which the premises of the factory are situate, or a person who is merely the owner of the premises in which the machinery is installed or who again is merely the owner of the machinery with the help of which the manufacturing process is carried on, cannot be deemed to be an owner such as is contemplated by sub-section (2) of s.85 of Factories Act.[176]

SECTION 2: CLAUSE (F): EMPLOYEE

Scope and Meaning of the term 'employee'

Meaning of the term 'employee' differs from statute to statute depending on the objectives they intend to achieve. The definition of "employee" in the social welfare legislation like the EPF Act, does not create the same sort of relationship of employer-employee as defined under the Industrial Disputes Act, 1947 or any other statutes for that purpose, and the contractor employees, without any distinction or discrimination, are deemed to be the employees of the principal employer for the limited purposes of the Employees' Provident Funds and Miscellaneous Provisions Act, 1952 if they satisfy the attributes as defined under s.2(f) of the Act.

Any kind of work – manual or otherwise

In *South India Research Institute v Regional Provident Fund Commissioner*,[177] the High Court held that the words 'in any kind of work, manual or otherwise" appearing in the definition of employee in s.2(f) would take in all kinds of work.

In *Kumar Bros.(Bidi) (P) Ltd. v Regional Provident Fund Commissioner*,[178] it was held that the definition of the word 'employee' as defined under s.2(f) of the Act is completely different from the definition of 'worker' and 'workman' respectively

---

[175] *Garware marine Indsutries Ltd. and others v Union of India and others*, 2005 (3) LLN 506 (Bom.HC)
[176] *Jamnabai Purshottam Asar v. State of Maharashtra*, (1964) 2 LLJ 7: AIR 1964 Bom 267
[177] (1981) 59 FJR 160
[178] 1968 Lab IC 1578 (Pat. HC)

in the Factories Act and the Industrial Disputes Act and decisions relating to the meaning of 'worker' or 'workman' under the said Acts may not be useful in interpreting the definition of 'employee' under the Employees' Provident Funds and Miscellaneous Provisions Act, 1952. The definition of the term 'employee' in s.2(f) includes all employees who are engaged in or in connection with the work of the establishment, including a person employed by or through a contractor in such work.

A Division Bench of the Calcutta High Court, in the case of *Bengal Ingot Co Ltd. v Regional Provident Fund Commissioner*,[179] was considering whether the part-time Medical Officer engaged by the Respondent will come within the meaning of 'employee' under s.2(f). The Court answered in the affirmative, observing as follows: :The term 'employee' as defined under s.2(f) of the Act means not only for performing any work in connection with the establishment, but also any other work for the employer-company manual or otherwise and that while construing the provisions of s.2(f) of the said Act we have to bear in mind the object of the Act and the principles of interpretation that have to be adopted in construing the provisions of the Act.

In *Tin Printers Pvt Ltd. v Regional P.F. Commissioner*,[180] the Calcutta High Court was considering whether the five directors who receive salary will come within the meaning of 'employee.' Taking note that those five directors had been receiving a salary as stated in the balance sheet of the company, and there has been master and servant relationship between the Company and the working partners, the High Court held that these directors are 'employees' for the EPF Act.

In *Gujarat State Civil Supplies Corporation Ltd. v Regional Provident Fund Commissioner & others*,[181] the High Court of Gujarat held that a person employed in or in connection with the work of an establishment is an 'employee' and a person having control over the affairs of the establishment is an 'employer, regardless of whether he has control or supervision over the functioning of the employees. The High Court observed that whatever may be the apprehensions about a person's employment through contractor before the amendment [inserting the words 'and includes any person employed by or through a contractor], there cannot be any further ambiguity in the face of clause (i) of s.2 (f). The Court also read the alternatives simply as follows: "Employee means any person (a) employed by a contractor in the establishment; (b) employed by a contractor in connection with the work of the establishment; (c) employed through a contractor in the establishment;

---

[179] (1996) IIILLJ 176 Cal
[180] 2000 LLR 1175 (Cal. HC).
[181] (2000) GLR 398, (1999) IILLJ 844 Guj

(d) employed through a contractor in connection with the work of the establishment." If a person falls 'in any one of the categories, he is to be treated as an employee in relation to the establishment in or in connection with the work of which he has been employed, and the owner, manager, managing director or managing agent of the establishment is treated as his employer. It becomes immaterial whether he is employed by the person treated as an employer within the meaning of s.2(c) or by any other person who receives his remuneration from such employer, under the terms of the agreement between the employer and the person who employs and supervises the work of such persons.

Homeworkers

In *P.M. Patel and Sons v Union of India and others*,[182] the question before the Supreme Court was whether the home workers were entitled to get the benefits of the EPF Act. The Court held that the terms of the definition of employee contained in s.2(f) are so wide as to include not only persons employed directly but also those employed by a contractor; it includes within its meaning not only the persons employed in the factory but also those engaged outside the premises of the factory but involved in an activity connected with the work of the factory. Following the *P.M. Patel & Sons*[183] case, the Patna High Court, in *S.K. Nasiruddin Bidi Merchant v Regional Provident Fund Commissioner*,[184] held that all the three categories of home workers, viz., (i) those directly employed by the manufacturer, (ii) those employed by the contractor for the manufacturer, and (iii) those supplying the finished products of persons known as independent contractors, are employees within the definition of s.2(f) of the Act. Thus, the decision in the case of *P.M. Patel and Sons* (supra) was considered and re-affirmed by the Supreme Court in the case of *S.K. Masiruddin Beedi Merchant Ltd. v Central Provident Fund Commissioner and another*,[185] and it was held that the EPF Act applies to those homeworkers engaged in rolling beedis through independent contractors.

In case of *Silver Jubilee Tailoring House v Chief Inspector of Shops and Establishments*,[186] the criteria which determined the relationship between master and servant were considered. It was held in that the workers who were tailors went to the tailoring shops and were given work as and when work was available and, when cloth was given for stitching to a worker he was told how he should stitch it, and if the instructions were not carried out the work was rejected, and he was

---

[182] (1986) 1 SCC (L & S) 155: (1986) 1 LLN 55.
[183] (1986) 1 SCC (L & S) 155: (1986) 1 LLN 55.
[184] 1990 (1) BLJR 348
[185] AIR 2001 SC 850
[186] AIR 1974 SC 37

asked to re-stitch it. Some of the workers were allowed to take the clothes home for stitching. The Court held that there was a relation of master and servant because of the right in the employer to reject the work done. It was reiterated that "the degree of control and supervision would be different in different types of work."

In *Padiyur Sarvodaya Sangh v Union of India*,[187] the Madras High Court held that the artisans who obtain the raw materials from the Petitioner society and convert these raw materials into finished products and return the finished products to the Sangh are 'employees' within the meaning of s.2(f). The Court observed, "it is clear that a section of these artisans, who are unable to pay for raw materials due to their financial position, are provided with raw materials by the Sanghs themselves, and the Sanghs collected their finished products by paying the difference of the value of finished products and raw material. If that is so, the difference in the value of the finished products and raw-materials is nothing but wages paid to the workers in the sense of the same being remuneration for the physical or mental effort in connection with the works, which are ultimately utilised by the Sanghs. In *Satish Plastics v Regional Provident Fund Commissioner*,[188] held, the definition of employee in s.2(f) is wide enough to take within its sweep a person permitted to work in his residence as well and further that even if a person is not employed but was principally employed in connection with the business of the shop, would be a person employed within the meaning of the statutory language.

Casual Employees

It is a settled legal position that the word 'employment' envisaged under s.2(f) and in s.1(3) of the Act would not include the employment of persons for a short period on account of some pressing necessity or some temporary urgency beyond the control of the company.[189]

The word 'employment' must, therefore, be construed as employment in the regular course of business of the establishment; such employment obviously would not include the employment of a few persons for a short period on account of some passing necessity or some temporary emergency beyond the control of the company. This must necessarily require determination of the question in each case in its own peculiar facts.[190]

---

[187] (2000) ILLJ 290 Mad
[188] 1981 (2) LLJ 277: (1982) 44 FLR 207: (1981) 22 Guj. LR 686
[189] *Saroj Oil and Dal Industries v Central Board of Trustees*, 2011 (176) DLT 150: (128) FLR 984: 2011(2) LLJ 735(Del.)
[190] *Regional Provident Fund Commissioner, Andhra Pradesh v T.S. Hariharan* 1971 2 SCC 68

In *Regional Provident Fund Commissioner v T.S. Hariharan*,[191] the Respondent was running a hotel, and due to the failure of water supply, he had to employ some persons to fetch water from the tank for a short period. The Provident Fund Commissioner sought to enforce the provisions of the Act by treating these temporary employees also as employees of the Respondent. The Supreme Court said, employment of a few persons on account of some emergency or for a very short period necessitated by some abnormal contingency which is not a regular feature of the business of the establishment and which does not reflect its business prosperity or its financial capacity and stability from which it can reasonably be concluded that the establishment can in the normal way bear the burden of contribution towards the provident fund under the Act would not be covered by this definition.

In *Sandeep Dwellers Pvt Ltd. v Union of India*,[192] the Bombay High Court (Nagpur Bench), following the decision of the Supreme Court in *T.S. Hariharan* case (supra), held that it is within the competence of the provident fund authorities to adjudicate on this issue whether the workers engaged for shorter duration are eligible to be included in the definition of 'employee' under s.2(f) of the Act. Likewise, the Hon'ble High Court of Madras observed, Para 26(1)(a) of the Scheme read with s.1(3) of the Act and the definition of the word 'employee' as contained in clause (f) of s.2, would cover only such of the persons who have been employed in or in connection with the work of the establishment in the regular course of business of the establishment or the factory as the case may be, and it would not include employment of the persons of a short period on account of some passing necessity or for some temporary need or emergency.[193]

In *East India Industries (Madras) Private Limited v Regional Provident Fund Commissioner*,[194] the Madras High Court held that the employment even for one day brought a factory within the scope of s.1(3)(a) and that the expression 'in which fifty or more persons are employed' in s.1(3)(a) did not envisage 'continuity of employment of all the fifty persons. This provision was also considered by a Division Bench of the High Court of Andhra Pradesh in *Nazeena Traders (P) Ltd. v Regional Provident Fund Commissioner.*[195] The Andhra Pradesh High Court differed from the view of the Madras High Court and held that the casual labour fell outside the scope of s.1(3), and hence the establishment in which employees did not come

---

[191] AIR 1971 SC 1519: 1971 Lab I.C.95
[192] 2006 (III) CLR 748
[193] *Joint Commissioner/Executive Officer, Arulmighu Subramaniaswamy Thirukoil, Tiruttani v EPFAT and others*, W.P. No.29158/2010, decided on June 7th, 2011 (Mad.HC)
[194] (1964) 1 MLJ 441
[195] AIR 1965 AP 200

up to twenty, excluding casual labourers did not fall within the purview of s.1(3) and the provisions of the EPF Act could not be applied to them.

Both these conflicting views were considered by the Supreme Court in the case of *Provident Fund Inspector, Guntur v T.S. Hariharan* and the Supreme Court did not accord approval to either the Madras High Court view or the Andhra Pradesh High Court view and observed as, "considering the language of s.1(3)(b) in the light of the foregoing discussion, it appears to us that employment of a few persons on account of some emergency or for a very short period necessitated by some abnormal contingency which is not a regular feature of the business of the establishment and which does not reflect its business prosperity or its financial capacity and stability from which it can reasonably be concluded that the establishment can in the normal way bear the burden of contribution towards the provident fund under the Act would not be covered by this definition. The word 'employment' must, therefore, be construed as employment in the regular course of business of the establishment, such employment obviously would not include employment of a few persons for a short period on account of some passing necessity or some temporary emergency beyond the control of the company."

Following the Supreme Court decision in the *T.S. Hariharan* case (supra), the Delhi High Court, in *Eastern Arts Corporation v S.P. Mehrotra*,[196] has held that the period of employment is not by itself a decisive factor, and that a person working for sixteen days in a leave vacancy could not be counted to determine the strength of employees under s.1(3)(b). Subsequently, in *G.V.V. Swamy v Regional Provident Fund Commissioner*,[197] a Division Bench of the Andhra Pradesh High Court considered the decision in *Hariharan case* as well as *Nazeena Traders* and held that the employees of contractors who continued to work in various contracts and were not appointed merely as casual labour, attracted the provisions of the Act. The Court observed that merely because the periods of various contracts between the contractors and the employees were limited periods or months, the employees did not become casual labour. Employees engaged in different work shifts should be included for the purpose of EPF Act.[198]

In *Laksmi Restaurant v Regional Provident Fund Commissioner*,[199] the Delhi High Court observed that the regular employment rests not on the nature of the terms of employment but the nature of the business of the establishment

---

[196] 1986 Lab IC 1402
[197] 1987 Lab IC 719 (AP)(DB)
[198] *American Express Bakery v Regional P.F. Commissioner*, 2011(131) FLR 1093 (Bom.HC)
[199] 1975 Lab IC 1186 (Del.)

and its commercial rooms. In *Lakshmi Restaurant v Regional Provident Fund Commissioner*,[200] casual workers were occasionally engaged by the petitioner restaurant for outside parties. It was held that the establishment in the regular course of its business did not employ them. Similarly, in *Ratan Lal v Regional Provident Fund Commissioner*,[201] a sweeper, a municipal employee, was being given *bakshish* (tipping or charitable giving) for doing work but no wages; a Chowkidar was working for community and not for the establishment, and a driver was the personal staff (though paid out of car expense account) of the proprietor of the establishment. The Court held that all these persons do not come within the meaning of 'employee.'

In *Chatram Agarwalla v Regional Provident Fund Commissioner*,[202] Orissa High Court observed that where an establishment employs temporary employees as a part of the regular feature of the establishment, such employees cannot be construed as casual employees. For instance, an establishment may be carried on daily by more than 20 temporary employees, and if they continue to work in the regular course of business for one year, then the establishment would come within the ambit of the definition in s.1(3) of the Act. If at least for one day in a year, the establishment employs more than 20 persons, the Act becomes applicable automatically to the establishment from that date.[203]

'Employee' under ESI Act is not in pari materia

The definition of the word employee under the EPF Act is not in *pan materia* with its definition of the Employees' State Insurance Act. While interpreting the provisions of one statute in *pari materia* with another statute the interpretation made of the same provision of a statute is a guiding factor, but the definition of employee in the two statutes is not in *pari materia* so as to import the same meaning as given to the word employee in the Employees' State Insurance Act.[204]

Coolies

In *ESI Corporation v Premier Clay Products*,[205] the Supreme Court held that where the work itself was of sporadic nature and the coolies engaged in performing that work worked for several others, such coolies could not even be called casual workers, and hence no contribution would be payable on the wages paid to such persons.

---

[200] 47 (1975) FJR 186
[201] 1977 Lab IC. 1765
[202] (1972) 1 LLJ 603: 1973 Lab IC 530 (Ori).
[203] *Deep Cycle Industries v Union of India*, (1971) 39 FJR 407
[204] *Union of India v Patna Tyre House Pvt Ltd* 2004 (101) FLR 666, (2004) IILLJ 778 Pat
[205] 1995 S.C.C. (L & S) 162

Bazaar Night watchman – Not an employee

A bazaar night watchman, who did not reside in the premise of the establishment and who looked after several shops in the vicinity of the establishment cannot be termed as 'employee.' The employment of a person should be dictated by the normal requirements of the establishment for the regular work which should also have a commercial nexus with its general financial capacity and stability.[206]

Proprietor's driver – Not an employee of the firm

In *Ratan Lal v Regional Provident Fund Commissioner*,[207] the question for consideration before the Delhi High Court was whether the driver of the proprietor of a firm whose salary was debited to the 'car expense account' can be treated as an 'employee' of the firm. The High Court held that as the proprietor was an individual, he was entitled to debit his personal expenses to the car account and deal with his accounts in any way he liked and the driver could not be said to be working in the establishment or in connection with the work of the establishment. It may be a different case if the establishment belongs to a limited company or a partnership firm.

Status of Trainees

In *Regional Provident Fund Commissioner v Hotel Highway Limited*,[208] held, the trainees undergoing training with the management and not paid wages will not fall within the definition of 'employee.' In *Regional Provident Fund Commissioner v Central Arecanut & Cocoa Marketing and Processing Coop Limited, Mangalore*,[209] it was held that the trainees who were paid stipend during the training period had no right to employment, nor were under obligations to accept any employment, even if offered by the employer. The Supreme Court held that 'apprentices' engaged under the Standing orders of the establishment could not be said to employees in terms of s.2(f) of the Act. The crux of the matter is whether there is an employer-employee relationship. If it is not there, it matters very little whether the qualification prescribed under the Apprenticeship Act are satisfied or not. Where only training is imparted, and no wages are paid, they cannot be called as employees at all.[210] The nominal payment made to the trainees does not make them regular employees, in the absence of any master-servant relationship between the establishment and the

---

[206] *Mysore State Cooperative Printing Works Ltd. v Regional P.F. Commisisoner* ILR 1976 KAR 1233, 1976 (1) KarLJ 277, (1976) IILLJ 300 Kant
[207] 1977 Lab IC 1765
[208] 2004 (3) LLN 397
[209] 2006 (1) LLN 529
[210] *Regional P.F. Commissioner v Hotel Highway Limited* ILR 1991 KAR 2381 1991 (79) FJR 190

trainees.²¹¹ Where only training is imparted, and no wages are paid, the trainees cannot be called employees at all.²¹²

Government Servant on deputation – Not an employee

In *Mysore State Coop Printing Works Ltd. v Regional Provident Fund Commissioner*,²¹³ the facts under consideration were that under the bye-laws of a co-operative society, the secretary was a government servant deputed to the society by the Registrar of Cooperative Societies, but he continued to remain as a government servant with all the conditions of service applicable to him including the rules of pension. The Karnataka High court held that he could not be considered as an employee of the establishment within the meaning of s.2(f) even though the establishment paid his salary. The payment of salary was necessitated by the terms of deputation and also perhaps as per bye-laws of the society, and it was certainly not by reason that he was an employee defined under s.2(f) of the Act.

In *Alwar Central Cooperative Bank Limited v Regional Provident Fund Commissioner and another*,²¹⁴ the Rajasthan High Court held that the managers of the primary agricultural cooperative society are employees of the particular bank though he acted under the control and supervision of the Managing Committee/ Sanchalak Mandal of the society.

Liaison Officer – Employee

A person doing liaison work in New Delhi for an establishment situated in Vijayawada would fall within the definition of employee as there is a direct connection or nexus with the work of the establishment and as he is part and parcel of the organisation.²¹⁵

Apprentices excluded from the meaning of 'employees.'

By the Amendment Act of 1988,²¹⁶ the definition of 'employee' has been so altered as to include any person engaged as an apprentice, not being an apprentice under the Apprentices Act, 1961, or under the standing orders of the establishment. In *Regional Provident Fund Commissioner, Mangalore v Central Arecanut & Coca Marketing and Processing Coop Ltd*,²¹⁷ the Supreme Court held, "an apprentice engaged under the Apprentice Act or the Standing Orders is excluded from the definition of an

---

211   Gandhi Vanita Ashram v Regional Provident Fund Commissioner., (1995) 111 PLR 237
212   Regional P.F. Commissioner v Hotel Highway Ltd., (1992) Lab. IC. 1201 (Karn).
213   1976 Lab IC 1307 (Kar HC)
214   2007 (113) FLR 310 (2007) 2 LLJ 347 Raj
215   South India Research Institute v Regional P.F. Commissioner., (1981) 59 FJR 160
216   With effect from 1ˢᵗ August 1988
217   (2006) 2 SCC 381

'employee' as per s.2(f) of the Act. The fact that by the Amendment Act of 1988, provision was inserted in the definition of the employee to include a person engaged as an apprentice subject to the exclusion therein, clearly demonstrates that before the amendment, there was no possibility of bringing in any category of apprentice into the definition of an employee.[218]

Apprentices – Model Standing order is sufficient

In *The Regional Provident Fund Commissioner v Central Arecanut and Cocoa Marketing and Processing Coop. Limited, Mangalore*,[219] the Supreme Court held that if the Standing Orders of the Company were not certified at the relevant point of time, the Model Standing Orders are deemed applicable virtue of clause 12A of the Industrial Employment (Standing Orders) Act, 1946. Under the Model Standing Orders, an apprentice is described as a learner who is paid allowance during the period of training and hence such a learner is excluded from the meaning of 'employee.' The decision of the Supreme Court will not be applicable if it is provided that the employer had not engaged apprentices and they were treated as regular employees and wages were paid for the actual days of their employment and only to circumvent the statutory liability, the employer had claimed the persons are engaged as apprentices.[220]

Priests and Nuns – Not 'employees.'

In *Reverend Father Agnelo Gracies vs Regional Provident Fund Commissioner*,[221] the Bombay High Court observed that the provisions of the Code of Canon Law indicate the absence of a relationship of employment between the seminary and the Priests. The Priests are not employees nor is there a relationship of employment. Control and direction which an employer possesses and which, in a conventional sense, is the prerogative of the employer, is absent in the case of Priests who render religious discourse at the seminary. They are not employees and do not meet the requirement of employment for the Act. In *Lohardaga Charitable Ursuline Society v Union of India*,[222] the Jharkhand High Court held that in the absence of records to prove that the nuns and sisters of a religious order are drawing a salary, they could not be brought within the meaning of 'employee.'

---

[218] *Regional PF Commissioner v Precise Wire Cloth Co (P) Ltd.*, 1992 (64)FLR 73
[219] 2006 (1) LLN 529 (2006) 2 SCC 381
[220] *N.E.P.C. Textile Ltd. v Assistant Provident Fund Commissioner, Coimbatore* 2007 LLR 535 (Mad.HC)
[221] 2005 (3) BomCR 308, 2005 (2) KLT 165, (2005) IILLJ 132 Bom, 2005 (1) MhLj 693
[222] 2003 (97) FLR 171, 2003 (1) JCR 476 Jhr, (2003) IILLJ 554 Jhar

Visiting doctors are not employees

In *Employees' Provident Fund Organisation v Employees' Provident Fund Appellate Tribunal and another*,[223] the Kerala High Court held that the consulting doctors providing services for some hours or so to different establishments without control over them by that establishment would not come under the meaning of 'employees.'

Deposit Collectors of Banks are employees

In *South Malabar Gramin Bank v Regional Provident Fund Commissioner*,[224] the Karnataka High Court, relying on the Supreme Court decision in *Indian Banks Association v Workmen of Syndicate Bank and others*,[225] held that the Nithya Nidhi Deposit Collectors engaged by the appellant Bank are 'employees' and the Commission earned by them forms part of 'basic wages' as defined in the EPF Act.

Partner receiving remuneration – Not an employee

The partners cannot be included in employees' category to satisfy the requirement of minimum number of employees as one person cannot at the same time be the employer and the employee.[226] The same view was endorsed by the Bombay High Court in *Prakash D. Shah and others v Union of India*.[227] The Bombay High Court relied on *Regional Director, ESIC v Ramanuja Match Industries*,[228] in which the Supreme Court observed, "A partner who belongs to the class of employer cannot rank as an employee because he also works for wages for the partnership. Undoubtedly the term employee is the co-relative of the employer. In common parlance the status of a partner qua the firm is different from employees working under the firm, it may be that a partner is being paid some remuneration for any special attention which he devotes, but that would not involve any change of status and bring him within the definition of employee." In *S.G. Tin Printers Pvt. Ltd. v Regional P.F. Commissioner*,[229] a Division Bench of the Calcutta High Court held that the same person could not hold dual capacity – one as an employer as well as the employee. Therefore, the partners could not be treated to be employees to attract the application of the Act.[230] In *Union of India v Patna Tyre House Private*

---

[223] 2012-II-LLJ-563 (ker)
[224] 2013 LLR 470 (Karn. HC)
[225] 2001 (3) SCC 36
[226] *Om Roller Flour Mill v Union of India* 2002 (3) LLJ 228
[227] 2004(I) LLJ 943
[228] 1985 AIR 278, 1985 SCR (2) 119
[229] 2001-I-LLJ-628 (Cal)
[230] *Om Roller Flour Mills v Union of India* 2002 (94) FLR 908, (2002) III LLJ 228 Cal

Limited,[231] the Patna High Court held that the directors are not 'employees' even if they get remuneration.

Directors are not 'employees'

The Director although getting remuneration shall not come within the definition of employee and the natural corollary of the same is that they shall not be counted as employees for calculating the employment strength.[232] It will also be a peculiar position if the same person is treated as both employer and an employee for the non-deduction and non-payment of provident fund amount from the remuneration payable to such a Managing Director, the very same Managing Director should be prosecuted.[233]

Part-time Workers

In *Railway Employees' Cooperative Banking Society v The Union of India*,[234] it was held that a sweeper engaged by the petitioner society who worked twice or thrice a week, a night watchman who kept a watch on other shops in the locality also, and a gardener who came for work ten days in a month – all 'employees' within the meaning of s.2(f) of the Act. Even if a person is not wholly employed, if he is principally employed in connection with the business of the shop, he would be a person employed within the meaning of the statutory language.[235]

Piece-rated women members of a charitable trust – employees

In *Shree Kutchi Visha Oshwal Mahila Mandal v Union of India and others*,[236] the Bombay High Court held that the device of obliging the women-members to make an application to become an associate member of the Society before they are allowed to work on wages at piece-rate could not change their legal status as employees.

Artisans and weavers of Sarvodaya Sangh

The weavers or artisans are provided with raw materials by the Sarvodaya Sangh, and those artisans or weavers converted the raw materials into finished products and after that returned the same to the Sanghs. The Madras High Court held that the difference in value of the finished products and raw-materials is nothing but wages paid to the workers in the sense of the same being remuneration for the physical or mental effort in connection the works, which are ultimately utilised

---

[231] 2004 (101) FLR 666, (2004) IILLJ 778 Pat
[232] *Union of India v Patna Tyre House Pvt Ltd* 2004 (101) FLR 666, (2004) IILLJ 778 Pat
[233] *Sanatan Ghosh v Regional Provident Fund Commissioner*, 1991-II-LLJ-466
[234] (1980) Lab IC 1212 (Raj.)
[235] *Satish Plastics v Regional P.F. Commissioner* (1982) 44 FLR 207
[236] 1992 (65) FLR 72, (1993) ILLJ 77 Bom

by the Sanghs, and that the workers or weavers undoubtedly fall under the ambit of the expression 'employees' as defined under s.2(f) of the Act.[237] In *Padiyur Sarvodaya Sangh v Union of India and another,*[238] the Madras High Court held that the artisans, weavers, workers of Sarvodaya Sangh are covered under the definition of employee.

Members of Self-Help Groups are 'employees'

In *P. Santhi and others v The Commissioner, Tiruppur Corporation and another,*[239] the facts of the case were that members of various Women Self-Help Groups were engaged through a tender process for collection and disposal of solid waste. When they were required to contribute the employees' share of Provident Fund contributions, they contended that they were engaged on daily wage basis and they engage not more than 16 workers; there was no reference to the EPF contributions in the tender notification issued by the Corporation; Self-Help Groups are not an establishment coming within the purview of the EPF Act. These contentions were rejected by the Madras High Court stating that the argument that the Act does not apply to the employees of the Self-Help Group does not stand to reason given s.2A of the Act read with s.2(f). The further argument that at the time of floating tender, the EPF liability was not mentioned also does not stand to reason because under the law when the Self-Help Groups are covered by the provisions of the Act; they are bound to deduct the amount from the wages of the workmen engaged by them. Since the work order itself stated that they are bound by the Rules and Regulations governed by the Government, they cannot feign ignorance of their legal obligations.

In *Springdale School and others v Regional Provident Fund Commissioner and another,*[240] the High Court held that an employee would be treated as working in or in connection with the work of the establishment if it can be ascertained that he is discharging his duties exclusively related to the work of the establishment.

In *Shahdol v Regional Provident Fund Commissioner and another,*[241] the Madhya Pradesh High Court held that the person coming in the truck to unload the bamboos in the factory premises falls under the definition 'employee' for all practical purposes.

---

[237] *Padiyur Sarvodaya Sangh v Union of India,* 2000 I LLJ 290 (Mad. HC)
[238] 1999 (2) LLN 224
[239] W.P. Nos.33748, 34410 to 34415, 34956 to 34962, 35162 to 35169 of 2012 and 3369, Decision dated February 13, 2013 (Mad. HC)
[240] 2006 (2) LLJ 321
[241] 2005 (4) LIC 4091

Excluded Employee

In terms of Para 2(f)(i) of the Employees' Provident Fund Scheme, 1952, an employee, having been a member of the EPF, withdraws the full amount of the accumulations on retirement after attaining the age of 55 years or leaving service for disablement, or for migration from India for permanent settlement aboard shall be deemed 'excluded employee' if he rejoins an establishment thereafter. But engagement of retired government employees (who are not governed by the provisions of the EPF Scheme during their government service) shall not qualify for the same, as held by the Supreme Court in *Orissa Cement Ltd. v Union of India*.[242]

Similarly, in *Central Provident Fund Commissioner v Modern Transportation Consultancy Services Pvt Ltd.*,[243] the Respondent Company was a contractor of the Damodar Valley Corporation for the supply of personnel for manning the cabins and gages on the Captive Railway System roads. It had engaged 28 persons who were retired employees of the Indian Railways on a lump sum honorarium basis, and all of them were over 58 years of age. As regards their enrolment under the EPF Scheme, the Respondent contended that they, being retired employees, did not come within the purview of the Act. It was stated that these employees while in the service of the Railways were not covered under the Employees' Provident Fund Scheme, 1952 but were covered under the General Provident Fund (GPF) and drew all the superannuation benefits including Provident Fund and Pension. It was claimed that these employees were 'excluded employees' under Paragraph 26 of the EPF Scheme, 1952. The High Court refused to accept these contentions and upheld that these retired employees are required to be enrolled as EPF members.

Employment versus Engagement

The Kerala High Court in the case of *Regional Director, E.S.I. Corporation v P.R. Narahari Rao*[244] took note of the distinction between an "employment" and "engagement." If a person is engaged casually in a process unconnected with the operations of the establishment, or some work which does not form an integral part of such operations, he may not be an employee since there would be no employer-employee relationship between them only in consequence of the casual engagement for purposes unconnected with the main operations of the establishment. On the other hand, if a person is employed, though casually and for a very short period, but in connection with the processes which are integral and connected with the

---

[242] AIR 1962 SC 1402; 1962–1 LLJ 400
[243] 2009 LLR 324(SN) (Cal HC)
[244] 1986 Lab IC 1981

incidental or preparatory to the operations of the establishment, then he may be an employee entitled to coverage under the Act.

Employee versus Independent Contractor

The definition of an 'employee' in sec.2(f) of the Act includes any person who is employed for wages in any kind of work or in connection with the work and includes a person employed by or through a contractor in or in connection with the work. The usual distinction between an employee and an independent contractor is thus abandoned in the Act.[245] In *Dharangadhra Chemical Ltd. v State of Saurashtra*,[246] the Supreme Court observed: "The broad distinction between a workman and an independent contractor lies in this that while the former agrees himself to work, the latter agrees to get other persons to work. Now, a person who agrees on himself work and does so work and is, therefore, a workman does not cease to be such by reason merely of the fact that he gets other persons to work along with him and that those persons are controlled and paid by him. What determines whether a person is a workman or an independent contractor is whether he has agreed to work personally or not. If he has, then he is a workman and the fact that he takes assistance from other persons would not affect his status."

The scope of the phrase "in connection with the work of an establishment"

In *Royal Talkies, Hyderabad v Employees' State Insurance Corporation*,[247] the Supreme Court held, "the expression "*in connection with the work of an establishment*" ropes in a wide variety of workmen who may not be employed in the establishment but may be engaged only in connection with the work of the establishment. Some nexus must exist between the establishment and the work of the employee, but it may be a loose connection. *'In connection with the work of an establishment'* only postulates some connection between what the employee does and the work of the establishment. He may not do anything directly for the establishment; he may not do anything statutorily obligatory in the establishment; he may not even do anything which is primary or necessary for the survival or smooth running of the establishment or integral to the adventure. It is enough if the employee does some work which is ancillary, incidental or has relevance to or link with the object of the establishment. Surely, an amenity or facility for the customers who frequent the establishment has a connection with the work of the establishment. The question is not whether without that amenity or facility the establishment cannot be carried on

---

[245] *Gopalan K. v Union of India*, 1973 LIC 287: 40 FJR 546 (Del.DB).
[246] AIR 1957 SC 264: (1957) 1 LLJ 477
[247] AIR 1978 SC 1478: 1978 LIC 1245

but whether such amenity or facility, even peripheral may be, has not a link with the establishment. Illustrations may not be exhaustive but may be informative.

There is no provision anywhere in the Act that before the Central Government issues a notification under s.1(3)(b), a notice is required to be given to all persons who would be affected by such notification to show cause against the extension of the provisions of the Scheme to their establishments. The question of such notice arises only where the Central Government intends to apply the provisions of the Act to any establishment employing a number of persons less than twenty.[248]

Coverage – Headcount includes all categories of employees

In *Nazeena Traders (P) Ltd. v Regional Provident Fund Commissioner*,[249] a Division Bench of the Allahabad High Court held that the clauses (a) and (b) of sub-section (3) of s.1 have to be interpreted in the light of the definition of the term 'employee' as contained in s.2(f) and not in isolation, independent of the definition. That being the real position, the definition brings in contract labour within the scope of s.1(3). s.1(3) is not confined to direct labour, and contract labour has also to be counted for determining the applicability of s.1(3). In *Bankim Chandra Chakravarty v Regional Provident Fund Commissioner*,[250] the Patna High Court held that "a plain reading of section 1(3) makes it perfectly manifest that all persons employed in an establishment whether drawing more or less than three thousand and five hundred rupees per month as pay, should be taken into account for finding out whether the establishment satisfies the test of numerical strength provided under s.1(3). If the number of all such persons is less than twenty, then only the provisions of the Act would be inapplicable."

SECTION 2: CLAUSE (G): FACTORY

The word 'factory' includes not merely the area comprised by the walls of the building in which a manufacturing process is carried on, but the whole area comprises within the boundaries of the premises.[251] In *Kokkalai Rice & Oil Mills Foundry v Regional P.F. Commissioner*,[252] the Full Bench of the Kerala High Court held that the word 'factory' in s.1(3) of the Act means the whole of the premises in any part of which a scheduled industry is carried on and not the particular unit thereof which is actually engaged in such industry. Though 'factory' stands defined

---

[248] *Bajranglal Padia v State of Orissa* (1974) 2 Cut.WR 735
[249] AIR 1965 AP 200: (1966) 1 LLJ 334
[250] AIR 1958 Pat 314, 1958 (6) BLJR 239, (1958) IILLJ 444 Pat
[251] *Regional P.F. Commissioner v Singhai Moujilal & Sons*, 1961 I LLJ 275 (MP. DB)
[252] 1960 II LLJ 528 (Ker. FB)

under s.2(g) of the Act, yet it falls within the general category of 'establishment,' and to such an 'establishment,' s.2-A of the Act would certainly be attracted.[253]

Difference between precinct and premise

In ordinary parlance 'precinct' means 'a bounded area,' and the 'premises' a built-up area.[254] The expression premises is a wide one and takes within itself not merely a building but a series of buildings also. Precincts mean a place which is bounded by metes and bounds. Therefore, the true test to determine whether a particular place is or is not 'premises, including the precincts thereof' is whether the place is such as is defined by metes and bounds.[255] Even if it is shifted from one place to another, it will continue to be an 'establishment' under s.1(3)(a).[256] When some manufacturing process is carried on in some premises, the whole premises become a factory even though the manufacturing process is being carried on only in a part of the premises.[257]

SECTION 2: CLAUSE (I): INDUSTRY

S.2(i) defines industry as meaning any industry specified in Schedule-I and includes any industry added to the Schedule by notification under s.4. This definition shows how entries in Schedule I assume significance.[258] Whenever a question arises as to whether the EPF Act covers any industry, the answer is to be found at looking at Schedule I. Once the prerequisites of s.1 (3) are satisfied, and the undertaking is shown to be engaged in a manufacture or manufacturing process, the Act applies. It is the manufacturing process which is the decisive factor.[259]

Industry and Factory

In case of a factory where an industry included in Schedule I of the Act and other industries not so included in the Schedule are carried on, the number of employees required for coverage under s.1(3) should be in the scheduled industry alone, or whether it can include the employees engaged in the other non-scheduled industries. In *Regional Provident Fund Commissioner v Great Eastern Electroplater Ltd.*,[260] the Allahabad High Court held that the said words relate to 'factories' and not to

---

[253] *Leos Mercantile Corporation v The Secretary, Ministry of Labour and others*, 1987 (2) LLJ 35
[254] *National Agricultural Coop Marketing Federation of India Ltd. v Regional P.F. Commissioner*, 1987 LIC 529 (Del. HC)
[255] *Swastik Textile Trading Co. Ltd. v Union of India*, 1965 II LLJ 254 (Guj. HC)
[256] *K. Gopalan v Union of India*, 1973 Lab IC 287 (Del).
[257] *Chinnaih (A.M.) Sangu Soap Works v State of Tamilnadu*, (1957)ILLJ280Mad
[258] *Regional P.F. Commissioner v Shibu Metal Works* (1965) 1 LLJ 473: AIR 1965 SC 1076
[259] *Regional P.F. Commissioner v Osmania University*, 1973 Lab IC 912 (AP)
[260] AIR 1958 All 474

'industry.' The Madras High Court also took the same view in *Madras Pencil Factory v Regional Provident Fund Commissioner.*[261] On the other hand, the Bombay High Court in *Oudh Sugar Mills Ltd. v Regional Provident Fund Commissioner*[262] held that the said words govern or qualify the phrase 'industry specified in Schedule-I' and not the word 'factories.'

Finally, a Division Bench of the Kerala High Court, in *Kokkalai Rice and Oil Mills v Regional Provident Fund Commissioner,*[263] observed that the real legislative intent was well manifested by the subsequent enactment of Act 94 of 1956 recasting s.1(3) of the Act as "Subject to provisions contained in Section 16, it applies to every establishment which is a factory engaged in any industry specified in Schedule I and in which fifty or more persons are employed." The Kerala High Court held that the addition of the word 'and' in this new section showed beyond any doubt that the expression 'engaged in any industry specified in Schedule-I' and the expression 'in which fifty or more persons are employed' both qualify the word 'factories.'

SECTION 2: CLAUSE (IC): MANUFACTURE

The definition of *'manufacture'* as in s.2 (ic) is somewhat wide. It includes not only making but also altering or otherwise treating or adapting any article to its use, sale, transport, delivery or disposal. In *Lawly Sen & Co v Regional Provident Fund Commissioner, Bihar and another,*[264] a Division Bench of the Patna High Court held that since the petitioner carried on the work of repair and servicing of cars and deals also in motor accessories, cars, trucks etc., it therefore followed that the workshop of the petitioner came within the definition of the expression 'manufacture' in s.2(ia)[265] read with the explanation in Schedule I of the Act. Citing the above, the Calcutta High Court, in *Metalizing Corporation v Regional Provident Fund Commissioner,*[266] held that metalising of the worn-out part is certainly treatment of an article and the petitioner establishment comes within the meaning of 'manufacture of electrical, mechanical or general engineering products.' Refuting the contention that the petitioner was merely repairing parts and components of machinery, already produced, by the process of moralizing and get remuneration for the work done, the Court held that the petitioner may not sell the goods reconditioned by it but only charge remuneration for repaid, but nevertheless, it treats the goods brought by other people for the purpose of repaid with a view that the worn-out parts may

---

[261] AIR 1959 Mad 235, (1959) ILLJ 262 Mad
[262] AIR 1957 Bom 149
[263] AIR 1961 Ker 57, (1960) IILLJ 528 Ker, (1960) IILLJ 528 Ker
[264] AIR 1959 Pat 271, 1958 (6) BLJR 722, (1959) ILLJ 272 Pat
[265] Re-lettered by Act 99 of 1976 as (ic) for (ia)
[266] (1966) IILLJ 528 Cal

ultimately be put to use and that brings the petitioner within the operation of the Act. (Handbook of Legal Clarifications, 1963). The definition of 'manufacture' or 'manufacturing process' in s.2(1a) includes various types of processes resulting in the manufacture or production of the basic article or substance mentioned in Schedule-I but does not include any process converting the basic article or substance into an altogether different article or substance.[267] Metalizing of worn-out parts of goods will come under 'manufacturing process.'[268]

SECTION 2: CLAUSE (J): MEMBER

A member of the provident fund continues to be a member even after he leaves the factory or establishment concerned until he withdraws the amount standing to his credit in the Fund.[269]

SECTION 2: CLAUSE (K): OCCUPIER OF A FACTORY

Managing Agent

The word *'managing agent'* is defined under s.2(25) of the Companies Act, 1956. "Managing agent" means any individual, firm or body corporate entitled, subject to the provisions of this Act, to the management of the whole, or substantially the whole, of the affairs of a company by an agreement with the company, or by virtue of its memorandum or articles of association, and includes any individual, firm or body corporate occupying the position of a managing agent, by whatever name called."

Official Liquidator is the Occupier

The expression 'ultimate control' used in the definition of the term 'employer' and 'occupier' in s.2(e) and 2(k) of the Act should be read to include the control exercised by the Official Liquidator appointed by the High Court to run the business of the factory with a view to sell it as a going concern. But if the Liquidator is asked to wind up the factory and close it down, he would not be liable because the factory would no longer be 'engaged' in the specified industry.[270]

POWER TO ADD TO SCHEDULE I

Factories engaged in industries other than those mentioned in Schedule I may also be brought within the ambit of the Act by a notification under s.4, thus adding

---

[267] *Kamalakar Shankar Warde v Central Board of Trustees*, 1966 I LLJ 553 (Bom.HC)
[268] *Metalizing Corporation Pvt Ltd. v Regional P.F Commissioner*, 1964 (9) FLR 253
[269] *Rameshwar Lal agarwala v Kuti mian*, 1969 Labour IC 790 (792) (Pat)
[270] *Mahalaxmi Cotton Mills v Regional P.F. Commissioner*, (1960) 1 LLJ 468: AIR 1960 Cal 199.

to Schedule I.[271] If, on the other hand, any establishment, factory or non-factory, whether engaged in industry or not, is to be brought within the scope of the Act, that can be done by issuing a notification under clause (b) of sub-section (3) of s.1. S.4(2) provides a safeguard by requiring that notifications issued under sub-section (1) of s.4 shall be laid before the Parliament, as soon as may be, after they are issued.

No overlapping between S.1(3)(b) and S.4

It is possible that to some extent the provisions of s.4 overlap the power under sub-clause (b), of s.1(3), but it cannot be said that both the provisions cover an identical matter. There might be considerations applicable to a class of establishments, and there might be particular circumstances on account of which the Central Government might contemplate to extend the provisions of the Act to a specified establishment or a class of establishments which would be permissible under clause (b) of sub-section (3). In such a case it would be necessary to take action under this clause and not under s.4. This shows that both the provisions, namely clause (b) of sub-section (3) and s.4 may fulfil a separate and distinct purpose and in this sense, it cannot be said that the two provisions would necessarily overlap in every case.[272]

Industrial Tribunal can direct institution of Provident Fund

In *Trichy Srirangam Transport Company (Pvt.) Ltd. V Industrial Tribunal*,[273] the Madras High Court held that the power of the Central Government under s.1(3)(b) to extend the provisions of the EPF Act to certain establishments does not preclude the industrial tribunal from directing a management to introduce a provident fund scheme, which may not however have certain statutory features like protection of monies from attachment, etc as available under the EPF Act.

PRIMARY AND SUBSIDIARY OR INCIDENTAL ACTIVITIES – COVERAGE

In *Regional Provident Fund Commissioner v Shree Krishna Metal Manufacturing Company*,[274] the Supreme Court held that the Act applies to establishments which are factories as well as to establishments which are not factories. An establishment may consist of different departments or may have different branches, whether they are situated in the same place or different places. Therefore, it cannot be said that a composite factory carrying on different industrial operations is outside the purview

---

[271] *Provident Fund Inspector, Quilon v Kerala Janatha Priners & Publishers (Pvt) Ltd.*, 1966(1) LLJ 491 (Ker. DB).
[272] *Ojas Corporation v. Regional P.F. Commissioner*, 1970 Lab IC 81.
[273] 1959(2)LLJ 515(Mad.)
[274] 1962 SC 1536: (1962) 1 LLJ 427

of s.1(3)(a). The expression 'engaged in any industry' does not mean 'exclusively engaged in any industry.' It should be interpreted to mean 'mainly engaged in any industry specified in Schedule-I." If a factory is engaged in two industrial activities one of which is its primary, principal or dominant activity and the other is a purely subsidiary, incidental, minor or feeding activity, then it is the primary or dominant activity which should determine the character of the factory under s.1(3)(a).

However, the question of a department or unit of a factory carrying out any subsidiary, minor or feeding industry or industries will arise only where the factory was started for running the primary industry and has undertaken other subsidiary industries only for supervising and feeding the purposes and objects of the primary industry. But if all the industries carried out in a factory are independent of each other and constitute separate and distinct industries, s.1(3)(a) will apply to the factory even if one or more, but not all, of the industries run by the factory fall under Schedule I. Thus, in *Associated Industries (P) Ltd. v Regional Provident Fund Commissioner*,[275] where a company was running a tile factory and an engineering industry on the same premises under one licence under the Factories Act and the engineering industry fell under Schedule I but the tile factory did not, it was held that the two industries being independent of each other, there was no question of any one of them being the principal or subsidiary. The contention that the factory did not attract the provisions of s.1(3) (a) was, therefore, rejected.

In *Nazeena Traders (P) Ltd. v Regional Provident Fund Commissioner*,[276] the Andhra Pradesh High Court held that the scope of s.1(3)(a) of the Employees' Provident Funds Act, 1952 is not limited to factories exclusively engaged in the industries enumerated in Schedule I to the Act and that the fact that a factory carries on one industry which is included in Schedule-I while the other industry carried on by the same factory does not come within its purview does not absolve the employer from the obligations impugned by the Act if the total strength of the employees in both the industries exceeds the required number.

Similarly, in *Andhra University v Regional Provident Fund Commissioner*,[277] the Supreme Court, overruled the Calcutta High Court order in *Visva Bharati v Regional Provident Fund Commissioner*,[278] observing that the Act being a beneficent piece of social welfare legislation is not to be narrowly interpreted so as to defeat that very object, held that an establishment which is a factory engaged in any 'industry' specified in Schedule I and employing 20 or more persons, will attract

---

[275] AIR 1964 SC 314: (1964) 2 SCR 905: (1963) 2 LLJ 652
[276] AIR 1965 AP 200: (1966) 1LLJ 334
[277] (1985) 4 SCC 509: 1986 SCC (L & S) 134: (1986) 1 LLJ 155
[278] 1983 Lab IC 38: (1983) 1 LLJ 332 (Cal).

the provisions of the Act even if being run by a larger organisation carrying on other activities not covered by the Act. The observations of the Supreme Court were made in the context that the Department of Publications and Press of the Andhra University and the Osmania University are factories within the meaning of s.2(g). They are carrying on printing work, which constitutes 'manufacture' within the meaning of s.2(i-c) and is also an industry specified in Schedule I. The said departments are 'establishments' and as they had employed more than 20 persons, the provisions of the Act are attracted.

In *Regional Provident Fund Commissioner v Madras Pencil Factory*,[279] the Respondent pencil factory employing more than 50 persons had a foundry and workshop attached to it in which certain spare parts required for the machinery employed in the manufacture of pencils were fabricated. Manufacture of pencils was not one of the industries notified in Schedule-I, but the fabrication of spare parts fell within the ambit of the schedule I. It was held that the requirement of the number of persons employed *relates to the factory and not to the industry*. It was further held that where a factory manufactures articles in which it does not trade but only uses those articles in enabling it to carry out its manufacturing process, the Act would apply only where the final product is within the schedule and not otherwise. Wholly irrational results would follow if the expression 'engaged in' is interpreted to mean to include any activity of a factory of whatever kind solely for the reason that such activity is carried on in the precincts of the factory.

In *Cemindia Co Ltd. v Bachubhai N. Raval*,[280] the Supreme Court, held that a workshop exclusively engaged in the work of maintaining and repairing the equipment of the main establishment is not a separate establishment. As illustrations, the Court explained that an establishment exclusively engaged in running a hospital does not cease to be an establishment exclusively carrying on the said business merely because it sets up a Pharmacy Section for preparing and compounding medicines to be used exclusively by the patients at its hospital. Similarly, an establishment which is exclusively engaged in providing shipping transport facilities does not cease to be an establishment exclusively carrying on the said business merely because it sets up an on-shore workshop for effecting repairs exclusively to its ships. The point which is made out by these illustrations is that where an establishment is engaged exclusively in carrying on a particular type of business by setting up any place of work with a view to carrying on the work of repairs etc., to the tools, equipments, vehicles, etc., used in its business or to carry on any other activity which is essential for its business effectively and which is not used to carry on the work for the benefit

---

[279] (1961) 2 LLJ 783 (Mad).
[280] 1987 AIR 1956, 1987 SCR (3) 784

of any third party but utilised exclusively for the business of the establishment, such establishment does not cease to carry on exclusively the business in which it is engaged. It cannot also be said that the establishment has commenced to carry on another industry by the setting up of such a place of work.

In *Oudh Sugar Mills Ltd. v Regional Provident Fund Commissioner*,[281] the Bombay High Court held that where while carrying on an industry certain products are produced, not with the object of marketing them separately but with the object of using them in the industry itself, then the production of those articles cannot result in the engagement in an industry of producing these articles. The word 'industry' should be understood in the sense in which it is understood in the business community. If the industry is the production of edible oil, then all the intermediate products which are produced for carrying on that industry cannot be regarded as separate industries. Thus the law is well settled that if a company carries on two manufacturing business, one of which falls in Schedule-I and the other not, and if the dominant activity falls within Schedule-I, the entire establishment will attract the provisions of s.1 (3)(a) subject to other conditionality.

---

[281] AIR 1957 Bom 149, (1957) 59 BOMLR 877, ILR 1958 Bom 438, (1957) II LLJ 654 Bom

Chapter V
DEPARTMENTS/BRANCHES AND COMPOSITE ESTABLISHMENTS

S.2-A was inserted by Act 46 of 1960 which came into force on 31st December 1960. It declares, for removal of doubt, that where an establishment consists of different departments or has branches, whether situated in the same place or different places, all such departments or branches shall be treated as part of the same establishment. Even before insertion of s.2-A, the provisions of the Act applied to a composite factory, as such a factory was factory within the contemplation of s.1(3)(b).[282]

S.2-A: EXPLANATORY IN NATURE

In *Andhra University and others v Regional Provident Fund Commissioner,*[283] the Supreme Court clarified that s.2-A of the Act was inserted merely to clarify the position that the Act applies to composite factories. It is not the intendment of the section to lay down even by remotest implication that an establishment, which is a factory engaged in an industry specified in Schedule I will not liable for coverage under the Act merely because it is part of a larger organisation carrying on some of the activities also which may not fall within the scope of the Act. In *Union of India v Ogale Glass Works,*[284] the Supreme Court held that the insertion of s.2-A merely clarifies the position and does not mean that before the said insertion, the Act was not applicable to composite factories. Thus, s.2-A is merely declaratory or explanatory, and it is not intended to amend or alter the law previously existing.[285] If the ingenious entrepreneurs so manage their affairs as to have separate factories, which on practical analysis can be said to be departments or branches of the other on account of certain well known interconnections, the clarification made in s.2-A would step in ultimately to realise the high objectives sought to be achieved by this Act.[286]

---

[282] *Union of India v Ogale Glass Works,* (1971) 2 SCC 678
[283] 1986 AIR 463, 1985 SCR Supl. (3) 582
[284] 1971 AIR 2577, 1972 SCR (1) 525
[285] *Uma Shankar Srivastava v State of U.P* SCN Vol No.VI, 14, Oct.16, 1964. P.19
[286] *Gujchem Distillers India Ltd. v Regional P.F. Commissioner,* 1985 LIC.1714

COMPOSITE ESTABLISHMENT

An establishment may well fall within the meaning of 'factory' under s.2(g), but any administrative or branch offices maintained by such an establishment for the working and running of the factory cannot be dissociated from the factory. Rather, such an establishment and such offices constitute a single unit for determining the number of persons employed.[287]

In *Regional Provident Fund Commissioner v Naraini Udyog and others*,[288] the facts for consideration before the Supreme Court were that the two establishments *viz.*, M/s Naraini Udyog, Kota and M/s Modern Steels, Kota were held a composite establishment for coverage under Sec.1(3)(a) of the Act. The Division Bench of the Rajasthan High Court held that they were registered under the Companies Act as two different individual identities, though they are represented by the members of the same family, and therefore they are two independent companies. Reversing the High Court order and restoring the order passed by the Provident Fund Commissioner, the Supreme Court observed that though they are registered as two independent units and represented separately by the members of a Hindu Undivided Joint Family, there is functional unity and integrity between the two concerns and consequently, they ought to be treated as 'composite establishment' keeping in view of the beneficial nature of the legislation.

In *P. Madhavan Thampi v Regional Provident Fund Commissioner*,[289] a partnership firm was dissolved, and on the date of dissolution itself, the owner gifted the shops and factory etc. to his spouse, son and daughters, who started running them as five different establishments. The Kerala High Court found that in spite of the gift deeds, the original places of business continued as such, either as branches or as independent concerns, and the original character of the business also continued. It was further found that what happened in the case was only a transfer of ownership to get out of the reach of the Act and not the creation of independent concern unconnected with one another. Thus, the High Court refused to accept the contention that the five concerns had taken birth in place of the old establishment.

In *Regional Provident Fund Commissioner and another v Dharamsi Morarji Chemical Co Ltd.*,[290] common ownership, by itself cannot be sufficient to hold that one unit is a branch of another unless there is clear evidence to show that there was an interconnection between the two units and there was common supervisory, financial or managerial control.

---

[287] *Leos Mercantile Corporation v Secretary, Ministry of Labour and others*, (1986) 2 LLN 965
[288] 1996 Supp(3) SCR 202
[289] (1978) 2 LLJ 467: (1978) 37 FLR 298 (Ker.)
[290] 1998) 2 SCC 446

In *Regional Provident Fund Commissioner v Raj's Continental Exports (P) Ltd.*,[291] the Supreme Court was considering whether the Respondent Company was a branch of already covered one. The Respondent argued that there was no financial integrity as both are separately registered under the Factories Act, the Central Sales Tax Act, 1956, the Income Tax Act, 1961 and the ESI Act. They have the separate balance sheets and audited statements. The High Court accepted the contention of the Company and held that there was total independence in exercise of power in the two concerns. The Supreme Court upholding the High Court order held that though the manufacturing of goods was in respect of the same article, that by itself was not sufficient to hold that it was a branch or department of M/s Continental Exporters.

Clubbing of establishments – Tests to determine

In *Eddy Current Controls (India) Ltd. v Regional Provident Fund Commissioner*,[292] the Kerala High Court elaborated the implications of s.2A holding that in order to determine the different parts, units, branches and so forth are mere constitutes of one establishment, the important tests which are enumerated below must be satisfied (however, with a note of caution that no hard and fast rule can be laid down as to how many of the following shall have to be satisfied). (i) The unity of ownership, management and control, unity of employment and conditions of service functional integrality and general unity of purpose (ii) The connection between the two activities is not by itself sufficient to justify an answer one way or the other, but the employer's conduct in mixing up or not mixing up the capital, staff and management may often provide a certain answer. (iii) The real purpose of the tests is to find out the true relationship between the two parts, branches, units etc. If they constitute one integrated whole, the establishment is one. If it is to the contrary, then each unit is a separate one. (iv) In one case the unity of ownership, management and control may be the important test; in another case, functional integrality or general unity may be the important test, and in still another case the important test may be the unity of employment. (v) Many enterprises may have functional integrality between factories, which are separately owned; some may be integrated in part with units or factories having the same ownership and in part with factories or plants, which are independently owned. In the midst of all these complexities, it may be difficult to discover the real thread of unity."

In *Andhra Cement Co. Ltd. v Regional P.F. Commissioner*,[293] the Andhra Pradesh High Court, while stating that there is no straight jacket formula, to hold that

---

[291] ((2007) 4 SCC 239
[292] 1993 (67) FLR 928: 1993 LLR 961
[293] (1998) II LLJ 453(AP)

different unit constitutes of one establishment, listed out certain salient features. They are (1) Unity of ownership, management and control, the unity of employment, conditions of service, functional integrity and general unity of purpose. (2) The connection between the two activities by itself is not sufficient, but the employer's conduct in mixing up or not mixing up the capital, staff and management may often provide a certain answer. (3) If the true relationship between the two parts constitutes one integrated whole, it is the same establishment. (4) Thread of unity must be there to constitute a single establishment.

Partition of the establishment – Effect on applicability

In *Regional Provident Fund Commissioner v K.K. Bhanumathy*,[294] the Kerala High Court held that 'members of the same family with close relationship, either as mother and son or as brothers or brother and sister, can conduct different establishments in the same premises and merely on the basis of locative proximity, all the establishments cannot be clubbed together as one establishment, falling under the Act, unless sufficient documentary evidence supports the integrity of function and management. Such a situation usually occurs, when single ownership divides by family partition. After family partition, different establishments cannot be clubbed together, though, earlier, they were owned and functioned singly. So, functional and managerial integrity are the twin conditions for clubbing different establishments together, as one, falling under the Act.' In *Mohmammed Kutti v Regional Provident Fund Commissioner*,[295] the Kerala High Court held that the estate partitioned on the death of its owner among his two sisters, should be treated as a separate establishment and the partitioned portion of the establishment, had it employed fewer than 20 persons, does not come within the purview of the Act.

In *Management of Pratap Press, New Delhi v Secretary, Delhi Press Workers' Union, Delhi*,[296] the Supreme Court held that where two units belong to the same proprietor there is most likely of unity of management and, in such cases, the Court has to consider as to how there is functional integrality between the two, meaning thereby, that one has to see functional inter-dependence between the two units. One has to find out as to whether both the units could exist conveniently and reasonably without the other. In the matter of finance and employment, the authorities were required to find out whether the two units were distinct or integrated and these two tests were to be applied before proceeding to consider the unit as one for the applicability of the Act of 1952. The same view has been

---

[294] 2016(2) LLJ 389: 2016(150) FLR 302: 2016(3) KLT 60: : 2016(3) CLR 547: 2016(3) Ker L.J. 67
[295] (1968) IILLJ 466 Ker
[296] A.I.R. 1960 SC 1213

expressed by the Supreme Court in various cases after that from time to time. In *Noor Niwas Nursery Pubic School v Regional Provident Fund Commissioner*,[297] the Supreme Court reiterated the three important factors to be considered for clubbing of establishments, viz., financial integrity between the two units (whether one unit cannot exist conveniently and reasonably without the other), financial matters and employment (has the employer kept the two units distinct or integrated).

In *Regional Provident Fund Commissioner, Jaipur v Naraini Udyog and others*,[298] the Supreme Court held that although the two firms are registered as two independent units and are represented separately by the members of a Hindu Undivided Joint Family, but since there is functional integrality between the two concerns (that is, some of the employees were working for both the units, offices of both the units are situated at the same premises and accounts being maintained by the same set of clerks etc.), the definition of 'establishment' which was widely defined would encompass within its ambit the two units as an establishment for the purpose of the Employees' Provident Funds and Miscellaneous Provisions Act, 1952.

Factor of inter-dependence for survival

In *South India Mill Owners' Association v Coimbatore District Textile Workers Union* the Supreme Court again held that several factors are relevant in dealing with such problem. However, the significance of several relevant factors would not be the same in each case. Unity of ownership, management and control would be a relevant factor. General unity or functional integrity may also be a relevant factor. Unity of finance may not be an irrelevant factor. Geographical proximity may also be of some relevance. In some cases, the test would be whether one concern forms an integral part of another so that together they constitute one concern. The Court held that the nexus of integration in the form of some essential dependence of the one on the other might assume relevance. Similarly, the unity of purpose or design or even parallel or co-ordinate activity intended to achieve a common object to carry out the business of the one or the other may also assume relevance and importance.

In *L.N. Gadodia and Sons and another v Regional Provident Fund Commissioner*,[299] the facts of the case were that the directors of the two petitioner-companies belong to the same family. The Managing Director is common. The two senior officers, i.e., Commercial Manager and Technical Manager are common. At the time of inspection, the Enforcement Officer noticed that the employees of the two companies were being swapped. Both of them have the same registered address and

---

[297] (2001) 1 SCC 1
[298] 1996 Supp(3) SCR 202
[299] AIR 2012 SC 273

common telephone numbers and a common gram number. The audited accounts revealed that the second petitioner-company had given a loan of 5 lakh to the first petitioner in the year 1988. The two companies are family concerns of the Gadodial family. In consideration of these factors, the Supreme Court held that there was the integrity of management, finance and the workforce in the two private limited companies. The Court further observed, 'the two companies have seen to it that on record each of these two entities engage less than twenty employees, although the number of employees engaged by them is more than twenty when taken together. The entire attempt of the petitioners is to show that the two entities are separate units so that the Provident Fund Act does not get attracted. The material on record, however, leads to only one pointer that the two entities are parts of the same establishment and in which case they get covered under the Provident Funds Act.'

In *Hotel Mahaveer and others v Regional Provident Fund Commissioner*,[300] the Karnataka High Court held that the filing of separate balance-sheets could not be pressed into service as proof of functional independence more so when there was common supervisory and managerial control. They only reveal that the establishment resorted to book adjustments, maybe, to overcome some fiscal burden in the form of taxes and duties which the establishment would have had to bear if it had continued to treat itself as one establishment.

Functional Integrality

In *Bells Controls Ltd. v Regional P.F. Commissioner*,[301] it was held by the Karnataka High Court that in order to determine whether several businesses constitute one establishment, the test to be applied is of integrality and commonness and that a person having different kinds of business in the same place, cannot be deemed to have a single establishment employing one set of employees. It was further held that if each business stands aloof and is not necessary or ancillary to the other, then each of them will be an independent establishment.

The question whether the business is being carried on at one place or at different places or in the same line or in the different lines, is neither material nor relevant for deciding the scope of an 'establishment.' The law takes into account only the existence of establishments and the employment of a certain number of persons in factories over a given period. It is for this purpose that change of location or change of composition of partners or even a change in the manufacturing process is not considered vital in the application of this law.[302]

---

[300] 2002 (92) FLR 1131, (2002) I LLJ 244 Kant
[301] 1988 (2) LLN 778
[302] *State of Punjab v Satpal and another*, AIR 1970 SC 655, 1970: (1970) II LLJ 64 SC, (1969) 3 SCC 910

The first and foremost test to establish the functional integrality would be whether one unit would survive in the absence of the order and whether the matters of finance, the employer had kept them distinct or integrated.[303] But the test of functional integrality is not the absolute test for holding the two establishments as one.[304] Merely having separate sales tax and income tax registrations, shall not change the unity of the establishment.[305]

Factory and Shops cannot be clubbed together

In *Regional Provident Fund Commissioner, Mangalore v B. Ganapathy Bhandarkar,*[306] a factory and two shops sought to be clubbed were having separate balance sheets, a separate set of employees, separate books of accounts etc., but owned by the common employer. While considering these facts, a Division Bench of the Karnataka High Court held that shops and factory could not be clubbed together, and the Act will not apply to these establishments. In *Khoja Lime Udyog v Regional Provident Fund Commissioner,*[307] the Provident Fund Commissioner sought to club the three establishments viz., Khoja Lime Udyog, Khoja Chemical Limes Industries, and Choudhary Lime Company for coverage under the Act. The Rajasthan High Court held that unless it is established that the employees of the three concerns get their wages directly or indirectly from the same employer, it will be difficult to hold that they jointly form an establishment within the meaning of the term 'establishment' under the Act. The Court further held that the members of a Joint Hindu family can have their own separate business, separate income and therefore, unless it is established that these three different owners of the three concerns pool their income and the employees are paid out of that joint or pooled income, their employees cannot form an establishment within the meaning of the Act. If the intendment of the Act were that every employer employing twenty or more employees was liable to pay the provident fund contribution irrespective of the fact whether they are all employed in the same establishment or not, the Act would have stated so and that there would have been no need to enact s.2A also.[308]

New establishment or part of the old one – Consideration of

In *Sayaji Mills Ltd. v Regional P.F. Commissioner,*[309] the Supreme Court observed that change in ownership of factory and subsequent temporary interruption in the

---

[303] *Nandhini Travels Pvt. Ltd. v Regional P.F. Commissioner,* 2003(2) LLJ 810
[304] *Regional P.F. Commissioner v Nath Traders and others,* 2007(1)LIC 826: 2007 LLR 378
[305] *Regional P.F. Commissioner v Nath Traders and others,* 2007 (1)LIC.826: 2007 LLR 278
[306] 2003 (3) LLN.371: 2003(3)LLJ.356].
[307] 1992(1)LLJ 903: 1991(62) FLR 252: 1991(1) CLR 75(Raj.)
[308] *Mahipal Singh Shankarsing Pawar v Regional P.F. Commissioner, 1972 Lab IC 1202 (Mys.)*
[309] 1985 SCC (C&S)310: 1985 Supp SCC 610: AIR 1985 SC 373

running of the factory does not amount to an establishment of a new factory. The mere fact that two of the erstwhile partners of a dissolved firm has started a new business in the same premises under a new name is not sufficient to conclude that the new establishment is a continuation of the old establishment.[310] In *Lakshmi Rattan Engineering Works v Regional P.F. Commissioner,*[311] the Supreme Court gave the test of 'continuity of working.' A mere change of ownership would make no difference to the date of set up of the establishment so long as there was continuity of working.

In *Devi Press, Madras v Regional P.F. Commissioner,*[312] a public limited company was running a printing press. The company was wound up as a result of voluntary liquidation, and the entire machinery with all fixtures and furniture were sold to the managing agents who later on formed a partnership and started the printing press. The licence under the Factories Act was transferred to the vendees. The services of all the employees were terminated, and their dues were settled. Most of the old employees were re-employed as fresh entrants by the vendees who commenced the business. When a dispute arose about whether the establishment was a new one or not, the Madras High Court observed that while in terms the business was not sold as a going concern to the petitioner-firm, in effect that was what was done. The entirely of the machinery, its accessories and the furniture were taken over. The very factory and corporation licences were transferred in the name of the petitioner-firm. The High Court held that the new establishment was a continuation of the old one. Besides these cases, there is a catena of judicial decisions enunciating the principles to decide whether an establishment is newly set up or part of the old one. These principles have been elucidated in *Sunder Transport and another v The Regional Provident Fund Commissioner,*[313] *Associated Polymers Ltd. v Union of India and others,*[314] *Allana Sons Private Limited v R.M. Gandhi and the Regional Provident Fund Commissioner.*[315]

Clubbing the units of Partnership Firms

For the purpose of ascertainment of applicability of the Act as well as for determination of the total dues of an establishment having different branches and/or departments in different places, all the departments and/or branches will be treated as a part of

---

[310] *Balaji Food Products v Central Board of Trustees and others,* 39 (1989) DLT 287, 1990 (60) FLR 428, (1991) ILLJ 52 Del
[311] 1966(1) LLJ 741
[312] 1965I L.L.J. 294
[313] 1992 II CLR 977
[314] 1997 II CLR 2941
[315] 1991 I CLR 743

the principal establishment.[316] A partnership firm or proprietor firm has no separate and independent identity. They are identified with the partners or proprietors.[317] An agreement between the partners to carry on a business and share its profits may be followed by agreement between the same partners to carry on another business and to share the profit therein. The intention may be to constitute two separate partnerships and, therefore, two distinct firms or it may extend merely a partnership originally constituted to carry on one business to the carrying on of another business. It will all depend on the intention of the partners which has to be decided with reference to the terms of the agreement between them and all the surrounding circumstances.[318]

An establishment which involves the running of a factory may also require a staff for procuring raw materials and disposing of the manufactured products and also for the maintenance of accounts. There can be integral relation between all these items of work and it may not be proper to separate the process of manufacture in the factory from the office establishment which attends to work connected with the factory and its raw materials or products and its accounts. Establishment for this purpose must be viewed in a larger sense than the process of manufacture.[319]

Common Provident Fund

Two conditions are necessary for the application of s.3 *viz.,* (i) The existence of a provident fund which is common to the employees employed in the establishment covered under the Act and the employees in any other establishment, and (ii) The existence of the common provident fund immediately before the Act became applicable to an establishment. The power of the Central Government for issuing a notification under this Section is discretionary and not mandatory. Though it is not necessary for the Central Government to take into account any representation which the employer may make against the coverage of its establishment under s.3, yet the Government has been informing the employer concerned of its intention to cover such an establishment and any representation made by an employee is taken into account before a notification is actually issued.

---

[316] *Belal Biri Factory Pvt. Ltd. and another v. Regional P.F. Commissioner and another,* (2006) III LLJ 532 Cal
[317] *Regional P.F. Commissioner v Nath Traders and others,* 2007(1)LIC 826: 2007 LLR 378
[318] *Deputy Commissioner of Sales Tax(Law) v K. Kelukutty,* 1985(60) S.T.C.7
[319] *P.S.N.S. Ambalavana Chettiar & Co v Regional P.F. Commissioner,* (1969) 2 MLJ 160, 1970(1) LLJ296

Chapter VI
EMPLOYEE-EMPLOYER RELATIONSHIP

The test of control over the manner of work if applied, may exclude many cases where the relationship of master and servant clearly exists, that there are many contracts of service where the master cannot control the manner in which the work is to be done as in the case of a certified captain of a ship, to whom the owner can tell him where to go, but he cannot tell him how to navigate.[320]

EMPLOYEE-EMPLOYER RELATIONSHIP

In *Annamalai Mudaliar & Bros. v Regional Provident Fund Commissioner*,[321] it was held that the inclusion in the statutory definition of an employee, the employee of a contractor in or in connection with the work of the establishment is certainly not based on any common law concept of master and servant. The question is, therefore, to be decided concerning the statutory definition of 'employee' in s.2(f).

In *Regional Director, ESIC v South India Flour Mills (P) Ltd.*,[322] the Supreme Court approved a rather peculiar interpretation of a Division Bench of the Punjab-Haryana High Court. Certain construction workers were casual workers, engaged for construction of an additional building for the Respondent mill. The Supreme Court observed, "In our opinion, the work of construction of additional building required for the expansion of a factory must be held to be ancillary, incidental or having some relevance to or link with the object of the factory. It is not correct to say that such work must always have some direct connection with the manufacturing process that is carried on in the factory. The expression 'work of the factory' should also be understood in the sense of any work necessary for the expansion of the factory or establishment or for augmenting or increasing the work of the factory or establishment. Such work is incidental or preliminary to or connected with the work of the factory or establishment."

Thus, the scope of the term used "employee" under the EPF Act has altogether different connotation, ambit and scope than that of other enactments and the facts of each case is to be tested on the anvil of the definition of employee

---

[320] *Cassidy v Ministry of Health*, [1951] 1 All. E.R. 574 at 5
[321] AIR 1955 Mad 387: (1955) 1 LLJ 674
[322] 1986-II-LLJ-304)(SC)

and other provisions of the EPF Act and in order to hold whether the provisions of the EPF Act are applicable to the persons of an establishment cannot be tested on the touchstone of the definition of the employee/worker/workman of the other Act.

In *Swamy G.V.V v Regional Provident Fund Commissioner*,[323] a Division Bench of the Andhra Pradesh High Court, relied on the interpretation of the Supreme Court and observed that the above interpretation was given in connection with the Employees' State Insurance Act, 1948. But, so far as the Employees' Provident Fund Act, 1952 was concerned, it is expressly mentioned that an employee includes any person employed by or through a contractor in or in connection with the work of the establishment. There can be no dispute that the employees of the contractor, though not directly employed by the principal employer, were however employed by the contractor in connection with the work of the principal employer.

Test to determine employer-employee relationship

In *Satish Plastics v Regional Provident Fund Commissioner*,[324] a Division Bench of the Gujarat High Court evolved certain principles to decide the question of employer-employee relationship. The Court observed, "...a master-servant relationship exists, and parties cannot make it a different relationship by applying the label of contract. An employee called by any other name remains an employee for the juridical relationship does not depend on the nomenclature devised in order to defeat the law. And [the] law will not countenance a slap in its face by its non-spectators who choose to flout it by disingenuous and circuitous devices. If [the] entry is prohibited, it is prohibited, regardless of whether on effects it is through the front door or the back door."

The Court further observed, to answer the question of employer-employee relationship, some other questions have to be asked and answered viz., (i) Was he doing the work for monetary payment? (ii) Was the work done by him the work of the establishment or had a nexus with such work? (iii) Was the payment made wages in the sense of being remuneration for the physical or mental effort in connection with such work? (iv) Was the work such that it had to be done as directed by the establishment or under its supervision and control to the extent that supervision and control are possible having regard to the specialised nature of the work or the skill needed for its performance? (v) Was the work of such a nature and character that ordinarily a master-servant relationship could exist and but for the agreement styling it as a contract, common practice and common sense would suggest a master-service bond? (vi) Was the relation indicative of master-servant status in substance

---

[323] 1987 LIC 719: 1987 I LLN 94 (AP.DB)
[324] 1981 (2) LLJ 277: (1982) 44 FLR 207: (1981) 22 Guj LR 686

having regard to the economic realities irrespective of the nomenclature devised by the parties? (vii) Was he required to do the work personally without the liberty to get it done through someone else? If these answers nod their heads, a master-servant relationship can be spelt out with safety and certainty.

TRANSPORTATION CONTRACTORS – LIABILITY OF THE PRINCIPAL EMPLOYER

A similar question of law came for judicial scrutiny before the High Court of Madhya Pradesh, in the case of *Orient Paper Mills v Regional Provident Fund Commissioner*.[325] In that case, the petitioner (M/s Orient Paper Mills) contended that the workers engaged by them through the transportation contractors to carry the bamboos to the mill were not its employees. Their contentions were that these transporters were free to hire their labourers, the mill was not obliged to engage any particular transporter for any particular period, any truck passing from the Forest Depot and coming towards the mill could load and transport the bamboo at a fixed rate, the mill had not kept any record of the drivers, conductors, cleaners, or labourers in the truck, the transporters are not engaged exclusively in the mill, it is not fixed that a particular truck of a particular transporter is engaged in the work, and the like. The High Court rejected the plea of the *Orient Paper Mills* and upheld that the employees engaged through the transport contractors to carry the bamboos to the mills were employees of the mill. In the above case, certain questions were framed by the Court and answered to it in the following the guidelines provided in the Satish Plastics case (supra).

(i) The person who is unloading the bamboos from the truck in the factory premises of the petitioner is doing work for monetary payment; (ii) the work of unloading the bamboos done by him is for the establishment and having nexus with the factory because unless and until the bamboos are brought in the factory premises, paper cannot be manufactured; (iii) the payment is made to that person, by the transporter to whom the petitioner makes the payment; (iv) the payment was made to that person in terms of money for his physical work and effort; (v) the person coming in the truck to unload the bamboos in the factory premises are unloading the bamboos personally and this work is not being discharged through someone else; (vi) that person since he is unloading the bamboos from the truck, therefore, he is mainly discharging the work for the petitioner's factory and (vii) unless and until the bamboos are unloaded the petitioner's factory cannot manufacture the paper, and therefore, the work of unloading the bamboos is in connection with the work of the establishment.

---

[325] (2006) I LLJ 1136 MP

In the case of *D.C.M. Limited vs Regional Provident Fund Commissioner*,[326] the High Court of Rajasthan discussed a similar case where it was held that the workers engaged through transportation contractors in connection with loading and unloading of material are the employees of the principal employer, viz., M/s D.C.M Limited. The Court observed: "The definition of *'employee'* under Section 2 (f) refers to any person who is employed for wages in any kind of work, manual or otherwise, in or in connection with the work of an establishment and who gets his wages directly or indirectly from the employer and includes any person employed by or through a contractor in or in connection with the work of the establishment. This definition makes it clear that even if the contractor has employed any person, then he will be an employee of an establishment and if it is in connection with a work of the establishment, then he will be the employee of the principal employer. It is not necessary that the order of employment would be issued by the principal employer. The work of transportation was in connection with the work of [the] establishment. Learned counsel for the petitioner has submitted that the employees of loading and unloading are already covered and, therefore, the dispute remains for the employees of the contractor who were engaged in transportation. Since the work is also in connection with the work of establishment though employed through a contractor, they will be considered to be employees as defined under Section 2(f) of the Act of 1952."

In *Ramala Sahkari Chini Mills Ltd. v EPF Appellate Tribunal and others*,[327] the Supreme Court remitted the case for consideration by the Regional Provident Fund Commissioner under s.7-A as to whether the employer is liable to contribute towards certain class of persons who are covered under an agreement to transport sugarcane, observing that no dues can be determined without discussing the material on records on this aspect.

PAYMENT OF WAGES – DIRECTLY OR INDIRECTLY

In *Basf India Limited and another v M. Gurusamy and another*,[328] the facts were that the petitioner company viz., M/s BASF India Ltd, permitted its managers to engage their car drivers, the wages/salary paid to them by the managers were reimbursed to the managers by the petitioner-company. It was the contention of the petitioner that the managers themselves selected the drivers and employed them; the managers called their 'domestic servants' at any day and instructed them to drive the car at any

---

[326] 1998(79) FLR 913, (1998) I LLJ 979 Raj, 1997 WLC Raj UC 665, 1997(2) WLN 10)
[327] 2000 (87) FLR 491, JT 2000 (10) SC 457, (2000) II LLJ 1371 SC
[328] 2004(2) LLJ500: 2004(105)FJR 199: 2004(101) FLR 724: 2004(2) LLN 221: 2004 Lab IC 1003: 2004 (1) CLR 995 (Bom.) (DB)

place with any passengers as per their requirements; the drivers were under exclusive supervision and control of the respective Managers in their individual capacity and not in the capacity of the Company's employees; the Company's role was confined only to the extent that as a part of service conditions agreed with the Managers, it will reimburse to the Managers the expenses incurred by them in utilizing their personal drivers services for to-and-fro drive between the residence and the office or any place outside for official work. The Company thus set up the case that there was no master-servant relationship of any kind between the Company and the drivers of the Company's Managers and that such drivers were not covered within the definition of 'employee' under s.2(f) of the Act of 1952. The Division Bench of the Bombay High Court confirmed and upheld the order of the Regional Provident Fund Commissioner, observing as follows: "Taking cumulative effect of these aspects the Commissioner held that there was no need for the establishment to have reimbursed the Managers towards the expenses for engaging the drivers had they not been engaged for the benefit of the establishment. The finding thus concluded by the Commissioner that these facts would prove that the concerned drivers are paid wages directly or indirectly by the establishment for the work carried out by them in or in connection with the establishment and therefore, they are nothing but employees as defined under Section 2(f) of the Act of 1952 cannot be faulted."

ELEMENTS OF SUPERVISION AND CONTROL

The test of control, in modern times, has taken a different perspective with changing modes of productions and division of labour. The nature of extent of control required to establish the relationship between employer and employee varied from business to business and was by its very nature incapable of precise definition.[329] When the employee is put to work under the eye and gaze of the principal employer, or his agent, where he can be watched secretly, accidentally, or occasionally, while the work is in progress, so as to scrutinize the quality thereof and to detect faults therein, as also put to timely remedial measures by directions given, finally leading to the satisfactory completion and acceptance of the work, that would be supervision.[330]

In *Silver Jubilee Tailoring House v Chief Inspector of Shops & Establishments*,[331] the Supreme Court held that for the purpose of deciding the question of relationship of master and servant, the test of control over the matter of work is unrealistic, that in its application to skilled and particularly professional work, the control test in

---

[329] *Dharangadhra Chemicals Works Ltd. v State of Saurashtra*, AIR 1957 SC 264: (1957) 1 LLJ 477
[330] *C.E.S.C. Ltd. v Subhash Chandra Bose* (1992) 1 SCC 441: AIR 1992 SC 572
[331] (1974) 3 SCC 498: 1974 SCC (L & S)31: (1973) 2 LLJ 495: AIR 1974 SC 37

its traditional form has really broken down, that the control test cannot be treated as the exclusive test, and that the search for a formula in the nature of a single test to tell a contract of service from a contract for service might not serve any useful purpose. The utmost that profitably can be done is to examine all the factors that have been referred to in the cases on the topic. The court can only perform a balancing operation weighing up the factors which point in one direction and balancing them against those pointing in the opposite direction. Control is no longer the decisive factor in every case.

Superintendence and Control – Not a decisive test

In *K. Gopalan v Union of India*,[332] it was contended before the Delhi High Court that the artistes working in the circuses are not employees but independent contractors. It was contended that the petitioners do not control the work or rather the method of the work of the artists. Rejecting the contention, the High Court held that superintendence and control could not be the decisive test when one is dealing with a professional man or a man of some particular skill and experience. Instances of that have been given in the form of the master of a ship, an engine driver, or a professional architect, or as in this case, a consulting engineer. In such cases, there can be no question of the employer telling him how to do work. Therefore the absence of control and direction in that sense can be of little, if any, use as a test.

PRINCIPAL EMPLOYER VIS-À-VIS CONTRACTORS RESPONSIBILITIES

Job-work Contracts

In *Rupa & Co and another v The Regional PF Commissioner, West Bengal*,[333] the Calcutta High Court observed that the term 'employee' under s.2(f) includes the employees of the contractors also, and the Act does not grant any exemption to an employee who works through a contractor doing work for other employers as well. The Court further identified certain problems to be addressed during the determination of dues in respect of an employer whose contractor works for diverse employers viz., the liability of an employer whose contractor engages employees but works for diverse employers; how are the employees to be identified?; how is the work of an employer which is done by a particular employee of the contractor to be apportioned? What part of the total wage of an employee is to be apportioned as the wage paid to him towards a particular employer's job work? The Court also suggested that in such cases, the Provident Fund authority should have considered

---

[332] 1973 Lab I.C.287
[333] 2016 LLR 1021

whether the job workers of the writ petitioner were independent contractors. Secondly, if the answer to the above question was in the negative, it was imperative for them to ascertain the number and the identity of the workers employed by the contractor or contractors. Secondly, the amount of work that each worker of this contractor did for the writ petitioner had to be determined. Thereafter, the proportion of the monthly or daily wage of each worker which was payable for the work of the writ petitioner had to be ascertained. Only then the Provident Fund liability of the principal employer could be fixed.

Contract-for-service vis-à-vis Contract-of–Service

On many occasions, it is contended by the principal employers that agreement made by them with the third-parties is a 'contract *for* service,' and not a 'contract *of* service.' The substance of such contention is that the employees engaged in the former case do not fall within the meaning of s.2(f) while those coming under the latter case do fall within the meaning of 'employees.' Of course, there is a distinction between these two terms in the common parlance. A contract of service is an arrangement whereby an employee agrees to work on a full-time or part-time basis for the other party to the contract (i.e., the employer) for either a specified or indeterminate period. Under such a contract, the employee serves the employer through an intermediary, in return for a salary or some other form of remuneration. The employer has the right to control and can direct the manner in which the employee carries out the duties to be performed. A contract for services, on the other hand, is an arrangement whereby one party agrees to perform certain specific work stipulated in a contract for another party; it usually calls for the accomplishment of a defined task but does not normally require the party paying for the service to do anything themselves. There is no right to control the methods of work and no direct "master-servant" relationship.

Pertinently, the Supreme Court of India, in *P.M. Patel and Sons v Union of India and others*[334] had an occasion to analyse and recapitulate the decisions and the inherent differences in a contract of service and contract for service and reiterated the need for an overall consideration without laying too much emphasis upon anyone factor by quoting with approval the *ratio decidendi* in *Silver Jubilee Tailoring House and others v Chief Inspector of Shops and Establishments and another*[335] in the following terms. It is exceedingly doubtful today whether the search for a formula like a single test to tell a contract of service from a contract for service will serve any useful purpose. The most that profitably can be done is to examine all the factors

---

[334] 1986-I-LLJ-88
[335] 1973-II-LLJ-495

that have been referred to in the cases on the topic. The Court can only perform a balancing operation weighing up the factors which point in the direction and balancing them against those pointing in the opposite direction.

The grammatical constructions and legal interpretations of the phrases "*by the contractor*" and "*through the contractor*" as mentioned in s.2(f) of the Act, are of vital importance here. Grammatically, the quaint distinction between the two phrases -- '*employed by a contractor*' and '*employed through a contractor*' encompasses the difference between the 'contract of service' and 'contract for service.' Thus, the definition of 'employee' under the Act is comprehensive enough to include both the categories of contract employees, within the meaning of 'employee.'

Role of Contractors

A combined reading of Para 30, 32, 36 and 36-B of the EPF Scheme 1952 makes it the statutory obligation of the principal employer to pay in the first instance the workers' share, as well as the employer's share of contributions (including those in respect of the workers engaged through or by a contractor) and the Principal employer, is vested with powers to recover the respective contributions from the money payable to the Contractor. This provision of law had been upheld in many judicial pronouncements. The employer is obliged to pay both contributions, namely, contribution payable by the employer as well as by members even in case of an employee engaged through a contractor. He cannot contend that as he is unable to realise from the contractor the amount of contribution payable by employees employed by a contractor, he is not liable to pay such contribution. The employer can recover the amount of such contribution from the contractor from the amount payable to the contractor or as a debt payable by the contractor.[336]

A Division Bench of Himachal Pradesh High Court in the case of *Rakesh Kumar v National Hydro Electric Power Corporation*,[337] considered a similar matter and held that though the contractor recovers the contribution payable by his employees and further pays it to the principal employer together with an equal amount of contribution and also administrative charges, yet it is the primary responsibility of the principal employer to pay both the contributions payable by him in respect of the employees directly employed by him and also in respect of the employees employed by or through a contractor, and also administrative charges. A similar view was taken by the High Court of Madras, in *The Tamil Nadu Small Industries*

---

[336] *Malwa Vanaspati and Chemical Co Ltd., v Regional Provident Fund Commissioner*, 1976 (1) LLJ 307; 1976(1) LLN 148(MP)(DB)

[337] 2001(2) CLJ(H.P.) 73: 2002 AIR (H.P.) 70: 2001(1) CLJ(Service) 461

Development Corporation Ltd. v The Regional Provident Fund Commissioner,[338] and observed, "as regards the liability of the principal employer, above quoted provisions are very clear to the effect that the liability is mainly on the principal employer. It is the duty of the principal employer to insist from the contractor to furnish all the details relating to the employees and there is also a corresponding duty cast upon the contractor to furnish all the particulars to the principal employer."

Independent Contractor

In *Chintaman Rao v State of M.P.*,[339] the Supreme Court had held that where the contractor is known as sattedar with whom manufacturing contract for the supply of bidis was recorded as independent contractors, and therefore the kulis employed by the sattedar could not be treated as an employee of the manufacturer for Factory Act. This distinction between the labour employed by the manufacturing and employed by an independent contractor was also brought out in *Orissa Cement Ltd. v Union of India*[340] and *D.C. Dewan Mohideen Sahib and Sons v Union of UB Workers*.[341] The law as laid down by Supreme Court took a major shift in *Silver Jubilee Tailoring House v Chief Inspector of Shops and Establishment Hyderabad*,[342] wherein the Supreme Court reviewed the entire law and pointed out that test of "control" was not an exclusive test and there can be no magic formula for all cases, and the court must perform a balancing operation weighing up factors which point in one direction and balancing them against those pointing in an opposite direction. The control test is not decisive. The degree of control would be different in different cases. The contractor the purpose of s.2(f) is a labour contractor and not an independent contractor who contracts to supply finished product to the establishment but for manufacturing of such finished products engages his labour for his own purpose.[343]

Principal employer can insist contractors have their own EPF Code

In *Transport Contractors, TASMAC Ltd. v Regional Provident Fund Commissioner*,[344] the Madras High Court held that once the principal employer is covered under the Act, then any employee engaged by the contractors in connection with the work of the Principal employer are indirectly covered by the EPF Act. In case of non-payment

---

[338] (2004)ILLJ67Mad
[339] 1958 (11) LLJ 252
[340] 1962 (1) LLJ 400
[341] (1964) 2 LLJ 633
[342] 1973 (2) LLJ 495
[343] *Karachi Bakery v Regional Provident Fund Commissioner*, 1990 (2) LLN 630
[344] Writ Petition Nos 24409, 25983, 25970 to 25972 of 2010

of contributions, and if the Provident Fund authorities fixed the responsibilities on the principal employer, it is always open to the Principal employer to safeguard their liability by entering into a specific contract with the contractors to get their liability removed.

Intermediate Contractor is not the employer

In *Hussainbhai v The Alath Factory Thozhilali Union and others*,[345] the Supreme Court observed: "Where a worker or a group of workers labour to produce goods or services and these goods or services are for the business of another, that other is, in fact, the employer. He has economic control over the workers' subsistence, skill and continued employment. If he, for any reason, chokes off, the worker is virtually laid off. The presence of intermediate contractors with whom alone the workers have immediate or direct relationship *ex-contractu* is of no consequence, when, on lifting the veil or looking it, the conspectus of factors governing employment, Courts discern the naked truth, though draped in different perfect paper arrangement, that the real employer is the management, not the immediate contractor."

Contractors' Liability

The employer pays the Contractor in a lump sum amount for the purpose of work and the Contractor out of this lump sum amount pays the wages to its employees. Therefore, the employer pays the Contractor overall lump sum from which determination cannot be made under s.7-A inasmuch as the employees of the Contractors are not available to the employer though the employer principally is responsible but the list of employees or the register of employees of the Contractors lie with the Contractors themselves. Therefore, unless the Contractors are summoned the dues cannot be determined under s.7-A.[346]

The Provident Fund authority should call upon the principal employer to submit the details of labour charges and also the break-up of the same through contract labourers. The principal employer should be afforded an opportunity to submit further details as to whether such contract labourers who are paid labour charges have complied with the provisions of the Act. If the contractors are covered by the Act and they have already made contribution for such purpose separately in their own account, there may not be double contributions for such purpose. If the contribution is not made by the contractors, then only the liability can be fastened upon the principal employer for compliance of the statutory provisions.[347] The

---

[345] [1978 SC 1410]
[346] *Regional Provident Fund Commissioner v Assam Biri Factories Pvt. Ltd. and another*, (2006) 3 CALLT 62 HC
[347] *Proto Pumps and Motors Pvt. Ltd. v Assistant Provident Fund Commissioner*, (2005) ILLJ 677 Guj

principal employer becomes responsible or liable to pay the dues of the Contractor's employees only when the Contractor fails to pay its employees their dues.[348] The action of the principal employer in attempting to shift the liability of obtaining code numbers for the workers engaged through the contractors, on the contractor, is unsustainable.[349]

---

[348] *Regional Provident Fund Commissioner v Assam Biri Factories Pvt. Ltd. and another*, (2006) 3 CALLT 62 HC

[349] *Ram Singh v Punjab State Co-operative Supply and Marketing Federation Ltd. and another*, (2007) IILLJ 631 P H

Chapter VII
LIABILITY TO CONTRIBUTE

A Division Bench of the Delhi High Court, in *SDB Infrastructure Pvt Ltd. v Union of India*,[350] held that the liability of the employer to make a deduction from the wage payable to an employee and with a matching contribution deposit the amount with the Provident Fund Commissioner is unconnected with how the employee can receive the benefit of the fund. The issue of portability of workers and how could a worker withdraw money lying to his credit in the fund did trouble the Division Bench of the Court because of the logistics problem which a worker could face. But that was dehors the liability of the employer to do the needful by complying with the employer's obligation as per the amended scheme.

Employer to pay both shares 'in the first instance.'

In *N.K. Industries (PR) Ltd. v Regional Provident Fund Commissioner*, the Allahabad High Court observed, "The petitioner should have made its own contribution and also that of the employees long before a demand was made from it. The petitioner could have, after making the contribution of the employee's share, recovered the same from the employee concerned. There is a duty cast upon the petitioner to contribute both the shares, i.e., his share as also that of the employee; inasmuch as the petitioner did not do so, it is to blame itself."

A similar proposition is contained in *Nagpur Glass Works Ltd. v R.P.F. Commissioner*.[351] It was held that the liability on the part of the employer to make contribution in respect of the basic salary as also dearness allowance of each of the employees "springs into existence" from the date the scheme has been extended to the particular establishment and it is not dependent on the issue of the notice envisaged in clause (5) of Paragraph 28 of the scheme. This view was supported by the decision in *Aluminium Corporation of India v Regional P.F. Commissioner*[352] (where it was held that neither s.6 nor paragraph 29 of the Scheme gives an option to the employees to pay or not pay their contribution) and *N.K. Industries (Private) Ltd. v Regional Provident Fund Commissioner*[353] (which laid down that paragraph

---

[350] LPA 727/2014 Decision dated 16th October 2015.
[351] (1960) II LLJ 301 Bom
[352] AIR 1958 Cal 570
[353] AIR 1958 All 474.

30 of the Scheme imposes a duty on the employer to contribute both the shares, namely his own as also that of the employee.)

Employees cannot opt out of the Schemes

In the *Changdeo Sugar Mills and another v Union of India and another*,[354] it was contended that even if the employer is made liable to pay the Provident Fund contributions, he should not be made to contribute the employees' share as he could not and have not deducted the same from the wages paid. The Supreme Court refused to accept the contention stating that the employer must contribute. The employer's agreement with the employee, not to deduct, does not discharge the employer of his obligation in law to make payment. The Employees' Provident Funds and Miscellaneous Provisions Act, 1952 is a social welfare legislation. A person, either the employer or employee, cannot contract out of the provisions of the Act. Even the beneficiary cannot relinquish his rights as provided under the Act. Any such relinquishment would be against public policy.[355]

Wages – Paid or payable

In *Calicut Modern Spinning and Weaving Mills Ltd. v Regional Provident Fund Commissioner*,[356] a Division Bench of the Kerala High Court held that the provisions of the Act and the Schemes cast an obligation on the part of the employer to make the contributions payable by him and on behalf of the member to the Fund in the first instance of every due date. The Court further held that the phrase "in the first instance" means payment by the employer for every month irrespective of the fact whether wages had been paid or not. The word 'payable' indicates the amount which becomes payable by which the employer's liability accrues. Nowhere from the scheme of the Act or the arrangement of the Scheme, it is possible to hold that the contributions are to be recovered or deducted only when the amount is paid. If such a proposition is accepted, in that event, the entire scheme would be stultified.[357]

Contract cannot override statutory provisions

The terms of such contract of employment, when contravening the provisions of the EPF Act, become void, to that extent. For instance, an employer and his employee cannot have a valid contract that they will not contribute towards the EPF Scheme, 1952, which otherwise is applicable. Simply because of the employer and the employee,

---

[354] [(2001)2 SCC 529]
[355] *Sunil Kumar v Rajendra Pillai and others*, 2007(114)FLR1016; (2007)IIILLJ1052Ker
[356] FLR 1982(45)92(Kerala HC(; 1982–1LLN 360; 1982 Lab.IC1422; (1982) I Lab.LN 360; ILR (1982) I Ker. 698;
[357] *Employees' Provident Fund Organisation v Birlapur Vidyalaya and others* 2007 (2) LLN 476

by agreement desired that contribution is not payable in respect of payment, liability under the Act cannot be avoided if such payment answers the definition of 'basic wages.' If the employer and the employee can, by agreement, avoid payment of contribution in respect of certain payment that would be against the provisions of the Act and in fact, would lead to very disastrous results.[358] Any such agreement is null and void.[359] Once there is a statutory definition of basic wages, and if certain amounts which are otherwise liable to be included in the term basic wages, but kept outside by the employer, such contracting out of statute cannot be permitted, and there cannot be any private arrangement in respect of such transaction. In essence, there cannot be estoppels against the statute.[360] Merely because an agreement was entered into between the employer and the employee, that will not take away the jurisdiction of the Provident Fund Commissioner in going into the real nature of payments.[361]

Financial stringency per se is no ground for non-compliance

In *Jagannath Prasad Jhalani v Regional Provident Fund Commissioner*,[362] the Delhi High Court held that financial stringency *per se* is no ground for not depositing the statutory dues particularly when the contributions of the employees had already been deducted from their salaries.

EPF benefits constitute an intrinsic part of the employees' right to life

In *Ralliwolf Ltd. v Regional P.F. Commissioner*,[363] the Bombay High Court observed: ""No industrial undertaking can work or operate without the work which is rendered by the employees. No work can be demanded save and except for the payment of wages and other statutory benefits. The payment of Provident Fund dues to the Fund, therefore, stands on the same footing as the payment of wages which is due to the employees. That is an entitlement to which the employees are entitled by dint of the work which they have put in. These are dues which are payable whether or not an undertaking is sick. They constitute an intrinsic part of the employees' right to life under Article 21 of the Constitution. In *Industrial Development Corporation Orissa Ltd. and another v Regional Provident Fund Commissioner and another*,[364] the Orissa High Court held that it could never be construed as the purpose or intention

---

[358] *Regional P.F. Commissioner v The Administrator, Cosmopolitan Hospital*, 2009 LLR 1272 (Ker.H.C)
[359] *Shree Changdeo Sugar Mills and others v Union of India and others*, 2001(2)SCC 519; AIR-2001 S.C. 557
[360] *The Management of Reynolds Pens India Pvt. Ltd. and others v Regional P.F. Commissioner*, 2011 LLR.876 (Mad.)
[361] *Stardust Enterprises, Chennai v The Employees' Provident Fund Commissioner*, 2011(5) LLN 318
[362] (1987)71 FJR 204 (Del.)
[363] 2001-I-LLJ-1423 (Bom)]
[364] 2002(1)LLJ 774

of the enactment, to deprive or defer the payment of wages to an employee during which the Company becomes sick.

Holding Company not liable for payment by Subsidiary Company

In *Regional Provident Fund Commissioner v A.B.S. Spinning Ltd., Orissa*,[365] the appellant Provident Fund Commissioner submitted that the Respondent No.2, being the holding company of Respondent No.1, is liable to pay the provident fund dues outstanding against its subsidiary company. The Supreme Court held that the subsidiary company has an independent existence as against the holding company and, therefore, Respondent No.2 is not liable to clear the provident fund dues of its subsidiary company. There is no provision in the EPF Act that a liability of one company could be fastened on the other company even by lifting the corporate veil, where the two companies are separate legal entities under the provisions of the Companies Act.[366] Though in law holding and subsidiary companies are two separate entities, the corporate veil can be pierced when the corporate personality is found to be opposed to justice, convenience and interest of revenue or workmen or against public interest.[367]

No Personal Liability of the owner or occupier of the public limited company

In *Vimalkumar Rajiv Shah v Employees' Provident Fund Organisation*,[368] the question before the Bombay High Court was – whether the dues of the provident fund can be recovered from the owner or occupier as defined in s.2 (e) of the Act. In *Employees' State Insurance Corporation v S.K. Agarwa*,[369] it was held that the word 'owner' or 'occupier' used in s.2 (e) of the said Act have been used disjunctively and therefore in a case where the owner in a public limited company, in that case, while construing the definition of it would not be necessary to refer to the word 'occupier.' Following the *ratio decetendi* of the Supreme Court, the Bombay High Court held that it is the company which is the principal employer and not a director who is liable to pay the dues of the provident fund.

Liability does not cease on closure of business

In *R.M. Lakshmanamurthy v The Employees' State Insurance Corporation*,[370] the Supreme Court held that the liability to pay the statutory arrears does not cease

---

[365] *Regional Provident Fund Commissioner v A.B.S. Spinning Ltd, Orissa* (Civil Appeal No.6928 of 2002)
[366] *Universal Pollution Control (I) Pvt. Ltd. v Regional P.F. Commissioner and another*, 2006(110) FLR 163: 2007 LLR 774
[367] *Bhaskar Tea and Industries Ltd. v Employees' Provident Fund Organisation*, 2014(3)WB LR 924(Cal.)
[368] 2009 LLR 953 (Bom. HC) (Writ Petition No.407 of 2003)
[369] 1998 LLR 806 (SC): II CLR 518
[370] [1974] 4 SCC 365

merely because of the closure of the business by the employer. The Court observed: "It is rather strange to conclude that the demand could not be enforced against a closed business. If this finding were to be accepted, it would not promote the scheme and avoid the mischief. On the contrary, it would perpetuate the mischief. Any employer can easily avoid his statutory liability and deny the beneficial piece of social security legislation to the employees, by closing down the business before recovery. That certainly is not the intendment of the Act."

Chapter VIII
CENTRAL BOARD OF TRUSTEES

CENTRAL BOARD OF TRUSTEES – BODY CORPORATE

In *Central Board of Trustees, EPF v EPF Appellate Tribunal and another*,[371] the Writ Petition filed by the CBT against the order passed by the EPF Appellate Tribunal was challenged on three grounds, viz., (i) there is nobody or authority by the name EPFO in the statute and it cannot have any Central Board of Trustees. (ii) challenging the order of the Tribunal falls outside the purview of the powers of the CBT and (iii) CBT, not being a party to the earlier stages of the proceedings, cannot figure as a petitioner in the Writ without obtaining leave of the Court.

The Calcutta High Court, while dismissing the appeals filed by the CBT as non-maintainable, observed the following. When a statute empowers a body corporate to sue, it must be in respect of the jurisdiction conferred upon it by the statute or in respect of a matter relating to its statutory functions. If the power to sue is sought to be interpreted in respect of any matter which does not fall within the jurisdiction of the Central Board of Trustees, such power plainly cannot be exercised by it encroaching upon the jurisdiction of some other authority under the Act. The statute nowhere says that recovering the dues from different establishments and augmenting the fund is a part of the duty. Recovery of dues, bringing different establishments within the coverage under the Act, determination of the amounts due from the employers, review of the orders passed by the Regional Provident Fund Commissioner or the Assistant Provident Fund Commissioner, determination of interest payable by the employer or levying damages do not come within the jurisdiction of the Central Board of Trustees.

When the statute lays down the subjects in respect of which a body corporate can delegate its powers, any purported delegation beyond the scope of the same must be held to be manifestly incompetent. The Central Board exercises no power relating to or, it is not concerned with, the recovery of dues from an individual establishment. Thus, there is no question of delegating any power which a person or a body does not enjoy. A person or authority or a body corporate may delegate only such powers which it enjoys. Even if the Central Board had the power, it could not delegate such power of recovery or institute a proceeding to the Regional Provident

---

[371] 17597 (W) of 2016 Decision dated 16 May, 2017

Fund Commissioner or Assistant Provident Fund Commissioner to challenge an order passed by the Tribunal as that is apparently beyond the scope of the power of delegation as provided in the Scheme. The Regional Provident Fund Commissioner is not empowered to represent the Central Board of Trustees so that any proceeding may be initiated in the name of the CBT through the Regional Provident Fund Commissioner.

However, in *Assistant Provident Fund Commissioner v S.K. Nasiruddin Biri Merchant Pvt. Ltd. and another*,[372] the Patna High Court has taken a different view. Here, the Court, placing reliance on the resolution dated May 25th, 1989 passed by the Central Board of Trustees, authorising the Additional Provident Fund Commissioner as well as some other officials to institute, file, conduct, prosecute and defend all civil and criminal proceedings, managed by, or against the CBT, and to act and appear in all these proceedings on behalf of the CBT, held that the Assistant Provident Fund Commissioner was competent to institute civil and criminal proceedings on behalf of the CBT.

The functions of the EPFO are 'governmental' in nature

Legal idea of a corporate body and that idea is that the corporate body is distinct from the persons composing it. It has a personality of its own. It has a corporate existence. In the eye of the law, it is a different person altogether.

In *Regional Provident Fund Commissioner v Karnataka Provident Fund Employees' Union*,[373] the question for consideration before the Supreme Court was whether the State Government could be the 'appropriate Government' in relation to any industrial disputes concerning the office of the Regional Provident Fund Commissioner. The Supreme Court observed, "...the activity carried on by the Central Board or the State Boards under the Provident Funds Act is not similar to the activity carried on by any private trade or manufacturing business like the one involved in the case of the *Heavy Engineering Corpn. Case*.[374] The activity is one traceable to Article 43 of the Constitution which requires the State to endeavour to secure by suitable legislation or economic organisation or in any other way to all workers, agricultural or industrial or otherwise, work, a living wage, conditions of work ensuring a decent standard of life and full enjoyment of leisure and social and cultural opportunities. It is a part of the programme of every welfare State which our country is. Institutions engaged in matters of such high public interest

---

[372] 2015(1) CLR 157: 2015(144) FLR 550: 2015(1) LLJ 521
[373] (1984)65FJR324, overruling *Karnataka Provident Fund Employees' Union v Addl. Industrial Tribunal*, (1983) 62 FJR 290(1983)2 LLJ 108
[374] (1969)1 SCC 765: AIR 1970 SC 82

or performing such high public functions, as observed by Mathew, J, in *Sukhdev Singh*[375] case, by their nature, performed governmental functions.

Prior approval of Central Government mandatory for deviation of rules

Under the proviso to s.5-D (7)(a) of the Act, where the Central Board is of the opinion that it is necessary to make a departure from the said rules or orders in respect of any of the matters enumerated therein, it is mandatory that it should obtain prior approval of the Central Government. *Ex-post facto* approval is not an approval in the eyes of the law.[376]

---

[375] (1975) 1 SCC 421: 1975 SCC (L&S)101: AIR 1975 SC 1331: (1975)1 LLJ 399
[376] *Union of India v Vinod Kumar* (1997) III LLJ (Suppl)493 (SC)

Chapter IX
DETERMINATION OF DUES

As far as the determination under s.7-A of the Act is concerned, the provision comprises two parts. Firstly, the authority has to decide whether the Act applies to the establishment and secondly, he has to determine the amount due from the employer. For this determination, the officer has to conduct such inquiry as deemed necessary. A reading of s.7-A(2) of the Act shows that the officer conducting the inquiry has to decide the issue as if he is trying a suit in a civil Court with powers under the Code of Civil Procedure. The inquiry shall be deemed to be judicial proceedings. Sub-section (3) shows that no order shall be made under sub-section (1) unless the employer concerned is given a reasonable opportunity of representing his case. Sub-section (3) empowers the officer to compel the attendance of the person concerned or the production of documents to decide the applicability of the Act or determination of the amount due from the employer. From the reading of these provisions, it is clear that no order under s.7-A of the Act can be passed without conducting a full-fledged inquiry as if the matter is decided in a suit and that the officer determining the question has to decide both the coverability as well as the determination of the amount."[377]

NATURE OF S.7-A AUTHORITY

No arbitrariness

The quasi-judicial powers may be exercised by two kinds of administrative authorities or tribunals, namely (i) by those whose jurisdiction depends on facts and preconditions, the existence of which is to be decided by the Civil Courts and (ii) those who are given power to decide even the jurisdictional facts on the proof of which their jurisdiction depends. The possibility of the arbitrary exercise of powers can exist with the latter but not with the former.

The power given to the Commissioner is for a beneficent purpose to enforce the social security given to the employees by the Act. It does not interfere with the liberties of the employer in any other way for any other purpose. S.7-A, therefore, does not impose any unreasonable restrictions on the rights of the employer guaranteed by Article 19(1) (f) and (g) of the Constitution. Article 14 of the Constitution is

---

[377] *Madathupatti Weavers Co-Operative Production and Sales Society Ltd., v Regional P.F Commissioner and others* (2003) 3 LLJ 795

not attracted at all since the Commissioner has no discretion to pick and choose any employers but is bound to act according to the provisions of the Act and the Scheme.[378] Further, the decision of the Commissioner is subject to review by the Tribunal under s.7-I and also by the High Court under Article 226 and 227 of the Constitution and by the Supreme Court under Article 136 of the Constitution.

Employers used to contend that the appeal mechanisms provided in s.7-A, 7-B and 14-B of the Act are unconstitutional for it is "almost like an appeal from Caesar to Caesar"- the Provident Fund commissioners acting as judges in their own cause. However, judicial interpretations of the above sections do not support this contention. In *Khushi Ram Raghunath Rai v Regional P.F. Commissioner*,[379] held, a Commissioner acting under s.7-A does not act as a judge in his own cause.

Inquiry Authority – No power of Investigation

No power of investigation has been conferred on any of the officers under s.7-A of the Act. There is no provision in the Act either expressly or impliedly authorising any officer to investigate matters arising under the Act. What is contemplated under s.7-A is only an inquiry to determine the amount due from any employer under any of the provisions of the Act or Scheme as the case may be.[380] In *Anandjiharidas and Co v S.P. Kasture*,[381] the Supreme Court held that a fact which was already there in records does not, by its mere availability, becomes an item of 'information' till the time it has been brought to the notice of the assessing authority.

S.7-A Inquiry is essentially inquisitorial, not adversarial

The Indian judicial system itself is based on the '*adversary system*' of justice, which is contra-distinct to the '*inquisitorial system.*' Adversary procedure is the procedure before a tribunal which should have both sides of the case presented to it and should judge between them, without itself having to conduct an inquiry of its own motion, enter into controversy and call evidence for or against either party.[382] As distinct from the adversary system, the inquisitorial system will empower the quasi-judicial authority further with the duty of leading evidence with the objective of seeking the truth. In *Uttarpara Children's Own Home v Union of India*,[383] the Calcutta High Court held that the quasi-judicial proceedings under s.7-A of the EPF Act are essentially inquisitorial and not adversarial.

---

[378] *Wire Netting Stores v Regional PF Commissioner* AIR 1970 Delhi 143
[379] ILR (1976) 2 Punj 481
[380] *Provident Fund Inspector v Mohammed* (Kerala) (DB) 1980 Ker LT 698 (DB)
[381] AIR 1968 SC 565
[382] *Administrative Law* (8th Edition) by HWR Wade and C.F. Forsyth
[383] W.P. No.20734 of 2005 Decision dated August 7th, 2009

Assessment under S.7-A is different from assessment of tax

In *Assistant Provident Fund Commissioner v Nand Lal and Company*,[384] a Division Bench of the Patna High Court, placing reliance on the Supreme court order in *Food Corporation of India* case, held that the assessment of dues payable under the Act is for the benefit of identified individuals. The Court further held that the assessment under s.7-A of the Act should not be confused with an assessment of tax. Unfortunately, these are provident fund dues which are to accrue to an individual and not a tax, and, not an amount payable to the Provident Fund Commissioner. Unless the nature of employment and the names of employees are identified with certainty, the assessment cannot be said to be in accordance with law. The collection of the amount under adjudication is not a collection to go to the purse of the Central Government or the State Government by way of a collection of tax. The collection of dues under the Employees' Provident Funds and Miscellaneous Provisions Act is for the benefit of the beneficiaries, in the absence of details of the beneficiaries and their salary components adjudication under s.7-A remains incomplete.[385]

S.7-A and S.14-B operate in two different spheres

In *Regional Provident Fund Commissioner and another v Shrine Velankanni Senior Secondary School*, the High Court of Madras brought out the difference between inquiries under s.7-A and s.14-B of the Act. The authorities empowered to take action to recover the damages under s.14-B are different from the authorities constituted to determine the dues under s.7-A of the Act. It is only when the employer fails to pay the amount determined by the authorities, the statutory authorities empowered under s.14-B takes recourse to the penalty proceedings." The contention of the EPFO that under s.7-A(1)(b) of the Act the order contemplated is one which determines the amount due from an employer and thus every order passed would be in exercise of the power under s.7-A of the Act was rejected by the Delhi High Court in *Jai Balaji Security Services v Assistant Provident Fund Commissioner, Delhi (North)*,[386] for the reason that s.7-I itself treats orders passed under s.7-A, s.7-B, s.7-C and s.14-B of the Act as separate and independent orders.

S.7-A order is like a money-decree

In *Employees' Provident Fund Organisation v Rollwell Forge Ltd. and another*,[387] a Division Bench of the Gujarat High Court opined that the order passed under s.7-A of the Act

---

[384] 2016(3) PLJR 373: 2016(151) FLR 724: 2017 LabLR 83: 2017 LabLR 197
[385] *General Manager, BSNL, Sambalpur v Assistant Provident Fund Commissioner*, 2015(144) FLR 175: 2014(118) CutLT 973: 2014(20) S.C.T. 830
[386] 2016(154) DRJ 110: 2016(2) CLR 84: 2016 LabLR 118: 2016(148) FLR 644: 2015(21) S.C.T. 234
[387] 2012(1) LLJ 773: 2011(131) FLR 525: 2011(23) S.C.T. 653

would be almost like a money decree. Though the provisions of the Civil Procedure Code may not be applicable so far as the proceedings under the Act is concerned, some clue can be taken from Order 41, Rule 5 of Civil Procedure Code, which relates to stay of proceedings and execution of judgment and decree. It provides that an appeal shall not operate as a stay of proceedings under a decree or order appealed from except so far as the Appellate court may order, nor shall execution of a decree be stayed by reason only of an appeal having been preferred from the decree. Order 41, Rule 5 provides that notwithstanding anything contained in the preceding sub-rules, where the appellant fails to make the deposit or furnish the security specified in sub-rule (3) of rule 1, the Court shall not make an order staying the execution of the decree. So far as the Act is concerned, s.7-O provides that even appeal cannot be entertained by a Tribunal unless 75% of the amount determined under s.7-A is deposited.

S.7-A of EPF Act is similar to S.45A of ESI Act

In *Bharat Heavy Electricals Ltd. v ESI Corporation*,[388] the Supreme Court pointed out the similarities between the EPF Act and the ESI Act. There is no significant difference in the purport and object of both the provisions. In the proceedings initiated under s.45-A of the Act, a next employer or principal employer may also show that they are not liable to deposit any contribution on behalf of the employees as the establishment in question did not come within the purview thereof. The purpose of the proceedings, both under the Act as also the Employees' Provident Fund Act, is to determine the amount due from any employer in respect of the employees under the statutory schemes. Both the Acts envisages compliance with principles of natural justice. The proviso appended to s.45A of the Act provides for a statutory mandate of giving a reasonable opportunity of being heard.

Powers cannot be delegated

In *Ganesh Das Kaluram v The Regional Provident Fund Commissioner, Orissa and another*,[389] the High Court held that the authorities competent to make a determination of dues under s.7-A of the Act are not authorised to delegate their powers. The Court further held that the Inspector could not determine the amount due from any employer under any provision of the Act.

THE CONSTITUTIONAL VALIDITY OF S.7-A UPHELD

In *Prakash Kothari v Regional Provident Fund Commissioner*,[390] a Division Bench of the Bombay High Court (Nagpur Bench), upheld the constitutional validity of

---

[388] Civil Appeal No.1271 of 2008 (Decision dated 14-2-2008)
[389] 1973(2)LLJ 465 (Ori)
[390] 1989 Mh.LJ 825: 1989(2) CLR 756: 1990(1) LLN 62: 1990(2) LLJ 217

s.7-A of the Act placing reliance on the Supreme Court decision in *Organo Chemical Industries v Union of India*.[391] In *Organo Chemical* case, the Supreme Court rejected the plea of absence of guidelines or appellate review to subvert the validity of s.14-B stating that an appeal is a desirable corrective but not an indispensable imperative and while its presence is an extra check on wayward orders, its absence is not a sure index of arbitrary potential. The Bombay High Court in the *Prakash Kothari* case (supra) held that what applies to s.14-B also applies to s.7-A.

The Full Bench of the High Court of Delhi in *Jay Prestressed Products Ltd. and another v Union of India and others*,[392] held that s.7-A of the Act is not violative of Article 14 merely because of the absence of provision for appeal from the order of Regional Provident Fund Commissioner in view of the subsequent insertion of sub-sections 7-A to 7-P of the Act and functioning of an Appellate Tribunal for orders passed under s.7-A of the Act. After the establishment of the Tribunal, the controversy has become merely academic. Various High Courts have considered the constitutional validity of s.7-A, and there is almost unanimity that the provision is *intra vires*. Decisions in *Interstate Transport Agency Sitamarhi v Regional Provident Fund Commissioner*,[393] *Prakash Kothari v Regional Provident Fund Commissioner*,[394] *Kshetriya Khadi Gramodyog Samiti Kumher v Union of India and others*,[395] *Sumedico Corporation and another v Regional Provident Fund Commissioner*,[396] held that after the establishment of the EPF Appellate Tribunal, the controversy has become merely academic.

Determination of dues is must before recovery action

It is only when the Regional Provident Fund Commissioner determines by an order that the establishment is covered under the PF Act and the Scheme, then he must hold a further enquiry to determine the amount due from the employer after affording an opportunity of being heard to the employer.[397] Making of an order under sub-section (3) of s.7-A determining the amount due from any employer is a condition precedent for serving a demand on the employer for payment of contribution is clear from a reading of Sections 7-A and 8 of the Act.[398]

---

[391] 1979 SC 1803
[392] 2001 LAB I.C. 1
[393] 1983 L.I.C. 940 (Patna)
[394] (1990) 2 LLJ 217
[395] 1995 L.I.C. 315
[396] (1999) ILLJ 1170 SC,
[397] *Oriental Agencies and others v Regional P.F. Commissioner and another* 1988WLN(UC)201
[398] *A.T. Union (P) Ltd. v Regional P.F. Commissioner* (1968) IILLJ 465 Ker

PRINCIPLES OF NATURAL JUSTICE

It cannot also be doubted that an order made in breach of principles of natural justice does not stand for that reason alone. The breach of principles of natural justice takes place in many forms. The order may not have been passed without affording an opportunity at all, the order may have been passed in violation of the fair procedure necessary for a fair adjudication, namely, where the accuser has acted as adjudicator or opportunity of cross-examination has not been granted, or opportunity of leading evidence has wrongly been denied or for that matter, no reasons have been recorded before passing the order affecting a person adversely. These are not the exhaustive circumstances in which breach of principles of natural justice is confined.[399] Refusal to consider the employer's documents on the pretext that some information already given by the employer operated as *estoppels* against the employer is a glaring disregard of the rules of natural justice.[400] In *Sandvik Asia Ltd. v Assistant Provident Fund Commissioner*,[401] the Gujarat High Court set aside the s.7-A order stating that the order was passed even before the expiry of the time given in the notice to the employer for production of material records, and hence it is a violation of principles of natural justice. The rules of natural justice aim to secure justice, or, to put it negatively, to prevent a miscarriage of justice.[402]

In *Gunvantrai Harivallabh Jani v Regional Provident Fund Commissioner*,[403] held, although s.7-A (2) of the Act gives to that authority certain powers of a civil court and the proceedings before it is judicial proceedings for specific specified purposes only, the authority is not a court. Even so, having regard to the rights involved and likely to be affected, the authority exercises quasi-judicial functions, and the procedure must be governed by equitable considerations in the sense that it must conform to the rules of natural justice.

Service of Summons

In *Vikram Poddar v Regional Provident Fund Commissioner*,[404] High Court of Calcutta observed that to pass a necessary order under s.7-A of the Act, no notice need be served upon every Director individually when the employer has been served. If in

---

[399] *Gujarat State Civil Supplies Corporation Ltd. v Regional P.F. Commissioner & others* (2000) GLR 398, (1999) IILLJ 844 Guj
[400] *Gunvantrai Harivallabh Jani v Regional P.F. Commissioner AIR 1970 MP 221*
[401] (2005) ILLJ 1049 Guj
[402] *A.K. Kraipak v Union of India*,(1969) 2 SCC 262: AIR 1970 SC 150
[403] AIR 1970 MP 221
[404] (2001) IILLJ 518 Cal

the absence of service of notice upon the employer, an order passed by the Regional Provident Fund Commissioner under s.7-A will be liable to be set aside.[405]

Presumption of Service

S.27 of the General Clauses Act, 1897 gives rise to a presumption that service of notice has been effected when it is sent to the correct address by registered post, unless and until the contrary is proved by the addressee, service of notice is deemed to have been effected at the time at which the letter would have been delivered in the ordinary course of business. The Supreme Court has held that when a notice is sent by registered post and is returned with a postal endorsement 'refused' or 'not available in the house' or 'house locked' or 'shop closed' or 'addressee not in station,' due service has to be presumed.[406]

Notice period

In *Sadidharan v Regional Provident Fund Commissioner*,[407] the High Court of Kerala held, 'under s.7-A, notice can be issued only to determine the amounts from the employer at the time of the issue of the notice and not the amounts that become due after the issue of the notice under s.7-A.'

Oral Hearing is not necessitated always

In *M.P. Industries v The Union of India*,[408] the Supreme Court observed: "It is no doubt a principle of natural justice that a quasi-judicial tribunal cannot make any decision adverse to a party without giving him an adequate opportunity of meeting any relevant allegations against him. However, the said opportunity need not necessarily be by personal hearing. It can be by written representation. Whether the said opportunity should be by written representation or by personal hearing depends upon the facts of each case and ordinarily it is in the discretion of the tribunal."

Ex-post facto Hearing

In *Swadeshi Cotton Mills v the Union Of India*,[409] the Supreme Court approved the ex-post facto hearing by citing the words of Prof. De Smith, the renowned author of '*Judicial Review*.' "Can the absence of a hearing before a decision is made be adequately compensated for by a hearing *ex-post facto*? A prior hearing may

---

[405] K.C. Mehra v The Regional PF Commissioner 1990 LLR 399 (Del HC)
[406] Jagdish Singh v Natthu Singh AIR 1992 SC 1604; State of M.P. v Hiralal and others (1996) 1 SCR 480 and VRaja Kumari v P. Subbarama Naidu and another 2005 Cri.L.J.127
[407] (1982) Lab IC597 (Ker.)
[408] AIR 1966 SC 675.
[409] 1981 AIR 818, 1981 SCR (2) 533

be better than a subsequent hearing, but a subsequent hearing is better than no hearing at all."

Grant of Adjournments

In *Camtex Mills v Assistant Provident Fund Commissioner*,[410] the Madras High Court held that a quasi-judicial authority like Provident Fund Commissioner should act reasonably, justly and should not act with undue haste and arbitrariness. When a request had been made well in advance for adjournment of proceedings by assigning reasons, the Commissioner should have, in fairness, accommodated the petitioner by granting a short adjournment. Hence the order passed *ex-parte* being an arbitrary exercise of power which was in violation of Article 14 of the Constitution cannot sustain. When the employer failed to avail as many as 34 opportunities of personal hearing, the Madhya Pradesh High Court held that the employer had to suffer the demand.[411]

Mandatory to divulge the report of the Enforcement Officer

In *Faze Three Limited v Employees Provident Fund Organisation*,[412] the Gujarat High Court set aside the order passed by the Regional Provident Fund Commissioner for the reason that he accepted the report submitted by the Enforcement Officer without furnishing a copy of it to the employer or affording him an opportunity to cross-examine the Enforcement Officer. In the light of the principles laid down by the Supreme Court in *Natwar Singh v Director of Enforcement and another*,[413] the Court held that it could not be said that the Provident Fund Commissioner followed a fair procedure before passing the impugned orders which are therefore liable to be set aside. However, in *Provident Fund Commissioner v Bena Garments*, the Bombay High Court observed that if the EPF Appellate Tribunal was of the opinion that non-supply of copy of Enforcement Officer's report vitiated the order of the Provident Fund Commissioner, then a direction could have been given to supply the report and to hear the matter afresh, instead of setting aside the order.

In *Aparna Construction and Estates v Regional Provident Fund Commissioner*,[414] the facts for consideration before the Andhra Pradesh High Court were that the Regional Provident Fund Commissioner passed orders under s.7-A of the Act on the report of the Enforcement Officers *ex-parte* requiring the petitioner to deposit provident fund contributions for the contract employees engaged by him, without any opportunity of

---

[410] 2003 LLR 553 (Mad HC)
[411] *Maya Spinners Ltd. v Assistant Provident Fund Commissioner*, 2004(101) FLR 175.
[412] 2014 1 C.L.R. 188
[413] (2010) 13 SCC 255
[414] 2012(6) ALT 72; 2012(3) CLR 1068; 2012(5) Andh LD 677; 2013(136) FLR 633; 2012(49) R.C.R.(Civil) 409

hearing. The petition made an application under s.7-A (4) of the Act to set aside the *ex-parte* order because even a copy of the report of Enforcement Officers was not furnished to him. Though the Provident Fund Commission gave a copy of the report, he again upheld the earlier order without giving any opportunity of hearing to the petitioner. The High Court held that the course adopted by the Respondent was illegal as he ought to have passed orders afresh by setting aside the earlier order, after giving the opportunity of hearing the petitioner after furnishing a copy of the report of Enforcement Officers.

Authority should divulge all documents

The Supreme Court, in *Natwar Singh v Director of Enforcement and another*,[415] held that the right to fair hearing is a guaranteed right and that nothing should be used against a person which has not been brought to his notice. It was held that the concept of fairness requires the adjudicating authority to furnish those documents upon which reliance has been placed and that it is only in cases where disclosure of evidential material might inflict serious harm on the person directly concerned or other persons or where disclosure would be in breach of confidence or might be injurious to public interest that an exception to the said rule can be taken.[416]

Cross-Examination of the Inspector – Allowed

In *Varhadi That v Assistant Provident Fund Commissioner, Nagpur*[417] the Bombay High Court (Nagpur Bench) was considering the case the Petitioner sought permission to cross-examine the Enforcement Officers about their report recommending clubbing of two units run by the petitioner. The High Court allowed cross-examination of the Enforcement Officer, observing that by depriving the petitioner of the opportunity of cross-examination, the Commissioner would not be able to come to a right conclusion.

Burden of Proof

In *Saraswati Construction Company v Central Board of Trustee*,[418] the Delhi High Court reaffirmed the settled legal position that if any establishment or employer is not covered under the said Act, then it is for the employer to place sufficient cogent and convincing material before the designated authority in an enquiry under s.7-A so as to satisfy the authority with regard to the non-applicability of the Act and on failure to place any such material, the onus cannot be shifted on the EPF

---

[415] (2010) 13 SCC 255
[416] *Faze Three Limited v. EPFO*, Special Civil Application No.9730 of 2013, decision dated 10th July 2013
[417] 2008(2) ALL MR 177: 2008(6) BCR 511: 2008(1) Mh.LJ 265: 2008(116) FLR 610
[418] 171(2010) DLT 3

authorities to prove the applicability of the Act, who under no circumstances, can be in possession of necessary records evidencing the extent of strength of employees in any particular establishment.

In *Bankim Chandra Chakravarty v Regional Provident Fund Commissioner*,[419] a Division Bench of the Patna High Court laid down that once the authorities under the Act have held the number of employees in the establishment to be more than required to bring it within the ambit of the Act, it is up to the person challenging the said findings to establish that in fact, the number is less. In *Lakshmi Restaurant v The Regional Provident Fund Commissioner, Delhi*,[420] also held that if anybody feels aggrieved by some order and files a petition in the High Court, he must bring sufficient material before the Court to displace the finding and the same has nothing to do with the question of onus of proof before the Provident Fund Commissioner.

IDENTIFICATION OF THE BENEFICIARIES

The amounts due *vis-à-vis* each employee, have to be quantified. The assessment under s.7-A of the Act should not be confused with an assessment of tax. These are provident fund dues which are to accrue to an individual and not a tax, and not an amount payable to the Provident Fund Commissioner. Unless the nature of employment and the names of employees are identified with certainty, the assessment cannot be said to be in accordance with law.[421] Unless the beneficiaries are identified the amount deposited with the Provident Fund Department will not be of any use to the employees whose benefit the Trust has been created for.[422]

In *Roxy Cinema v State of Bihar and another*,[423] the Patna High Court held that in the absence of the identified workmen or employees, who are entitled to the benefit, liability could not be saddled upon an establishment in the name of compliance or enforcement of the law. The Provident Fund authorities can make no collection for the faceless, nameless or non-identifiable workers on mere head-count or herd count. The same view was endorsed in *Raj Kumar Gupta v Assistant Provident Fund Commissioner*.[424] In *H.P. State Forest Corporation v Regional P.F. Commissioner*,[425]

---

[419] AIR 1958 Patna 314
[420] 10(1974) DLT 369
[421] *Assistant Provident Fund Commissioner v Nand Lal & Co.*, 2015(3) PLJR 373: 2016(151) FLR724(Pat.DB)
[422] *Service Club v Presiding Officer*, 2013(1)SCT 433 (P & H).
[423] Writ Petition No. 11499 of 2006. Decision dated July 20, 2012.
[424] 2013(3)PLJR464:2013(139)FLR207(Pat.)
[425] 2008(2) S.C.T. 724: 2008(3) Recent Apex Judgments (R.A.J.) 377: 2008(3) LLJ 581: 2009(1) LLJ 141: 2008(5) SCC 756: 2008(6) JT 203: 2008(6) Scale 124: 2008(3) LLN 43: 2008(119) FLR 50: 2008(2) SCC (L&S) 158: 2008(3) CLR 82: 2008(3) RSJ 101

it was contended before the Supreme Court that the employees are seasonal employees and as the inquiry period pertains to long back, the records were not available, and in many a case, the beneficiaries were not even traceable. The Supreme Court recommended that the amounts due from the Corporation would be determined only concerning those employees who are identifiable and whose entitlements can be proved on the evidence. Unless a beneficiary is identified, the employer cannot be fastened with any liability. However, the identification of the beneficiary would require the employer to produce their records with the Commissioner.[426]

In *Regional Director, ESI Corporation v Kerala State Drugs and Pharmaceuticals Limited*,[427] the Supreme Court observed, "as regards the findings that the workmen were unidentifiable, what is forgotten is that under the Act, once an establishment comes to be covered by the Act, the employer becomes liable to pay the contribution in respect of the employees in his employment directly or indirectly. The contribution which had become payable for the relevant period has to be paid even if the employees concerned are no longer in employment. Whether the employees are unidentifiable today or not is, therefore, irrelevant so long as the contribution was liable to be paid on their behalf when they were in employment." In *Food Corporation of India v Provident Fund Commissioner and others*,[428] the Supreme Court held that the Commissioner is authorised to enforce attendance in person and also to examine any person on oath. He has the power requiring the discovery and production of documents. This power was given to the Commissioner to decide not abstract questions of law, but only to determine actual concrete differences in payment of contribution and other dues by identifying the workmen."

Provident fund dues had to be kept in the account of individual home workers. Their name and address and/or their identity is required to be known by the provident fund authorities otherwise the person in whose favour the money is kept would not get it back when he was entitled to get it. Such sum could not be kept with reference to the contractors inasmuch as the contractors are not the recipient of the benefit under the Act.[429]

Assessment should be of independent finding

S.7-A enjoins the officers not below the rank of Assistant Provident Fund Commissioner to conduct the inquiry. The determination of dues under sub-section (3)

---

[426] *SDB Infrastructure Pvt Ltd. v Union of India*, 2015 (224) DLT 166 (Del)(DB)
[427] 1995 Supp (3) SCC 148
[428] (1990) 1 SCC 68
[429] *Mantu Biri Factory (P) Ltd. and another v The Regional P.F. Commissioner and another*, 1994 vol. (2)CHN, p. 75

is to be made by such authority and not by the Inspector.[430] The investigation made by the inspector or the report submitted by him was no substitute for a quasi-judicial enquiry envisaged by s.7-A.[431] In *Regional P.F. Commissioner v Glamour-Proprietor Sethhassaram and Sons,*[432] a Division Bench of the Delhi High Court held that the Inspector's report, apart from being no substitute for a proper enquiry, should be made available to the employer to enable him to disprove it based on facts. Thus, determination of dues based on the report of the Provident Fund Inspector is not by the provisions of the Act. An independent inquiry by the competent authority is necessary.[433]

Commissioner to exercise his powers to collect all evidence

In *Food Corporation of India v Provident Fund Commissioner and others,*[434] the Supreme Court while considering the nature of inquiry by the authority under s.7-A of the Act observed, "the Commissioner is authorised to enforce attendance in person and also to examine any person on oath. He has the power requiring the discovery and production of documents. This power was given to the Commissioner to decide not abstract questions of law, but only to determine actual concrete differences in payment of contribution and other dues by identifying workers. The Commissioner should exercise all his powers to collect all evidence and collate all material before coming to a proper conclusion. That is the legal duty of the Commissioner. It would be a failure to exercise the jurisdiction particularly when a party to the proceedings requests for summoning evidence from a particular person." In *Panchhi Food Pvt Ltd. v Assistant Provident Fund Commissioner,*[435] the Allahabad High Court further held that issuance of a summons or notice to appear would not be sufficient, but the authorities concerned are bound to force them to appear in the exercise of the power conferred in sub-section (2) of the s.7-A as the authorities concerned had to collect material to discharge their statutory duties and responsibilities imposed under the law.

In *Prem Motors Pvt Ltd. v Employees' Provident Fund Organisation and others,*[436] the Madhya Pradesh High Court observed that the cardinal principle of rules of natural

---

[430] *Ganesh Das Kaluram v Regional Provident Fund Commissioner, Orissa and another* 1973(2)LLJ 465 (Ori)
[431] *Glamour v Regional P.F. Commissioner* (1975) ILLJ 514 Del
[432] 20(1981)DLT424; 1982LabIC1787
[433] *Minerva Stores v Regional P.F. Commissioner* 1978 Lab IC 1160
[434] (1990) 1 SCC 68
[435] 2015(147) FLR 997: 2016 LabLR 176: 2015(23) S.C.T. 517
[436] 2016(2) M.P.L.J. 148: 2016(149) FLR 789: 2016(150) FLR 109: 2016 LabLR 968: 2017(1) CLR 73: 2015(77) R.C.R.(Civil) 377

justice is that no one should be condemned unheard, which in its fold encompasses the requirement of supply of documents to the delinquent which are likely to be acted upon by the enquiry officer to the detriment of the delinquent. Therefore, if the enforcement officer has relied upon the documents procured from various departments in respect of the establishment, the same is required to be confronted to the petitioner before any finding is arrived at against him in the matter of raising of demand of the amount due in the enquiry under s.7-A of the Act of 1952.

Arrest – Not allowed for non-production of records

In *Vinod Tiwari v Employees' Provident Fund Organisation*,[437] a Division Bench of the Madhya Pradesh High Court held that clause (d) of s.32 of the Civil Procedure Code is the only provision providing for detention of a person in civil prison. It stated that the Court might compel the attendance of any person to whom a summons has been issued under s.30 of the Civil Procedure Code and for that purpose may order him to furnish security for his appearance and in default commit him to civil prison. The expression '*for that purpose*' clearly indicates that the detention in civil prison can be ordered only for compelling the attendance of a person and not for non-production of the records summoned. Thus, the power under Order XVI, Rule 18 of the Civil Procedure Code can be exercised by the Court only to ensure the appearance of the person and not when he fails to produce any document or record.

In *Vignan Education Development v. Assistant Provident Fund Commissioner*,[438] the Andhra Pradesh High Court held that the authority under s.7-A does not have the power to arrest an employer on the sole ground that the later did not respond to the notice issued by the authority.

But the Madhya Pradesh High Court, in *Devi Ahilya Bai Ghatge Uccha Shiksha Samiti v. State of Madhya Pradesh*,[439] held that the authority conducting inquiry under s.7-A of the Act of 1952 is empowered to take recourse to the coercive step contemplated under s.32 of the Code of Civil Procedure and when it is also found that the power is exercised on proper consideration of the facts and circumstances of the case, no case for interference is made out by this Court.

SPEAKING ORDER

The Provident Fund Commissioner exercises judicial functions. His order must be supported by reasons.[440] In *S.N. Mukherjee v Union of India*,[441] the Supreme

---

[437] 2006 III LLJ 308 (M.P. DB)
[438] 2005 (3) ALD 770, 2005 (2) ALT 618, (2005) II LLJ 728 AP
[439] (2007) ILLJ 78 MP
[440] *Mohd. & Sons v J.M. Pandya*, 1979 Lab IC NOC 115 (Raj)
[441] 1990 AIR 1984, 1990 SCR Supl. (1) 44

Court held that an administrative authority exercising judicial or quasi-judicial functions is required to record the reasons for its decision. Quoting this, in *Gurbir Kaur v Regional Provident Fund Commissioner*,[442] the High Court of Calcutta held that the authority under s.7-A has to record the reasons for his decisions. Non-disclosure of such particulars in the order leads to the conclusion that the decision arrived at, was based on surmise and conjecture. In *Kathayee Cotton Mills Private Ltd. v Regional Provident Fund Commissioner*,[443] the Kerala High Court held that an order must be speaking one containing at least some indication that there has been a consideration by the authority the relevant aspects governing such adjudication and a brief statement of the reasons that weighed with the authority for the imposition of damages. In *Cannore Shop v Regional Provident Fund Commissioner*,[444] held, the authority is bound to state in its order the reasons for the quantification of the damages having due regard to the facts and circumstances, and if this is not done, the order is liable to be quashed. The Court further held that the reasons mentioned in the order could not be allowed to be supplemented by fresh reasons by way of affidavit in a Writ. If that is permitted the order which is invalid at the admission stage for lack of reasons will become valid at the state of final hearing.

In *Travancore Rayon Ltd. v Union of India*,[445] the Supreme Court mentioned why the Courts do insist upon disclosure of reasons in the order. One, the party aggrieved in the Court proceedings has the opportunity to demonstrate that the reasons which persuaded the authority to reject his case were erroneous; the other, the obligation to record reasons operates as a deterrent against possible arbitrary action by the executive authority invested with the judicial power.

Non-speaking orders

In *Samy Company v Presiding Officer, EPFAT and others*,[446] the Madras High Court set aside the order of the Tribunal observing that except adding one-word 'appeal is dismissed,' there is no discussion, nor had the Presiding Officer adverted to the factual matrix as well as the contentions raised in the appeal. Thus, the proceeding suffers from an error apparent on the face of the record, and it is a failure to exercise the jurisdiction vested in it.

---

[442] (2006) 1 CALLT 566 HC, 2006 (1) CHN 547, (2006) III LLJ 98 Cal
[443] (1970) I LLJ 77 Ker
[444] (1995) III LLJ 134 Ker
[445] [1970] 3 SCR 4
[446] (2000)III LLJ 119 Mad

Vague reasons can be summarily rejected

In *Regional Provident Fund Commissioner v Allahabad Canning Co.,*[447] a Division Bench of the Allahabad High Court held that for vague nature of objections raised by the appellant, the findings given by the Regional Provident Fund Commissioner that the plea advanced by the employer was 'untenable' is a sufficient compliance with the requirements of a reasoned order. The Court further vowed to what other reasons could conceivably be given to the vague nature of objections. The reasons expected to be recorded in a speaking order must necessarily depend on the nature of contentions raised in reply to the show cause notice.

No power of waiver

In *K.R. Subbier Tape Factory v Regional Provident Fund Commissioner,*[448] the Madras High Court observed: "Section 7-A(1) of the Act merely refers to the determination of the amount due under any of the provisions of the Act, and so long as the employer's share of the contribution is due under the provisions of the Act, Section 7-A can have nothing whatever to do with the waiver or remission of any such amount, and admittedly neither the Act nor the Scheme confers any power on the authorities to waive any such amount. It is one of the basic principles of administration of the law that the creature of a statute will have to function within the four corners of the statute, and it has no power or authority to do anything outside the scope of the statute."

Principle of Best Judgment Assessment

In *Brij Bhushan Lal Parduman Kumar v Commissioner of Income-Tax,*[449] the Supreme Court observed that the authority making the best judgment assessment must make an honest and fair estimate of the income of the assessee and though arbitrariness cannot be avoided in such estimate, the same must not be capricious but should have a reasonable nexus to the available material and the circumstances of the case. About determination of contribution payable under s.45-A of the Employees' State Insurance Act, 1948, the Supreme Court in *Employees' State Insurance Corporation v C.C. Santhakumar,*[450] held that on non-cooperation by the employer, judgment on *"best assessment,"* as is known in taxing statutes, can be passed. Following this, the High Court of Orissa, in *Bidi Supply v Regional PF Commissioner,*[451] upheld the order passed under s.7-A of the Act applying the principle of best judgment assessment in case of non-cooperation by the employer.

---

[447] 1978 L.I.C. 998
[448] (1970) IILLJ 109 Mad
[449] [1978] 115 ITR 524
[450] (2007) 1 SCC 584
[451] W.P. No.14712 of 2005, judgment dated 1.7.2016

Inspector cannot override the decision the Commissioner

In *Patel Narshi Thakershi v Pradyumansinghji Arjunsinghji*,[452] the Supreme Court observed that the power to review is not an inherent power but has to be provided explicitly by the statute. When the Regional Provident Fund Commissioner himself has not been given any reviewing power under the statute and therefore could not review the order of his predecessor, the Inspector could not review the decision of the Regional Provident Fund Commissioner.

Non-rejoinder of Employees as necessary Parties

When the order passed by the Assistant Provident Fund Commissioner under s.7-A (resolving the dispute regarding the applicability of the Act and in which the employees' union was a party) was challenged by the employer before the EPF Appellate Tribunal, the employees' union was not pleased as a party. Setting aside the order of the EPF Appellate Tribunal, a Division Bench of the Calcutta High Court held that the Tribunal ought not to have passed any order affecting the interest of the employees without hearing them and that the appeal should have been dismissed for non-joinder of necessary parties.[453]

Dispute regarding Applicability should be resolved first

Before determining the amount due from the employer as envisaged in s.7-A(1)(b) of the Act, the authority has to decide the dispute relating to the applicability of the Act as envisaged in s.7-A(1)(a) of the Act.[454]

Admissibility of illegally gathered material

In *Pooran Mal v Director of Inspection (Investigation)*,[455] the Supreme Court held that materials gathered by illegal means could not be rejected in an adjudication. Following the *ratio decidendi*, the Madras High Court held that even assuming (not admitting) that the Enforcement Officer had illegally conducted an inspection or that they have called for records without any legal authority, that will not invalidate the orders passed under s.7-A.[456]

---

[452] AIR 1970 S.C. 1273
[453] *Employees' Provident Fund Organisation v EPF Appellate Tribunal*, 2015(144)FLR 481: 2014(4) LLJ 537 (Cal.)(DB)
[454] *Sri Mayur Biscuit Co.(P) Ltd. Regional P.F. Commissioner*, 1999 (81) FLR 581, (1999) IILLJ 163 Ori (DB).
[455] (1974) 1 SCC 345
[456] *Sree Gokulam Sizing Mills v Regional Provident Fund Commissioner and others*, W.P.11063 and 11064 of 2010, decided on April 27, 2011

Order, having attained finality, cannot be challenged

In *Amarjit Singh v Devi Rattanam*,[457] the Supreme Court held that challenging the consequential order without challenging the basic order is not permissible. In *Bengal Services Society (School) and another v Regional P.F. Commissioner*,[458] a Division Bench of the Calcutta High Court held that the liability to pay the contributions cannot be challenged at a later date once the employer had accepted the jurisdiction of Provident Fund Commissioner and no appeal was preferred against the order passed under s.7-A of the Act within prescribed time. If the employer fails to make use of the appeal mechanism under s.7-B or 7I, he cannot dispute the correctness of the s.7-A assessment order at the time of recovery action, long after passing of the s.7-A order. In *Esemar Chits(Madras) Pvt Ltd. v The State of Tamilnadu & others*[459] ruled that so long as the petitioner has not challenged the proceedings under s.7-A of the Act, the enforcement proceedings initiated under s.8F of the Act cannot be challenged. When the proceedings under s.7-A of the Act have become final, it is not open to the petitioner to challenge the recovery or enforcement proceedings after that.

Appeal lies only against the Composite order under s.7-A

In *Autogrinx Engineers (P) Ltd. v Regional P.F. Commissioner*,[460] a Division Bench of the Rajasthan High Court held that s.7-A of the Act enjoins upon the authority to pass a composite order, that is, immediately after deciding the dispute regarding the applicability of the Act to the establishment forthwith to undertake the exercise to determine the amount due from the employer. The order which is appealable or reviewable is the complete order (composite order) made by the authority under clauses (a) and (b) of s.7-A and the order passed under clause (a) of s.7-A of the Act at that stage, is not challengeable by way of review or the appeal.

Contractor can also dispute applicability under S.7-A

In *Parvati Construction Company v Rajasthan Housing Board*,[461] the High Court of Rajasthan held when the applicability of the Act and payment of provident fund contribution is disputed by the contractor, unless and until the dispute is adjudicated under s.7-A of the Act, the principal employer, by a unilateral order, cannot direct deposit of the amount towards the provident fund contribution nor has authority to deduct it from the running bills of the contractor.

---

[457] 2010 1 SCC (L & S) 1108
[458] 2008 (1) CHN 614
[459] W.P. No.2361/1998 Mad HC
[460] 2004 (102) FLR 846, (2004) IIILLJ 139 Raj, 2004 (2) WLC 681
[461] (1998) IILLJ 970 Raj

The principal employer, though he does not undertake any activity, and all works are entrusted to the contractors, the liability of the petitioner under the provisions of the Act will still be there.[462]

Contractor is a necessary party

In *Panchhi Food Pvt Ltd. v Assistant Provident Fund Commissioner*,[463] the Allahabad High Court held that the question whether the workers were employed by the Corporation directly or through the Contractor has to be determined on the basis of the contracts and that for ascertaining the name and address and the particulars of the workers, it would be necessary for summoning the contractor and/or examining them for getting materials for making efficient determination. It is the contractors who are in a position to know the name and address of the workers, who are engaged by the contractor for the work which was entrusted by the Corporation.

In *General Manager, BSNL, Sambalpur v Assistant Provident Fund Commissioner*,[464] the Orissa High Court held that since the adjudication was in relation to casual and Non-Muster Roll (NMR) employees of the contractors following the provisions contained in the aforesaid Section, it was incumbent upon the authority to summon the contractors and to find out the particulars before arriving at the final assessment. In *Chennai Petroleum Corporation Ltd. v Assistant Provident Fund Commissioner (Exemp.), Chennai*,[465] the Madras High Court held that when it is brought to the notice of the respondent the available details of the contractors, the respondent should have impleaded the contractors and proceeded against them for determining the quantum of provident fund contribution payable by them as per the provisions of the Act.

Quasi-Judicial authority cannot challenge the order on appeal

In *Regional Provident Fund Commissioner, West Bengal v Sathi Traders*,[466] the Provident Fund Commissioner preferred a Writ Petition against the order of the EPF Appellate Tribunal setting aside the order passed by him. The Calcutta High Court dismissed the petition observing that the Regional Provident Fund Commissioner cannot be said to be the person aggrieved. The said authority is a part of the establishment and is exercising quasi-judicial authority. He is bound by the order passed by the appellate authority and cannot question the same by filing the Writ Petition. The Court further observed that when the Regional Provident

---

[462] *Himachal Pradesh Nagar Vikas Pradhikaran v Regional P.F. Commissioner*, 1998 II LLJ 267 (HP. DB)
[463] 2015(147) FLR 997: 2016 LabLR 176: 2015(23) S.C.T. 517
[464] 2015(144) FLR 175: 2014(118) CutLT 973: 2014(20) S.C.T. 830
[465] 2006 II CLR 1036
[466] 2014 LabLR 963: 2014(143) FLR 259: 2014(14) S.C.T. 341

Fund Commissioner decides the matter under s.7-A, it has a trapping of a judicial order and such authority cannot be a judge in its own cause and feel aggrieved by any order that may be passed by the appellate authority.

Similarly, in *Assistant Provident Fund Commissioner v Nirmitee Holidays (P) Ltd.*,[467] the Bombay High Court also held that authorities discharging quasi-judicial functions are not permitted to challenge the order passed by the Appellate Authority reversing their orders. The Court observed, 'permitting such an exercise would be subversive of judicial discipline,' and referred to the observations of the Supreme Court in *Syed Yahoob v K.S. Radhakrishnan and others*,[468] that the Tribunal is not supposed to defend his own orders unless allegations are made against them.

Inquiry Officer comes under Judges (Protection) Act, 1985

In *E.S. Sanjeeva Rao v Central Bureau of Investigation*,[469] the Bombay High Court held that no criminal prosecution could be launched against the Regional Provident Fund Commissioner merely on the ground that he made a wrong assessment. The facts of the case were that the Central Bureau of Investigation conducted an enquiry and concluded that the assessment made by the Regional Provident Fund Commissioner was wrong and the liability of the employer was much higher than the assessment. The Central Bureau of Investigation (CBI) filed prosecution complaints against the Commissioner under s.420 of the Indian Penal Code and the Prevention of Corruption Act. The Bombay High Court, quashing the prosecution, held that the Regional Provident Fund Commissioner, while passing an order under s.7-A, is a judge within the definition under s.19 of the IPC and s.2 of the Judges (Protection Act, 1985) and that the prosecution of the Provident Fund Commissioner only by the order passed under s.7-A is barred given s.77 of the IPC or s.3(1) of the Judges (Protection) Act, 1985.

In *Swapan Kumar Bankura v Union of India*, the facts of the case for consideration before a Division Bench of the Calcutta High Court were that disciplinary proceedings were initiated against an officer who conducted an inquiry under s.7-A on the grounds that he concluded the inquiry by exercising powers beyond his jurisdiction. The Calcutta High Court, relying on the Supreme Court order in *Union of India and another v R.K. Desai*,[470] struck down the disciplinary proceedings holding that no proceedings should have been initiated against the

---

[467] 2011(2) LLJ 469: 2010(11) S.C.T. 222
[468] AIR 1964 SC 477)
[469] 2012 CriLJ 4053: 2013(1) R.C.R.(Criminal) 284: 2013(1) S.C.T. 92: 2013(1) R.C.R.(Civil) 535: 2013 ALL MR(Cri) 933: 2013(1) CCR 4: 2012(4) Mh.LJ (Crl.) 257
[470] 1993 SCC (L&S)

petitioner in the absence of any specific allegation of misconduct, as the petitioner had exercised his juridical function under s.7-A without any corrupt or improper motive. Thus, in the absence of specific allegation regarding the discharge of the judicial or quasi-judicial function of an officer under corrupt or improper motive, no disciplinary action can be initiated.

S.7-A Proceedings – Judicial Proceedings

In *Amit Vashistha v Suresh and another*,[471] the Supreme Court held that the proceedings under s.7-A are deemed to be a judicial proceeding by fiction, and such a judicial proceeding can well be equated for that purpose with a Court under s.195(1)(b)(i) of the Criminal Procedure Code. Citing a previous case *Lalji Haridas v State of Maharashtra*,[472] the Supreme Court held that if a person offers an insult to a public servant sitting in a judicial proceeding under s.7-A or causes interruption to him while he is so sitting at any stage of judicial proceeding, the complaint has to proceed from the public servant himself. That is the effect of s.195(1)(b) of Cr.P.C.

REVIEW OF ORDERS PASSED UNDER S.7-A
Review of own Orders – Permissible

The Supreme Court has laid down that review of its own order by a quasi-judicial authority is permissible where there is a procedural mistake or procedural illegality. In *Rajender Singh v Lt. Governor, Andaman & Nicobar Islands and others*,[473] the Supreme Court clarified that the power of review extends to correct all errors to prevent a miscarriage of justice and when the interest of the justice so demands in appropriate cases.

S.7-A order cannot be challenged in Special Appeal

In *P.G.T. Components Pvt. Ltd. v Assistant Provident Fund Commissioner*,[474] a Division Bench of the Allahabad High Court, referring to a previous decision in *India Thermit Corporation Ltd. v Regional Provident Fund Commissioner*,[475] held that the Regional Provident Fund Commissioner functions as a Tribunal (and not as a Court) while discharging the duties under the provisions of the Act, and accordingly, no Special Appeal could lie against his order as provided in Chapter VIII Rule 5 of the Rules of the Court.

---

[471] Crl. Appeal No.245/2010, decided on August 31st, 2017
[472] (1964) 6 SCR 700
[473] AIR 2006 SC 75
[474] 2003(1) LLJ 1033: 2003(96) FLR 473: 2003(1) All WC 508: 2003 ILR (Allahabad) 64
[475] Special Appeal No.567 of 1994, decided on March 23rd, 1994.

Period of review petition pendency excluded

In *Rameshwar Jute Mills v Union of India and others*,[476] the review petition filed by the appellant under s.7-B of the Act was dismissed, after an extended period of pendency, on the ground of absence of the power of review. After that, the appellant resorted to the remedy of Writ Petition which was also dismissed on the ground of delay. The Supreme Court held that the period of pendency of the review petition should not have been treated as a period of delay, even if any specific period of limitation is prescribed for filing the writ petition.

Review by the same officer who passed the S.7-A Order

In *Deccan Education Society v Union of India and others*,[477] the facts of the case were that the order under s.7-A was passed by the Assistant Provident Fund Commissioner and the review application filed under s.7-B was dismissed by the Regional Provident Fund Commissioner. Karnataka High Court held that according to s.7-B of the Act, the review application has to be decided by the very same officer who had passed the assessment order under s.7-A of the Act.

Hearing is mandatory for adjudicating review application under S.7-B

In *Ashmit Motors Private Limited v Assistant Provident Fund Commissioner*,[478] the Bombay High Court held that the review petition under s.7-B has to be decided after issuing a notice to the review petitioner and all other parties concerned, and naturally after hearing them. There has to be an adjudication of the review petition. Therefore, whether the authority gave a reasoned order or not will not make any difference. The Court further cited the case of *Lok Vikas Sahakari Bank Limited v Assistant Provident Fund Commissioner*,[479] in which the High Court reasoned out that "the words 'appears' and 'no sufficient ground' employed in sub-section (3) of s.7-B cast an obligation upon the authority to record findings at least *prima facie* about availability or non-availability of such grounds. Sub-section (4) permits that authority to grant the review. The proviso to sub-section (4) then stipulates that such review shall not be granted without previous notice to all parties before the authority. It is therefore evident that at the stage when review application is being considered under sub-section (3), the aggrieved party alone needs to be given a hearing to find out whether a case for review is made out or not. If, according to the

---

[476] 1999 SCC (L&S) 1231: 2002(sup4) LLJ 997
[477] 2016(150) FLR 646: 2016 LabLR 1185
[478] 2016(4) LLJ 315: 2017(1) CLR 41: 2017 LabLR 10: 2017(1) Mh.LJ 885: 2017(152) FLR 459: 2017 LIC 1234
[479] *Lokvikas Sahakari Bank Ltd. v The Assistant Provident Fund Commissioner*, Writ Petition No. 3389 of 2011 dated 2-5-2011.

authority, no such case is made out there is no question of proceeding further to hear all other parties, as contemplated by clause (1) of sub-section (4) thereof." S.7-B of the Act expressly provides for review and the same will have to be decided after issuing a notice to review petitioner and all concerned parties, and apparently after hearing them. There has to be an adjudication of the review petition. Therefore, whether the authority gave a reasoned order or not will not make any difference.[480]

Personal hearing for admission of application for review – Not mandatory

Unlike a hearing on a Review application as is contemplated under Oder XL VII Rules 1 to 4 of the Civil Procedure Code, 1908, the EPF Act makes no provision for any hearing on the Review application, if the same is to be rejected. Only when a Review application is likely to be allowed, that a hearing is contemplated, to ensure that the beneficiaries of the order under s.7-A have no grievance of having not being heard.

Previous Notice to all the parties necessary

In *Thikedar Mazdoor Union v State of Jharkhand*,[481] the Jharkhand High Court held that power of review being a creature of the statute is to be strictly conformed to by the authority exercising it. When the petitioner, who was a party to the s.7-A proceeding, was not heard during the review proceedings under s.7-B, the High Court struck down it as it suffers from error of jurisdiction and failure to comply with the procedure laid down, that is, previous notice upon a party in the proceedings.

7-B – Time Limit for Appeal

In *Anurag Board and Mills (P) Ltd. v Regional Provident Fund Commissioner*,[482] the Allahabad High Court held that the starting point of limitation for filing review under s.7-B is 45 days from the date of original order and since the application was filed under s.7-B, the benefit of s.7-A(4) providing 3 months time from the date of communication of the order is not available. When the law debars explicitly the person concerned to accept an application for review beyond 45 days from the date of passing of the original order, the question of entertaining the application for review beyond 45 days does not arise.[483] However, the authority, having *suo moto* powers to correct the errors, is not debarred from taking *suo moto* action, notwithstanding the time limit prescribed under Para 79A of the EPF Scheme, 1952.[484]

---

[480] Shri Gajanan Maharaj Sansthan v Regional P.F. Commissioner, Writ Petition No. 1002/2008 Decision dated 27-8-200 (Bom.HC)
[481] 2016(151) FLR927 (Jhar.)
[482] 2005 All. LJ 1172: 2005(3) UPLBEC 2699: 2005(105) FLR 11: 2005(23) LCD 1061
[483] Gulati Packaging Pvt Ltd. v Assistant P.F. Commissioner 2012(135)FLR 917 (Uttar)(DB)
[484] Perfect Borng Pvt. Ltd. v Employees' Provident Fund Organisation 2016(1)LLJ 446 (Guj)

No coercive action when the application for review is pending

In *Laxmi Devi Shroof Adarsh Sanskrit College v Regional Provident Fund Commissioner*,[485] the Jharkhand High Court held that when the review application is pending, no coercive action should be taken for recovery of the assessed amount.

'For any other sufficient reasons' – Scope of

The phrase 'other sufficient reasons' means the reasons within the parameter of the review. It cannot be unconnected with the ingredients of review. When the ingredients of appeal are already available for due disposal by the appellate authority under s.7I, such provision for any other sufficient reasons cannot independently override the same.[486]

Recording of reasons necessary

In *Choithram Hospital & Research v Assistant Provident Fund Commissioner*,[487] a Division Bench of the Madhya Pradesh High Court observed that there was no satisfaction recorded by the Commissioner, as was required to have been recorded under the provisions of s.7-C of the Act and in the absence of reasons in conformity with the provisions contained in s.7-C of the Act, the order should have been quashed.

DETERMINATION OF ESCAPED AMOUNT

Period of Limitation applies to S.7-C

In *Satnam Singh Ahluwalia v Regional Provident Fund Commissioner*,[488] the Calcutta High Court held that the 'continuing offence' principle had no application about the proceedings under s.7-A of the Act and s.7-C put an explicit prohibition against reopening any case of s.7-A after the expiration of five years.

Section 7-C – not applicable to S.14-B levy

In *Regional P.F. Commissioner v Maharaja Shree Umaid Mills Ltd.*,[489] the Rajasthan High Court (Jaipur) held that the determination of escaped amount under s.7-C of the Act applies to the assessment of dues under s.7-A and not for the orders passed under s.14-B of the Act.

---

[485] (2009)IV LLJ 730Jhar
[486] *Innovative Classic Export (P) Ltd. v Regional P.F. Commissioner*, 2004 (1) LLJ 666 (Cal.)
[487] 2012(132) FLR 1097: 2012(1) CLR 514: 2012(3) LLJ 510: 2012(7) S.C.T. 748
[488] 2007(6) SLR 627
[489] 2015(1)WLC 633: 2015 LLR 839 (Raj.)

Chapter X
EPF APPELLATE TRIBUNAL

After the 33rd Amendment Act of 1988, s.7-D was inserted, and a statutory remedy of appeal before the Appellate Tribunal was made available for challenging the orders under s.7-A of the Act. Such a Tribunal is also established vide notification dated 30.6.1997. A Southern Bench of the EPF Appellate Tribunal was constituted in Bengaluru vide notification dated November 7, 2014, in compliance of the directions issued by the Karnataka High Court in Mandamus Writ Petition 14378/2006 and started functioning from April 29, 2016. However, by the Finance Act, 2017 the Government of India has wound up eight tribunals, including the EPF Appellate Tribunal, and transferred the remit to the Central Government Industrial Tribunals that examine matters under the Industrial Disputes Act of 1947. By s.185(4) of the Finance Act, 2017, the pending cases in EPFATs shall stand transferred to the CGITs with effect from May 26, 2017, and any fresh case of an appeal under the EPF Act shall be filed in the respective CGITs.[490]

By the Finance Act, 2017, s.2 (m) has been amended to read: "Tribunal" means the Industrial Tribunal referred to in s.7-D. The amended provision of s.7-D reads, "The Industrial Tribunal constituted by the Central Government under sub-section (1) of s.7A of the Industrial Disputes Act, 1947 shall, on and from the commencement of Part XIV of Chapter VI of the Finance Act, 2017, be the Tribunal for the purposes of this Act and the said Tribunal shall exercise the jurisdiction, powers and authority conferred on it by or under this Act." Sections 7-E, 7-F, 7-G, 7-H, 7-M, 7-N and 21(2)(a) have been deleted. S.18-A has been amended to read, "The authorities referred to in section 7-A and every inspector shall be deemed to be a public servant within the meaning of section 21 of the Indian Penal Code."

THE APPEAL BEFORE EPF APPELLATE TRIBUNAL (NOW, CGITS)

Appeal under S.7I – a statutory remedy

The statutory remedy of appeal under s.7-I of the Act available to the petitioner-company would be in the nature of the substantive remedy. The Appellate Tribunal

---

[490] The legal validity of Section 156 to 189 of the Finance Act has been challenged by the Madras Bar Association in Writ Petitions 15147 and 15148 of 2017 and the matter is pending before the High Court of Madras, as of date of publication of this book.

is obliged to consider the matter independently and to deal with all the contentions raised in the appeal.[491]

Order of the Appellate Tribunal

7-L (1) gives powers to the Tribunal to decide the appeals which are preferred before it, after hearing the parties. The Tribunal has the power of confirming, modifying or annulling the order appealed against or referring it back to the authority with cardinal directions.

Tribunal reserves its right to correct procedural errors

The expression ' review' is used in the two distinct senses, namely (1) a procedural review which is either inherent or implied in a Court or Tribunal to set aside a palpably erroneous order passed under a misapprehension by it, and (2) a review on merits when the error sought to be corrected is one of law and is apparent on the face of the record. The Supreme Court in *Patel Narshi Thakershi v Pradyamansinghji Arjunsinghji*[492] held that the power of review is not an inherent power and must be conferred by law either expressly or by necessary implication. This sort of review relates to review on merits. Obviously, when a review is sought due to a procedural defect, the inadvertent error committed by the Tribunal must be corrected *ex debito justitiae* to prevent the abuse of its process, and such power inheres in every Court or Tribunal.[493]

In *Employees' Provident Fund Organisation v Mahila Griha Udyog Lijjat Papad*,[494] the facts of the case were that the EPF Appellate Tribunal passed an adverse order without referring to a specific contention raised by the EPFO at the time of hearing before the Tribunal and it was not even referred to in the order. The Gujarat High Court clarified that in such circumstances, the petitioner department must, in the first instance, approach the Tribunal with an appropriate application seeking necessary clarification before the Tribunal.

Tribunal can only rectify the mistake but cannot review the order

7-L (2) empowers Tribunal to rectify any mistake apparent on the record, amend any order passed by it under sub-section (1). Such a mistake may be brought to the notice of the Tribunal by the parties to the appeal. The Tribunal cannot make such correction or amendment if the effect of the same is to enhance the amount due from the employer or increase the liability of the employer unless the employer

---

[491] *Kot Kapura Bus Service Pvt Ltd. v Presiding Officer, EPFAT* 2015(1) PLR 336 (P & H).
[492] AIR 1970 SC 1273, (1971) 3 SCC 844
[493] *Modern Public School Education Society v Presiding Officer, EPF Appellate Tribunal*, (2007) II LLJ 772 Del
[494] 2016(151) FLR 313: 2016 LabLR 1263: 2017(1) CLR 1047

is heard. The section provides that this power can be exercised within five years from the date of passing of the order. Such an extended period has been provided to exercise this power because the legislature thought that if there was any factual mistake or calculation mistake apparent in the order, the same could be corrected as and when mistake came to notice within five years. This section does not provide for review of the order. If the legislature intended that the Appellate Tribunal could review the order, the legislature would have provided for review of the order also. It is apparent that s.7-L (2) does not vest the power of reviewing its own order in the Appellate Tribunal. The power is limited and can be exercised only to make corrections which are apparent on the record. In the garb of this power, Tribunal cannot reverse or recall its own order, even if the order is bad in law. In the absence of an express provision in the Act, Tribunal cannot recall or review its own orders.[495]

A similar view was taken by the Delhi High Court, in *Food Corporation of India v Regional Provident Fund Commissioner*,[496] where it was held that the presiding officer was not invested with a power of review on merits under s.7L(2) and his power is limited to procedural review.

Dismissal for non-prosecution cannot be on merits

In *Shiv Shakti Shetkari Sahakari Sakhar Karkhana Ltd. v Union of India*,[497] the petitioner had challenged the s.7-A order contending that it was passed without considering the documents on record. He, however, failed to pursue the case in the EPF Appellate Tribunal which dismissed the case on merits in the absence of the petitioner. A Division Bench (Aurangabad Bench) of the Bombay High Court held that if the appellant remains absent in an appeal, the course open to the Appellate Authority would be to dismiss the appeal for non-prosecution or default but ought not to have decided it on merits.

EPFAT can grant instalments

In *Regional Provident Fund Commissioner v Sylee Tea Estate*,[498] a Division Bench of the Calcutta High Court held that the Employees' Provident Fund Appellate Tribunal could direct mode in which relief can be granted and to modify or vary the order passed under s.7-A. The Tribunal had considered the genuine financial difficulty of the establishment of remitting huge amount towards Provident Fund and rightly directed payment in 36 equal instalments.

---

[495] *Modern Public School Education Society v Presiding Officer, EPF Appellate Tribunal*, (2007) II LLJ 772 Del
[496] 2015 LabLR 482: 2015(146) FLR 207: 2015(7) S.C.T. 846
[497] 2016(151) FLR 1020
[498] 2017 LIC 992: 2017 LabLR 518

PRE-DEPOSIT UNDER S.7-O OF THE ACT
Pre-deposit not applicable for penal damages

In *Writer Safeguard Pvt. Ltd. v Regional P.F. Commissioner,*[499] the Bombay High Court held that s.7-O of the EPF Act is not applicable to an order made under s.14-B of the Act. In *The Regional P.F. Commissioner and another v Shrine Velankanni Senior Secondary School,*[500] a Division Bench of the Madras High Court, while dealing with a different aspect, held that proceedings contemplated under s.7-A is a primary proceeding for determining the contribution from the employer, but proceeding under s.14-B is entirely different. The Division Bench has further held that the authorities empowered to take action to recover damages from the under s.14-B, are different from the authorities constituted to determine the dues under s.7-A of the Act.

In *Naga Nanthana Mills Ltd. v Presiding Officer, EPFAT,*[501] the Madras High Court refused to accept the contention that the officer who has issued s.14-B order is the officer referred to in s.7-A of the Act and therefore s.7O applies to order for recovery of damages passed by such officer. The High Court clarified that a close reading of s.7-O of the EPF Act would make it abundantly clear that s.14-B has not been brought within the ambit of s.7-O of the EPF Act. Going by a plain reading of the said provision, one can readily perceive that the Parliament did not intend to bring s.14-B within the purview of s.7-O. Had the Parliament intended to bring an order made under s.14-B of the EPF Act also within the purview of s.7-O, the Parliament would have indeed, in unequivocal terms, stated so in s.7-O of the EPF Act. While the Parliament has specifically mentioned s.7-A in s.7-O, it has omitted to mention s.14-B in s.7-O, which is a conscious omission.

Similarly, in *Old Village Industries Ltd. v Assistant Provident Fund Commissioner,*[502] the Delhi High Court held that if the appeal is preferred against the order passed under s.14-B, then the Tribunal cannot insist for pre-deposit of assessment amount as provided under s.7O of the Act. The Court observed that the provisions of s.14-B of the Act are attracted only if there is default on the part of the employer. It, being a consequential liability essentially, must fall into a category of not the principal liability to attract stringent provisions of pre-deposit to the hearing of the appeal. Such provisions being related to revenue would be construed strictly whether to the advantage or disadvantage of the person upon whom the liability is sought to be fastened. Once the provisions of s.7-O does not include an appeal against an order

---

[499] 2011 II CLR 846
[500] 2009 Writ L.R. 326
[501] 2014 LabLR 204; 2014(140) FLR 1047; 2014(1) CLR 136; 2013(15) R.C.R.(Civil) 922
[502] 2005 (3) LLN 572

under s.14-B, then it would be in no way permissible to include such an order by implication or otherwise.

Placing reliance on the *Old Village Industries* case (supra), the Bombay High Court in *Writer Safeguard Pvt Ltd. v Regional Provident Fund Commissioner*,[503] set aside an order of the Presiding Officer, EPF Appellate Tribunal directing the appellant to deposit 30% of the amount assessed under s.7-C of the Act, observing that the counsel for the Provident Fund Commissioner failed to point out any provision under the Act requiring pre-deposit of the amount if the appeal is preferred against the order passed under s.7-C of the Act.

In *Bedi & Bedi Associates v Central Board of Trustees*,[504] the Delhi High Court held that the requirement of pre-deposit under s.7-O of the Act is confined to the determination of dues under s.7-A of the Act and does not apply to the damages levied under s.14-B of the Act. The Court further held that the inherent powers conferred upon the EPF Appellate Tribunal by Rule 21 of the Employees' Provident Fund Appellate Tribunal (Procedure) Rules, 1997, is confined to give effect to its orders and it does not confer any discretionary powers upon the Tribunal to insist for pre-deposit in appeals pertaining to determination of the damages levied under s.14-B of the Act. The discretion cannot be exercised to supplant the substantive law. A similar view was taken in the case of *Jai Balaji Security Services v Assistant Provident Fund Commissioner, Delhi (North)*[505] also. In *Shiv Herbal Research Laboratory v Assistant P.F. Commissioner*,[506] the Supreme Court held that there is nothing in the Act to indicate that any part of the amount levied under s.14-B is required to be deposited at the time of filing an appeal under s.7I with the EPF Appellate Tribunal.

---

[503] 2012(2) LLJ 34: 2011(130) FLR 1097: 2011(23) S.C.T. 932
[504] 2015(147) FLR 537: 2016 LabLR 7: 2015(22) S.C.T. 209
[505] 2016(154) DRJ 110: 2016(2) CLR 84: 2016 LabLR 118: 2016(148) FLR 644: 2015(21) S.C.T. 234
[506] 2016 LabLR 55

Chapter XI
LEVY OF PENAL DAMAGES AND INTEREST

PENAL DAMAGES – LEGISLATIVE HISTORY

S.14-B was brought on the statute by Act 37 of 1953 with an object of imposing exemplary or punitive damages to prevent employers from committing defaults. The provision for imposition of damages at 25% of the amount of arrear, however, did not prove to be effective. Accordingly, by Act 40 of 1973, the words '*not exceeding the amount of arrear*' were substituted for the words '25 percent.' Before November 1, 1973, s.14-B read as "Where an employer makes default in the payment of any contribution to the fund...the proper Government may recover from the employer such damages not exceeding 25% of the amount of arrears as it may think fit to impose." Thus, the power to levy damages rested with the appropriate governments. With effect from 1-11-1973, it was amended to read as "where an employer makes default in the payment of any contribution to the Fund... the Central Provident Fund Commissioner or such officer as may be authorised by the Central Government by notification in the Official Gazette in this behalf, may recover from the employer such damages not exceeding the amount of arrears as it may think fit to impose; Provided that before levying and recovering such damages the employer shall be given a reasonable opportunity of being heard."

After the Amendment Act of 1973, the Central Government had framed a table of damages which were to be recovered in case of defaults depending upon the period over which the default continued and the number of times that such a default occurred. The quantum of damages levied by this table gave rise to certain difficulties. As a result, the 'Employees' Provident Fund Review Committee' was appointed on 5th April 1980 for considering the question of levy of damages under s.14-B. The Committee, headed by G. Ramanujam (INTUC), submitted its report to the Union Minister for Labour and Planning (Shri. N.D. Tiwari) on 28th January 1981. The Ramanujam Committee recommended that instead of imposing damages on the employers for the belated payment of the EPF and allied contributions, the defaulting employer should be asked to pay penal interest at the maximum lending rate of banks plus 3% if the employers are occasional defaulters and at the maximum lending rate plus 5% in case of employers who are habitual defaulters. The Central Board of Trustees of the EPF considered this recommendation and decided that keeping in view the frequent fluctuations in the bank lending rates and the consequential difficulties in calculating the damages if the same were linked to the bank lending rates, the damages should be charged at a flat rate of 25% per annual on all belated remittances subject to the condition that the total damages levied do not exceed the actual amount of arrears. The recommendations of the Ramanujam Committee were placed before the CBT, in its 88th meeting held on 1-3-1981 and the Board by majority endorsed most of the recommendations of the Committee.[507]

Amendment Act 33 of 1988 made two amendments to s.14-B viz., the words "from the employer such damages, not exceeding the amount of arrears as it may think fit to impose" were replaced with "from the employer *by way of penalty* such damages, not exceeding the amount of arrears, *as may be specified in the Scheme.*"

The amended provision was brought into force with effect from 1-9-1991 by Notification No. SO 2259 dated 7-8-1991, published in the *Gazette of India* dated 24-8-1991. On a comparison of the pre-amended Section and the amended Section, it is to be noted that for the words "from the employer such damages not exceeding the amount of arrears as it may think fit to impose," the words "from the employer by way of penalty such damages not exceeding the amount of arrears as may be specified in the scheme" were substituted. Along with this amendment, the legislature brought in an additional Section also in the Act, namely, s.7-Q, providing for imposition of interest for delay in payment of amounts due under the Act. By these amendments, the legislature consciously wanted to segregate the compensatory portion of the damages under s.14-B, making s.14-B purely punitive in nature leaving the compensatory part of the damages under the erstwhile s.14-B to be taken care of by the newly introduced s.7-Q.

Both before and after the amendment it has been optional with the Regional Provident Fund Commissioner to levy and to recover the damages by way of penalty. Before the amendment, he had the power to levy the damages at the rate he thought to be fit, the maximum of which was fixed at 100%. It did not, however, prescribe any minimum rate. After the amendment, his power to levy the damages up to the maximum rate of 100% appears to have been curtailed by incorporating a sliding table in Paragraph 32-A of the EPF Scheme, 1952 for applying the rates for levy of damages according to the period of default specified therein even though the liability or the right to enforce the liability for such damages had been accrued long before the amendment was effected.[508]

---

[507] *Union Of India And others vs Super Processors* (1993) IILLJ 203 Bom
[508] *Atal Tea Company Ltd., and another v Regional Provident Fund Commissioner* – 1997 (2) LIC.1207 (Cal.HC)

CONSTITUTIONAL VALIDITY – ABSENCE OF APPEAL PROVISION DOES NOT VITIATE

In *Organo Chemical Industries and another v Union of India*,[509] it was contended that s.14-B was unconstitutional since it conferred unguided and uncontrolled discretion upon the government to impose such damages and therefore violated Article 14 of the Constitution. While upholding the constitutional validity of s.14-B, the Supreme Court laid down that while passing orders under s.14-B, the authority was acting in a quasi-judicial capacity and was bound to give reasons for its orders. The mere absence of provision for an appeal does not imply that the Regional Provident Fund Commissioner is invested with arbitrary or uncontrolled power, without any guidelines.

In *Atlantic Engineering Services v Union of India and another*,[510] a Division Bench of the Delhi High Court upheld the constitutional validity of s.14-B by observing that the method of determining damages is entirely reasonable, and it shows that no officer acting under s.14-B can act arbitrarily, but must follow this reasonable guideline made by the Government. Further, this is only a guideline. It is not a determination. The actual decision as to what the damages should be in a particular case is made only after hearing the employer and assessing the particular facts of his case.

Meaning of 'damages'

The word 'damages' has not been defined under the Act and has, thus, given rise to disputes regarding its interpretation. The expression "makes default" is synonymous with failure to pay,[511] within the time prescribed under the Scheme framed in pursuance of the Act.[512] Not only the failure to make payment but even the failure to make timely payment amounts to default for the purposes of s.14-B.[513]

Before the Supreme Court decision in *Organo Chemical Industries and another v Union of India*, the High Courts were divided as to the meaning of the word 'damages' in s.14-B. According to the High Courts of Calcutta,[514] Kerala[515] and Orissa,[516] it is different from 'fine' and 'penalty' and intended to compensate the

---

[509] 1979 AIR 1803, 1980 SCR (1)61
[510] 1979 (39) FLR 176, ILR 1979 Delhi 402, (1979) IILLJ 136 Del
[511] *Calicut Modern Spinning Weaving Mills v Regional P.F. Commissioner* (1982) ILLJ 440 Ker
[512] *Sea Shore Traders v Regional Provident Fund Commissioner* (1998) II LLJ 841 (Mad.)
[513] *Bharat Heavy Electricals Ltd. v Regional P.F. Commissioner* 1985 Lab IC 282 (Ker.)
[514] *Murarka Paint and Varnish Mrks Ltd. v Union of India* (1978) 52 FJR 51
[515] *Bharat Plywood and limber Products v Employees' Provident Fund Commissioner* (1977) 50 FJR 7
[516] *Prajatantra Prachar Samiti v RPC Commissioner* (1979) 1 LLJ 136

actual loss to beneficiaries of the scheme. On the other hand, the High Court of Patna[517] held that the damages were penal in nature. The Supreme Court, in *Organo Chemical* case (supra), resolved the controversy by holding that the very object of the legislation would be frustrated if the word 'damages' in s.14-B was not construed to mean penal damages. However, s.14-B as amended by Act 33 of 1988 postulates recovery of damages by way of penalty.

PRINCIPLES OF LEVY OF PENAL DAMAGES

In *Hindustan Times Ltd. v Union of India*,[518] the Supreme Court reviewed various judicial precedents on the subject and laid down the following principles:-

1. The Act does not contain any provision prescribing a period of limitation for assessment or recovery of damages. The monies payable into the Fund are for the ultimate benefit of the employees, but there is no provision by which the employees can directly recover these amounts. The power of computation and recovery are both vested in the Regional Provident Commissioner or other officers as provided in s.14-B.

2. It is not the legislative intent to prescribe any period of limitation for computing and recovering the arrears. As the amounts are due to the Trust Fund and the recovery is not by suit, the provisions of the Indian Limitation Act, 1963 are not attracted.

3. The position under s.14-B of the Act of an employer is different. The employer who has defaulted in making over the contributions to the Trust Fund had, on the other hand, the use of monies which did not belong to him at all.

4. In cases under s.14-B, if the Regional Provident Commissioner has made computations earlier and sent demand immediately after the amount fell due, the defaulter would not have been able to use these monies for his own purposes or his business.

5. There is no period of limitation prescribed by the legislature for initiating action for recovery of damages under s.14-B. The fact that proceedings are initiated or demand for damages is made after several years cannot by itself be a ground for drawing an inference of waiver or that the employer was lulled into a belief that no proceedings under s.14-B would be taken; mere delay in initiating action under s.14-B cannot amount to prejudice inasmuch as the delay on the part of the department, would have only allowed the employer to use the monies for his own purposes or for his business especially when there is no additional provision for charging interest. However, the employer can claim prejudice if there is proof that between the period of default and the date of initiation of action under s.14-B, he has changed his position to his detriment to such an extent that if the recovery is made after a large number of years, the prejudice to him is of an irretrievable nature.[519]

---

[517] *B.H.N. Jute Mills v R.PE Commissioner* (1958) 1 LLJ 59
[518] J.T. 1998(1) S.C. 18
[519] *Swastika Woolens v Presiding Officer, EPFAT*, (2003) ILLJ 241 P H

Meaning and Scope of the word 'May.'

Regarding the meaning and use of the word 'may' in s.14-B, the Supreme Court observed in *Regional P.F. Commissioner v S.D. College, Hoshipur and other,*[520] that the Regional PF Commissioner has no power to waive the penalty altogether. This decision draws to the meaning that the word 'may' has to be construed the meaning of 'shall.' Going by the General Clauses Act also, the word 'may' takes the meaning of 'shall' in case of public authorities vested with obligations.[521]

A different view was taken by the Kerala High Court in *Puthiyara Tile Works v Union of India*[522] while considering the scope of s.14-B. The Court observed: "The words "may recover" occurring in s.14-B will clearly show that the authority under the Act is vested with the discretion to decide whether damages are liable to be recovered from the defaulter, and if so to what extent. [The] Penalty would not also be imposed merely because it is lawful to do so. Whether penalty should be imposed for failure to perform a statutory obligation is a matter of discretion of the authority to be exercised judicially and on a consideration of all the relevant circumstances. Even if a minimum penalty is prescribed, the authority competent to impose the penalty will be justified in refusing to impose penalty, when there is a technical or venial breach of the provisions of the Act or where the breach flows from a *bona fide* belief that the offender is not liable to act in the manner prescribed by the statute. Though the quantum of damages that can be levied has been indicated in the statute, the question as to whether any recovery of damages has to be made by way of penalty is entirely at the discretion of the authority which proposes to impose such a penalty. The said discretionary power vested in the authority has to be exercised in a fair, reasonable and just manner. If the authority which is vested with the discretionary power as indicated in s.14-B does not act with an open mind, the entire adjudicatory process will lose its authenticity and judicial approval."

In *Assistant Provident Fund Commissioner v Hi-Tech Vocational Training Centre,*[523] a Division Bench of the Delhi High Court observed, 'a perusal of Para 32A of the EPF Scheme, 1952 would show that the legislature has once again used the word '*may*' in the phrase 'may recover from the employer by way of penalty.' The Court further held that the table referred to in Para 32A of the Scheme would mean that the damages indicated in the table of said paragraph fix the upper limit and leave it to the discretion of the authority to determine in each case as to whether or not

---

[520] 1997 (1) LLN 520
[521] *Sankar Chemical Lime v Assistant P F Commissioner* [W.P.4636 of 2008] decision dated 3rd September 2010 9 (Mad. HC)
[522] 2003 (3) KLT S.N. 74
[523] 2015 SCC Online Del 12215

damages have to be levied, and if yes the extent thereof. Para 32(B) mirrors the power conferred on the Central Board under the second proviso to s.14-B and thus the argument that since power to waive or lower the penalty is conferred on the Central Board as per Para 32B of the Scheme, the Commissioner would have no power to waive or lower the penalty as per Para 32A of the Scheme, has to be rejected."

'Default' in law is a failure to perform an act at a time assigned; it is with reference to the time so assigned. Hence, the difference sought to be made between 'default in payment' and 'default in paying' for the purpose of confirming the ambit of s.14-B of the Act to cases of total failure of payment and not coverage cases of delayed payment, was found to be unacceptable by the Madras High Court in *Sea Shore Traders v Regional Provident Fund Commissioner*.[524]

Doctrine of Double Punishment – Not attracted

Article 20(2) of the Indian Constitution says that no person shall be prosecuted and punished for the same offence more than once. This principle is called Doctrine of Double Jeopardy related to the law maxim – *nemo debet bis vexari*. This means that no man shall be put twice in peril for the same offence. The objective is to avoid harassment, which must be caused for successive criminal proceedings, where the person has committed only one crime.

In *R.B.H.N. Jute Mills v Regional Provident Fund Commissioner*,[525] a Division Bench of the Patna High Court held that the employer is not entitled to invoke the protection of Article 20(2) on the ground that s.14-B deals with the same offence as Paragraph 76 of the EPF Scheme. The protection of Art.20 (2) can be invoked only if there is a prosecution and punishment in respect of the same offence before a court of law or a judicial tribunal.

In *The Deposit Manager, APSRTC v Regional Provident Fund Commissioner*, the High Court of Andhra Pradesh, relying on the judgment of Justice Krishna Iyer in *Organo Chemical Industries v Union of India,* held that

In *Hindustan Times Ltd. v Union of India*,[526] the Supreme Court laid down that the authority under s.14-B has to apply his mind to the facts of the case and the reply to the show-cause notice and pass a reasoned order after following principles of natural justice and giving a reasonable opportunity of being heard; the Regional Provident Fund Commissioner usually takes into consideration the number of defaults, the period of delay, the frequency of default and the amounts involved;

---

[524] (1998) II LLJ 841 (Mad.)
[525] (1958) 1 LLJ 598 (Pat.HC DB)
[526] (1998) 2 SCC 242

default on the part of the employer based on the plea of power cut, financial problems relating to other indebtedness or the delay in realization of amounts paid by the cheques or drafts, cannot be justifiable grounds for the employer to escape liability.

Another line of argument advanced by some employers is that the penal damages under s.14-B and simple interest mandated under s.7-Q result in double jeopardy. This contention was rejected by a Division Bench of the Karnataka High Court in *Ratna Polypack (India)Ltd. v Union of India and others*,[527] observing as follows: "There is a difference between the provisions of Sections 7-Q and 14-B. The action of authorities requiring the employer to pay interest for the belated payment does not require any opportunity of being heard. On the other hand under s.14-B of the Act it is provided that the employer shall be given a reasonable opportunity of being heard before levying and recovering damages. It is therefore clear that if the employer can give a convincing explanation for the belated payment, the employer is not liable to pay damages, in which event the argument advanced by the learned Counsel that in view of s.14-B of the Act, s.7-Q, which renders the employers liable to pay simple interest amounts to double jeopardy, fails."

There is a distinction between a penalty and damages. s.14 envisages penalty, which is a personal liability to which the principles of Article 20(1) may be applicable. s.14-B governing damages in default if attempted to be brought within the purview of Article 20(1), it would be an extremely strenuous effort. At the same time, Article 20(1) provides that the penalty is to be imposed on the basis of the law prevailing on the date of commission of the offence. Subsequent enhancement of punishment by a change in law would not affect such cases, and the offenders would be liable for the punishment provided in law at the time of the commission of the offence.[528]

Element of Mens rea or actus reus

According to the doctrine of criminal law, it is the coincidence of *actus reus* (guilty act) and *mens rea* (guilty mind) which constitutes and justifies criminal liability. It means that there must be a combination of external and mental elements concerning the commission of the offence.

In *Mcleod Russel India Limited v Regional Provident Fund Commissioner, Jalpaiguri and others*,[529] the Supreme Court observed that the presence or absence

---

[527] 2009 (1) KarLJ 515: (2009) III LLJ 584 Kant: 2009(1) AIR Kar 453
[528] *Dalgaon Agro Industries Ltd. v Union of India and others* (2006) 1 CALLT 32 HC, 2005 (3) CHN 428, (2005) IIILLJ 356 Cal
[529] (2014) 15 SCC 263

of *mens rea* and/or *actus reus* would be a determinative factor in imposing damages under s.14-B, as also the quantum thereof since it is not inflexible that 100 percent of the arrears have to be imposed in all the cases. Alternatively stated, if damages have been imposed under s.14-B, it will be only logical that *mens rea* and/or *actus reus* was prevailing at the relevant time.

In *Regional Provident Fund Commissioner, EPFO, Madurai and another v Sree Visalam Chit Funds Ltd., Palathur and another*,[530] a Division Bench of the Madras High Court was considering the scope of levying damages under s.14-B, held that for claiming damage sunder s.14-B, *mens rea* is required to be proved. The Court held, "unless it is established that such failure to pay the contribution was attributable to the *mens rea* or *actus reus* on the part of the employer, [the] question of levying damages under s.14-B of the Act does not arise. The Supreme Court has repeatedly held that merely because the statutory provision enables an authority to impose a penalty, it does not mean that such penalty should be imposed mechanically without looking into the attending circumstances and the facts as to whether there was any *mens rea* or *actus reus* on the part of the employer.

The said decision was rendered taking note of the judgments of the Supreme Court in *Prestolite (India) Ltd. v Regional Director, ESIC and another*,[531] *Hindustan Times Ltd. v Union of India*,[532] *Dilip N Shroff v Joint Commissioner of Income Tax, Mumbai and another*,[533] *Employees' State Insurance Corporation v HMT Ltd*.[534] Following the *ratio decidendi* of the Supreme Court in *ESI Corporation v HMT Limited and another*, the Madras High Court, in *Terrace Estate v HMT Limited and another*,[535] held that the existence of *mens rea* or *actus reus* to contravene a statutory provision must also be held to be a necessary ingredient for levy of damages and/or the quantum thereof.

On the plain language of s.14(1) of the Act, it is evident that there is an element of *mens rea* and therefore the burden is on the authority prosecuting the person to prove the offence. Under s.14(1A) of the Act, only the employer who contravenes or makes default in complying with the provisions of the Act or the Scheme is punishable. Under s.14(1B), only the employer who contravenes or makes default in complying with certain provisions of the Act is punishable. Under

---

[530] 2010 (4) LLN 706
[531] 1995 (2) LLN 667
[532] 1998 (2) SCC 242
[533] (2007) 6 SCC 329
[534] (2008) 3 SCC 35
[535] Writ Petition No 29465 of 2004 decided on 7th October 2009

s.14(2-A), any person, i.e., including the employer, who contravenes or defaults in complying with any provisions of the Act or of any condition subject to which exemption was granted under s.17, shall, if no other penalty is elsewhere provided by or under the Act, is punishable. Thus, it could be seen that for the first offence, *mens rea* is an essential ingredient, but for other offences, mere contravention or default with the relevant provisions of the Act or the Scheme is sufficient to punish the person or the employer as the case may be. That is to say, the offences under s.14(1-A), (1-B) and (2-A) of the Act attract the principle of strict liability under the law, and these offences are committed as soon as the infringement occurs, or default is made. Similarly, s.14-B which provide for damages on default of the provisions contained therein attract strict liability under the law, and the employer becomes liable for damages the moment he makes a default but the explanation or excuse for such default, good or bad, will be relevant for recovery and assessment of damages.

The Supreme Court, in *ESI Corporation v HMT Ltd*,[536] considering *pari material* provisions of the Employees State Insurance Act, 1948, held that existence of *mens rea* or *actus reus* to contravene a statutory provision must also be held to be a necessary ingredient for levy of damages and/or quantum thereof. Since the provident fund authority, before levying damages had not returned a finding of *mens rea* or *actus reus* on the part of the employer, applying the ratio of the said decision, the Delhi High Court quashed the order levying damages, in *Hi-Tech Vocational Training Centre v Assistant Provident Fund Commissioner*.[537] In *Regional Provident Fund Commissioner, Mangalore v Jamiyyatul Falah, Mangalore & another*,[538] the Karnataka High Court, following the decision of the Supreme Court in the *ESI Corporation v HMT Limited* case, observed that the provisions of s.85-B of the Employees' State Insurance Act, 1948 read with Regulation 31-C of the Employees' State Insurance (General) Regulations, 1950, in the matter of recovery of damages being *pari materia* with that of s.14-B of the Act and paragraph-32A of the Scheme, held that, existence of *mens rea* or *actus reus* to contravene a statutory provision must also be held to be a necessary ingredient for levy of damages and/or the quantum thereof, while rejecting the petition filed by the Regional Provident Fund Commissioner and confirmed the levy of damages at 15% per annum on the arrears of contribution by the Appellate Tribunal.

---

[536] (2008)3 SCC35
[537] 2011 LLR231:2011(1)CL689:2011(129) FLR274:2011(3)LLJ554:2011(4) LLN273(Del.)
[538] 2010 (3) LLJ 652 (Kant): 2010 (1) AIR Kar R 812

In *Radhanath Cooperative Press Ltd.v Regional P.F. Commissioner*,[539] the Orissa High Court did not agree that *mens rea* was a necessary ingredient for awarding damages under s.14-B of the EPF Act, as the words used in the section are not 'wilful' but only 'default' in payment of contribution.

In *Assistant Provident Fund Commissioner v Management of RSL Textiles India Pvt Ltd*,[540] the Supreme Court considered whether presence of *mens rea* and/or *actus reus* would be a determinative factor in imposing damages under s.14-B, as also quantum thereof since it is not inflexible that 100 percent of arrears have to be imposed in all cases. The Supreme Court held that this issue is now wholly covered in the decision in *Mcleod Russel India Limited v Regional Provident Fund Commissioner, Jalpaiguri and others*,[541] where it was held, "the presence or absence of mens rea and/or actus reus would be a determinative factor in imposing damages under s.14-B, as also the quantum thereof since it is not inflexible that 100 percent of the arrears have to be imposed in all the cases. Alternatively stated, if damages have been imposed under Section 14-B, it will be only logical that *mens rea* and/or *actus reus* was prevailing at the relevant time."

The Madras High Court in *V.S. Murugan v Regional P.F. Commissioner*[542] held that conducting enquiry and recording of specifying findings that there was *men's rea* to delay the payment of provident fund contribution was mandatory before imposing damages. In *Solidaire India Limited v EPF Appellate Tribunal*,[543] the Madras High Court observed that the imposition of penalty was made mechanically and when the company has pleaded explicitly that they have no funds and they should have made some consideration towards the levy of damages as the Supreme Court held it was not automatic and there must be *mens rea* in the default. The Court further observed that when these facts were pointed out, the Tribunal also did not apply its mind and exercised its jurisdiction which obliged the High Court to interfere with the impugned order. It is pertinent to mention here that in *Chairman, SEBI v. Shriram Mutual Fund*,[544] considering the provisions contained in Securities and exchange Board of India Act, 1992, the Supreme Court held that penalty is *sine qua non* of the violation; *mens rea* is not essential element for imposing penalty for breach of civil obligation.

---

[539] (1998) III LLJ (Suppl)1160 (Ori.)
[540] 2017(1) JT 460: 2017(2) Scale 33: 2017(1) Law Herald (SC) 322: 2017 AIR (SCW) 679: 2017 AIR (SC) 679: 2017 LIC 928: 2017(3) SCC 110: 2017 LabLR 337: 2017(1) SCC (L&S) 543: 2017(153) FLR 214
[541] 2015(1) S.C.T. 465: (2014) 15 SCC 263
[542] 2012(1) LLJ 579: 2012(2) S.C.T. 445: 2012(132) FLR 903
[543] 2012(2) LLJ 280: 2012(134) FLR 359: 2011(10) S.C.T. 939
[544] AIR 2006 SC 2287

LEVY OF PENAL DAMAGES – LIMITATION ACT DOES NOT APPLY

In *Hindustan Times v Union of India*,[545] the Supreme Court reasoned that as the legislature did not think fit to make any provisions prescribing a period of limitation over a period of more than thirty years, it is not the legislative intent to prescribe any period of limitation for computing and recovering the arrears. The Supreme Court further held, 'as the amounts are due to the Trust Fund and the recovery is not by suit, the provisions of the Indian Limitation Act, 1963 are not attracted. In *Nityanand M. Joshi v Life Insurance Corporation of India*,[546] it has been held that the Limitation Act, 1963 has no application to Labour Courts and in our view that principle is equally applicable to recovery by the concerned authority under s.14-B."

In *Fenwick and Ravi, Bangalore v Employees' Provident Fund Organisation*,[547] the Karnataka High Court held that the Act does not contain any provision prescribing the period of limitation for assessment or recovery of damages or interest. The contributions are required to be remitted by the employer for the benefit of the employees. The Commissioner under the Act, by s.14-B and s.7-Q, has been vested with the power of computation of recovery of the damages and the interest respectively. As the petitioner did not deposit the amount due within the time allowed and there being no provision stipulating any period of limitation for recovering arrears, the provisions of the Limitation Act, 1963 has no application. The Bombay High Court took a similar view in *Mathur Alloy Steels Pvt. Ltd. v Union of India*.[548]

Act does not prescribe any time limitation

In *Regional Provident Fund Commissioner v Allahabad Canning Co.*,[549] a Division Bench of the Allahabad High Court held that s.14-B of the Act does not provide any limitation during which action against an erring employer can be taken for delayed deposits under the Act. In the absence of any bar of limitation, there is no principle of law which debarred the Provident Fund Commissioner from exercising the statutory powers available to him under s.14-B of the Act. The test whether the lapse of time is reasonable or not will depend upon the fact that whether the employer in the meantime has changed his position to his detriment and is likely to be irretrievably prejudiced by the belated issuance of such a show cause notice.

---

[545] 1998 (2) SCC 242: AIR 1998 SC 688
[546] (1970) 1 SCR 396
[547] 2016(4) Air Kar R 743: 2017 LabLR 72: 2017 LIC 225: 2017(152) FLR 777
[548] (1993) II LLJ 471 (Bom)
[549] 1978 L.I.C. 998

If such defence is not pleaded and proved, challenge on the ground of late issuance of notice must stand rejected.[550]

In *Regional Provident Fund Commissioner v K.T. Rolling Mills Pvt Ltd.*,[551] the Supreme Court pointed out that though s.14-B has not laid down any period of limitation, the power has to be exercised within a reasonable time. The Supreme Court while admitting that there was an undue delay in levy of penal damages, observed further that, "it is also kept in mind that the default-related even to the contribution of the employees, which money the respondent (after deducting the same from the wages of the employees) must have used for its own purpose and that too without paying any interest, at the cost of those for whose benefit it was meant. Any different stand would encourage the employers to thwart the object of the Act, which cannot be permitted."

S.14-B prescribes no period of limitation for the authority to initiate action for levy of damages against the erring employers. It confers a statutory right without the prescription of limitation, and the plea of waiver or acquiescence cannot operate against the rule that there could be no estoppels against the statute.[552] In *S.H. Salvekadam & Co. v Regional Provident Fund Commissioner*,[553] the Karnataka High Court observed that under the Act, the default lies in not remitting the Contribution of the employers' and employees' shares and since the employees have no right of action under the Act, though they may have suffered an injury by the delayed contributions, the concepts of 'strict liability and strict interpretation' are attracted by s.14-B of the Act.

Undue Delay in Levy of Penal damages – Effects of

In *Presidency Kid Leathers (P) Ltd. v Regional Provident Fund Commissioner*,[554] a Division Bench of the Madras High Court, while refusing to accept the contention that the failure in initiating the s.14-B proceedings within a reasonable time will render the impugned order *non-est* in law, further held that the delay of 4 ½ to 8 years cannot at all be easily ignored. Hence, the High Court ordered reduction of the damages by 50% to meet the ends of justice. In *Sushma Fabrics Pvt Ltd. v Union Bank of India and another*,[555] the Bombay High Court observed that absence of a prescribed period within which s.14-B becomes operational does not mean that

---

[550] *Gandhidham Spinning & Manufacturing Co. V Regional P.F. Commissioner* 1987 LIC 659: 1987(1) GLR 337: 1987(1) LLN 813 (Guj. DB)
[551] AIR 1995 SC 493
[552] *S.H. Salvekadam & Co. v Regional Provident Fund Commissioner*, ILR 1995 Kar. 4244.
[553] ILR 1995 Kar. 4244
[554] (1999) IIILLJ 980 Mad
[555] (1993) IIILLJ 316 Bom

the authorities can initiate action at any time. They must move within a reasonable interval of the commission of the lapse.

A different aspect of prejudice was referred to in *Sushma Fabrics* case (supra). In some cases there could be serious prejudice on account of abnormal delay in taking proceedings under s.14-B, either because the records or accounts of the defaulter are lost or on account of the personnel concerned acquainted with the facts of a past period no longer being available for unearthing the facts. However, such pleas must be raised before the Department and strictly proved. In case such facts are proved, it is possible in some cases that there is irretrievable prejudice.[556] Lapse of an extended period from the delayed remittance would give the employer opportunity to raise excuses that it would have immediately compensated the loss of the employees had it been called upon to show cause for the delay in remittance within a required time.[557]

Delayed payment of contributions on retaining allowance – Penalty

In case of a permanent seasonal employee who, after the crushing season is paid retaining allowance, the retaining allowance forms part of wages and, therefore, levy of damages for delay in payment of contribution on such payment would be valid.[558]

Power to reduce damages

The Regional Provident Fund Commissioner is given discretion only to reduce a percentage of damages, and he has no power to waive penalty altogether.[559] In *South India Flour Mills Pvt Ltd. v Regional Provident Fund Commissioner*,[560] the Madras High Court, observed, 'it is not a mere arithmetical computation or a rigid application of law by which damages could be recovered. There must be an exercise of the mind, and there must be an examination of the merits of each case.

Personal hearing – Not a formality

In *Kasthuri Mills (P) Ltd. v Assistant Provident Fund Commissioner*,[561] a Division Bench of the High Court observed: "The Legislature had intended for an opportunity of being heard before such damages are levied. This is obvious from the First proviso to s.14-B which contemplates that provided before levying and

---

[556] *Hindustan Times Ltd. v Union of India* (1998) 2 SCC 242
[557] *Vinson Engineering Co. v Regional P.F. Commissioner*, 1995(2)LLJ 1224 (Mad.)
[558] *Keshorai Patan Sahkari Sugar Mills Ltd. v Regional P.F. Commissioner*, 1993 (67)FLR 1044: 1993(83)FJR 487(Raj.)
[559] *Regional Provident Fund Commissioner v S.D. College* (1997) II LLJ 55 (SC)
[560] (1978) 52 FJR 62
[561] (2007) IILLJ 956 Mad

recovering such damages, the employer shall be given a reasonable opportunity of being heard. The opportunity contemplated under the said provision cannot be construed to be one of formality and in our view, is not only a precondition but also mandatory. Failure to comply with the above condition would vitiate the very order passed under Section 14-B."

In *Regional Provident Fund Commissioner v South India Flour Mills (P) Ltd*,[562] a Division Bench of the Madras High Court observed that the proviso under s.14-B would emphasise the fact that the Provident Fund Commissioner is required first to determine, after hearing the defaulter, as to whether the defaulter is liable to pay any damages at all, and if he comes to the conclusion that the defaulter has given valid reasons acceptable to the Commissioner which explains the delay in depositing the contribution under the Scheme or the Act, then the further question of recovering any damages or determining the quantum of damages does not arise.

Speaking order

The power of the Regional Provident Commissioner to impose damages under s.14-B is a quasi-judicial function. It must be exercised after notice to the defaulter and after giving him a reasonable opportunity of being heard. The Regional Provident Fund Commissioner has not only to apply his mind to the requirements of s.14-B, but he is cast with the duty of making a 'speaking order' after conforming to the rules of natural justice. The authority assessing the damages is obliged to write a speaking order of his assessment setting out the reasons for it so that it was readily exposed to the scrutiny of a Court exercising writ jurisdiction. This is the guarantee against arbitrariness.[563] The order by itself should give an indication of the consideration and application of mind by the commissioner. The writing of a speaking order indicating the applicability of mind does not mean that order should be equated with the judgment of a Court containing detailed reasons.[564] In case the explanation offered by the employer in reply to the show-cause notice was not considered, the order cannot be termed as a 'speaking order.'[565]

In *T.C.M. Woollen Mills Pvt. Ltd. v Regional P.F. Commissioner*,[566] the Punjab and Haryana High Court observed that where the employer filed no reply against the notice issued to him under s.14-B of the Act, he cannot complain that the Commissioner did not make a speaking order as required by law. Unless objections

---

[562] 1985-I-LLJ-283
[563] *Josts Engineering Limited v Union of India and another*, (1983) II LLJ 436 Bom
[564] *Bhopal Dugdha Sangh v Regional Provident Fund Commissioner, Indore* 1984 LIC 1542
[565] *Haryana State Corporative Supply & Marketing Federation Ltd. v Regional P.F. Commissioner*, 1983 (2) LLN 501 (All.DB)
[566] 1980 (57) F.J.R. 222

and the factual matters are pressed before the Commissioner, he cannot imagine the same and adjudicate thereon. Where the objections raised are vague and devoid of necessary particular, a finding that a plea is untenable would be sufficient compliance with the requirements of a reasoned order. This view was endorsed by the Bombay High Court in *Super Processors v Union of India*,[567] holding that when the petitioners have chosen not to file a reply to the show cause notice and not to lead evidence in support thereof, there was nothing to be adjudicated upon.

Application of Mind

Where the establishment has been afforded sufficient opportunity of being heard, and in the proceeding, the default has been admitted by the establishment, it cannot be argued that the order has been passed without application of mind.[568] In *Bhopal Dugdh Sangh v Regional Provident Fund Commissioner*,[569] held, a speaking order which indicates the application of mind is good enough for it need not contain detailed reasons like a court judgement. Before imposing any penalty, the authority must see whether the employer is a chronic defaulter and must also see the nature and frequency of default as also the period of delay and the amount involved. It is at such points that the authority is required to apply its mind.[570]

Maximum is only a guiding factor

In *Prestolite (India) Ltd. v Regional Director, ESIC*,[571] the Supreme Court observed, "even if the regulations have prescribed general guidelines and the upper limits at which the imposition of damages can be made, it cannot be contended that in no case, the mitigating circumstances can be taken into consideration by the adjudicating authority in finally deciding the matter, and it is bound to act mechanically in applying the uppermost limit of the table." Following this, the Madras High Court, in *Terrace Estate v HMT Limited and another*,[572] held that the regulations under Para 32(A) of the EPF Scheme could be termed only as a guideline and the authority cannot pass the order mechanically applying the regulations. Subsequently, the Supreme Court in *ESI Corporation v HMT Limited and another*[573] accepted the proposition above and held, "a penal provision should be construed strictly. Only because a provision has been made for levy of penalty, the same by itself would

---

[567] (1994) III LLJ (Suppl)564 (Bom).
[568] *Bhatter Solvent Extraction Udyog Ltd. v Regional P.F. Commissioner*, 2016 (3) LLJ 472 (Ori.).
[569] 1984 (65) FLR 714
[570] *Commonwealth Trust (India) Ltd. v Regional P.F. Commissioner*, 1994(2)LLN 1262 (Ker.)
[571] AIR 1994 SC 521: (1994) Supp 3 SCC 690: LNIND 1993 SC 834: 1995-II-LLJ-622
[572] Writ Petition No 29465 of 2004 decided on 7th October 2009
[573] 2008 (3) SCC 35

not lead to the conclusion that penalty must be levied in all situations. Such an intention on the part of the legislature is not decipherable from s.85-B of the Act. When a discretionary jurisdiction has been conferred on a statutory authority to levy penal damages because of an enabling provision, the same cannot be construed as imperative. Even otherwise, an endeavour should be made to construe such penal provisions as discretionary, unless the statute is held to be mandatory in character."

Power under s.14-B of the Act, being a quasi-judicial one, the discretion exercised must be for sound and objective considerations. Paragraph 32 of the Scheme is only a guideline and not intended for a mechanical application.[574] A quasi-judicial authority is not expected to conform to the tables but to use his own judgment and support it by a speaking order.[575] In *Kirloskar Electric Co. v Regional Provident Fund Commissioner*,[576] held that there is no doubt that paragraph 32-A and 32-B of the EPF Scheme prescribes general guidelines over the limits to which the imposition of damages is permissible and mitigating circumstances can be taken into consideration by the adjudicating authority in entirely deciding the quantum of damages and is not bound to apply the uppermost or lowermost table as the limit mechanically.

Guidelines cannot once and for all bind the hands of the Provident Fund Commissioner. However, where the authority wants to depart from the guidelines, he must give valid reasons which may be tested if an occasion arises.[577] Table of damages provided by the Government for determination of damages though it is a salutary measure for the guidance of the Commissioner under s.14-B of the Act is nevertheless only guidance. It is not a determination. The actual decision is to be made only after hearing the employer and taking into consideration the facts of each case. Administrative directions cannot control the Commissioner who is a statutory authority.[578]

Not a mechanical process

Mechanical computation of damages based on standard tables or slabs without reference to any mitigating circumstances has been held to be improper in several cases. The award of damages cannot be undertaken as a mechanical process in all cases. Depending on the facts of each case, the authority is vested with the discretion to decide whether or not to levy the damages.[579] Determination of

---

[574] *Cable Corporation of India Ltd. v Union of India* 2006(3)CLR 349 (Bom)
[575] *Josts Engineering Limited v Union of India* (1983) II LLJ 436 (Bom)
[576] 2014(1) AIR Kar R 329: 2014 ILR (Karnataka) 3184: 2013(9) S.C.T. 179
[577] *Regional P.F. Commissioner v South India Flour Mills (P) Ltd* (1985) I LLJ 283 (Mad.)
[578] *Avon Scale Company v Regional Provident Fund Commissioner* (1993) II LLJ 226 (P & H DB).
[579] *The Quilon Automobile Employees Cooperative Society v Employees' Provident Fund Organisation*

damages is not an inflexible application of any rigid formula, and the authority must apply his mind to the facts and circumstances of each case.[580] The provision under the slab-system by which one authority automatically levies certain amounts by way of penalty without reference to any mitigating circumstances, leaving the employer to move the appellate forum, is not a substitute for the usual rule of natural justice.[581]

In *Hindustan Malleable and Forgings Ltd. v The Regional Provident Fund Commissioner and others*,[582] a Division Bench of the Patna High Court has taken the view that the determination of damages is not an inflexible application of a rigid formula, and the competent authority must apply its mind to the fact, and circumstances of the case. The order should be a speaking order containing at least indication or the consideration of relevant aspects and a statement and reasons that weighed in the imposition of damages. Damages have to be found and ascertained, and then something more should be added to it by way of penalty.[583]

Damages referred to in s.14-B are not by way of compensation but by way of penalty.[584] The damages levied under s.14-B of the Act do not correlate with the loss suffered as a result of the delayed payment because damages levied and recovered under s.14-B go to the general account of the Fund and not into the employees' account.

In *Telangana Spinning & Weaving Mills v Regional Provident Fund Commissioner*,[585] the Andhra Pradesh High Court held that determination of quantum of damages, though discretionary, depends upon various factors, such as, amount of arrears, the persistent or habitual nature of the employer in committing default, the length of default, explanation submitted by the employer and the interest lost by the Provident Fund Organisation due to not investing the amount in time. So, in the very nature of things, the quantum of damages cannot be predetermined to be mentioned in the show cause notice. Indeed it has to be determined only after giving an opportunity of being heard to the employer and after considering his explanation.

The order must contain specific indication that a judicial and objective mind has been applied to the facts of a particular case. He must not only refer to the reply

---

2010 LLR 1037 (Kerala HC)

[580] *Hindustan Malleables & forgings Ltd. v Regional P.F. Commissioner.*, 1978 Lab IC 930(Pat.)
[581] *Madras-Bangalore Transport Co. v Regional P.F. Commissioner* (1969) 2 LLJ 136
[582] 1978 Lab. I.C. 930
[583] *Aditya Agro Industries Private Ltd. v Regional P.F. Commissioner* (1997) I LLJ 118 (Mad).
[584] *Avon Scale Company v Regional P.F. Commissioner, Haryana* 1993-II-LLJ-226 (P & H)
[585] AIR 1992 AP 128

and the material submitted by the employer in response to the show-cause notice for assessment of damages but should also record its reasons as to how he arrived at these findings.[586]

Tribunal can reduce penal damages

The Madras High Court, in *Assistant Provident Fund Commissioner v EPF Appellate Tribunal*,[587] held that the Tribunal while hearing the appeal under s.7I of the Act is entitled to grant relief with reasons of fair play and justice, and it is not trapped by the limitation prescribed under the Second proviso to s.14-B of the Act. The High Court also upheld the order of the Tribunal in reducing the quantum of damages imposed by the department.

Tribunal cannot dictate the percentage of penal damages

In *Regional Provident Fund Commissioner v Orissa State Road Transport Corporation*,[588] the EPF Appellate Tribunal remanded the case to the Provident Fund Commissioner with a direction to levy penal damages @ 10% inclusive of interest. When the order of the Presiding Officer, EPFAT was challenged, the Orissa High Court observed: "The Tribunal has never been conferred with any power to sit over the statutory provision on whatsoever ground may be. Otherwise, there will be no sanctity of the statutory provision. Moreover, it is not the duty of the Court or Tribunal to sit over the statutory provision, rather it is the duty of the Court of law to see as to whether the order passed is in accordance with law, and certainly if the order is not in accordance with law, the Tribunal or Court of law has got power to rectify the same in consonance with the statute or direct the authorities to rectify the mistake."

Exonerating Factors

It is obligatory on the part of the employer to place before the authority sufficient and reliable materials to establish his inability to send in the contribution payable under the Act. Mere strike or lockout or power cut etc., would not be sufficient explanation unless it is also possible for the employer to show that the employees' salaries had not been paid and therefore deductions were not made or that even that much of funds to be remitted were not available on due dates. Authority has to consider the relevant factors quasi-judicially and has to ascribe reasons for the conclusions arrived.[589] That the power cut which has immobilised the industry for a considerable period is not only a pertinent but a relevant factor before even damages are assessed, and that the factors

---

[586] *Avon Scale Company v Regional Provident Fund Commissioner* (1993) II LLJ 226 (P & H DB).
[587] W.P. No.17518 to 17521 of 2004
[588] 2016(3) CLR 882
[589] *Regional P.F. Commissioner v South India Flour Mills (P) Ltd* (1985) I LLJ 283 (Mad.)

which are not within the control of industry are responsible for the non-functioning of the factory like total strike in all industries; flood, power-cut, which is imposed every year; direction by law and order authorities to close down factories during public unrest, etc. they would be relevant circumstances for sympathetically considering the claims of such industries in non-payment of contributions and other remittances under the Act.[590] Timely deposit of Provident Fund is a statutory obligation which cannot be allowed to be diluted by such extraneous factors as financial difficulties.[591] Financial stringency is no ground for making delay in payment of a contribution to the Fund.[592] The fact that there had been the imposition of a penalty for the earlier period would be a relevant consideration for determining the quantum of damages for a subsequent period.[593]

In *Regional Provident Fund Commissioner v. S.D. College, Hoshiarpur and others*,[594] the college authorities continued to deposit the provident fund contributions with the University instead of with the Provident Fund authorities. Taking into account the special features involved, the Supreme Court reduced the penal damages to 25% of the amount levied by the Provident Fund Commissioner. In similar circumstances, in *Holwasia Vidya Vihar v Regional Provident Fund Commissioner*,[595] the Supreme Court reduced the penal damages to 25% of the amount levied by the Commissioner.

Delay in transit by the bank – exonerating factor

If the employer furnishes sufficient cause for delay, as delay in transit by the bank, the authority may not levy damages.[596]

Penalty – No special concern for Government Corporation

In *India Tourism Development Corporation Ltd. v Regional Provident Fund Commissioner*,[597] the Delhi High Court held that merely because the establishment is a Government Corporation is no reason why damages should not be levied in the event of default in deposit of the provident fund dues by the employer.

The power under s.14-B of the EPF Act is a quasi-judicial power and the discretion exercised must be for sound and objective considerations. Para 32A of the

---

[590] *Sri Rajendra Mills Ltd. v Regional P.F. Commissioner* (1982) I LLJ 352 (Mad).
[591] *Nav Bharat Industries v Regional P.F. Commissioner and another* (1997)IIILLJ216P& H; (1996)113PLR786
[592] *S.K. Machinery (P) Ltd. v Regional P.F. Commissioner* 1988 Lab.IC 2258 (Orissa)(DB)
[593] *Sivaramakrishna Iyer v Regional P.F. Commissioner*, 1988 (1) LLN 635: 1988 (1) CLR 454 (Ker.)
[594] (1997) (1) SCC 241)
[595] AIR 2006 SC 1767
[596] *Bhubaneswar City Distribution Division v Union of India and another*, 85(1998)CLR198.
[597] (CWP No. 1100/1989)

Scheme is only a guideline and not intended for a mechanical application. Reliance was placed upon the Kerala High Court order in *Indian Telephone Industries Ltd. v Assistant Provident Fund Commissioner and others,*[598] and of the Bombay High Court in *Cable Corporation of India Ltd. v Union of India.*[599] In both the judgments, it was held by the High Court that the liability to pay damages on belated remittances of Provident Fund dues does not arise automatically, but the same will have to be decided by the Provident Fund authorities by applying mind to the merits of the case, and no arithmetic calculation can be made. The Supreme Court, in *Organo Chemical Industries and another v Union of India and others,*[600] had observed that while fixing the amount of damages, the Provident Fund authorities generally take into consideration the various factors, viz., the number of defaults, the period of delay, the frequency of defaults and the amount involved. Subsequently, a similar view was taken by the Orissa High Court in *Bhubaneswar City Distribution Division v Union of India.*

In *K. Streetlite Electric Corpn. v Regional Provident Fund Commissioner,*[601] the Supreme Court did not remand the matter for fresh consideration. It held that the direction issued by the Central Government under s.20 could not be binding on the department in assessing the damages. In the matter of imposition of damages, the authorities must levy damages commensurate with the situation on hand.

Offences under s.14-B are continuous in nature

In *Regional Provident Fund Commissioner v K. Mohammed,*[602] the Supreme Court held that the offence under s.14-B is a continuing one and given otherwise, in a case of this nature, the Courts should give due weight to s.473 of Cr.PC to condone the delay in the interest of justice.

Liability to pay penal damages

In *McLeod Russel India Limited v Regional Provident Fund Commissioner, Jalpaiguri and others,*[603] the Supreme Court affirmed the decision of the RPFC, and held that the Transferee Company could be made liable for 'damages' as the language in s.17-B specifically speaks of "contributions and other sums due from the employer."

---

[598] 2006 (3)KLJ 698
[599] 2006(3)CLR 349 (Bom)
[600] AIR 1979 SC 1803
[601] AIR 2001 SC 1818: (2001) 4 SCC 449: LNIND 2001SC 911: 2001-I-LLJ-1703.
[602] 1994(Sup3) SCC 673: 1995(2) LLJ 631: 1995 SCC (L&S) 195
[603] 2014 (8) SCALE 272

Stay period – inclusive for penal damages & s.7-Q interest

In *Sushil Choudhury v Union of India*,[604] the facts were that the petitioner had not deposited the EPF contributions because of the stay order granted by the Court. When the case was finally decided against him, he was required to pay not only the contributions due but also the interest thereon under s.7-Q of the Act. When the petitioner challenged it, a Division Bench of the Tripura High Court held that 'the stay order was granted at the asking of the petitioner. The matter has been finally decided against the petitioner. Therefore, the petitioner cannot now contend that for the period when the petition was pending in the Court, he is not liable to pay interest or not liable to pay the amount.'

Effect of payment before issue of Show Cause Notice

In *Birla Cotton Spinning & Weaving v Union of India and others*,[605] a Division Bench of the Delhi High Court, refused to accept the view that s.14-B is applicable only if any arrears of contributions are still outstanding at the time of issue of show cause notice and not if the dues had been remitted before issue of the notice. The Court observed, "to accept the argument of the petitioner would amount to an open invitation to the employer to defeat the purpose of s.14-B by not depositing the contributions within the prescribed time, and utilize the funds for his business and still avoid the penal damages under s.14-B by merely depositing the contribution before show cause notice is issued. This would make a mockery of Section 14-B of the Act." However, the payment though made after default but before notice is issued, may be a circumstance which the competent authority can take into account in considering the quantum of damages with regard to default.[606]

Wages paid or payable

In *Calicut Modern Spinning & Weaving Mills Ltd. v Regional Provident Fund Commissioner*,[607] the Kerala High Court held that even in a case of lockout and strike, the failure to make the EPF contributions should be visited by damages under s.14-B of the Act. Justifying this view, the Court observed, "to allow the employer to make the contribution only when he pays the wages would be to stultify the project. To accept the petitioner's contention, in this case, would be to enable the employer to divert remittances to the Fund to suit his convenience putting forward sometimes reasonable grounds, sometimes justifiable grounds and most often unjustifiable grounds."

---

[604] 2015(146) FLR 66: 2015(3) CLR 243: 2015 LabLR 986: 2015(9) S.C.T. 630
[605] ILR 1984 DELHI 60
[606] *Hindustan Malleables & Forgings Ltd. v Regional P.F. Commissioner*, 1978 Lab IC 930 (Pat).
[607] 1982 LAB.I.C. 1422(2): (1982) I LLJ 440 (Ker.)

In *Apex Security and Detective Force Ltd. v Central Board of Trustees, EPF,*[608] the Delhi High Court rejected the contention that in the absence of arrears of provident fund contributions on the date of issue of notice, no damage could have been levied. Damages under s.14-B can be levied not only for arrears but also for the late payments as the requirement of arrears on the date of computation is not provided under the Act. Otherwise also, if such contention is permitted, then in all cases the defaulter would make provident fund contributions after a delay and would claim that since on the day of notice under s.14-B of the Act no arrears were pending and hence he is not liable to damages, which would make the provisions nugatory.

Income Tax Liability on Penal damages

In *Rohtak Textiles Mills Ltd. v Commission of Income Tax,*[609] the Delhi High Court, following the *ratio decidendi* of the Supreme Court in *Haji Aziz and Abdul Shakoor Bros v Commission of Income Tax,*[610] heldthat damages paid under s.14-B of the Employees' Provident Funds and Miscellaneous Provisions Act, 1952, are penal in nature, therefore, the same cannot be allowed as deduction under s.37 of the Income Tax Act, 1961. In *Haji Aziz and Abdul Shakoor Bros v Commission of Income Tax* case, the Supreme Court had held that no expense which was paid by way of penalty for a breach of law, even though it might involve no personal liability, could be said to be an amount wholly and exclusively laid out for the purpose of the business of the assessee within the meaning of s.10(2)(IX) of the Indian Income Tax Act,1922 and the fine paid by the assessee was not an allowable deduction under that section. S.37 of the Income Tax Act, 1961 corresponds to s.10(2) (XV) of the Indian Income Tax Act, 1922. The levy under s.14-B of the EPF Act is predominantly a penal levy imposed by the PF Commissioner depending on the circumstances. If the levy is a penal levy, there can be no doubt that the same cannot be claimed as a deduction to compute the taxable income under s.37 of the Income-Tax Act.[611]

Income Tax Liability on EPF trust

The recognition of the fund either under Income Tax Act or the Employees' Provident Funds Act is a pre-condition for allowing any contribution to the provident fund as a deduction given s.2(38) of the Act and s.36 of the Act. S.2(38) of the Act defines recognised provident fund as meaning a provident fund which has been and continues to be recognised by the Chief Commissioner or Commissioner in accordance with the rules contained in Part A of the Fourth Schedule, and includes a provident fund

---

[608] 2015 LLR. 900 (Delhi H.C)
[609] 1997 (91) FJR 118: (1997) 226 ITR 0485: (1998) 146 CTR 0336
[610] 1961(41)ITR 350: 1961 AIR 663, 1961 SCR (2) 651
[611] *Commissioner of Income Tax v A. Albuquerque & Sons* (1993) I LLJ 571 (Kant-DB).

established under a scheme framed under the Employees' Provident Funds Act, 1952. Under s.2(38) of the Act, it is only a scheme framed under the Employees' Provident Funds Act which is deemed to be an approved provident fund for the Income-tax Act even though such a fund has not received the express approval of the Commissioner of Income-tax. The very object of exemption granted under section 17 of the Employees' Provident Funds Act is to render the scheme immune from the application of the provisions of the Employees' Provident Funds Act, subject to such conditions as may be prescribed while granting such exemption. The scheme referred to in s.2(38) of the Income-tax Act is a scheme either framed under the Employees' Provident Funds Act or a scheme approved by the Commissioner of Income-tax. A scheme which has been exempted from the provisions of the Provident Funds Act does not become a scheme framed under that Act. The scheme to which an Act is rendered inapplicable by exemption is not a scheme framed under the Act.[612]

Penal damages reduced 7-Q already ingrained in 14-B levy table

In *System and Stamping and another v. EPF Appellate Tribunal and others*,[613] a Division Bench of Delhi High Court held that the damages under s.14-B of the Act were inclusive of interest chargeable under s.7-Q of the Act up to 26th September 2008, as the mechanism to charge interest separately was not enforced by modifying the existing table and this step was taken only in issuing fresh table making effective from 26th September 2008. In *Roma Henry Security Services Pvt. Ltd. v Central Board of Trustees, EPFO*,[614] the Delhi High Court held that up to September 26th, 2008, the earlier table continue to govern the assessment, which included the element of interest under s.7-Q of the Act and from 26th September 2008 onwards, the damages and interest are segregated. Thus, the interest as provided under s.7-Q of the EPF Act is ingrained under the order for damages as computed under s.14-B of the said Act for the period above.

Waiver of Penal damages

The Act provides for consideration of an application for waiver of the damages by the Central Board of Trustees. When the Legislature says that an application for waiver of the damages requires being considered only by the Central Board of Trustees, it is that authority which has to consider the application and not someone else.[615]

---

[612] *Commissioner of Income Tax v. Kattabomman Transport Corporation Ltd.*, (2004)192CTR(Mad)168; [2004]268ITR507(Mad)
[613] (2008) 2 LLJ 939
[614] (2013) 1 LLJ 29 Del
[615] *Assistant Provident Fund Commissioner and others v Indian Telephone Industries Ltd. and another* Writ Appeal 2182 of 2006, Order dated 28th August 2008 (Ker. HC DB).

Sick Industrial Companies – Waiver of penal damages

By the Amendment Act 33 of 1988 the provisions of s.14-B of the EPF Act has been amended by addition of a further proviso to the effect that the Central Board may reduce or waive damages levied under that section in relation to an establishment which is sick Industrial Company and in respect of which a scheme for rehabilitation has been sanctioned by the Board of Industrial and Financial Reconstruction (BIFR) established under s.14 of the Sick Industrial Companies (Special Provisions) Act 1985 subject to such terms and conditions as may be specified in the rehabilitation scheme. If the Central Board does not exercise this jurisdiction properly, the writ court can interfere and set aside the order of the Central Board.[616]

Provident Fund Commissioner – a delegatee of the Central Government under s.14-B

In *Regional Provident Fund Commissioner v EPF Appellate Tribunal and another*,[617] the Gujarat High Court held that the very language of s.14-B signifies that the Regional Provident Fund Commissioner is only a delegatee of the Central Government, while exercising powers under s.14-B as the powers are directly conferred by the Act on the Central Provident Fund Commissioner only. In the alternative, such powers could also be vested in an officer as notified by the Central Government. When the Central Government names the authority by way of notification, such officer acts as a delegate of the Central Government. In such cases, the repository of powers would be the Central Government. As a delegate, the specified authority cannot claim an independent status."

Provident Fund Commissioner cannot challenge EPFAT order

In *Regional Provident Fund Commissioner v EPF Appellate Tribunal and another*,[618] the Gujarat High Court placing reliance on the Supreme Court order in *Mohtesham Mohd. Ismail v Special Director, Enforcement Directorate and another*[619] held: "A person may have *locus standi* without having any litigative interest. There is a subtle distinction between 'to have a *locus standi*' and 'to have a litigation interest.' For instance, in the matters of Public Interest Litigation, the petitioner is perceived in law to have been clothed with a locus standi even though a public interest litigant cannot be said to have a litigation interest *strict sensu*. The statutory authority which functions as 'Adjudicating Authority' and discharges quasi-judicial powers cannot claim for itself either a *locus standi* or a litigation interest to challenge the order of

---

[616] *Poysha Industrial Company Ltd. v Union of India* (1995) II LLJ 137 (Cal).
[617] Special Civil Application 8574 of 2013 Decision dated 7th March 2014
[618] Special Civil Application 8574 of 2013 Decision dated 7th March 2014
[619] (2007) 8 SCC 254

the Appellate Forum/Court which considers its own order."

Citing a Wrong Provision – Effect of

A Division Bench of the Gujarat High Court, in *Gandhidham Spinning & Manufacturing Co. V Regional P.F. Commissioner*,[620] citing the decision of the Supreme Court in the case of *State of Karnataka v Muniyalla*,[621] held that merely because an order is purported to be made under a wrong provision of law, it does not become invalid so long as there is some other provision of law under which the order could be validly made. The mere recital of a wrong provision of law does not have the effect of invalidating an order which is otherwise within the power of the authority making it. A clerical error about mentioning of the period in relation to the dues cannot be taken advantage by the employer when the dates have been clarified.[622]

Scope of Writ Jurisdiction is Limited

In *Arvind Mills Ltd. v R.M. Gandhi*,[623] a Division Bench of the Gujarat High Court has considered the scope and ambit of the proceedings under Article 227 of the Constitution *vis-à-vis* the order passed under s.14-B of the EPF Act. The Bench observed, "The High Court in exercising powers under Article 227 of the Constitution will not convert the proceeding virtually into an appeal against the impugned order. The High Court will not substitute its determination in place of the determination made by the competent authority. It is not for the High Court to consider to what extent damages should have been levied by the High Court if it was exercising the powers which have been exercised by the Competent Authority in passing the impugned order." Where the Regional P.F. Commissioner, after affording the opportunity to the employer, imposed penal damages, the reasoning adopted by that authority for imposing the damages, unless perverse, could not be questioned before the High Court.[624]

Grant of instalments will not affect levy of penal damages

In *Calicut Modern Spinning Weaving Mills v Regional P.F. Commissioner*,[625] the Kerala High Court rejected the argument that the permission granted to the petitioner to liquidate the arrears would absolve him of his liability for damage under s.14-B.

---

[620] *1987 LIC 659: 1987(1) GLR 337: 1986 GujLH 1130: 1987(1) LLN 813 (Guj. DB)*
[621] AIR 1985 SC 470
[622] *TTG Industries Ltd. v Regional P.F. Commissioner*, 2014 (4) LLJ 645 (Mad)(DB)
[623] (1981) 22 Guj. LR 994
[624] *Balaji Structurals v Regional P.F. Commissioner* (1991) 63 FLR 85 (Kant).
[625] (1982) ILLJ 440 Ker

The instalments granted were as a resulted of a sympathetic consideration, and for that, the Respondent Commissioner should not be deemed to have waived his rights to proceed under s.14-B.

INTEREST PAYABLE UNDER S.7-Q
Validity of Section 7-Q

Interest under s.7-Q is an inbuilt mechanism of the Act itself to compensate the loss of interest owing to the delayed investment of Trust monies owing to the default on the part of the employer. The constitutional validity of the relevant provision has also been upheld by the High court of Karnataka, which was pleased to observe that, "while declaring that Section 7-Q of the Act is very much constitutional, and it stands the test of reasonableness under Articles 14, 19(1)(g) and 20(1) of the Constitution."[626] Upholding the legal validity of s.7-Q, the Delhi High Court, in *Apex Security and Detective Force Ltd. v Central Board of Trustees, EPF,*[627] observed: "Absence of an expressed provision of appeal against Section 7-Q of the EPF Act is not sufficient enough to make its provisions nugatory. It is well-settled law that right of appeal is a creature of statute, for the right of appeal inheres in no one and, therefore, for maintainability of an appeal there must be the authority of law."

No appeal provision

In *Road Transport Corporation v Central Board of Trustees, EPF Organisation,*[628] the Delhi High Court held that the appeal challenging the order passed under s.7-Q of the Act is not sustainable under s.7-I of the Act. An appeal against an order passed under s.7-Q of the EPF Act would not lie under s.7-I of the said Act. However, the Supreme Court in *Arcot Textile Mills Limited v Regional Provident Fund Commissioner and others*[629] has held that when a composite order is passed under s.7-A and 7-Q of the EPF Act, it can be challenged under s.7-I of the said Act. However, when an independent order under s.7-Q of the EPF Act is passed, the affected person should have a right to file an objection if he intends to do.

S.7-Q has its independent footing

In *Road Transport Corporation v Central Board of Trustees,*[630] the Delhi High Court held that no fetters could be placed on the power of the competent authority to pass an independent order under s.7-Q of the Act, and it is not proper to limit

---

[626] *Khodyas Systems Ltd. v Regional Provident Fund Commissioner* (2008) I LLJ 329 Kant.
[627] 2015 LLR. 900 (Delhi H.C)
[628] 2015 LabLR 697: 2015(2) CLR 812: 2015(3) LLJ 135: 2015 LabLR 910
[629] (2013) 16 SCC 1
[630] 2015 LabLR 697: 2015(2) CLR 812: 2015(3) LLJ 135: 2015 LabLR 910

the applicability of s.7-Q to cases where it has been levied along with the damages under s.14-B of the Act. s.7-Q of the Act stands on its own independent footing.

In *Arcot Textile Mills Limited v Regional Provident Fund Commissioner and others*,[631] the Supreme Court held that when a composite order is passed under s.7-A and s.7-Q of the EPF Act, it can be challenged under s.7-I of the said Act. However, when an independent order under s.7-Q of the EPF Act is passed, the order cannot be challenged under s.7I.

---

[631] (2013) 16 SCC 1

Chapter XII
PROTECTION AGAINST ATTACHMENT

LEGISLATIVE HISTORY

The immunity from attachment of the Provident Fund benefits is provided on consideration of the public policy under the benevolent legislation that the subscriber in case of retirement should have something to live on, or in case of death have something to leave. A provision similar to s.10 of the EPF Act, 1952 was extant in s.3 of the Provident Fund Act, 1925. The protection under s.10 was extended to the members of the exempted provident fund trusts, by the Amendment Act 37 of 1953. It was further extended to the monies payable under the Pension Scheme and Insurance Scheme, with effect from 23.4.1971 by the Amendment Act of 1971. With effect from 1.8.1988, the words "*and shall not be liable to attachment under any decree or order of any court*" were added by the 33 Amendment Act, 1988.

In *Som Prakash Rekhi v Union of India and others*, the Supreme Court was considering the provisions s.10 of the Employees' Provident Funds and Miscellaneous Provisions Act, 1952 as also the Payment of Gratuity Act, 1972. "The public policy behind the provisions of Section 10, 12 and 14 of the respective statutes are clear. We live in a welfare State in a 'socialist' republic under a Constitution with a profound concern for the weaker class including workers (Part IV). Welfare benefits such as pensions, payment of provident fund and gratuity are in fulfilment of the directive principles. The payment of gratuity or provident fund should not occasion any deduction from the pension as a 'set-off.' Otherwise, the solemn statutory provisions ensuring provident fund and gratuity become illusory."

Provident Fund is not a part of Contract of employment

In *Balbir Kaur and another v Steel Authority of India Ltd. and others*,[632] the Supreme Court held that the provident fund and gratuity, etc. are rights of an employee under the provisions of social security legislation, and a person or his dependants cannot be deprived thereof. S.10 of the EPF Act, 1952 envisages protection against attachment of an employee's provident fund and an employee would be entitled to payment of the same irrespective of any dues which might be recovered from him and due to the employer. The amount admissible on account of provident fund

---

[632] (2000) 6 SCC 493: (AIR 2000 SC 1596)

dues is not a part of remuneration or wages arising out of a contract of employment but is a liability on the employer by the beneficial provisions of the Act, and the Schemes envisaged thereunder. A similar view was taken by the Rajasthan High Court in *M.L. Sharma v University of Rajasthan and another.*[633]

Protection extends to members of Private Trusts also

In *Tata Iron and Steel Co Ltd. v Bir Singh,*[634] the Full Bench of the Patna High Court held that the protection granted by s.10 of the Act extends to a fund created under a scheme framed by an establishment exempted under s.17 of the Act. In *Punjab National Bank v Sunil Kumar Poddar,*[635] the complainant bank was having its own Provident Fund Scheme and exempted from the EPF Scheme, 1952, and it attached the Provident Fund benefits of its employee. The District Consumer Forum held that the bank could not attach the PF amount and directed release of the PF amount with interest. In the revision petition, the National Consumer Disputes Redressal Commission, New Delhi, while upholding the decision of the District Forum, held that 'exempted establishment does not mean the Bank is exempted from complying with the provisions of the Act.'

Immunity continues till the amount is paid

In *Mettur Industries Ltd. v Velayutha Mudaliar,*[636] it was held that when under the terms of the provident fund amount standing to the credit of a member became payable on the expiry of six months from the date of discharge of the member concerned, the order of attachment made two days after the resignation of the employee, was illegal and prohibited by law, and that so long as the amount does not cease to have the character of provident fund either by payment of the same to the employee or by removing it from his credit in his provident fund ledger, the immunity against attachment continues. Similarly, in *A. Subbian v Thiruvenkataswami,*[637] the High Court of Madras held that so long as the amount regarding Employees' Provident Fund is in deposit with the employer and has not been paid over to the employee even after his retirement, it does not become the employee's property and is exempt from attachment. The court further held that the provident fund amount is a compulsory deposit and will continue to be a deposit and not the property of the employee until it is paid. In *Rameshwar Lal Agarwala v Kuti Mian,*[638] the Patna High Court held that the amount standing to the credit

---

[633] 1998 (2) LLJ 203
[634] 1982 AIR (Patna) 130: 1982 BLJ 312: 1982 PLJR 273: 1979(58) ILR (Patna) 1110: 1982 BBCJ 307
[635] 2008(4) C.P.J. 58: 2008(3) C.P.R. 211: 2009(1) CLT 22: 2008(3) C.P.C 509
[636] 1961 (1) LLJ 279)(Madras)
[637] 1971 Lab IC 1595 (Mad HC)
[638] 1969 Lab.IC 790(Pat.)

of the member, even though he has ceased to be an employee cannot be attached or any receiver appointed under the Provincial Insolvency Act, 1920 shall not be entitled to or have any claim on such amount.

In *Union of India v Hira Devi and another*,[639] the Supreme Court held that the provident fund amount not paid to the subscriber after the date of his retirement is also 'compulsory deposit' and that it is exempt from attachment and sale under s.60(1)(k) of the Civil Procedure Code. The Court held that a receiver could not be appointed in execution in respect of provident fund money due to a judgment-debtor as it cannot be assigned or charged and is not liable to any attachment. Attachment of the EPF benefits payable to the legal heirs after the death of the employee is not sustainable.[640]

No immunity once the amount is paid

In *Pearly Andrew Franz v Official Assignee*,[641] a Division Bench of the Bombay High Court held that even when the employee has become an insolvent, the amount standing to his credit – so long as it is with the Regional Provident Fund Commissioner and has not been paid to the insolvent – does not vest in the Official Assignee and the Official Assignee cannot lay any claim to it. The Court, however, stated that the immunity given by s.10(1) of the Act would not continue after the amount has been paid to the insolvent. In *Joseph Benjamin Bonjour v Official Assignee*,[642] a Full Bench of the Madras High Court laid down that the protection afforded by the Provident Funds Act from the attachment of the money in such deposit will not continue after the money in such compulsory deposit has been paid over to the subscriber or the depositor. The Court further observed that money thus paid over could no longer be described as 'compulsory deposit.' Thus, it is implicit that so long as the money continued to be in deposit, it will not cease to have the character of a provident fund, and will not be the property of a judgment debtor.

Group Insurance benefits cannot be attached

In *Vallabhaneni Ratnakumar and another v Katta Subbaravamma*,[643] the Andhra Pradesh High Court held that a combined reading of sub-sections (1) and (2) of s.10 makes it abundantly clear that the amount payable to the nominee of the deceased member under the General Insurance Scheme is not liable to be attached, and the

---

[639] (1952) S.C.J. 326: (1952) S.C.R. 765: (1952) 2 M.L.J. 265: A.I.R. 1952 S.C. 227,
[640] *Sathiambama and others v M. Palanisamy and others* – 2004 LIC 2964: 2004(2)LLJ 403: 2004 LLR 270
[641] AIR 1966 Bom 121: 67 Bom LR 654
[642] (1956) 69 L.W. 105: (1956) 1 M.L.J. 166: I.L.R. (1956) Mad. 491: A.I.R. 1956 Mad. 283
[643] 1993 (3) ALT 464, 1993 (3) ALT 464, 1994 (68) FLR 1048, (1994) II LLJ 81 AP, (1994) II LLJ 81 SC

nominees or, where there are no nominees, the legal representatives, are entitled to receive the amount "free from any debt or other liability incurred by the deceased."

Protection does not extend to LIP benefits

In *Rajam v Parameswara Ayyar*,[644] a government servant subscribing to the General Provident Fund subscribed a life insurance policy, and as per the rules of the provident fund, the premiums of the LIP was paid out of his Provident Fund account, and he mortgaged the insurance policy to the Provident Fund to that extend. He died without making a valid nomination. His creditors attached the insurance benefit amount. The widow contended that the insurance amount deposited by the Insurance company represented the provident fund of the deceased judgement debtor, at least to the extent of the amount withdrawn from the provident fund to pay the premiums, and that part of the insurance amount partook the same character as the provident fund and therefore it could not be attached in execution of the decree. It was held that the insurance benefits should be regarded as an asset of the deceased in the hands of his widow and the amount is not exempt from attachment, etc. under the Act, and it could not partake of the character of provident fund.

Immunity from Court attachment

In *Thomas George v Soudamini Manakkal and others*,[645] a Division Bench of the Kerala High Court held that the Provident Fund amount standing to the credit of the subscriber or member of the Fund is entirely immune from attachment under any decree or order of the civil court.

PF money cannot be withheld for extraneous reasons

In *Shailesh Manjulal Jadav v Gujarat State Land Development Corporation Ltd.*,[646] the Respondent Corporation withheld part of the EPF benefits payable to its retired employee on the pretext that the Regional Provident Fund Commissioner has levied penal damages/s.7-Q interest which has been challenged, and the benefits due to the retired employee will be settled only after disposal of the petition. The Gujarat High Court held that withholding of Provident Fund for the pendency of such dispute is irrational and unreasonable. In *Motilal Sharma v the University of Rajasthan*,[647] the Rajasthan High Court held that the provident fund could not be withheld for non-payment of arrears of rent from an employee.

---

[644] AIR 1945 Mad 267: (1945) 1 MLJ 433
[645] (1997) ILLJ 1178 Ker
[646] 2015 LIC 3088: 2015(14) S.C.T. 789
[647] 1998) 1 WLC 440: 1998 II LLJ 1021 (Raj HC).

SCOPE OF ENTITLEMENT OF THE NOMINEE

S.10(2) of the Act provided *exmajoure cautela*[648] that the provident fund amount shall be free from any debt or other liability incurred by the deceased or the nominee before the death of the member of the provident fund etc. It does not follow therefrom that on the death of subscriber the nominee becomes the owner of the provident fund amount to the exclusion of heirs or legatees and the fund does not form part of the estate of the deceased. The history of the law of provident fund and its object of rendering social justice to widow or children of deceased or some such very close relatives cannot be ignored while interpreting s.10(2) of the Act.[649]

In *Lalitaben Bhanabhai v Laliben Bhanabhai*,[650] Gujarat High Court held that the nominee of the Provident Fund member does not get the benefits exclusively. Other legal heirs of the deceased member can claim it by the law of succession. The sole purpose of s.10 is to afford protection to the member of the Provident Fund Scheme against the creation of any debt by the member so that after retirement he gets something to survive or in case of his death, his heirs get something to live on. Therefore, the word "vest" is required to be given a limited meaning to the effect that as against attachment of the said amount for the debt or other liability incurred by the deceased member or the nominee, it shall vest in the nominee. The Supreme Court in *Sarabati Devi and another v Usha Devi*,[651] and *Vishin N. Kanchandani v Vidya Lachmandas Kanchandani*[652] held that a mere nomination did not confer any beneficial interest in favour of the nominee. The nominee is mere to receive money for and on behalf of the successor. In *Narayanan Pai v Aesha*,[653] the Kerala High Court held that the amount received by the nominee does not vest in the nominee as his absolute property.

Status of Nominee under s.39 of Insurance Act vis-à-vis s.10(2) of EPF Act

In *Usha Majumdar and others v Smriti Basu*,[654] the Calcutta High Court discussed the most striking difference about the status of a nominee under s. 39 of the Insurance Act and s.10(2) of the EPF Act. The Court held that s.10(2) of the Provident Fund Act expressly provides that the amount standing to the credit of a member of the

---

[648] Means 'for greater caution'
[649] *Nozer Gustad Commissariat v Central Bank of India and others,* 1993 (2) BomCR 8, (1993) 95 BOMLR 4, (1993) II LLJ 98 Bom, 1993 (1) MhLj 228
[650] (1992) 1 Cur LR 164: 64 FLR 520 (Guj)
[651] AIR 1984 SC 346
[652] AIR 2000 SC 2747
[653] AIR 1964 Ker.197
[654] AIR 1988 Cal 115, (1988) 1 CALLT 35 HC

Fund at the time of his death shall vest in the nominee and it shall be free from any debt or liability incurred by the deceased or the nominee before the death of the member. Thus, immediately after the death of the member, the provident fund money becomes part of the asset of the nominee whereas under the Insurance Act after the death of the assured, the money continues to be his asset.

In *C.S. Clarke and others v State (Govt. of NCT of Delhi) and another*,[655] the Delhi High Court referred to a previous decision in *Omwati v Delhi Transport Corporation and others*[656] where the Court drew the distinction between the provisions of s.5(1) of the Provident Fund Act, 1925 and the EPF Act, 1952 and held that the *non-obstante* clause in s.5 of the 1925 Act did not find place in the EPF Act 1952, and since the latter was a subsequent legislation, the departure must be deliberate. It was therefore held that a nominee under the EPF Act, 1952 was only entitled to receive the money lying in the Fund which is to be disbursed to the legal heirs. The High Court of Bombay in *Antonio Joao Fernandes v The Assistant Provident Fund Commissioner and others*[657] approved the above view and declined to follow the view taken by the Calcutta High Court in *Usha Majumdar* case (supra).

In *Nozer Gustad Commissariat v Central Bank of India and others*,[658] the Bombay High Court considered the legislative antecedents of s.10(2). Before the amendment by Act 11 of 1946, s.5 of the Provident Funds Act, 1925 read as "Any nomination which purports to confer upon any person the right to receive the whole or any part of such sum on the death of the subscriber shall be deemed to confer such right absolutely." By the 1946 Amendment, the expression 'absolutely' occurring in s.5 was omitted. The object was to make it clear beyond doubt that the nominee would have no title to the amount. S.10(2) of the Act of 1952 does not use the word "absolutely" and hence the nominee cannot claim under s.10(2).

Nominee has a right to money

The nominee under the Provident Fund Act, unlike the nominee under the Insurance Act, gets a right to the money, because in sub-section (2) of s.10 of the Provident Fund Act, it is stated *inter alia*, that any amount standing to the credit of a member in the Fund or of an exempted member any of the provident fund at the time of his death and payable to his nominee under the scheme or the rules, subject to any deduction authorised by such scheme or rule, vest in the nominee.

---

[655] 2013(1) PLR (Delhi) 9: 2013 LIC 13: 2012(17) S.C.T. 505
[656] (1987) 61 Comp Cas 801 (Delhi).
[657] 2010 (4) Bom CR 208
[658] 1993 (2) BomCR 8, (1993) 95 BOMLR 4, (1993) II LLJ 98 Bom, 1993 (1) MhLj 228

In *Rama Chakraborty v Manager, Punjab National Bank and others,*[659] the Calcutta High Court was dealing with s.10(2) of the EPF Act, held *inter alia*, referring to s.270 of the Indian Succession Act, 1923 and Sections 45ZA(2), 45ZC(3) and 45ZE of the Banking Regulation Act, 1949 that a nominee, notwithstanding a valid nomination in his favour, would not acquire any right, title or interest in the property itself to the exclusion of the heirs unless the law governing such nomination clearly vest the same in the nominee. A nomination under s.39 of the Insurance Act does not have the effect of conferring on the nominee any beneficial interest in the amount payable, but only indicates the hand which is authorised to receive the amount on the payment of which the insurer gets a valid discharge. Under s.10(2) of the Employees' Provident Fund Act, however, the amount is to vest in the nominee in respect of the deposit of money, not only the right to receive the amount but also the right to the amount itself.

Protection extends to nominees

In *Vallabhaneni Ratnakumar and another v. Katta Subbaravamma,*[660] the High Court of Andhra Pradesh held that under s.10(1) of the Employees Provident Fund Act, the amount standing to the credit of any member of the Fund is not liable to attachment. The expression "fund" is defined by s.2(h) of the Act. A combined reading of sub-sections (1) and (2) of s.10 of the Act makes it abundantly clear that the amount in question is not liable to be attached, and the nominees or where there are no nominees, the legal representatives, are entitled to receive the amount free from any debt or other liability incurred by the deceased.

MEANING OF THE TERM 'VEST'

In *The Fruit and Vegetable Merchants' Union v The Delhi Improvement Trust,*[661] the Supreme Court held that the expression 'vest' did not mean in all cases that the property was owned by the person or the authority in whom it is vested. It may vest in the title, or it may vest in possession, or it may vest in a limited sense, as indicated in the context in which it may have been used in a particular piece of legislation.

Taking a cue from the above, the Bombay High Court, in *Nozer Gustad Commissariat v Central Bank of India and others,*[662] held that the word 'vest' in the context of the EPF Act means mere possession of the property for a particular purpose. The Court observed that the use of the word 'vest' in s.10(2) of the Employees' Provident Funds and Misc. Provisions Act, 1952 does not clothe a

---

[659] 1991 (1) CHN 75: CAL. LT. 1991 (1) HC 324
[660] HC (AP) II LLJ 81–82.
[661] 1957 AIR 344, 1957 SCR 1
[662] 1993 (2) BomCR 8, (1993) 95 BOMLR 4, (1993) II LLJ 98 Bom, 1993 (1) MhLj 228

'nominee' with an absolute title or a beneficial title in respect of provident fund amount lying to the credit of the deceased. The nominee is merely authorised to receive the amount for the benefit of heirs of the deceased. In other words, vesting of the amounts in the nominee is for the limited purpose of receiving the amount from the employer and handing over the same to the heirs entitled to it.

Chapter XIII
PRIORITY OF PAYMENT OVER OTHER DEBTS

PRIORITY AGAINST STATUTORY & NON-STATUTORY AS WELL AS SECURED & UNSECURED DEBTS

In *Maharashtra State Cooperative Bank Limited v Assistant Provident Fund Commissioner and another*,[663] the Supreme Court considered whether the dues payable by the employer would have priority over debts due to the bank in terms of s.11 of the EPF Act. The Supreme Court, referring to various judgments including those in *UCO Bank v Official Liquidator*,[664] *A.P. State Financial Corporation v Official Liquidator*,[665] *Textile Labour Association v Official Liquidator*,[666] held: "The priority given to the dues of provident fund, etc. in Section 11 is not hedged with any limitation or condition. Rather, a bare reading of the section makes it clear that the amount due is required to be paid in priority to all other debts. Any doubt on the width and scope of Section 11 qua other debts is removed by the use of expression 'all other debts' in both the sub-sections. This would mean that the priority clause enshrined in Section 11 will operate against statutory as well as non-statutory and secured as well as unsecured debts including a mortgage or pledge. Sub-section (2) was designedly inserted in the Act for ensuring that the provident fund dues of the workers are not defeated by prior claims of secured or unsecured creditors."

In a Company Application (C.A. No. 899/2012) in Company Petition C.P.230/2001, in the matter of *Murugan Mills Private Limited (Company in liquidation)*, the High Court of Madras, in its order dated January 31ˢᵗ 2013, directed the Official Liquidator to adjudicate the claim of the Recovery Officer for recovery of EPF contributions, interest, penal damages and compensation if any, and further directed him to re-compute the amounts payable to respective parties afresh in accordance with law by giving priority to EPF dues over other debts and to recover the amount, if any paid in excess to the secured creditors and workmen and others, and to make re-appropriation of the same to the respective parties in accordance with law.

---

[663] JT 2009 (13) SC 106
[664] JT 1994 (6) SC 350
[665] JT 2005 (12) SC 156
[666] JT 2004 (Suppl.1) SC 1

Provident Fund dues - More than 'Crown Debt'

In *KMECCO Engineering Service Pvt Ltd. v IAEC Industries Madras Ltd.*,[667] the Delhi High Court observed that as per s.11(2) of the Act, arrears of Provident Fund enjoy special protection and can be treated as 'Crown Debt.' The EPF Act being a welfare legislation, while balancing the claim of a private party against the judgment debtor as against a debt owed by the judgment debtor towards Provident Fund arrears, the scales ought to tilt in favour of the employees, who ought not to be put to any hardship in respect of Provident Fund contributions, as is manifest from the incorporation of Sections 10 and 11 in the EPF Act, both of which seek to protect the interests of the employees against any such hardships.

Though the Delhi High Court has termed the Provident Fund dues as 'Crown Debts,' the interpretation of the Supreme Court proves that the Provident Fund dues are more than the 'Crown debts.' In *Union of India and others v Sicom Ltd. and another*,[668] the Supreme Court observed, "Generally, the rights of the crown to recover the debt would prevail over the right of a subject. Crown debt means the debts due to the State or the king; debts which a prerogative entitled the Crown to claim priority for before all other creditors. Such creditors, however, must be held to mean unsecured creditors. The principle of Crown debt as such pertains to the common law principle. A common law which is a law within the meaning of Article 13 of the Constitution is saved in terms of Article 372 thereof. Those principles of common law, thus, which were existing at the time of coming into force of the Constitution of India, are saved because of the provision above. A debt which is secured or which because of the provisions of a statute becomes the first charge over the property having regard to the plain meaning of Article 372 of the Constitution of India must be held to prevail over the Crown debt which is an unsecured one. It is trite that when a Parliament or State Legislature makes an enactment, the same will prevail over the common law."

In *B.M.G. Pharmaceuticals (P) Ltd. v The Official Liquidator*,[669] the Calcutta High Court took a different view that the Provident Fund dues have an equal footing with those of the secured creditors of the company in liquidation, and the quantum of secured creditors' dues and provident fund dues of workmen have to be ascertained and to be paid out by the official liquidator to the secured creditors and the provident fund authorities on a *pro rata* basis. The Court observed, "Section 530(1)(f) of the Companies Act refers to sums being due to an employee, *inter alia*, from a Provident Fund. Section 530(8)(b) provides that the expression 'employee'

---

[667] 2008(4) S.C.T. 218: 2008 LIC 2297: 2008(3) LLJ 950
[668] 2009 (1) SCALE 10
[669] 2007(140) Comp Cas 237: 2007(3) WBLR 727: 2008(116) FLR 751: 2007(3) Cal. L.T. 620

in such section not include a workman. The opening words of Section 530 make the entirety of the provisions that follow subservient to Section 529A. Workmen's dues are covered by Section 529A and by the definition of 'workmen's dues' contained in Section 529(3)(b), the provident fund dues of a workman are included in the expression "workmen's dues" appearing in Section 529A(1)(a). Section 529(3)(b)(iv) and Section 530 (1)(f) are similarly worded except that the former covers provident fund and related dues of workers and the latter covers provident fund and like dues of all employees not being workmen. Upon Section 529A being introduced, all of the workmen's dues, including on account of provident fund, are to rank *pari passu* with those of a secured creditor to the extent the dues of such secured creditor are covered by any security. Other employees' dues, including on account of provident fund and like matters, are ranked below the secured creditors' and workmen's dues."

Provident Fund dues constitute Actionable Claim

S.3 of the Transfer of Property Act, 1882 defines *'actionable claim,'* as "a claim to any debt, other than a debt secured by mortgage of immoveable property or by hypothecation or pledge of moveable property, or to any beneficial interest in moveable property not in the possession, either actual or constructive, of the claimant, which the Civil Courts recognise as affording grounds for relief, whether such debt or beneficial interest be existent, accruing, conditional or contingent." A right to the credit in a provident fund account has also been held to be an actionable claim in *Official Trustee, Bengal v L. Chippendale,*[670] *Bhupati Mohan Das v Phanindra Chandra Chakravarty and another.*[671]

Priority over State Financial Corporation Acts

In *Indus Agro Products v Union of India and others,*[672] the facts of the case were that a purchaser in a sale conducted by the State Financial Corporation has challenged an attachment levied under the EPF Act. The Bombay High Court declined to accept the contention that the charge cannot be enforced in the hands of a purchaser in a sale conducted under the State Financial Corporation Act. The Court held, 'the first charge on the assets of the establishment created by the Parliament while enacting s.11(2) of the EPF Act, 1952 and the priority enunciated there is given an overriding effect, notwithstanding anything to the contrary contained in any law for the time being in force. The charge and the priority are founded on overriding social welfare principles, protecting the terminal benefits of industrial workers over other competing claims."

---

[670] AIR 1944 (Cal.) 335
[671] AIR 1935 (Cal.) 756
[672] (2006) III LLJ 598 Bom, 2006 (44) MhLj 136

In *Sicom Limited v Union of India*,[673] a Division Bench of the Bombay High Court held that the Provident Fund dues have priority of claim over the dues under the provisions of the State Financial Corporation Act and irrespective of the provisions of the mortgage under the Transfer of Property Act. Once an English mortgage does not create a conveyance in favour of the mortgagee then considering s.11(2) of the EPF Act, there will be a first charge on the said property to the exclusion of all other creditors including secured. The law thus would be that the PF dues under the EPF Act would have the priority of claim irrespective of the provisions of the mortgage under the Transfer of Property Act or a sale under the provisions of the State Financial Corporation Act.

In *Recovery Officer and Assistant Provident Fund Commissioner v Kerala Financial Corporation*,[674] the Kerala High Court held both s.46-B of the State Financial Corporation Act and s.11(2) of the EPF Act declare their intent by usage of the *non-obstante* clause. However, since s.11(2) of the EPF Act has been enacted later, it overrides the earlier legislation also. It is, therefore, clear that s.11(2) of the EPF Act overrides all provisions of other enactments including s.46-B of the State Financial Corporation Act.

In *Mahendra Jain v Assistant Provident Fund Commissioner*,[675] the Madhya Pradesh High Court (Gwalior Bench) held that the Provident Fund Organisation has a right to recover the dues as a first charge from the financial institution, FICI Ltd., and further observed the following: (i) The EPF dues cannot be recovered from the auction purchaser who is a *bona fide* purchaser. (ii) As per the scheme of EPF Act, it cannot be held that the Provident Fund contributions of the employees stand waived because of inaction or delay on the part of the PF Organisation, and the liability to pay the contribution has not come to an end just because the erstwhile employer is closed down and the property is auctioned. (iii) The financial institution which sold out the properties to realise the dues under the SARFAESI Act is under a legal obligation to pay the PF dues to the EPFO.

Priority of dues under the Companies Act

The Supreme Court in *Employees' Provident Fund Commissioner v Official Liquidator of Esskay Pharmaceuticals Limited*,[676] dealt with the question as to whether 'priority given to the dues payable by an employer under s.11 of the EPF Act is subject to s.529-A of the Companies Act, 1956,' the Court observed that 'it is also important

---

[673] 2008(5) BCR 515
[674] (2002 (2) KLT 723): 2002 (95) FLR 1024 (Ker.)
[675] 2013(139) FLR 182: 2012(29) S.C.T. 832
[676] 2011(10) SCC 727

to bear in mind that even before the insertion of proviso to Sections 529(1), 529(3) and s.529A and amendment of s.530(1), all sums due to any employee from a provident fund, a pension fund, a gratuity fund or any other fund established for the welfare of the employees were payable in priority to all other debts in a winding up proceedings (s.530(1)(f)). The Court further held, 'even the wages, salary and other dues payable to the workers and employees were payable in priority to all other debts. What the Parliament has done by these amendments is to define the term 'workmen's dues' and to place them at par with debts due to secured creditors to the extent such debts rank under clause (c) of the proviso to s.529(1). However, these amendments, though subsequent in point of time, cannot be interpreted in a manner which would result in diluting the mandate of s.11 of the EPF Act, sub-section (2) whereof declares that the amount due from an employer shall be the first charge on the assets of the establishment and shall be paid in priority to all other debts. The words "all other debts" used in s.11(2) would necessarily include the debts due to secured creditors like banks, financial institutions, etc. The mere ranking of the dues of workers at par with debts due to secured creditors cannot lead to an inference that the Parliament intended to create the first charge in favour of the secured creditors and give priority to the debts due to secured creditors over the amount due from the employer under the EPF Act.

In *Bowreah Cotton Mills Co Ltd. v Industrial Development Bank of India*,[677] the Calcutta High Court held that the liabilities of the petitioner-mill to its employees could not be ignored given provisions of s.529A of the Companies Act, and allowed the public auction sale of the properties and assets of the mills.

S.11(2) priority – Not confined to insolvency and winding up

In *Indus Agro Products v Union of India and others*,[678] it was contended by the Petitioner that sub-section (2) of s.11 must apply only in those situations which are covered by sub-section 1, namely, where an employer is adjudged insolvent or where the employer, being a company, is being wound up. The High Court of Bombay held that 'to read sub-section (2) as subservient to sub-section (1) or as a provision which operates in the same field as sub-section (1) would render sub-section (2) largely otiose. Such a construction cannot be accepted since it would be contrary to the plain and grammatical meaning that attaches to the words used in sub-section (2) of s.11. The words "if any amount is due from the employer" must be given a full and untrammelled construction. The deeming fiction in sub-section (2) by

---

[677] 2013(1) Cal. L.T. 458: 2013(3) BC 51: 2013(2) CalLJ 44: 2013(128) AIC 574: 2013(1) D.R.T.C. 502: 2013(3) Cal. H.C.N. 85: 2013(2) BankJ 168: 2012(26) R.C.R.(Civil) 118

[678] (2006) III LLJ 598 Bom, 2006 (44) MhLj 136

which a first charge is created on the assets of the establishment must be taken to its logical conclusion and must comprehend within its ambit all the consequences which can reasonably be construed to emanate therefrom, sub-section (2) is not a proviso to sub-section (1) but is a provision that stands by itself to lend teeth to the recoverability of the dues of the employees by way of contribution.

In *Regional Provident Fund Commissioner v Ramgopal Paper Mills Ltd*,[679] the Karnataka High Court, referring to the Supreme Court order in *Maharashtra State Cooperative Bank Ltd. v Assistant Provident Fund Commissioner*[680] held that the provident fund dues, being workmen's dues, must be paid in priority to all other debts of the company under liquidation. The Court further directed the Official Liquidator to make payment to the workmen on a priority basis as soon as funds are realised.

In *Employees' Provident Fund Organisation v Government of Andhra Pradesh*,[681] the question involved was whether the dues towards the provident fund would get priority over debts vis-à-vis the provisions of s.12-A(9) of the Andhra Pradesh Cooperative Societies Act, 1964. The Supreme Court upheld that the dues payable to workmen shall include the provident fund dues also and hence, the priority will be covered under s.12-A(9)(ii)(a) of the 1964 Act, though the item 'provident fund' is not explicitly mentioned in that section but in s.12-A(9)(ii)(c).

Application of Sick Industrial Companies (Special Provisions) Act, 1985

The Sick Industrial Companies (Special Provisions) Act, 1985 was enacted to revive the sick industrial companies and the Board for Industrial and Financial Reconstruction (BIFR) was formed under the SICA Act to determine the sickness of such industrial companies and to prescribe measures for revival through rehabilitation scheme, if possible. However, the SICA has been repealed by the Sick Industrial Companies (Special Provisions) Repeal Act, 2003 which has resulted in the dissolution of the BIFR and the Appellate Authority for Industrial and Financial Reconstruction with effect from December 1, 2016. The net effect of this is that BIFR and the Appellate Authority became *functus officio* (i.e. defunct) with effect from 1-12-2016. In terms of the Eighth Schedule of the Code, it means that any appeal preferred to the Appellate Authority or any reference made to the BIFR or any inquiry pending before the BIFR or any other authority or any proceeding of whatever nature pending before the Appellate Authority or the BIFR immediately before the commencement of the SICA Repealing Act stand abated. Any company in

---

[679] 2012(5) KantLJ 187: 2012(17) S.C.T. 389
[680] 2009 (10) SCC 123: (2009) 2 SCC (L and S) 743: 2009 AIR SCW 6784
[681] 2017(3) LLJ 197

respect of which such an appeal or reference or inquiry stands abated has been given an option to make an application to the National Company Law Tribunal (NCLT) under the Code within 180 days from the commencement of the Insolvency and Bankruptcy Code by the provisions therein.

INSOLVENCY AND BANKRUPTCY CODE, 2016

The Insolvency and Bankruptcy Code, 2016 is a comprehensive compilation of laws, rules and regulations about the subject of bankruptcy law in India and seeks to repeal the Presidency Towns Insolvency Act, 1909 and Provincial Insolvency Act, 1920. Also, it seeks to amend various laws, including the Companies Act, 2013, Recovery of Debts Due to Banks and Financial Institutions Act, 1993 and Sick Industrial Companies (Special Provisions) Repeal Act, 2003, amongst others. The Bankruptcy Code attempts to harmonise the process of insolvency, restructuring and rehabilitation under the umbrella of the "corporate insolvency resolution process." Under the Bankruptcy Code, the process for corporate insolvency may be initiated by a financial creditor, an operational creditor or the company (irrespective of whether the same owns an industrial undertaking or not) itself. Briefly understood, the corporate insolvency proceeds when there is a debt, in respect of which the corporate debtor has committed a default. The amount of default should be Rs.1 lakh or more.

Priority of Provident Fund dues under the Insolvency and Bankruptcy Code, 2016

During the deliberations for enactment of the Code, the representative of the EPF pleaded before the Joint Parliamentary Committee and stated that the priority of payment of debts under the Code is changed, and EPF dues in the Bill have been placed on a lower priority, and the Eleventh Schedule of the code proposes that s.326 and 327 shall not be applicable in the event of liquidation under the Code. By this, the provision of s.11 of the EPF Act is rendered null and void. The EPFO's representative had also drawn the Committee's attention to the Supreme Court judgments upholding that the EPF dues shall get priority over all other debts including secured creditors.

The observations made by the Joint committee on the IB Code, after taking into due consideration of the EPFO's concerns, are as follows:

"The Committee after in depth examinations are of the view that provident fund, pension fund and the gratuity fund provide the social safety net to the workmen and employees and hence need to be secured in the event of liquidation of a company or bankruptcy of partnership firm. The Committee, therefore, feel that all sums due to any workman or employee from the provident fund, the pension fund and the gratuity fund should not be included in the liquidation estate assets and estate of the bankrupt.

In view of the above, the Committee decides that the Clause 36(4)(a)(iii) may be substituted by the following: "*all sums due to any workman or employee from the provident fund, the pension fund and the gratuity fund.*" Similarly, the following new sub-clause 155(2)(d) may be added after Clause 155(2)(c), "*all sums due to any workman or employee from the provident fund, the pension fund and the gratuity fund.*" Clause 155(2) (c) may accordingly be renumbered 155(2) (d).[682]

Section 36(4) of the Insolvency and Bankruptcy Code, 2016 provides *inter alia* that "*all sums due to any workman or employee from the provident fund, the pension fund, and gratuity fund*" shall not be included in the liquidation estate assets and shall not be used for recovery in the liquidation. Similarly, sub-clause (2) of Clause 155 of the Code reads as follows: 155. (2) The estate of the bankrupt shall not include— (a) excluded assets; (b) property held by the bankrupt on trust for any other person; (c) *all sums due to any workman or employee from the provident fund, the pension fund and the gratuity fund;* and (d) such assets as may be notified by the Central Government in consultation with any financial sector regulator.

Thus clause 36(4) and 155(2) of the I & B Code, 2006 expressly provides that the workmen's dues (including the provident fund dues) should not constitute part of the 'liquidation estate assets' of the corporate debtor and that the estate of the 'bankrupt' shall not include the workmen's dues. Thus, the provident fund dues have been deliberately kept out of the confine of the liquidation process to protect the interest of the workers.

---

[682] *Report of the Joint Parliamentary Committee* submitted to the Lok Sabha on April 28th 2015

Chapter XIV
RECOVERY OF ARREARS

LEGISLATIVE HISTORY

The National Commissioner on Labour (1967) under the chairmanship of Justice P.B. Gajendragadkar recommended that the Provident Fund Commissioner should be vested with powers to issue Recovery Certificates to the District Collectors to recover the provident fund arrears as 'arrears of land revenue.' Thus, the recovery certificate was commonly termed as Revenue Recovery Certificate (RRC).

The Amendment Act of 1988 has substituted the words "in the manner specified in Sections 8-B to 8-G" for the words "by the Central Provident Fund Commissioner or such other officer as may be auhorised by him, by notification in the Official Gazette, in this behalf, in the same manner as an arrear of land revenue." The amended provision came into effect from 1.7.1990.

The legislature has incorporated the provisions of II and III Schedule to the Income Tax Act and Certificate Proceeding rules for a specific purpose, and the intention appears to be that instead of reproducing those provisions *verbatim* in this Act, the provisions under the IT Act have been incorporated in s.8G in a consolidated manner. S.8-G is therefore in legal phraseology, '*legislation by reference.*' Thus, s.8B (analogous to s.222 of the Income Tax Act, 1961) and schedules II and III, and the Income Tax (Certificate Proceedings) Rules, 1962, together constitute a self-contained code prescribing the various modes for the recovery and arrears of under the EPF Act.

The Second Schedule to the Income-tax Act is a detailed and self- contained Schedule which deals thoroughly with the modes for the recovery of tax arrears. Rule 2 of the Second Schedule provides that when a certificate is received by the Tax Recovery Officer from the Income-tax Officer for the recovery of arrears under the Schedule, the Tax Recovery Officer shall cause to be served upon the defaulter a notice requiring the defaulter to pay the amount specified in the certificate within 15 days from the date of service of the notice and intimating that in case of default, steps would be taken to realise the arrears. Rule 16(1) of the same Schedule provides that when a notice has been served on a defaulter under Rule 2, the defaulter or his representative-in-interest shall not be competent to mortgage, charge or lease or otherwise deal with any property belonging to him except with the permission of the Tax Recovery Officer, nor shall any civil court issue any process against such property in execution of a decree for the payment of money.[683]

Under s.8F (Other modes of recovery), the Recovery officer is not authorised to invoke the powers of attachment.

Sections 8-B and 8-G of the Employees' Provident Funds Act enable the authorities functioning under the provisions of the said Act to resort to various measures that are available under the provisions of the Income Tax Act for recovery of the contribution from the defaulting employees. S.222 enables the Tax Recovery Officer on receipt of a certificate to resort to the recovery by one or more of the methods mentioned therein and by the rules laid down in the second schedule. Part IV of the second schedule deals with the mode of recovery by way of appointment of Receiver. Part V of the second schedule describes the mode of recovery by way of arrest and detention of the defaulter. Paragraph 82 of Part VI of the second schedule states that every Tax Recovery Officer or other officer acting under Second Schedule shall in the discharge of his functions under the said schedule be deemed to be acting judicially within the meaning of Judicial Officers' Protection Act, 1850.[684]

Constitutional Validity of S.8(B)(2) upheld

In *Chindan A. Rajan v Union of India*,[685] the Petitioner challenged the constitutional validity of s.8 (B)(2) of the EPF Act contending that it confers unguided and arbitrary powers to the executives to arrest a person. The Karnataka High Court observed that the rules provided under the Income Tax Act viz., s.189 (procedure to be followed to the III Schedule to the Income Tax Act), s.73 (notice to show cause why the defaulter should not be arrested) etc., provided sufficient safeguard against arbitrary exercise of powers and hence held that the said provisions are not in violation of Article 21 of the Constitution.

RECOVERY CERTIFICATE

It is always open to the Income-tax Officer to amend the certificate already issued by including the partner whose name was left out in the Certificate as a defaulter.[686] If there are more than one Certificates received from the authorised officer in respect of the same defaulter, the Recovery Officer has to serve as many notices of demand as there are recovery certificates.

---

[683] *Palani Gounder (Decd.) and others V Income Tax Revenue Department and others* 1998 (229) ITR 59 (Mad.)

[684] *Guru Vittal P.and others v Regional P.F. Commissioner* 2001 (90) FLR 649, (2001) III LLJ 1244 Mad, (2001) 2 MLJ 287

[685] 2007 (3) KarLJ 233, (2007) III LLJ 42 Kant

[686] *Kethmal Parekh v Tax Recovery Officer and another* 1973 87 ITR 101 AP

Issue of Recovery Certificate – a Must

In *Navnit Motors Pvt. Ltd. v Union of India and another*,[687] the Bombay High Court quashed the recovery proceedings stating that the Respondent without following the procedure prescribed under s.8B of the Act, without issuing any recovery certificate and without declaring the petitioner as a defaulter, recovered the amount. The Court directed the Provident Fund Commissioner to refund the amount recovered by him from the petitioner's bank account, observing that he has the liberty to follow the procedure as prescribed under the Act for implementing their order under s.7-A and s.7-B of the Act if they want.

Correctness of the Recovery Certificate

Recovery proceedings based on a certificate for an amount more than the arrears due from the assessee (defaulter) would be wholly invalid. In *Income-tax Officer, Kolar Circle v Seghu Buchiah Setty*,[688] the Supreme Court quashed the recovery proceedings because a fresh notice of demand had not been served upon the assessee after his tax liability had been reduced in appeal. Similarly, in *Vimlaben Khimji and others v Manivikar*,[689] *Sriramiah v Income Tax Officer*,[690] and *Collector of North Arcot v Kannan*,[691] the recovery proceedings were quashed by the Courts because the real amount of arrears had not been specified in the Recovery Certificate. In *Sriramiah v Income-tax, Officer, Kolar*,[692] it was held that if the amount for the recovery of which an assessee's properties are sold in tax recovery proceedings is higher than what is really due from the assessee, the sale would be invalid and the Collector could be restrained by an order from confirming the sale. In *Collector of North Arcot v VK. Kannan*,[693] the certificate for recovery was for a sum, which was substantially in excess of what was actually due, and it was held that the error would go to the root of the jurisdiction of the Collector to recover the arrears, and the proceedings taken by the Collector for recovery of the arrears would be invalid.

Certificate showing excess amount – Invalid

In *Collector of North Arcot v VK. Kannan*,[694] a Division Bench of the Madras High Court, held that the under the Revenue Recovery Act, the Collector had no

---

[687] 2012(3) CLR 575: 2013(136) FLR 334: 2012(132) FLR 518: 2011(13) S.C.T. 799
[688] (1964) 52 ITR 538:AIR 1964 SC 1473
[689] (1964) 51 ITR 29 (Bom)
[690] (1965) 52 ITR 408 (Mys)
[691] (1967) 65 ITR 302 :AIR 1967 Mad 249
[692] , [1964] 52 I.T.R. 408 (Mys.)
[693] [1967] 65 I.T.R. 301 (Mad.)
[694] (1967) 65 IRT 301 (Mad.)

jurisdiction either to attach or to bring to sale properties to recover a sum higher than what was legally due on the date of the notice of attachment. When the amount mentioned in the order of attachment and the subsequent sale proclamation is higher than the actual dues, then the attachment and the sale become vitiated.[695] If the amount, for the recovery of which an assessee's properties are sold, is higher than what is due from him, the sale is invalid.[696] The prohibitory order issued under Order 21, Rule 54 of the CPC in pursuance of a certificate for recovery of tax is invalid if the amount sought to be recovered by the said prohibitory order is more than the actual liability of the assessee.[697] On the Assessment order being revised on appeal, the default based on it and all consequential proceedings must be taken to have been superseded, and new proceedings have to be started to realise the dues as found by the revised order.[698]

Assessment – a precondition for recovery

Any amount due from such employer as is specified in s.8 may, if the amount is in arrear, be recovered in the manner specified in Sections 8B to 8G. For order of demand under s.8, it is necessary that there should be a determination of the amount due if the liability is disputed. An order under s.7-A(3) is a condition precedent to the making of a demand under s.8.[699] Before asking the establishment to deposit any amount, the Commissioner was required to determine the liability, and it was to be done by initiating proceedings under s.7-A of the EPA Act. Without determining the liability, if any, the establishment cannot be called upon to deposit an unspecified amount.[700]

DEMAND NOTICE

The Tax Recovery Officer's competence is attributable only to the Recovery certificate which is the foundation of his jurisdiction to proceed with the assessee's person or property. It not only vests in his jurisdiction but defines its limits.[701]

In *Sheo Prasad v Hira Lal*,[702] a Full Bench of the Allahabad High Court laid down that an attachment would not abate on the death of the judgment-debtor.

---

[695] S. Santosha Nadar v First Additional Income-Tax Officer 1961 42 ITR 715 Mad
[696] Sriramiah v Income-Tax Officer, Kolar, [1964] 52 I.T.R. 408 (Mys.)
[697] Vimlaben Khimji v H.S. Manvikar, [1964] 51 I.T.R. 29 (Bom.)
[698] Income-Tax Officer v Seghu Buchiah Setty (1964) 52 ITR 538: AIR 1964 SC 1473
[699] A.T. Union (P) Ltd. v Regional Provident Fund Commissioner, (1968) (2) LLJ 465 Ker
[700] Tapan Kumar Battacharyya v Assistant Provident Fund Commissioner and others 2010(3) LLJ 700: 2010(125) FLR 24
[701] Kethmal Parekh v Tax Recovery Officer 1973 87 ITR 101 AP
[702] ILR 12 All 440 (FB)

The property under attachment must be considered to be in the custody of the law. There is no provision in the Civil Procedure Code requiring notice to be given personally to a judgment-debtor or his legal representative of a sale of property under the attachment. If the sale damnifies the legal representative, his remedy is by application under s.311 of the CPC.

No need for service of notice on the partners when it is served on the firm

If a notice of demand (CP-1) is served on the partnership firm, no further notice is mandatory to be served upon the partners to render them liable for recovery of the dues. In *Sahu Rajeswar Nath v Income Tax Officer*,[703] the Supreme Court observed: 'Under the Partnership Act the liability of the partners of a firm is joint and several, and it is open to a creditor of the firm to recover the debt of the firm from any one or more of the partners. However, the name of the partners should be mentioned in the Recovery Certificate and the Notice of Demand. The effect of Rule 16 is that a defaulter can not grant even a lease after the receipt of the certificate by the Tax Recovery Officer. In cases where the firm alone is named as a defaulter, the result of the theory of constructive liability under the certificate would be that a partner who is unaware of the issue of the certificate and who may have dealt with his property *bona fide* suffers from the disability arising under Rule 16. This may affect a large number of *bona fide* transactions entered into with partners by third parties, reasoned a Division Bench of the High Court of Andhra Pradesh in *Kethmal Parekh v Tax Recovery Officer and another*.[704] It is, however, open to the Income-tax Officer to amend the certificate already issued by him naming the individual partner also as a defaulter.

Recovery Officer not to demand Interest on certified dues

In *Indian Drilling and Mining (P) Ltd. v Regional Provident Fund Commissioner*,[705] the petitioner had challenged an order passed by the Recovery Officer demanding interest and costs under the provisions of s.7-Q of the Act, in addition to the amount mentioned in the Recovery Certificate. The High Court held that the Recovery Officer could recover only the amount specified in the Certificate. The provision contained in s.7-Q of the Act merely enables the authorised officer under s.7-A to charge interest, but if such interest is not included in the certificate, it is beyond the competence of the Recovery Officer to demand such interest.

---

[703] AIR 1969 SC 667, 1969 72 ITR 617 SC, 1969 1 SCR 999
[704] 1973 87 ITR 101 AP
[705] 2001-II-LLJ-450

Service of Notice of Demand

When the law requires that a notice of demand should issue, the mode of compliance by a letter is excluded. It may be that the letter is a good substitute for a notice of demand, but the section demands that it should be 'in the prescribed form.'[706] Notice by way of telegram cannot be said to be a substitute for notice by post, and it is mandatory that notice must be served only in the manner provided in s.282 of the Income Tax Act.[707]

In *M.X. De Nornha & Sons, Cawnpore v Commissioner of Income Tax*,[708] a notice to a firm, sent by registered post, was served on a clerk and it was held that there was a presumption of good service which would prevail unless the assessee could rebut it by competent evidence. In *L.C. De Souza*,[709] the notice sent by registered post was received by a minor son of the assessee. It was established that the minor had nearly attained the age of majority, was an intelligent person and had, on previous occasions, also received registered letters addressed to his father. On those facts, the Court held that the presumption under s.27 of General Clauses Act, had not been rebutted. The notice served upon the brother of the assessee (who had no authorisation to receive it on his behalf) is a good service considering the presumption of service under s.27 of the General Clauses Act.[710]

The Recovery Officer should investigate objection to attachment

Any objection to the attachment of the property could be investigated by the Recovery Officer under Rule 11 of Schedule II to the Income Tax Act, 1961. Recovery Officer is required to pass a speaking order after such investigation. Given the existence of alternative remedy, the writ will not usually be issued by the High Court.[711] The investigation contemplated in Rule 11 is *pari materia* with an enquiry usually held by Civil Courts under Order 21, Rule 58 of the code of Civil Procedure. The Recovery Officer should ultimately decide as to whether any item of property is exempt or not from attachment and sale and his decision is final. An application for review also cannot be filed against such orders.[712]

---

[706] *Income-Tax Officer, Kolar and another v Seghu Buchiah Setty*, 1964 AIR 1473, 1964 SCR (7) 148
[707] *Commissioner of Income-Tax v Sattandas Mohandas Sidhi* 1998 230 ITR 591 MP
[708] AIR 1952 All 137, 1950 18 ITR 928 All
[709] 54 ALL. 548
[710] *Commissioner of Income Tax v Malchand Surana* AIR 1956 Cal 537, 1955 28 ITR 684 Cal
[711] *Keshav Deo Poddar v Tax Recovery Officer and others*, 1992 193 ITR 480 All
[712] *Jatin Estates (P) Ltd. v Tax Recovery Officer*, (1975) ITR 343 (Cal.)

Refusal of Demand Notice – Presumption of Service

In *Shri Bhagwan Radha Kishen v Commissioner of Income-Tax, UP*,[713] the Allahabad High Court held that the endorsement by the postal authorities that the addressee refused to accept the postal article is sufficient to raise a presumption of service on the assessee.

Property cannot be alienated after service of Demand Notice

In *Employees' Provident Fund Organisation v Inspector General of Registration, Chennai*,[714] the Madras High Court held that alienation to property under attachment is void as per Rule 16(2) of Second Schedule to Income Tax Act, and any dealing in relation to property is prohibited by Rule 16(1) of Second Schedule to Income Tax Act. The Court has further directed the Additional Central Provident Fund Commissioner, Tamilnadu and Kerala, Chennai to issue suitable instructions to the Recovery Officers that they can ignore any sale or alienation, if any, made by the defaulter establishment after the issue of certificate by the Authorised Officer, in view of Rule 16 of the Second Schedule to the Income Tax Act which declares such sale as void, and that they can proceed further to bring the property to sale, etc.

Recovery Proceedings against Legal Representatives

There is also no provision for issue of certificates in the name of a deceased assessee, and for the Tax Recovery Officer proceeding against his legal representatives in the Income-tax Act, 1922 or 1961. Rule 84 in the Second Schedule to the Income-tax Act, 1961, provides that no certificate shall cease to be in force by the death of the defaulter. Rule 85 says that if at any time after the issue of the certificate, the defaulter dies, proceedings may be continued against the legal representative of the defaulter, and the provisions of the Schedule shall apply as if the legal representatives were the defaulter. When the assessee (employer) dies, the efficacy of the certificate comes to an end, and the recovery proceedings cannot be continued against the successor-in-interest on the strength of the certificate. The only method by which the successor could be proceeded against was by a new certificate naming him as the defaulter.[715]

Notice to Legal Representative of the deceased defaulter

In a case where the recovery proceedings are to be continued against the defaulter's legal representative, a fresh notice of demand should be served on the legal representative. However, if the legal representative himself happens to be one of the joint defaulters along with the deceased, then there is no necessity to issue a fresh demand notice on the death of the defaulter.

---

[713] AIR 1952 All 857, 1952 22 ITR 104 All
[714] 2013(8) MLJ 363: 2014(140) FLR 595: 2013(33) R.C.R.(Civil) 817
[715] *Kethmal Parekh v Tax Recovery Officer and another* 1973 87 ITR 101 AP

However, the High Court of Karnataka made a different interpretation in consonance with the object of the Act and held that no fresh notice of demand is required to be served on the legal representative. The Court observed: Rule 60 of the Rules requires the issue of a notice to the legal representative of a deceased defaulter under Rule 85 read with rule 2 of Schedule II in Form No. ITCP 29, before further coercive steps, may be taken to recover arrears of tax. If on such a legal representative a notice under s.156 of the Act has to be served again, then he would cease to be a defaulter immediately after such service is made because under the scheme of the Act an assessee would become a defaulter only when he has not paid the tax mentioned in the notice of demand issued under s.156 within the time prescribed by s.220(1) of the Act. The illogicality lies in the fact that, whereas Rule 85 treats such a legal representative as a defaulter forthwith, s. 220(4) does not treat a person on whom a notice under s. 156 has been issued until the time prescribed in s. 220(1) has expired.[716]

Law imposes no obligation on the part of the Recovery Officer to recover the arrears first by the sale of movables, or by arrest and detention of the defaulter before immovable property of the defaulter may be proceeded with for sale.[717] There is no provision for issue of a certificate in the name of the deceased assessee, and hence the sale in pursuance thereof is void.[718]

Attachment – deemed withdrawal on payment of the dues

Rule 12(a) of Schedule II provides that if the amount due, with costs and charges and expenses resulting from the attachment of the property are paid to the Recovery Officer, the attachment shall be deemed to be withdrawn. Property can be brought to sale after it has been duly attached, and if the attachment comes to an end upon the payment of the entire arrears before the date of sale, the property was not duly attached at the time of sale and hence the sale is *ab initio* void.[719]

Civil Court has no jurisdiction once notice under Rule 2 is served

Rule 16 of the Second Schedule to the Act has the effect of depriving the civil court of any jurisdiction to issue any process against the property of a defaulter on whom a notice under Rule 2 of the said Second Schedule had been served.[720]

---

[716] *K.R. Prasanna Kumar and others v Income Tax Officer* ILR 1974 KAR 581, 1977 106 ITR 701 KAR, 1977 106 ITR 701 Karn, 1974 (1) KarLJ 541

[717] *Padrauna Rajkrishna Sugar Works Ltd. v Land Reforms Commissioner, UP and another*, 1969 AIR 897, 1969 SCR (3) 468

[718] *Isha Beevi and others v Tax Recovery Officer and others*, 1971 80 ITR 82 Ker

[719] *Sorabji Coovarji v Kala Raghunath*, (1911) 13 BOMLR 1193, 12 Ind Cas 911

[720] *Tax Recovery Officer vs VA. Ramaswami and others* [1978] 114 ITR 408 (Mad)

In *Sriniwas Pandit v S. Jagjeet Singh Sawhney and another*,[721] held, the effect of Rule 16 of Schedule II is that as soon as it was brought to the notice of the court that the Recovery Officer had issued a notice it becomes the duty of the court to desist from any further process for realising the money sought to be realised in execution of a decree for the payment of money. Any order of attachment and subsequent order of sale by a civil court in respect of a property of a defaulter, on whom a notice under Rule 2 has been served, are without jurisdiction.[722]

JUDICIAL POWERS OF THE RECOVERY OFFICER

The powers conferred on the Recovery Officer by Rule 83 are far-reaching, and the proceedings thereof are strictly civil court proceedings. Rule 83 of Schedule confers on the Income Tax Officer all the relevant powers which the civil courts have under the code of Civil Procedure regarding the production of books of account and other documents. Since Order XIII, Rule 10 confers such power on the civil court to call for documents from other courts, the Income Tax Officer also has such powers.[723] The material furnished by the statement of a person whose attendance is enforced by the Income-tax Officer or any other officer of the Department, is good material, although the person does not make that statement on an oath or affirmation. The provisions of this section do not compel the authorities mentioned therein to take statements of persons only upon oath.[724]

Recovery Officer is a Judicial Officer

A reading of Rule 69 of part IV of the Second Schedule along with Rule 82, discloses that a Tax Recovery Officer when discharging his functions under the Schedule-II, should be deemed a judicial officer.[725]

Recovery is a civil process

In *Binod Kumar Biyala v Regional Provident Fund Commissioner*,[726] the Calcutta High Court made a distinction between the recovery process and prosecution. The Court held that s.8B to s.8E related to a civil process for recovery of the amount due payable under the EPF Act. S.14 to s.14C deal with punishment which may be imposed in connection with the offence by an employer under the Act. Recovery Certificate

---

[721] 1976 104 ITR 20 Delhi
[722] *Union of India v G.J. Baga* (1978) 115 ITR 741 (Mad.)
[723] *Jhabarmull Agarwalla v Kashiram Agarwalla and others*, 1969 71 ITR 269 Cal
[724] *Chowkchand Balabux v Commissioner of Income-Tax*, 1961 41 ITR 465 Gauhati
[725] *Guru Vittal P.and others v Regional P.F. Commissioner* 2001 (90) FLR 649, (2001) IIILLJ 1244 Mad, (2001) 2 MLJ 287
[726] (2000) 2 CALLT 443 HC, 2001 (88) FLR 216, (2001) ILLJ 305 Cal

is equivalent to a money decree, and it should be executed as it is. There is no bar under s.8B to the Recovery Officer recovering the amount due by attachment and sale of any movable and immovable property of the establishment and detention of the defaulter in prison. This detention is not a detention under the finding of guilt under s.14 but a mode of recovery similar to s.51 of the Civil Procedure Code.[727] In *Auchtel Products Ltd. v Regional Provident Fund Commissioner*,[728] the Bombay High Court observed that the very purpose behind giving show cause notice is to afford an opportunity to the person concerned to submit his explanation, and the moment such an explanation is submitted, the authority issuing show cause notice is duty bound to consider the explanation submitted, and to give reasons for rejecting that explanation. Failure to consider the explanation of the employer in recovering arrears of Provident Fund will vitiate the entire recovery proceedings.

Jurisdiction of the Recovery Officer

Order 21, Rule 46 deals with the attachment of debt, share and other property, not in possession of the judgment-debtor. Where the garnishee resides outside the Recover Officer's geographical jurisdiction and also the debt is payable outside such jurisdiction, he is not competent to issue a prohibitory order under Rule 46 to the garnishee. In such a case, the proper course is to transfer the certificate to the Recovery Officer in whose jurisdiction the garnishee resides.[729] Similarly, in *Satyapriya Banerjee v Kundunmuli Babu*,[730] a Division Bench of the Calcutta High Court while referring to Order 21, Rule 46 held: A debt payable to the judgment-debtor outside the jurisdiction of the Court by a person not residing within the jurisdiction of the Execution Court cannot be attached. However, if the debt is payable within the Recovery Officer's jurisdiction, he is competent to prohibit the garnishee even if such garnishee resides outside his jurisdiction.[731]

ATTACHMENT AND SALE OF MOVABLE AND IMMOVABLE PROPERTIES

Distinction between movable and immovable properties

In *Jagdish v Mangal Pandey*,[732] a Division Bench of the Allahabad High Court observed: "Anything attached to the certain would normally be treated as immovable

---

[727] *Sanatan Ghosh and others v. Regional Provident Fund Commissioner*, 95 CWN 115, 1991 (62) FLR 97, (1991) II LLJ 466 Cal
[728] 1998 LLR 377: 1998 (78) FLR 900 (Bom HC).
[729] *Padmanabha Pillai Bhaskara Pillai v Bank of Kerala*, 1956 Travencore-Cochin 100
[730] AIR 1939 Cal. 428
[731] *British Transport Co Ltd. v Suraj Bhan and others* AIR 1963 All 313
[732] AIR 1986 All 182

property and a tree which is attached to the earth and seeks its nourishment and sustenance from the soil in which it stands will be deemed to be attached to the earth with the only distinction that if the tree of the kind which is usually used as timber and is of sufficient size so as it can be used as such and is intended to be severed from the soil reasonably thereafter, it may not be treated as immovable property."

Attachment and sale of movable properties

Proviso to Order 21, Rule 43 of the Code of Civil Procedure provides that when the property seized is subject to speedy and natural decay, or when the expense of keeping it in custody is likely to exceed its value, the attaching officer may sell it at once, without waiting for completion of the period of 15 days. In *Rangoon Municipality v Ram Behari*, an objection was raised against the attachment of the grains belonging to the judgment-debtor. The Court held that once the grain is separated from the chaff, it ceases to be agricultural produce and there is no protection against its attachment and the grain as well as the straw both can be attached.

Warrant of attachment

The order of attachment is an order whereby the judgment-debtor and all other persons are directed not to deal with the property attached either by way of transferring or charging after the attachment. The order of attachment is an order like a direction, and it cannot be said to be effective unless it is brought to the notice of all concerned in the manner provided by law.[733] When several properties are sought to be attached in pursuance of an order of attachment, there must be proof of affixture on every one of the properties. It was laid down in *Rukminiamma v Ramayya*,[734] that where there are several lots of property, an order of attachment affixed only to one such lot cannot be deemed to be the effective attachment of other lots of properties.[735] If a valid attachment has not been made, subsequent execution proceedings by the attachment are liable to be quashed.[736]

Attachment of a Debt

The procedure in connection with the attachment of a debt not secured by a negotiable instrument is regulated by Order 21 Rule 46. The attachment is made by a written order prohibiting the creditor from receiving the debt and the debtor from making payment thereof until the further order of the Court. In the case of moveable property, when the property is in possession of the judgment-debtor at

---

[733] *Jagannath Prasad v Mahabir Ram Kumar and another* AIR 1955 Pat 231, 1954 (2) BLJR 444
[734] (1943) 2 M.L.J. 189
[735] *Murugappa Chettiar v Thirumalai Nadar and others*, (1947) 2 MLJ 310
[736] *Sahul Hameed Rowther v P.R.S.A. Arunachalam Pill and another* AIR 1944 Mad 561

the time the order of attachment is made, the procedure is by seizure – actual or constructive. When the property is not in possession of the debtor the procedure is by way of prohibitory order. In the case of any negotiable instrument to which that rule applies, the attachment must be made by actual seizure whether the instrument is in possession of the judgment-debtor or not.[737]

An attachment can be made under Rule 26 of Schedule II only when the defaulter happens to be the full owner of the debt; and not merely a co-owner of the debt along with other joint creditors. In the latter case, the attachment has to be made under Rule 28 and not under Rule 26.[738]

Demand against third-party should be made with due caution

The contribution which the employer is obliged to make under the provisions of the Act could not be fastened on anyone else except as directed by the Act itself and the Commissioner could raise the demand under sub-section 3(i) of s.8F against a third party, only when he finds the money of the employer in the hands of such third party to whom the notice is sent or in course of time, required money will become due to the employer. The provisions of sub-section 3(i) of s.8F and provisions of sub-section (2) of s.11 should be read harmoniously and reasonably.

Contingent Debt cannot be attached

The word 'debt' occurring in the rules means a present obligation to pay (*debitum in praesenti*) and not any contingent liability. A contingent debt is, strictly speaking, not a debt at all. It has no present existence because it is payable only when the contingency happens and ex-hypothesi that may or may not happen.[739] An anticipatory attachment made before the money has reached the public officer is invalid.[740] The expression 'may become due' or 'may subsequently hold money' suggest a subsisting relationship between a person served with a notice and the assessee; e.g., assessee's employer, or banker, or debtor, or a person paying an annuity to him. They do not suggest a bank with which he has never dealt with, a person he has never lent money to or dealt with, or all persons who may in the future employ an assessee.[741]

Fixed Deposit can be attached

The Recovery Officer has jurisdiction to attach the fixed deposit and the bank is under obligation to make the payment of the amount even before the maturity

---

[737] *Yellammal v Ayyappa Naick* 22 Ind Cas 870, (1914) 26 MLJ 166
[738] *Moideen Batcha Rowther v Sulaiman Saheb* 1955 (2) MLJ 522
[739] *Shanti Prasad v Director of Enforcement* (1963)(2)SCK 297
[740] *Ramanathan Chettiyar v Chidambaram Chettiyar* (1938)65 MLJ 347
[741] *Income Tax Officer v Budha Pictures*, 1967 AIR 1547, 1967 SCR (3) 425

of the fixed deposit receipt, according to the instructions which are issued by the Reserve Bank from time to time if a depositor wants to encash the fixed deposit receipt before its maturity.[742]

Overdraft amount cannot be attached

Where a banker lends money on an overdraft and the customer is always in debit, there is no stage at which the banker is a debtor to the customer, nor any point of time at which he holds any money of the customer on the latter's account. In the case of unutilized overdraft account, s.46 (5A) of the Income Tax Act cannot be resorted to as a credit freeze, and it was beyond the jurisdiction of the Income Tax Officer to issue such an order under s.46(5A) of the Act. In *K.M. Adam v The Income Tax Officer*,[743] the Madras High Court held that unless the bank was a debtor, there could be no attachment and as an unutilized overdraft account does not render the bank a debtor, nor does the bank in such a case falls within the expression 'person from whom money may become due,' the unutilized portion of the overdraft facility could not be attached.

Attachment of Decree

A plain reading of Rule 31 of the Schedule II, Income Tax Act, 1961 shows that where the property to be attached is in the custody of any Court or public officer, the attachment shall be by notice to such Court or officer requesting that such property or any interest or dividend becoming payable therein may be held subject to further orders of the Tax Recovery Officer by whom the notice is issued. As per the proviso to Rule 31 when any question of title or priority arises between the Recovery Officer or any other person not being a defaulter, the said question shall be determined by the Court in whose custody the property vests.[744]

Attachment of property in custody of Court

The Recovery Officer may always request the Court with whom any money lies in a deposit on account of the defaulter for payment of such money to the Recovery Officer. A written request of the Recovery Officer is sufficient, and no suit is necessary for the purpose.

---

[742] *Vysya Bank Ltd. and another v Joint Commissioner of Income Tax and another*, 2000 241 ITR 178 KAR, 2000 241 ITR 178 Karn.

[743] (1958) 1 MLJ 34

[744] *Syndicate Bank v Andhra Pradesh Steels Limited and others*, 2002 (6) ALD 662, 2003 113 CompCas 129 AP, 2003 41 SCL 301 AP

Intangible properties cannot be attached

Membership of the Stock Exchange is a personal permission from the Exchange to exercise the rights and privileges attached to it. It is not a private asset.[745] The membership right in question is not the property of the assessee, and therefore, it could not be attached under s.281-B of the Income Tax Act.[746]

Provisional Attachment

An order under s.281B cannot last beyond six months and the total period for which extensions can be granted under s.281B is two years, and the attachment cannot survive beyond that.[747] A reading of the provisions quoted above shows that an order of provisional attachment passed under s.281B(1) ceases to operate after the expiry of six months from the date of order. However, under the first proviso to s.281B(2) the Chief Commissioner, Commissioner, Director General or Director can extend that period by such further period or periods as he may think fit, but the total period of extension cannot exceed beyond two years. In other words, the maximum period for which an order of provisional attachment can remain effective is two years and six months.[748] Extension of period of attachment without recording reasons would be invalid.[749]

Properties exempt from attachment

As per Rule 10(1) of the second Schedule of the Income tax Act, all such property as is by the Code of Civil Procedure, 1908, (s.60 – Exemption from attachment and sale in execution of a decree of a Civil Court) shall be exempt from attachment and sale under the said schedule.

In *Udharam Delumal v Rozi Shambe*,[750] held, the meaning of 'implements of husbandry' is not limited only to primitive implements, and that the needs of progressive agriculture require that a broader meaning should be given. The agriculturists should not be forced to go in for substitute implements of an inferior character when the law itself gives him the right to pursue his livelihood in the same manner as he was pursuing it before the attachment was made with the help of his existing implements.[751] A sewing machine was held to be an artisan's tool.[752]

---

[745] *Vinay Bubna v Stock Exchange, Mumbai and others* (1999) 6 SCC 215
[746] *Stock Exchange, Ahemadabad v Asst. CIT* (2001) 248 ITR 209(SC)
[747] *Shrimati Majjo v Assistant Commissioner of Income Tax and another*, [1991]187ITR642(All)
[748] *Tek Chand v Income Tax Officer*, (2001)169CTR(P& H)204
[749] *Seshasayee Paper and Boards Ltd. v Commissioner of Income-Tax*, (2003) 261 ITR 63(Mad.)
[750] AIR 1939 Sind 96 (B)
[751] *Dwarka Prasad v Municpal Board, Meerut*, AIR 1958 All 561
[752] *Ahmad Sayeed v Kamizak Sahra* A.I.R. 1941 All.

A tractor used by a farmer was held to be an implement of husbandry.[753] In *Bindeshari v. Banshilal*,[754] an extended meaning was given to the word artisan as including a person who works in the production of commodities, and it was held that a soap boiler who practised making soaps was an artisan and the paraphernalia of his soap factory were the tools of an artisan. In *Union of India v Smt. Hira Devi and another*,[755] the Supreme Court held that the compulsory deposit made in the Provident Fund under s.2(1) of the Provident Fund Act, 1925 is not liable to attachment.

In *T.R. Punnavanam Pillai v Muthuswami Achari*,[756] the Madras High Court held that the judgment-debtor who was a goldsmith was an artist and his machines which consisted of a cutting press, machine for processing plates and dies were tools of an artisan. In *Harjiram v Ghanshyam Da*[757] held that the mechanic is an artisan and the machines like lathe, welding machine etc., used by him are not liable to attachment under proviso (b) of s.60(1) of the Code of Civil Procedure.

Right of membership in Stock Exchange cannot be attached

It was held in *Stock Exchange v ACIT*[758] and *Vinay Bubna v Stock Exchange*[759] that on plain and combined reading of rules relating to membership of the Ahmedabad Stock Exchange, it is clear that the right of membership is merely a personal privilege granted to a member, it is not transferable and incapable of being alienation by the member or his legal representatives and heirs except to the limited extent as provided in the rules on the fulfilment of conditions provided therein. Hence, the garnishee notice against stock exchange was set aside.

Recovery Officer cannot attach the properties with the Liquidator

In *Recovery Officer, Coimbatore v Official Liquidator*,[760] the Recovery Officer issued a prohibitory order attaching the properties under the custody of the banker for the Official Liquidator. The Madras High Court struck down the order as not legally valid as it had attached the entire funds of the Official Liquidator and not necessarily the funds arising out of the assets of the company-in-liquidation. Ultimately, it is only when the entire process of liquidation is complete, the Recovery Officer may have priority over other claims for recovery of the amount.

---

[753] *Dwarka Prasad v Municipal Board, Meerut*, AIR 1958 All 561
[754] *Bindeshari v Banshilal* AIR 1932 All 344 (C)
[755] AIR 1952 SC 227
[756] AIR 1962 Mad 444
[757] AIR1972Raj62; 1971(4)WLN422
[758] (2001) 248 ITR 209(SC)
[759] (1999) 97 (Comp Cases) 874 (SC), (1999) 97 (Comp Cases) 874 (SC),
[760] 2013(3)MLJ305(Mad.HC)

Attachment of properties held in trust or by benami on defaulter's behalf

Under s.82 of the Indian Trusts Act, 1882, a benamidar holds the property for the benefit of the real owner who provided the consideration of the purchase. S.222 of the Income Tax Act, 1961 and Rule 4 of the Schedule II authorise the Tax Recovery Officer to realise the arrears of tax by attachment and sale of the defaulter's movable or immovable properties. The properties that are exempt from attachment and sale are set out in Rule 10 which reads, "(1) all such property as is by the Code of Civil Procedure, 1908 (V of 1908), exempted from attachment and sale in execution of a decree of a civil court shall be exempt from attachment and sale under this Schedule, (2) The Tax Recovery Officer's decision as to what property is entitled to exemption shall be conclusive." Therefore, on a plain reading of Rules 4 and 10, it is evident that properties held in the name of the defaulter or by another in trust or on his behalf are liable for attachment and sale. Such a power also could be inferred from Rule 11 of the Second Schedule.[761] The property standing in the name of some other person benami for the defaulter and property in possession of some other person in trust for the defaulter or the benefit of the defaulter could not be attached and sold for realising the arrears of income-tax due from the defaulter. The Supreme Court has however taken a different view that the properties of the defaulter transferred to his spouse and daughter, shall not be attached against the dues payable by the defaulter.

In *TRO v. Gangadhar Vishwanath Ranade*,[762] the Tax Recovery Officer issued notice under Rule 11 of the Schedule II to the Income Tax Act and attached a residential house of the assessee. Objections were filed by the assessee, his wife and his daughter, that the assessee had executed a trust deed in respect of the said house in favour of his wife and daughter well before the order of attachment. They contended that on the date of issuance of notice under Rule 2, the assessee's wife and daughter had become full owners and was in possession of the property. The question before the Supreme Court was whether in proceedings under Rule 11 of the Schedule II to the IT Act, the TRO could have declared such transfer as void under s.281. The Court held as follows: "The TRO, therefore, has to examine who is in possession of the property and in what capacity. He can only attach property in possession of the assessee in his own right, or in possession of a tenant or a third party on behalf of/for the benefit of the assessee. He cannot declare any transfer made by the assessee in favour of a third party as void. If the Department finds that

---

[761] *Iqbal Begum and others v Tax Recovery Officer and others*, 1974 97 ITR 310 Mad
[762] AIR 1999 SC 427, 1998 234 ITR 188 SC, JT 1998 (6) SC 277, 1998 (5) SCALE 241, (1998) 6 SCC 658

a property of the assessee is transferred by him to a third party with the intention to defraud the Revenue, it will have to file a suit under Rule 11(6) to have the transfer declared void under Section 281."

Attachment is not a bar against registration of the properties

The order of attachment cannot be a bar to register a document. The sale of any property, pending the order of attachment, is void only against the claims enforceable under the order of said attachment and not in respect of other claims. Hence, if a document is presented for registration in compliance with the provisions of the Registration Act, the Sub-Registrar cannot deny the registration of the same unless there is interim order from the competent Court restraining him from registering the document and he is empowered to deny the registration of the document within the provisions of the Registration Act and Rules framed thereunder, particularly, on the grounds enunciated under Rule 55 viz., if the document is forged, impersonation by the parties, if the executive party is a minor or a lunatic, etc. Therefore, in the absence of any interim order from the competent Court nor any of the grounds available under Rule 55, the Sub-Registrar cannot deny the registration.[763]

CONFIRMATION OF SALE AND ISSUE OF SALE CERTIFICATE

The scheme of Part III of Second schedule indicates that the sale proceedings terminate on their becoming absolute after that all that remains to be done is the issuance of sale certificate. However, an order confirming the sale by the Tax Recovery Officer is a must. The efficacy of sale by public auction in favour of the highest bidder has been made to depend on the order of confirmation by the Tax Recovery Officer by incorporating Rule 56 in the Schedule. It is true that ordinarily if there is no application filed for setting aside the sale under Rules 60, 61 or 62 and 30 days from the date of sale have expired, the Tax Recovery Officer has to make an order confirming a sale. Nevertheless, an order shall have to be made. The combined effect of sub-section (3) of s.225 of the Act and Rule 56 and Rule 63 of Second Schedule is that if before the Tax Recovery Officer actually passes an order confirming the sale, the demand of tax consequent upon an order made in appeal or other proceedings under the Act has been reduced to nil, the Tax Recovery Officer is obliged to cancel the certificate and as soon as the certificate is cancelled, he shall have no power to make an order confirming the sale. The sale itself is subject to confirmation by the Tax Recovery Officer would fall to the ground for want of

---

[763] *State Bank of India v The Tax Recovery Officer and another*, (W.P. No.6685 of 2016, decision dated 12-4-2016) (Mad. HC)

confirmation.[764]

In *Balram, son of Bhasa Ram v Ilam Singh and others*,[765] the Supreme Court held that the deposit of 25 percent of bid amount under Rule 84 is mandatory and the non-compliance of it renders the sale a complete nullity. The Supreme Court had relied upon its earlier judgment in *Manilal Mohanlal Shah and others v Sardar Sayed Ahmed Sayed Mohamad and others*,[766] where it was held that when the auction purchaser failed to deposit 25 percent of the amount immediately on the date of sale and that Order 21 Rule 84 is mandatory and there is no option for the Recovery Officer except to bring the property for resale.

PROCLAMATION OF SALE

The Sale Proclamation should include the estimate. Service of notice on the judgment-debtor under Order 21 Rule 66(2) is a fundamental step. The absence of notice causes irremediable injury to the judgment debtor. Equally, publication of the proclamation of sale under Rule 67 and specifying the date and place of sale of the property under Rule 66 (2) are intended so that the prospective bidders would know the value so as to make up their mind to offer the price and to attempt that sale of the property and to secure competitive bidders and fair price to the property sold. A sale made, therefore, without notice to the judgment debtor is a nullity since it divests the judgment debtor of his right, title and interest in his property without an opportunity.[767]

Each stage of the sale is governed by the provisions of the Code. At each stage of the execution of the decree, when a property is sold, it is mandatory that notice shall be served upon the person whose property is being sold in execution of the decree, and any property which is sold, without notice to the person whose property is being sold is a nullity, and all actions pursuant thereto are liable to be struck down/ quashed. The question of non-service of notice under Rule 66 of Order 21 CPC and the effect of non-service was the subject of numerous judicial decisions – in some cases it was held a 'mere irregularity' if no substantial injury was shown to have occurred to the interest of the judgmenet-debtor, and in other cases, the sale itself has been declared *ab initio* void.

---

[764] *Mohan Wahi v Commissioner, Income Tax* (Civil Appeal No.2488 of 2001 decision dated 30 March 2001)
[765] (1996) 5 SCC 705
[766] AIR 1954 SC 349.
[767] *Mahakal Automobiles and another v Kishan Swaroop Sharma*, Civil Appeal No.2598 of 2005 decided on April 2, 2008.

Sale without publication of Sale Proclamation is void

In *Chinna Venkatanarayana v Pannapati Elias*, held, a sale without any publication whatever of the proclamation of sale is void. The same view has been taken in the case of *Venkateswara Ettu Naciker v Ayyammal and others*,[768] that a sale held without a proclamation as required under Order 21, Rule 66 of Civil Procedure code is void. In *Arjanavarma v China Appalaswamy*,[769] held, the sale which was held on a date other than the notified date without any order of adjournment and a further sale proclamation, amounted to an irregularity. The mere publication in a local newspaper would not do away with the necessity of the proclamation of sale by a beat of drum and by affixation of copies on the 'village chavdi' or court-house.[770] The law requires that an impending execution sale should be proclaimed by beat of drum or another customary mode, and failure to do so is a material irregularity.[771]

Sale must be by Public auction

In *Gulabsingh Bachhusingh Thakur v Chandrapalsingh Sheonathsingh Thakur and others*,[772] the Supreme Court held that the sale had to be carried out by public auction alone, and the sale by inviting offers through a public advertisement was a nullity.

Settling a Sale Proclamation

Under Rule 53 of the Schedule II to the Income-Tax Act, 1961, a notice is required to be issued for settling a sale proclamation. If the notice did not fix any date for drawing up the proclamation of sale and giving the opportunity of hearing for settling the terms thereof, it is void.[773]

It is by means of the proclamation of sale that notice of the sale is given to the public. To constitute a sale under the Act it must be preceded by a proclamation, and it must be by public auction to the highest bidder. A sale without proclamation being one not contemplated by the Revenue Recovery Act will be a nullity. Similarly, a sale held against the notice of proclamation will also be null and void. If, for example, the notice is that the sale will take place in a particular place and at a particular time and if it is held in a different place or at a different time it will be as good as a sale without a proclamation. Such a sale will be void even under the Code of Civil Procedure.

---

[768] AIR 1950 Mad 367
[769] 1958 Andh LT 456
[770] *Kummathi Narayanappa v Talari Akkulappa and others*, AIR 1965 AP 215
[771] *Rajendra Behari Lal v Gulzari Lal and others*, (1933)ILR55ALL182
[772] 1988(Supp.) Bom.C.R. (N.B.)535: 1987 Mh.L.J. 301
[773] *Manchhabhai Fakirbhai v Tax Recovery Officer*, 1997 228 ITR 393 Guj

In *Basharutulla v Uma Churn Dutt*,[774] the property that had been advertised for a particular date was sold on that date, but at an earlier hour than that stated in the proclamation, and the court held that there was no sale within the meaning of the Code and that the proclamation of the time and place and the holding of the sale at such time and place were conditions precedent to its being a sale under the Code. This decision was followed by *Jayarama Iyer v Vridagiri Iyer*,[775] where the property was sold at a time and by an officer different from those mentioned in the proclamation and this vitiated the sale.

Sale without attachment – not a nullity but only a material irregularity

In *Swaminatha Iyer v Krishnaswami Iyer*,[776] it was pointed out that though an attachment is necessary preliminary to a judicial sale, a sale without attachment is not a nullity. The omission to attach the properties is only a material irregularity which renders the sale liable to be set aside under Order 21 Rule 90 CPC if the substantial injury is proved. If that was not done, the purchaser obtained a title which could not after that be attached by the sons of the judgment-debtor. When a sale is held on a date different from that notified, without an order of adjournment and without a further sale proclamation that would amount only to an irregularity and the only remedy open to the party aggrieved is to apply to set aside the sale under Order 21, Rule 90 on proof that substantial injury has resulted therefrom.[777] To the same effect is the decision of the Calcutta High Court in *Gangadhar Das v Bhikari Charan Das*.[778] The Cochin High Court also has taken the view that failure to comply with the provisions of the Revenue Recovery Act relating to the proclamation of sale is only an irregularity and that it would not make the sale void.[779] As per Order 21, Rule 90 CPC, when an immovable property has been sold in execution of a decree, a person, whose interest is affected by the sale, may apply to Court to set aside the sale on the ground of material irregularity or fraud in publishing or conducting it. The condition to set aside the sale is that the person must prove to the satisfaction of the Court that he had sustained a substantial injury because of such irregularity or fraud.

---

[774] (1889)) I.L.R., 16 Calc., 794
[775] (1921) ILR 44 Mad 35
[776] (1946) 2 Mad LJ 307 = (AIR 1947 Mad 213)
[777] *Vasudeva Kavu Patteri v Mani Naicka and others*, 1954 CriLJ 1239
[778] 16 CWN 227
[779] *Kunhunni Kartha v Diwan of Cochin*, (17 Cochin 391) and *Inchunni Thambayi v Jayantha Namboori*, (22 Cochin 334).

Mere inadequacy of price cannot cancel the Court sale

In *State Bank of Travancore v Recovery Officer, EPFO and others*,[780] the petitioner sought for setting aside of the sale of properties made by the Recovery Officer because it was sold for a rate very lower than is the actual value. The Karnataka High Court relying on the Supreme Court decision in *Desh Bandhu Gupta v N.L. Anand and Rajinder Singh*[781] held that a mere inadequacy of price itself could not be a ground to set aside the auction sale held by law. In *Desh Bandhu Gupta* case (supra), the Supreme Court citing its earlier decision in *Kayjay Industries (P) Ltd. v Asnew Drums (P) Ltd.*,[782] held that if there were any material irregularities in the conduct of sale and if it causes sufficient injury to the judgment debtor the same could be set aside. For instance, where the Court mechanically conducted the sale not bothering to see that the offer is too low and the better price could have been obtained. The Supreme Court further observed that there is always a considerable difference between the Court sale price and the market price. The Court sale is a forced sale, and notwithstanding the competitive element of a public auction, the best price is not always forthcoming. If the Court sales are too frequently adjourned to obtaining a still higher price, prospective bidders will lose faith in the actual sale taking place and may not attend the auction. What is expected of the Court is to make a realistic appraisal of the factors pragmatically and if satisfied that in the given circumstances the bid is acceptable, it should conclude the sale.

Material Irregularity alone is not sufficient to set aside sale

In *Radhey Shyam v Shyam Behari Singh*,[783] the Supreme Court, while construing Order 21, Rule 90 of the CPC held that, in order to set aside an auction sale, mere proof of a material irregularity such as the one under Rule 69 and inadequacy of the price realised in such a sale, in other words, injury, was not sufficient. What had to be established is not the mere inadequacy of the price, but that inadequacy was caused because of the material irregularity or fraud, thus establishing a connection between the inadequacy of the price and the material irregularity. Rule 61 of Schedule II to the Income Tax Act is in *pari material* with Rule 90 of Order 21 of the CPC. Hence, no sale shall be set aside on the ground of any material irregularity in publishing or conducting the sale unless the applicant satisfied the TRO that he has sustained a substantial injury because of such material irregularity in the conduct of the sale.[784]

---

[780] 2003(1) LLJ 88 (Kant.)
[781] (1994)1SCC131
[782] (1974)3 SCR 678
[783] 1971 AIR 2337, 1971 SCR (1) 783
[784] *M.R. Anthony Swamy v Commissioner of Income Tax* (1981) 24 CTR Kar 1, 1982 135 ITR 424 KAR, 1982 135 ITR 424 Karn.

Common Sale Proclamation for more than one defaulter – Invalid

The rules in the second Schedule do not permit the Recovery Officer to club together the recovery certificate issued against one assessee with that of another, and to issue a single sale proclamation. Such sale proclamation is contrary to the provisions of Rule 53.[785]

Interests of the auction-purchaser is protected in case the order is set-aside

In *Padanathil Ruqmini Amma v P.K. Abdulla*,[786] the Supreme Court observed that if in a court auction sale in execution of a decree, the properties are purchased by a *bona fide* purchaser who is a stranger to the court proceedings, the sale in his favour is protected, and he cannot be asked to restitute the property to the judgment-debtor if the decree is set aside. The ratio behind this distinction between a sale to a decree-holder and a sale to a stranger is that the court, as a matter of policy, will protect the honest outside purchasers at sales held in the execution of its decrees, although the sales may be subsequently set aside, when such purchasers are not parties to the suit. However, for such protection, the properties which are sold in court auctions would not fetch a proper price and the decree-holder himself would suffer. The same consideration does not apply when the decree-holder is himself the purchaser, and the decree in his favour is set aside. He is a party to the litigation and is very much aware of the vicissitudes of litigation and needs no protection.

Law makes a clear distinction between a stranger who is a *bona fide* purchaser of the property at an auction sale and a decree-holder purchaser at a court auction. The strangers to the decree are afforded protection by the court because they are not connected with the decree. Unless the protection is extended to them, the court sales will not fetch the market value or the fair price of the property.[787]

Default by Auction purchaser

Rule 57(1) of the II Schedule to the Income Tax Act, 1961, states that on every sale of immovable property, the person declared to be the purchaser shall pay immediately after such declaration, a deposit of 25%, of the amount of purchase money, to the Officer conducting the sale. As per Rule 57(2), the auction purchaser has to pay the remaining 75% of sale amount on or before the 15th day from the date of the sale of the property. In default of payment under Rule 57(2), the Recovery Officer has got power to forfeit the amount in favour of the Government after defraying the

---

[785] *Precision Instruments (Pvt.) Ltd. v Union of India and others*, [1976]104ITR723(All)
[786] (1996) 7 SCC 668
[787] *Janatha Textiles and others v Tax Recovery Officer and another* (2008) INSC 970

expenses of the sale, and the property has to be resold. The language in Rule 57(1) and (2) is identically worded as that of Order 21 Rules 84 and 85 of Code of Civil Procedure.

The Supreme Court interpreted the rules 84, 85 and 86 of Code of Civil Procedure in *Manilal Mohanlal Shah and others v Sardar Sayed Ahemd Sayed Mahmad and another*,[788] and it was held that the provisions of the rules requiring the deposit of 25% of the purchase money immediately, on the person being declared as a purchaser and the payment of the balance within fifteen days of the sale are mandatory and upon non-compliance with the said provisions, there is no sale at all. Non-payment of the price on the part of the defaulting purchaser renders the sale proceedings as a complete nullity. This decision of the Supreme Court holds the field till date and has been followed in numerous judgments subsequently including in *Balram Son of Bhasa Ram v Ilam Singh and others*,[789] and *Gangabai Gopaldas Mohata v Fulchand and others*.[790]

In *Rosali.V v Taico Bank*,[791] the Supreme Court interpreted the word 'immediately' appearing in Oder 21; Rule 84 CPC should be construed to mean 'within a reasonable time.' In that case, the auction was concluded at 4 p.m. on a particular day, and the Court permitted the auction purchaser to deposit the money on the next day, as the Banks had been closed at that time. In *P. Kumaran v Debts Recovery Appellate Tribunal*,[792] a Division Bench of the Madras High Court held that the Recovery Officer has no power to extend the time for payment of balance 75% of the bid amount, in the absence of a clause in the auction sale notice, empowering him to do so.

In case of default by the successful bidder to pay the bid amount in time, the amount already deposited by him is liable to be forfeited by the Government under Rule 58, after the Recovery Officer adjusts the amount incurred towards the expenses in conducting the sale. However, such forfeiture is not mandated, given the expression 'may' appearing in Rule 58.

In *P. Mohan Reddy and others v Debts Recovery Appellate Tribunal and others*,[793] the facts of the case before the Andhra Pradesh High Court were that the Debt Recovery Officer while issuing auction notice deviated from Rule 57 (which mandates payment of 25% of the bid amount by the purchaser immediately after

---

[788] [1955]1SCR108
[789] AIR1996SC2781
[790] AIR1997SC1812
[791] (2009) 17 SCC 690
[792] (2011) 6 CTC 369
[793] AIR2004AP94; 2004(1)ALD199; 2004(1)ALT417; II(2004)BC76; (2004)189CTR(AP)256

declaration of the successful bidder) by incorporating in the auction notice that the deposit of 25% bid amount shall be paid within seven days.

CERTIFICATE OF SALE

Under Rule 2 of the Second Schedule, on a certificate being received by the Tax Recovery Officer, he has to serve on the defaulter a notice requiring him to pay the amount specified in the certificate within 15 days from the date of the service and intimate that in default steps would be taken to realise the amount otherwise. In the event of non-payment of the amount mentioned in the notice, the Tax Recovery Officer is empowered to realise the arrears by attachment and sale of the defaulter's movable and immovable, property or by arrest or appointing a receiver for the management of the defaulter's movable and immovable property. Rule 9 provides that all questions arising between the Income-tax Officer and the defaulter or their representatives relating to the execution, or satisfaction of a certificate duly filed under the Act or relating to the confirmation or setting aside by an order under the Act of a sale held in execution of such certificate have to be determined by the Tax Recovery Officer before whom the question arises, and not by suit. A proviso makes provision for filing a suit on the ground of fraud to Rule 9. Under Rule 53, a sale proclamation has to be drawn, which is after notice to the respondent. The form of sale certificate is set out in Form No. ITPC 17 which has been framed under the Income-tax (Certificate Proceedings) Rules. A perusal of the form indicates that notice is given to the defaulter of the date on which the sale proclamation is to be drawn up and the defaulter can in those proceedings draw the attention of the Tax Recovery Officer to the encumbrances, charges, claims or liabilities attaching to the said properties or any portion thereof. Under Rule 53 the property to be sold, revenue assessed thereon, the amount for the recovery of which sale is ordered and any other thing which the Tax Recovery Officer thinks is material for a purchaser to know, to judge the nature and value of the property are to be mentioned. Rule 56 makes it incumbent to hold the sale by public auction. On the auction taking place, the auction purchaser is to deposit 25 percent of the purchase money and in-default thereof the property can be put for resale. Rule 60 provides for applications to set aside the sale of immovable property on deposit. Under Rule 63 the Tax Recovery Officer has to confirm the sale in case the full purchase money has been paid. The sale certificate is granted to the purchaser under Rule 65.

Registration is optional once Certificate of Sale is issued

The Recovery Officer under the Recovery of Debts due to Banks and Financial Institutions Act will fall within the meaning of Revenue Officer as enumerated under Article 18 of the Indian Stamp Act and a Sale Certificate issued by him will squarely within the said provision.[794] Under Order 21 Rule 92 of Civil Procedure Code, a sale becomes absolute, the moment an order confirming the sale is passed by the Court. Similarly, the sale made by the Recovery Officer becomes absolute, the moment an order of confirmation of sale is made under clause 63 of the Second Schedule to Income-Tax Act. A sale certificate issued by the Recovery Officer under Clause 65 of the Schedule II is not an instrument of conveyance (sale deed), and it is only a document evidencing conveyance which had already taken place. S.17(2)(xii) of the Registration Act, 1908 expressly provides that a Certificate of Sale granted to any purchaser of any property sold by a public auction by a Civil or Revenue Officer does not fall under the category of non-testamentary documents, which require compulsory registration under sub-sections (b) and (c) of s.17(1) of the said Act. Thus, the registration is purely optional in respect of a Certificate of Sale issued by a Civil or Revenue Officer. The only legal implication is, if the Certificate of Sale is not registered, it is not admissible in evidence under s.35 of the Indian Stamp Act and s.49 of the Registration Act.[795] Moreover, s.89(2) of the Registration Act reads that every court granting a certificate of sale of immovable property under the code of Civil Procedure, 1908 shall send a copy of such certificate to the registering officer within the local limits of whose jurisdiction and such officer shall file the copy in his Book No.1 or get is scanned.[796]

Priority can be claimed on sale proceeds and not on property after court sale

In *C. Madanraj v Regional P.F. Commissioner and another*,[797] the Madras High Court held that one property on which there could be several charges and attachments could be brought to sale only once. If at all, people claim priority of payment or ratable distribution, it could be only on the sale proceeds and not on the property after a pucca court auction sale.

Rule 60 and 61 – persons whose interests are affected

The expression 'persons whose interests are affected' occurring in Rule 60 and 61 has to be understood in the light of the meaning assigned to it under s.54 of the Transfer of Property Act, which says that a mere contract does not by itself create any interest in the property.[798]

---

[794] Dr. Meera Thinakaran v The State of Tamilnadu and others, 2012 (2) CTC 759
[795] Dr. Meera Thinakaran v The State of Tamilnadu and others, 2012 (2) CTC 759
[796] Dr. Meera Thinakaran v The State of Tamilnadu and others, 2012 (2) CTC 759
[797] 2016 LLR 738(Mad.HC).
[798] D.V. Sathyanarayana and others v Tax Recovery Officer and others 1992 194 ITR 409 KAR, 1992 194 ITR 409 Karn.

Recovery Officer can adjudicate disputes over properties attached (Rules 66)

In *Sankar Chemical Lime v Assistant Provident Fund Commissioner and another*,[799] the Madras High Court refused to exercise its discretionary powers with regard to finding out whether the properties attached by the Recovery Officer belongs to the employer or someone else, holding that the EPF Act provides a complete safeguard in case of an improper attachment of the properties and also sale of third party rights towards the execution of the recovery of amount from the defaulting employer. S.66 of the Second Schedule to the Income Tax Act, 1961 enables the Sale Officer to postpone the sale, if there is any dispute regarding the property of the defaulter.

Person holding interest in the property under attachment

It is axiomatic that mere agreement to sell creates no legal interest or right in the property which is the subject-matter of the agreement. A Division Bench of the Karnataka High Court, in *D.V. Satyanarayana and others v Tax Recovery Officer and others*,[800] has taken a view that a person who had obtained an agreement to sell which is hit by Rule 16 of the Schedule II cannot make an application under Rule 61 for setting aside the sale as a person holding interest in the property. On the same analogy, such an agreement holder cannot equally apply under Rule 60 in his own right to get such auction sale set aside.[801]

Property should be in possession of the defaulter in his own right

In *Tax Recovery Officer v Gangadhar Vishwanath Ranade*,[802] the Recovery Officer attached a residential house of the assessee. Objections were filed by the assessee, his wife and daughter stating that the assessee had, by a registered deed, conveyed that the property to them. The TRO overruled the objections filed by the objectors and held the conveyance of the property in their favour to be illegal and void. The Supreme Court observed: "The TRO, therefore, has to examine who is in possession of the property and what capacity. He can only attach property in possession of the assessee in his own right, or in possession of a tenant or a third party on behalf of/for the benefit of the assessee. He cannot declare any transfer made by the assessee in favour of a third party as void. If the Department finds that a property of the assessee is transferred by him to a third party with the intention to defraud the Revenue, it will have to file a suit under Rule 11(6) to have the transfer

---

[799] W.P.(MD)No.1513 of 2009, judgment dated 11th December 2011 (Mad.HC)
[800] (1992) 197 I.T.R 407
[801] *K. Basavarajappa v Tax Recovery Commissioner, Bangalore and others* [1996] INSC 1289
[802] [1998]234ITR188(SC)

declared void under Section 281." In *P.K. Kunjamma v Tax Recovery Officer*,[803] the Kerala High Court also dealt with a similar case where the property of the wife was attached to realise the tax dues of her husband. The Court struck down the attachment of the property.

Income Tax rules are similar to CPC

Rules 11(1) and (2) of the Second Schedule to the Income Tax Act correspond to Rule 58 of Order 21, Civil Procedure Code, Rule 11(3) corresponds to Rule 59, Rule 11(4) corresponds to Rule 60, Rule 11(5) corresponds to Rule 61, and Rule 11(6) corresponds to Rule 63 of Order 21 of the Civil Procedure Code. The provisions of Rule 11 of the Second Schedule to the Income Tax Act, therefore, have to be interpreted in the same manner as the erstwhile provision of Rules 58 to 63 of Order 21, of the Code of Civil Procedure. A third party objecting to the attachment of the property could either file a suit or prefer a claim before the execution court, which the execution court was required to decide, albeit summarily, upon evidence, subject to the decision of the court in the suit which could be preferred under Rule 63 against such decision of the execution court on the claim.

Time-limit for sale of attached properties

Rule 68B was introduced in Schedule II by Finance Act, 1992 specifically to prescribing time limit of 3 years for sale of attached immovable properties. The proviso to Rule 68B (1) provides for the extension of one more year in certain cases where the sale falls through. Rule 68B (2) provides for the exclusion of the period during which any Court stays the demand. The period of limitation under Rule 68B (1) for sale of the attached property commences from the date on which the demand of any tax interest, fine, penalty or any other sum for the recovery of which the immovable property has been attached has become conclusive under the provisions of section 245 I or the provisions of Chapter XX of the Income Tax Act. In the absence of any order staying the recovery, the mere filing of a Miscellaneous Application would not fall in any of the categories specified in rule 68B (2) of the Second Schedule to the I.T. Act and, therefore, the period during which the Miscellaneous Application was pending cannot be excluded while computing the period of limitation under Rule 68B of the I.T. Act.[804]

---

[803] [1997]227ITR852(Ker)
[804] *M.U. Joshi v The Tax Recovery Officer*, 2005 (6) BomCR 17, (2005) 199 CTR Bom 249, 2006 281 ITR 289 Bom, 2006 (1) MhLj 95 (Bom.DB).

Private Limited Company - attachment of personal properties

In *Mohan v Regional Provident Fund Commissioner and another*,[805] Punjab & Haryana High Court held that proviso to s.8-B (1) lays down that if the Recovery Officer intends to resort to the mode of attachment and sale of property, then it should be first qua the properties of the establishment and the properties of the employer shall be touched only if the amount collected from the sale of properties of the establishment is not sufficient for recovering the whole of the arrears. A similar view was taken by the Court earlier in the case of *Sobhag Textile Ltd. v The Regional Provident Fund Commissioner, Haryana and another*.[806]

ARREST AND DETENTION IN CIVIL PRISON
Recovery Procedure and relevant rules for arrest and detention

Rule 2 of the Second Schedule provides for service of notice upon the defaulter requiring him to pay the amounts specified therein within 15 days from the date of service of the said notice and intimating that in default, steps would be taken to realise the amount under the Schedule. Rule 73(1) of the Second Schedule provides that no order for the arrest and detention in civil prison of a defaulter shall be made unless the Tax Recovery Officer has issued and served a notice upon the defaulter calling upon him to appear before him on the date specified in the notice and to show cause why he should not be committed to the civil prison, and unless the Tax Recovery Officer, for reasons recorded in writing is satisfied. That the defaulter, has, or has had since the drawing up of the certificate by the Tax Recovery Officer, the means to pay the arrears or some substantial part thereof and refuses or neglects or has refused or neglected to pay the same. Rule 73(2) provides that notwithstanding anything contained in sub-rule (i), a warrant for the arrest of the defaulter may be issued by the Tax Recovery Officer if the Tax Recovery Officer is satisfied, by affidavit or otherwise, that with the object or effect of delaying the execution of the certificate, the defaulter is likely to abscond or leave the local limits of the jurisdiction of the Tax Recovery Officer. Sub-rule (3) of Rule 73 empowers the Tax Recovery Officer to issue a warrant for the arrest of the defaulter if appearance is not made in obedience to such a notice. Sub-rule (4) of Rule 73 contemplates bringing of the arrested person as soon as practicable and in any event within 24 hours of his arrest. However, regarding the proviso, the defaulter may be released in the event the amount entered in the

---

[805] (2002) III LLJ 779 P H
[806] 2000(3) R.S.J. 178

warrant of arrest as due, and the cost of the arrest to the officer arresting him is paid. Rule 74 provides for an opportunity to show cause by the defaulter as to why he should not be committed to civil prison. Rule 75 provides for custody pending hearing or the Tax Recovery Officer, who, however, may also release the arrested person on his furnishing security to his satisfaction for his appearance when required. An order of detention can be passed under Rule 76 regarding which the Tax Recovery Officer upon conclusion of the enquiry/order for the detention of the defaulter in the civil prison and that in that event cause him to be arrested if he is not already under arrest. The proviso appended to the said rule empowers the Tax Recovery Officer to give the defaulter an opportunity of satisfying the arrear before making the order of detention for a specified period not exceeding 15 days or release him on his furnishing security to his satisfaction for his appearance at the expiration of the specified period if the arrears are not so satisfied. Rule 77(1) provides for the period of detention and the proviso appended thereto specifies that the persons so detained shall be released if the amount mentioned in the warrant of detention is paid to the officer-in-charge of the civil prison or on the request of the Tax Recovery Officer on any ground other than the grounds mentioned in Rules 78 and 79. Rule 78 empowers the Tax Recovery Officer to release a defaulter upon being satisfied that he has disclosed the whole of his property and has placed it at the disposal of the Tax Recovery Officer and that he has not committed any act of bad faith.[807] By Order 21 Rule 30(e) of the Code of Civil Procedure, simultaneous execution both against the property and person of the judgment-debtor is allowed.[808]

Arrest and Detention in Civil Prison

As long as there is no dishonesty and *mala fides* on the part of the judgment-debtor to discharge his obligation, committing him to civil prison would amount to a violation of Article 11 of the International Covenant on Civil and Political Rights and Article 21 of the Constitution of India.[809] Power to arrest a person is a drastic power vested with the Recovery Officer under the Act by recourse to Rule 73 of Schedule II to the Income Tax Act, 1961 as enabled by s.8(G) of the Act. It is needless to state that the power of arrest is required to be strictly by law as it affects personal liberty enshrined under Article 21 of the constitution as held by the Supreme Court in *Jolly George Varghese and another v The Bank of Cochin*.[810] The *non obstante* clause

---

[807] *Gajendra Kumar Banthia v. Union of India*, 1996 222 ITR 632 Cal
[808] *Padrauna Rajkrishna Sugar Works Ltd. v Land Reforms Commissioner, UP and others*, 1969 AIR 897, 1969 SCR (3) 468
[809] *Jolly George Varghese and another v Bank of Cochin*, 1980 AIR 470, 1980 SCR (2) 913: (1980) 2 SCC 360.
[810] *R. Vijayendra Babu v K. Narayana*, 2012 LLJ KANT 2 303

in Sub-Rule 2 of Rule 73 mandates the Recovery Officer to be satisfied by affidavit or otherwise, that with the object of delaying the execution of the certificate the defaulter is likely to abscond or leave the local limits of the jurisdiction of the recovery officer then and then alone by recording reasons in writing an order of arrest and detention in civil prison of the defaulter is permissible.[811]

Woman cannot be arrested

A judgment debtor who is a woman enjoys a statutory protection against her arrest and detention in civil prison in execution of a decree for money given the embargo under s.56 of the Civil Procedure Code, 1908. Even a notice to show cause under Order 21, Rule 37 of the CPC cannot be issued to the judgment debtor who is a woman.[812]

Due process of law should be followed scrupulously

In *Kanaiyalal Prabhudas Maru v Regional Provident Fund Commissioner*,[813] held, before issuance of warrant of arrest against the defaulter under s.8B of the Act, the conditions specified in Rule 73(1)(a) and (b) of Part V of Schedule II to Part V Rule 73 are required to be complied with, and the non-compliance thereof vitiates the proceedings of issuance of warrant. Arrest and detention in prison by an order beyond the authority of law, or not supported by the due process of law will entitle the defaulter to get relief under Article 21 of the Constitution by way of a writ of *Habeas Corpus*.[814]

Inability to pay due to adverse market conditions – No Excuse

The inability of an employer to make the PF contributions due to adverse market conditions or defaulting customers etc. has been held as no excuse by the Karnataka High Court in *Chandan A. Rajan v Union of India and others*. In that case, the employer was put in prison under s.8-B(1)(b) of the Act for failure to pay provident fund contribution though he narrated the facts and circumstances of his default due to market recessions, slump in the off take, his customers' default in making payment, lack of funds and mounting interest liability, and as such he was compelled to defer the statutory obligations. The High Court upheld the action of

---

[811] R. Vijayendra Babu v K. Narayana, 2012 LLJ KANT 2 303
[812] VM. Abdul Hameed v Ramani, 2014 ILR KER 4 64
[813] 2002–1-LLJ-297
[814] Annamma Kunjacko v Tax Recovery Officer and others, 1967 64 ITR 85 Ker

the Provident Fund authority. Arrest and detention in civil prison for non-payment of provident fund dues is neither illegal nor unconstitutional.

Arrest – Not justified when appeal is pending

In *Jivraj Mehta Smarak Trust Sanchalit v Provident Fund Commissioner*,[815] the petitioner had challenged the assessment order before the EPF Appellate Tribunal and had also deposited 40% of the assessed dues under s.7-O of the Act. When the appeal was pending, the action of the Provident Fund Commissioner in issuing a warrant of arrest and freezing the bank of the petitioner was quashed.

Writ against Show Cause Notice of arrest (CP 25) – Premature

In *ATV Projects India Ltd. v Office of the Regional Provident Fund Commissioner, Mumbai*,[816] the Bombay High Court held that it is too premature to entertain the grievance of the petitioners about the show cause notice. The Recovery Officer is yet to apply his mind to the facts of the case. He is yet to hear the petitioners and the petitioners will have ample opportunity to put forth their say in the case before the officer concerned who is also in a position to assess the factual situation and to arrive at the proper finding on the materials to be placed by the petitioners in response to the show cause notice, bearing in mind the provisions of law contained in Rule 73, and thereupon to invite a proper order from the Recovery Officer in relation to the show cause notice issued by the Tax Recovery Officer requiring the petitioners to show cause against their arrest and detention in civil prison.

Director can be arrested

In *Sayan Ghosh and another v Regional Provident Fund Commissioner*,[817] the Calcutta High Court held that there is no bar under s.8B to the Recovery Officer recovering the amount due by attachment and sale of any movable and immovable property of the establishment as well as by the arrest of the employer and their detention in prison. This detention is not a detention under the finding of guilt under s. 14 but a mode of recovery similar to section 51 of the Civil Procedure Code.

Arrest – Compliance with Rule 73 of the IT Act

In *Vikram Poddar v Regional Provident Fund Commissioner*,[818] the High Court of Calcutta held that to recover any amount mentioned in s. 7-A of the Act, Rule 73

---

[815] 2004 (102) FLR 828, (2004) 3 GLR 2628, (2004) IIILLJ 990 Guj
[816] 2005(1) Mh.LJ 791: 2005(1) LLJ 1046: 2005(2) BCR 242: 2005(105) FLR 992
[817] W.P. No. 1095 of 1998
[818] (2001) IILLJ 518 Cal

of the Income Tax Act, 1961 should be strictly followed. According to the said rule, warrant of arrest cannot be issued unless the Recovery Officer, for reasons recorded in writing, is satisfied that the defaulter with the object or effect of obstructing the execution of the certificate, has, after the drawing up of the certificate by the Recovery Officer, dishonestly transferred, concealed, or removed any part of the property, or that the defaulter has or has had since the drawing up of the certificate by the Recovery Officer the means to pay the arrears or some substantial part thereof and refuses or neglects or has refused or neglected to pay the same. In the case of execution of certificates, the Calcutta High Court in *Sri Jagadish Roy v The Regional Provident Fund Commissioner, West Bengal and others*,[819] was of the view that the right to arrest the defaulter should not be exercised unless the Provident Fund authority is satisfied that he was neglecting to pay the dues despite his ability to do so or was acting in bad faith. Even the show-cause notice issued by the Recovery officer, if it does not reflect the grounds to justify the issuance of an arrest warrant, is liable to be quashed.[820]

In *Jugal K Jhunjhunwala v Assistant Provident Fund Commissioner*,[821] the Uttarakhand High Court held that the recovery of an outstanding amount under the Act should be made by attachment and sale of the property of the establishment. However, when amount recovered by sale of assets of the establishment falls short of the outstanding amount, outstanding balance amount can be recovered against the employer of the establishment. Without exhausting the remedy of attachment and sale of property for the realisation of the outstanding amount, no proceeding can be initiated against the employer of the establishment under the Act.

Recourse to arrest only when other modes of recovery fail

In *Sobhag Textile Ltd. v The Regional Provident Fund Commissioner, Haryana*,[822] the High Court of Punjab and Haryana held that sub-section (1) of s.8-B of the 1952 Act prescribes alternative modes of recovery of the arrears by a certificate issued by the authorised officer. Attachment or sale of movable or immovable property of the establishment or, as the case may be, and arrest of the employer and his detention in prison are two of the three modes which can be adopted by the Recovery Officer. Proviso appearing below clause (c) of s.8-B(1) of the 1952 Act lays down that attachment and sale of any property under s.8-B shall first

---

[819] (2006) 3 CAL LT 411 (HC)
[820] *Carona Ltd. and another v Regional Provident Fund Commissioner and others*, 2007 LLR 921 (Bom HC).
[821] 2014(3) CLR 470: 2014 LabLR 1212: 2014 LIC 4227: 2014(143) FLR 999: 2014(17) S.C.T. 839
[822] 2000(4) SCT 508 (P&H): 2000(3) RSJ 178

be effected against the properties of the establishment and proceedings against the property of the employer can be taken only if the amount due cannot be recovered from the properties of the establishment. However, there is nothing in the said proviso from which it can be inferred that the Recovery Officer is not entitled to have recourse to the mode prescribed in clause (b) of Section 8-B (1) before taking recourse in the sale of property under s.8-B (1)(a) of the Act. This legal position was reiterated by a Division Bench of the High Court of Punjab and Haryana in *Mohan Lal v Regional Provident Fund Commissioner*.[823]

A Division Bench of the Andhra Pradesh High Court, in *Regional Provident Fund Commissioner v Deccan Foam Plastics Pvt. Ltd.*,[824] held that under s.8B of the Act even the movable and immovable properties of the employer cannot be attached and sold for recovery of the arrears without first exhausting the remedy of attaching and bringing the properties of the establishment for sale, and if that is so, it would be absurd to hold that the employer can be arrested for the purpose for sending him to prison without even finding whether the attachment and sale of the properties of the establishment for realization of the arrears is sufficient or not. Thus, the arrest of the employer and his detention in prison cannot at all be made without exhausting the remedy of attachment and sale of properties of establishment for the realisation of amounts of arrears.

In *Hotel Horizon Pvt. Ltd. v Union of India*,[825] the Bombay High Court held that only when there is sufficient material available with the Recovery Officer or Executing Court that the assessee or the judgment debtor in the case of civil suit tries to escape the clutches of law by resorting to unfair means of selling his property clandestinely or surreptitiously or where he fails to pay the decretal amount though he has means to pay that amount, only in such cases the extreme step of arrest of the employer has to be resorted to.

The power of the recovery officer to attach and sale of immovable property is a drastic power, and unless and until the same is exhausted, the power to arrest the employer may not be available to the Recovery Officer. For instance, if steps are taken for the sale of the moveable/immovable property after attachment and such mode of recovery is sufficient to satisfy the amount mentioned in the certificate of recovery, there would not be any necessity to arrest the employer.[826]

---

[823] 2002(5) SLR 577: 2002(1) CLJ(Service) 364: 2002(3) S.C.T. 350: 2002(3) PLR 1: 2002 LIC 2602: 2002(4) RSJ 402: 2002(2) RLR 129
[824] 2005 LIC 2534: 2005(1) ALT 645: 2005(105) FLR 1184
[825] 2007(3) LLJ 584: 2008 BCR 614: 2007 LIC 3494
[826] *D.R. Venkatesh v Regional P.F. Commissioner, Hyderabad and another* (2004) III LLJ 952 AP

Negligence to pay – Arrest

In *Ali v Recovery Officer, Employees' Provident Fund Organisation*,[827] the Kerala High Court held that Sections 8, 8B and 8-G, if read together, would show that a defaulter can be arrested only on the following conditions: (i) the defaulter with the object or effect of obstructing the execution of the certificate, has after the drawing up of the certificate by the Tax Recovery Officer, dishonestly transferred, concealed, or moved any part of his property, or (ii) the defaulter has or has had since the drawing up of the certificate by Tax Recovery Officer the means to pay the arrears or some substantial part thereof and refuses or neglects or has refused or neglected to pay the same." In the absence of any finding of having sufficient means of the petitioner to satisfy the certificate dues and the substantial part thereof, the finding regarding the petitioner's neglect and failure to satisfy the certificate dues becomes illusory.[828] In *Nath Kumar v Assistant Commissioner, Employees' Provident Fund*,[829] the Calcutta High Court observed, "Para 72 of the Second Schedule to the Income Tax Act provides a right of hearing to a person proposed to be committed to civil prison. This paragraph stipulates that the defaulter would be 'called upon to appear before the Tax Recovery Officer and to Show-Cause why he should not be committed to civil prison.' The order of the Officer has to contain reasons. His satisfaction has to be recorded on two points. First, the defaulter with the object or intent of obstructing the execution of the certificate was dishonestly transferring the assets. Alternatively, he was refusing or neglecting to pay the amount."

Element of dishonesty to evade payment necessary for arrest

In *Kanaiyalal Prabhudas Maru and others v Regional Provident Fund Commissioner, Maharashtra & Goa and others*,[830] held, the warrant of arrest was vitiated due to the failure of the competent authority under the Act to record its satisfaction, with reasons in writing, that would demonstrate, that the conditions which are specified in Clauses (a) or (b) of sub-rule(1) of Rule 73 of the Rules contained in Schedule II to the Income Tax Act, 1961 have been satisfied. The authority, before issuing a warrant of arrest, should be satisfied that the defaulter had either dishonestly transferred, concealed or removed any part of his property or that despite having the means to pay the arrears, had refused and neglected to do so.

---

[827] 2007 LabIC 899
[828] *Jagdish Roy v Regional P.F. Commissioner, West Bengal and others* (2006) 3 CALLT 411 HC, 2006 (4) CHN 605
[829] 2016(2) Cal. L.T. 303: 2016(3) WBLR 170: 2016(2) CLR 1020: 2016(150) FLR 594: 2016 LabLR 1118: 2016(4) Cal. H.C.N. 369: 2015(30) S.C.T. 470
[830] 2002 I LLJ 297

Relying on the above case, the Calcutta High Court in *Sri Jagadish Roy v Regional Provident Fund Commissioner, West Bengal and others*,[831] held that Rule 73(1)(b) can be invoked only when the defaulter despite having sufficient means, failed and neglected to satisfy the certificate dues or any substantial part thereof. Mere failure and neglect to pay the certificate dues cannot attract the provision of Rule 73(1)(b) as neglect or refusal implicates an element of bad faith reflecting a dishonest attempt to evade the payment of dues. The Calcutta High Court placed reliance on *Bikram Poddar v Regional P.F. Commissioner*[832] and *Kanaiyalal Prabhudas Maru and others v Regional P.F. Commissioner*.

Arrest cannot be made when property is already under attachment

The legislature makes the employer personally liable for paying the PF arrears only in the event of the properties of the establishment being insufficient. The personal liability, therefore, is not straightaway attracted. There is no dispute on the aspect that the three modes of recovery mentioned in s.8B of the Act are mutually exclusive. However, the Recovery officer, having resorted to the first mode of recovery, namely, attachment, could not issue a notice of arrest. The proviso clearly says that the attachment and sale of any property under this section shall first be effected against the properties of the establishment and where such attachment and sale is insufficient for recovering the whole of the amount of arrears specified in the certificate, the Recovery Officer may take such proceedings against the property of the employer for recovery of the whole or any part of such arrears.[833]

Hearing of the defaulter – Necessary before arrest

In *ATV Projects India Ltd. v Office of the Regional Provident Fund Commissioner*,[834] the Bombay High Court held that when the Recovery Officer was yet to hear the defaulter and the latter has ample opportunity to put forth their say in the case before the Recovery Officer, interference of the High Court at this stage is not warranted.

Managing Director cannot be arrested for default

In *Vijay Aggarwal v The Recovery Officer*,[835] the High Court of Punjab and Haryana held that 'if the amount for recovery by attachment of the immovable or movable properties of the Company could not be made, then the provisions

---

[831] 2007(112) FLR 216: 2006(2) CalLJ 506: 2006(3) Cal. L.T. 411: 2006(6) Cal. H.C.N. 605
[832] 2001(1) CHN 476
[833] *D.R. Venkatesh v The Regional P.F. Commissioner*, (2004)III LLJ 952 AP
[834] 2005(2) Bom. CR 242
[835] 2009(3) S.C.T. 686

for arrest could be exercised only against the employer, which in this case is the Company. If the company itself could not be arrested in the absence of any specific provision empowering the authorities to proceed personally against the Director, there was no scope for proceedings against the Director of the Company. The provisions that allow for the imposition of penalties and the mode of inflicting punishment for the offences committed by the Companies provided under s.14 and 14-A of the Provident Fund Act contain distinct provisions relating to criminal prosecution that would extend punishment with imprisonment. It must be noticed that the impugned proceedings are not taken under s.14-A by pinning down the Director as a person responsible to the Company in the conduct of the business of the Company. The recovery proceedings should be issued only against the employer which in this case cannot be said to be a Director or the Managing Director.'

Karta of the HUF cannot be arrested for default

In *Kapurchand Shrimal v Tax Recovery Officer, Hyderabad*,[836] the facts of the case were that a Hindu Undivided Family committed default in the payment of income tax and a recovery certificate was issued under Rule 76 of Schedule II of the Income Tax Act, 1961. The Tax Recovery Officer directed the arrest and detention in prison of the Karta[837] of the family for non- payment of tax. Setting aside the order of arrest, the Supreme Court observed: "The Legislature having treated a Hindu undivided family as a taxable entity distinct from the individual members constituting it, and proceeding for assessment and recovery of tax having been taken against the Hindu undivided family, it was not open to the Tax Recovery Officer to initiate proceedings against the manager of the Hindu undivided family for his arrest and detention." The manager by his status is competent to represent the Hindu undivided family, but on that account, he cannot for s.222 of the Act of 1961 be deemed to be the assessee when the assessment is made against the Hindu undivided family and certificate for recovery is also issued against the family.

In *Kapurchand Shrimal v Tax Recovery Officer, Hyderabad*,[838] a Division Bench of the Andhra Pradesh High Court held that the alienation to the property under attachment should be void as per Rule 16(2) of the Schedule II to the Income Tax Act. In fact, it is held that even before the attachment, after the issuance of a certificate by the Authorised Officer to the Recovery Officer, any dealing about the property by the defaulter is prohibited by Rule 16(1) of the Schedule II to the

---

[836] 1969 AIR 682, 1969 SCR (1) 691
[837] *Karta* is that adult male coparcener of a HUF who has the responsibility and authority to manage the affairs and assets of the HUF.
[838] 1967 64 ITR 1 [AP]

Income Tax Act. The Bench observed: "We are, therefore, of the view that once a notice has been served and as a matter of fact, even before any attachment is made, the defaulter cannot deal with his properties in any manner. If there is any dealing with the property, whether movable or immovable, after the receipt of the notice, the defaulter would be contravening the provisions of [the] rule." The restriction placed under the rule is a reasonable restriction, and it is not a violation of the fundamental rights guaranteed under Article 19(1)(g) to carry on business or to hold property.[839]

ATTACHMENT OF BUSINESS AND APPOINTMENT OF RECEIVER

Attachment of business and appointment of receiver – purpose of

As regards the power relating to attachment of the administration of a business is concerned, the whole purpose seems to be to continue the business as before, with a view to generate income and thereby provide scope for the recovery of the arrears while simultaneously sustaining the operation of the business activities without bringing it to a grinding halt.[840]

Attachment of business should precede appointment of receiver

There should be an order of attachment of business under the said Rule 69(2), by the Recovery Officer prohibiting the defaulter from transferring or changing the business etc., before the appointment of a Receiver to manage the said business. In other words, the attachment of a business should precede the appointment of a Receiver for running the said business. Therefore, Para 69 of 2nd schedule postulates two independent actions in the matter of attachment of business and appointment of Receiver. The attachment of a business when mandated to be made by a separate proceedings, it is in contemplation of one form of notice to the defaulter to make him realise that the resort to recovery through such a mode has become so very imminent that in order to get oneself relieved of such an extreme mode of recovery, all efforts should be made by the employer to discharge the arrears so as to enable the Recovery Officer to resort to Para 72 for withdrawal of its attempt to take over the management of the business. In such circumstances any resort had by the Recovery Officer by abruptly depriving of the employer of its business by initiating proceedings without giving a reasonable opportunity to the

---

[839] *Recovery Officer, EPFO v The Inspector General of Registration and others* W.P.(MD)No.11726 of 2010 Decision dated September 30, 2013 (Mad. HC)

[840] *Guru Vittal P. and others v Regional Provident Fund Commissioner and others*, 2001 (90) FLR 649, (2001) III LLJ 1244 Mad, (2001) 2 MLJ 287

employer would be wholly unjustified and cannot be resorted to in such an abrupt and arbitrary manner.[841]

Recovery – Business should not be paralysed

In *Radhamani v Enforcement Officer, Kollam*,[842] the High Court of Kerala held that merely because the employer or his transferee is liable to pay any arrear to the Employees' Provident Fund, that does not mean that the employer or his transferee should be prohibited from running the establishment. That is not what is meant by Section 8A or 8B of the Act. The purpose of attachment is to bring the movables for sale and to recover the dues to the extent possible. That should not result in the employer or his transferee being prohibited from running the factory, which would affect not only the employer or his transferee but the employees as well. Paralyzing the establishment is not what is meant by the process of recovery. As regards the power relating to attachment of the administration of a business is concerned, the whole purpose seems to be to continue the business as before, with a view to generate income and thereby provide scope or the recovery of the arrears while simultaneously sustaining the operation of the business activities without bringing it to a grinding halt.[843]

Appointment of Receiver

Appointment of Receiver is governed by the rules under Part IV of Schedule II to the Income Tax Act. Rule 69 of the IT Act reads, (1) where the property of a defaulter consists of business, the Tax Recovery Officer may attach the business and appoint a person as Receiver to manage the business. (2) Attachment of business under this rule shall be made by an order prohibiting the defaulter from transferring or charging the business in any way and prohibiting all persons from taking any benefit under such transfer or charge, intimating that the business has been attached under this rule. A copy of the order of attachment shall be served on the defaulter, and another copy shall be affixed on a conspicuous part of the premises in which the business is carried on and on the notice board of the office of the Tax Recovery Officer.

Under Rule 73 of Part V of the Second Schedule, it is expressly provided that no order for the arrest and detention in civil prison of a defaulter should be made unless the Tax Recovery Officer issued and served a notice on the defaulter calling

---

[841] *Guru Vittal P. and others v Regional Provident Fund Commissioner and others* 2001 (90) FLR 649, (2001) III LLJ 1244 Mad, (2001) 2 MLJ 287
[842] 2011 LIC 2965: 2011(4) S.C.T. 554: 2011(1) Ker L.J. 9
[843] *Guru Vittal P.and others v Regional P.F. Commissioner* 2001 (90) FLR 649, (2001) III LLJ 1244 Mad, (2001) 2 MLJ 287

upon him to appear before him on the date specified in the notice to show cause why he should not be committed to civil prison. There is no such provision made in the matter of appointment of a Receiver. Rule 72 of Part IV of the Second Schedule stipulates that the attachment and management under the preceding rules can be withdrawn at any time at the discretion of the Tax Recovery Officer or if the arrears are discharged by the receipt of such profits and rents or otherwise paid.

Procedure for appointment of Receiver

The Recovery Officer has been vested with ample powers to recover the arrears of contribution by resorting to one or several modes of recoveries provided under the Act. The same did not mean that the first respondent should act in haste and without preparing the necessary basis for resorting to such extreme step of the appointment of a Receiver. The attachment of a business should precede the appointment of a Receiver for running the said business. While resorting to the attachment of business and consequential appointment of a Receiver for running of the said business, there should and must be a fair and minimum opportunity to the concerned defaulter before resorting to such mode of recovery.[844]

In *Kanhaiyalal v Dr.D.R. Banaji and others*,[845] the appellant was the auction-purchaser of the property at a revenue sale held under the provisions of the Berar Land Revenue Code, 1928, for recovery of land revenue. The property at the time of the attachment and sale was in possession of a Receiver appointed under Order 40 Rule 1 of the CPC. No notice to the receiver was given of the sale of the property, nor was any leave of the Court taken for the sale. Declaring the sale as illegal, the Supreme Court observed, the general rule that property in *custodia legis* through its duly appointed Receiver is exempt from judicial process except to the extent that the leave of that Court has been obtained, is based on a very sound reason of public policy, namely, that there should be no conflict of jurisdiction between different Courts. If a Court has exercised its power to appoint a Receiver of a particular property, it has done so to preserve the property for the benefit of the rightful owner as judicially determined. If other Courts or Tribunals of coordinate or exclusive jurisdiction were to permit proceedings to go on independently of the Court which has placed the custody of the property in the hands of the Receiver, there was a likelihood of confusion in the administration of justice and a possible conflict of jurisdiction."

---

[844] *Guru Vittal P.and others v Regional P.F. Commissioner* 2001 (90) FLR 649, (2001) III LLJ 1244 Mad, (2001) 2 MLJ 287
[845] 1958 AIR 725

COMPANY UNDER LIQUIDATION

S.446(1) of the Companies Act mandates that when a winding up order has been made, or the Official Liquidator has been appointed as provisional liquidator, no suit or any other legal proceeding shall be commenced, or if pending at the date of the winding up order, shall be proceeded with, against the company, except by leave of the Court and subject to such terms as the Courts may impose. Recovery proceedings under the Income Tax Act is a legal proceeding within the meaning of s.446(1) of the Companies Act, and therefore, such recovery proceeding cannot be commenced or proceeded with against the Company in liquidation without the leave of the Court. Any recovery proceeding in such cases without prior leave of the Court would tantamount to contempt of court. However, this provision does not constrain the assessment of the arrears, and hence no leave of Court is necessary for any assessment proceeding of the company.[846] The Supreme Court, in *S.V. Kondaskar, Official Liquidator v VM. Deshpande, Income Tax Officer*,[847] held that there is no provision by which the liquidation court should be vested with the power to stop assessment proceedings for determining the amount of tax payable by the company which is being wound up.

Filing of additional claim with the Liquidator barred by Order 2, Rule 2 of CPC

Order 2 Rule 2 of Code of Civil Procedure states that where a plaintiff omits to sue in respect of or intentionally relinquishes, any portion of his claim, he shall not afterwards sue in respect of the portion so omitted or relinquished. In *Usha Spinning and Weaving Mills Pvt. Ltd. v EPF Appellate Tribunal and another*,[848] the High Court of Punjab and Haryana held that where the demand against a company in liquidation has become statutorily final, any further demand is barred under Order 2, Rule 2 of Civil Procedure Code.

Liquidator cannot pay the Provident Fund dues directly to the workers

In *Vishwanath Namdeo Patil and others v Official Liquidator and others*, the Bombay High Court held that the provident fund contributions could not be claimed by the workmen directly from the Official Liquidator, but the claim will have to be made by the Provident Fund authorities. The Official Liquidator cannot merely take a stand that the provident fund dues will be paid as and when the Provident Fund

---

[846] *Official Liquidator, High Court v Commissioner of Income Tax, West Bengal* AIR 1970 Cal 349, 1971 80 ITR 108 Cal
[847] AIR 1972 SC 878, 1972 42 CompCas 168 SC, 1972 83 ITR 685 SC, (1972) 1 SCC 438, 1972 2 SCR 965
[848] 2013(2)CLR 493(P&H)

Commissioner makes an application. Even if the Commissioner has not moved an application, the Official Liquidator should move the provident fund authorities and assist the workers in the recovery of their dues.

Recovery from Sick Undertakings

In *Gowri Spinning Mills (P) Ltd. v Assistant Provident Fund Commissioner, Salem and another*,[849] a Full Bench of the Madras High Court held that the dues payable under the provisions of the EPF Act are payable by the Company despite the fact that the proceedings regarding the said company are pending under the Sick Industrial Companies (SP) Act, 1985. The Court observed, "...both the statutes are special statutes. Whereas the object of enactment of the SICA was to provide for the revival and rehabilitation of sick industrial companies, the object of the EPF Act, as indicated hereinbefore, was a measure to provide social security to the employees. The contribution of the employees, as well as the employer towards provident fund, is not a tax due. It is also not an amount recoverable under a contract. The money, which has been deducted from the wages of the employees as well as the amounts, which the employer is required to pay as its contribution, belong to the employees and constitute their rightful and just entitlement for the eventual payment of provident fund benefits."

The Bombay High Court took a similar decision in *Baburao P Tawade and others v HES Ltd., Bombay and others*.[850] It was held that notwithstanding that the company has been either declared sick and being revived in a scheme, or its matter is pending before the Board or before the appellate authority, yet the money is liable to be recovered under the EPF Act against the said company and the company will not get protection under s.22 of the SICA, 1985. The Allahabad High Court has again held a similar view in *Modi Industries Ltd. v Additional Labour Commissioner*.[851]

In *Jalpac India Ltd. v Regional Provident Fund Commissioner*,[852] High Court of Uttarakhand observed that although the Madras High Court, Bombay High Court and the Allahabad High Court in their judgements, have not explicitly dealt with s.32 of the SICA, 1985 while deciding the controversy, yet by implication all these judgements imply that a *non-obstante* clause as contained in the 1985 Act will not protect a sick industry qua the legitimate claim of the workmen under the 1952 Act.

---

[849] [2006] 4 MLJ 1261
[850] (1997) III LLJ 265
[851] (1994) I LLJ 482 All
[852] 2013(1) U.D. 609: 2013(21) S.C.T. 204

In *Maruthi Textiles v Board for Industrial & Financial Reconstruction and others*,[853] the Andhra Pradesh High Court was considering whether the sale of properties belonging to the petitioner-Company (a sick unit) by the EPFO for recovery of Provident Fund arrears is vitiated by s.20(4) of the Sick Industrial Companies (Special Provisions)Act, 1985 when winding up was ordered by the BIFR. The Court, taking into consideration the labour welfare elements of the Act, held that even after winding up proceedings are concluded, the dues payable to the EPF are to be cleared first before clearing any other debts. The Court further held that non-compliance of s.20 (4) of the SICA would not affect the purchaser's interests. However, the Court directed the EPFO to approach the BIFR duly intimating the sale of the assets and seek its ratification for the appropriation of sale proceeds towards the Provident Fund dues.

OTHER MODES OF RECOVERY

S. 8-F(3)(vi) of the EPF Act would cover the situation, where a person to whom notice has been issued, objects to the notice by a statement on oath that the sum demanded or any part thereof is not due to the employer or that he does not hold any money for or on account of the employer and if it is found that the said statement was false in any material particular, such person shall be personally liable to the officer authorised to that extent of his own liability to the employer on the date of notice, or to the extent of the employers liability for any sum due under this Act, whichever is less.

The provisions of Section 8F(3) of the EPF Act provide for machinery to recover amounts which are due from an establishment by directly recovering the same from its debtors. Thus if any person owes any amount or an asset to the establishment, the authorised officers of the Provident Fund Organisation can directly recover the same from such persons.

Section 8F (3) – Inquiry is mandatory

In *Ferro Concrete Construction (I)Pvt Ltd. v Regional Provident Fund Commissioner*,[854] the Madhya Pradesh High Court pointed out the similarity between Section 8F(3) of the EPF Act and s.226(3) of the Income Tax Act, and quoted the observations of the Supreme Court, in *Biharilal Ramcharan v Income Tax Officer*,[855] in which the scope and ambit of s.226(3) of the Income Tax Act came up for discussion. The Supreme Court held that it is mandatory on the part of the Recovery Officer

---

[853] 2014(3) LLN 49: 2014(143) FLR 209: 2014(5) Andh LD 415: 2014(12) S.C.T. 559
[854] 2002 (93) FLR 883, (2002) I LLJ 986 MP
[855] 1984 (131) ITR, 129, 136 (SC)

before passing any order under these two sections to hold an inquiry after giving due opportunity to the person concerned, allow him to state on oath whether he has to pay any amount to the defaulter and if so under what head, against which transaction or whether he holds any money on account of defaulter and if so, how much, whether any money is due or not and if so, its extent. Thus, holding of an inquiry into the requirement of s.8F (3) (iv) is mandatory, and any deviation from the compliance will result in vitiating the order.

All future deposits liable for attachment

In *A.P. Enterprises Pvt. Ltd. v Regional Provident Fund Commissioner*, the High Court of Punjab and Haryana clarified that 'not only on the date when the notice is served but subsequently also if any money becomes due to the employer or he subsequently holds money for or on account of the employer jointly, the same has to pay such amount to the authorised officer forthwith if it is available on the date the notice is received or on the date the same becomes due.' This condition, however, is limited to the amount which has to be recovered. Once the said amount as has been specified in the certificate of recovery issued against the employer is satisfied, no further remittance has to be made to the authorised officer.

Garnishee order

No attachment can be made when there is no existing debt due by the garnishee to the judgment debtor, and if the judgment debtor has already parted with his interest in the debt by assignment or created an equitable charge in respect of the same in favour of another person, the attaching creditor acquires no more substantial rights than his debtor.[856]

In *Vijaya Bank v Employees' Provident Fund Organisation*,[857] the Delhi High Court held that the provisions of s.8F(3) of the EPF Act provides for machinery to recover amounts which are due from an establishment by directly recovering the same from its debtors. Thus if any person owes any amount or an asset to the establishment, the authorised officers of the Provident Fund Organisation can directly recover the same from such persons. The proceedings under s.8F(3) of the Act are similar to garnishee proceedings and the authorised officer of the Employees Provident Fund Organisation is placed in a position similar to that of a garnisher, and can directly reach out to the funds owed to or held on account of the establishment by other persons. However, the precondition to proceeding under

---

[856] *Canara Bank v Tecon Engineers and others* 1994 207 ITR 691 Ker
[857] 2015(144) FLR 103: 2015(1) CLR 485: 2015(1) BankJ 672: 2015(1) D.R.T.C. 226: 2014(213) DLT 741: 2014(50) R.C.R.(Civil) 220

s.8F(3) is a conclusion that the third parties hold money for or on account of the establishment, which is liable to pay the provident fund dues.

Un-utilized Bank loan cannot be attached

The un-availed portion of a bank loan cannot be termed 'an amount due from the bank' to the employer. Hence, the bank cannot be said to be in the position of a garnishee in respect of the unutilized portion of the overdraft or cash credit facility and hence, the same cannot be attached under s.8F of the Act.[858]

S.8, 8-B and 8-G should be read together

S.8-G says explicitly that the provisions of the Second and Third Schedule to the Income Tax Act, 1961 and the Income Tax (Certificate Proceedings) Rules, 1962, as in force from time to time, shall apply with necessary modifications as if the said provisions and the rules referred to the arrears of the amount mentioned in s.8 of the EPF Act instead of to the Income Tax. So, Section 8, 8-B and 8-G have to be read together. If so read, the provisions of the Second and Third Schedule to the Income Tax Act, 1961 and the Income Tax (Certified Proceedings) Rules, 1962 will have to be applied.[859]

S.8F (3) is counterpart of S.226(3) of Income Tax Act

S.8F(3) which consists of ten sub-sections (i) to (x) is a counterpart of s.226(3) of the Income Tax Act. These two sections are identically worded and are enacted for one object. It is as if s.226(3) of the Income-Tax Act which also consists of ten sub-sections (i) to (x) is bodily lifted and inserted in the EPF Act as s.8F(3) (i) to (x). Therefore the interpretation of s.226(3) of Income Tax Act made by the Supreme Court explaining its scope and ambit will equally apply to cases falling in s.8F(3) of the EPF Act.[860]

The scope and ambit of s.226(3) of the Income-Tax Act came under the judicial scrutiny in the case of *Biharilal Ramcharan v Income-Tax Officer*.[861] The Supreme Court held that it is mandatory on the part of the Recovery Officer before passing any order under this section to hold an inquiry after giving due opportunity to the person concerned, allow him to state on oath whether he has to pay any amount to the defaulter and if so under what head, against which transaction or whether he holds any money on account of defaulter and if so how much, whether any money

---

[858] *Canara Bank v Regional PF Commissioner*, 1998 II LLJ 839 (Karn. HC)
[859] *Ali v Recovery Officer, EPF Organisation* 2007 LablC 899
[860] *Ferro Concrete Construction India Ltd. v Regional Provident Fund Commissioner and others*, 2002 LLJ MP 1 986: 2002 FLR 1 883
[861] 1984 (131) ITR, 129, 136 (SC)

is due or not and if so, its extent. It is only after the person concerned files and makes a statement on oath on any of the facts referred supra, then depending upon the statement so made, the Recovery Officer will proceed to pass an order. In other words, holding of inquiry to the requirement of s.8F(3)(vi) is mandatory, and any deviation from the compliance will result in vitiating the order.[862] Such a notice and such an enquiry are required to be afforded to the person, who is allegedly holding the money belonging to the employer. There is no necessity to issue any notice to the employer.[863]

The only exception is that the amount exempted from attachment under section 60 of the code of civil procedure, 1908, is protected by way of this provision.

EMPLOYER CANNOT REDUCE THE WAGES, ETC

A careful reading of s.12 shows that the employer is not to reduce wages, etc. In other words, no employer because of his liability for payment of contribution can reduce the various benefits such as old age pension, gratuity, provident fund or life insurance which the employee would have been entitled to under the terms of his employment. In the instant case, under the original scheme, what was provided for the employees was 10% contribution. Merely because the Act says the contribution will be at 8% such a reduction is not warranted. If the contention of the respondent is accepted, it will render the benefit conferred under s.12 of the Act illusory. There is a strict direction that the employer shall not be allowed to reduce his contribution to statutory level. S.12 is absolute in its terms.[864]

A benignant provision must receive a benignant construction. The total quantum of benefits like old age pension, gratuity, or provident fund, shall not be reduced by reason only of the liability of the employer for payment of a contribution to the fund. The section prevails over the Trust Deed. The provident fund accrues by legal force, and s.12 overrides any agreement authorising deduction.

---

[862] *Ferro Concrete Construction India Ltd. v Regional Provident Fund Commissioner and others*, 2002 LLJ MP 1 986: 2002 FLR 1 883
[863] *Sri Ganapathy Mills v Regional Provident Fund Commissioner and others*, W.P(MD)No.2905 of 2007, decided on Nov25, 2008 (Mad. HC (Madurai))
[864] *Regional P.F. Commissioner v Harihar Polyfibres*, (1995) III LLJ (Suppl)862 (Kant.)

Chapter XV
INSPECTORS

POWERS OF THE INSPECTOR

The Act does not provide as to what the Inspector will do after the inspection. It only empowers him to do the things mentioned in s.13. There is nothing to show that he has to place the report before the Commissioner or he has to issue any notice. In *Regional Provident Fund Commissioner v Lux Hosiery Industries Ltd*,[865] the Calcutta High Court observed, "when the legislation is enacted, and certain powers are given, the powers are meant to be exercised. It cannot become redundant or rendered into oblivion because it does not provide any specific rules. The Act prescribes for framing of rules in Section 21. At the same time, the scheme also provides for framing of rules. We are told that no such rules have been framed. In the circumstances, we are to give a harmonious construction of the provisions of the Act to interpret s.13 as to the power conferred by it on the officers mentioned therein under s.13."

In *Regional Provident Fund Commissioner v Lux Hosiery Industries Ltd*,[866] the Calcutta High Court held that mere issue of a notice by the Inspector does not create any liability on the employer except raising a dispute if he disputes the applicability of the Act. When such a dispute is raised, the Inspector has to place the matter before the authority under s.7-A together with his report and then s.7-A is invoked and the entire process under s.7-A is to be undergone. In *Indian Chamber of Commerce and Industry v Regional Provident Fund Commissioner*,[867] Kerala High Court held that even if exemption is granted under s.17 (1) of the Act, authorities under the Act can still conduct regular inspections to ensure compliance of the conditions of exemption and it is only if compliance of conditions is made, the exempted establishment will be entitled to continue enjoying the benefit of exemption.

Issuance of Notice

In *J & J Dechane v Regional Provident Fund Commissioner and another*,[868] a Division Bench of the Andhra Pradesh High Court rejected the argument that s.13 does not

---

[865] 2005 LIC 1998: 2004(4) Cal. H.C.N. 531
[866] 2005 LIC 1998: 2004(4) Cal. H.C.N. 531
[867] 2015 LabLR 577: 2015(3) LLN 719: 2015 LIC 2230: 2015(147) FLR 284: 2015(1) KHC 715: 2015(6) S.C.T. 659
[868] (1960) ILLJ 765 AP

give the Inspectors the power to decide when there is a dispute and that it is an arbitrary exercise of the powers to the prejudice of the employer. The appellant invited references to the corresponding provisions of the Employees' State Insurance Act, 1948 and the Minimum Wages Act, 1948 which provide for adjudication of disputes and claims. The High Court declined to accept the reasoning stating that the test of reasonableness, wherever prescribed, should be applied to each statute and no abstract standard, or general pattern of reasonableness can be laid down as applicable to all cases. Held, there is no unreasonableness or arbitrariness in s.13 which confers certain powers on the inspector to implement the provisions of the Act.

Under s.13, the appropriate Government shall appoint by notification in the Official Gazette Inspectors of the Act and the Scheme including Pension or the Insurance Scheme. Under s.13(2) of the Act, the Inspector so appointed has been empowered to inquire into the correctness of any information furnished or to ascertain whether any of the provisions of the Act have complied.

Appointment by State Government does not violate Article 258-A

Article 258 provides for the power of the Union to confer powers on States in specified cases. The President may, with the consent of the Government of a State, entrust either conditionally or unconditionally to that Government or to its officer's functions about any matter to which the executive power of the Union extends. In *Sree Gokulam Sizing Mills v Regional Provident Fund Commissioner and others*,[869] the Madras High Court dismissed the contention that the notification issued by the State Government appointing the officers of the Provident Fund Department as Inspectors under s.13 without the consent of the Central Government is in violation of Article 258A of the Constitution. The High Court observed that the petition itself is based on a wrong notion that the officers of the EPF Department were appointed by the Central Government and therefore the State Government by exercise of its powers under s.13 cannot notify those offices, and clarified that the officers of the EPFO (except the Central Provident Fund Commissioner and the Financial Advisor and Chief Accounts Officer) are appointed by the Central Board of Trustees in terms of s.5-D(3) of the Act, and hence there is no violation of Article 258-A of the Constitution.

No Suit against Inspectors without prior Notice under S.80 CPC

In *Union of India v Narayan Bannappa Pakkanavar*,[870] the Karnataka High Court held that the appropriate Government appoints a Provident Fund Inspector and that

---

[869] (2011) (4) LLJ 640 (Mad.)
[870] 1989 Lab IC 854 (Kant.)

Government controls his services. He performs public duties. Hence, notwithstanding that he is paid from the Central Provident Fund and not by the Government, he is a public officer within the definition contained in s.2(17)(h) of the Civil Procedure Code. Therefore a suit filed without notice under s.80 of the CPC, for restraining him from enforcing the provisions of the Act, is not maintainable.

Search and Seizure – No Violation of Article 20(3)

In *M.P. Sharma v Satish Chandra*,[871] the Supreme Court held that unless there is a formal accusation, any statement or information given would not be hit by Article 20(3) of the Constitution. Ordinarily, an enquiry made by an inspector to ascertain that the provisions of the Act have been complied with would not amount to a formal accusation and as such the enquiry could not be hit by Article 20(3) of the Constitution. The Court further held that the guarantee under Article 20(3) would be available to persons against whom a First Information Report has been recorded as accused therein. It would extend to any compulsory process for the production of evidentiary documents which are reasonably likely to support a prosecution against them. However, there is nothing unconstitutional in Section 96 of the Code of Criminal Procedure which provides for 'search and seizure' of documents on failure to produce documents in compliance with a summons for production under Section 94 of the Code as there is no prohibition in our Constitution against search and seizure."

Search and Seizure – Not a testimonial compulsion under Article 20(3)

In *Mohammed Hussain v Provident Fund Inspector*,[872] a Division Bench of the Madhya Pradesh High Court, in discussing the question of search warrants issued by Magistrates for production of documents in the possession of the accused, remarked that, "the constitutional protection under Article 20(3) is not defeated by the statutory provisions for searches contained in Sections 94 and 96, Criminal Procedure Code. Searches are under the authority of a Magistrate (excepting in the limited class of cases falling under Section 165 of the Cr.P.C). Therefore, issue of a search warrant is normally the judicial function of the Magistrate. When such judicial function is interposed between the individual and the officer's authority for search, no circumvention thereby of the fundamental right is to be assumed." The Court further held that, "having regard to the historical background regarding the Indian Criminal Procedure law regarding searches, interposition of the judicial function while ordering searches and the person to whom the orders regarding

---

[871] AIR 1954 SC 300
[872] AIR 1957 Madh-B 68: 1957 CriLJ 195

searches are addressed, searches are not tantamount to testimonial compulsion to the accused persons and for that reason there is no invasion of any fundamental right guaranteed under Article 20(3)."

Search and Seizure governed by S.94 of the new Criminal Procedure Code of 1973

Sub-Section 2(B) of s.13 stipulates that the provisions of the Code of Criminal Procedure, 1898 (as they apply to any search or seizure made under the warrant issued under s.98 of the said Code) shall apply to any search or seizure to be made in terms of sub-section (2) of s.13. However, the old Criminal Procedure Code of 1898 was repealed and replaced by the Code of Criminal Procedure, 1973, with effect from 1.4.1974 (without concurrent amendment of the corresponding provision in the EPF Act). Therefore, references to s.98 of the old code of 1898 should be construed as references to s.94 of the new Code of 1973.

Testimonial compulsion under Article 20(3)

In *State v Prabhu Singh and others*,[873] the facts were that prosecution complaints were filed against the Chairman and Managing Director of Loharu Motor Service Pvt. Ltd., and the complainant Inspector did not examine any evidence in support of his case, but relied solely on the records kept by the employer (accused) and applied to the Court under s.94 of the Cr.P.C for production of the records by the accused. The accused resisted the application given the prohibition under Article 20(3) of the Constitution against testimonial compulsion and that they could not be forced to produce the relevant documentary evidence against themselves. The trial Court upheld their objection holding that the accused could not be compelled to be witnesses against themselves and in the absence of any other material to support the case, acquitted them. Upholding the decision, the Punjab and Haryana High Court observed that where an order under s.94 of Cr.P.C. to an accused person, it is apparently an order compelling him to produce documents which the prosecution seeks to use as evidence against him, which is not permissible under Article 20(3) of the Constitution.

---

[873] 1964 CriLJ 199

Chapter XVI

PENAL PROVISIONS

PROSECUTION CASES

Constitutional validity of penal provisions

In *T. Marimuthu Handloom Factory and others v The Regional Provident Fund Commissioner*,[874] the Madras High Court relying on the Supreme Court decision in *Pannalal Binjraj and others v Union of India and others*,[875] observed that there is a broad distinction between discretion which has to be exercised with regard to a fundamental right guaranteed by the Constitution and other rights given by the statutes. It was laid down in that case that if the statute deals with a right which is not fundamental, the statute can take it away. However, a fundamental right the statute cannot take away. The determination of the amount payable by the employer under the provisions of the Act does not affect any fundamental right of the employer. Even if s.7-A can be constructed as one imposing restrictions on the right to carry on trade or profession, it does not impose any unreasonable restriction on the rights guaranteed under Art. 14 of the Constitutions of India.

Period of Limitation and the Concept of 'Continuing Offence'

S.468 of Criminal Procedure Code prescribes the period of limitation for various offences, a smaller period of limitation having been prescribed for offences punishable with smaller imprisonment and larger period of limitation being prescribed for offences punishable with greater imprisonment. The period of limitation for offences punishable up to three years is three years. S.469 relates to the commencement of the period of limitation. S.470 and s.471 deal with the exclusion of time in some instances. S.472 stipulates that in the case of a continuing offence, a fresh period of limitation shall begin to run at every moment of time during which the offence continues. Moreover, s.473 empowers the Court to take cognisance of an offence after the expiry of the period of limitation if it is satisfied, on the facts and circumstances of the case, that the delay has been adequately explained or that it was necessary to do in the interest of justice.

---

[874] (1990) I LLJ 555 Mad
[875] 1957 AIR 397, 1957 SCR 233

In *Bhagirath Kanoria v State of Madhya Pradesh*,[876] the Supreme Court considered whether the non-payment of the contributions to the statutorily created provident fund was a continuing offence within the meaning of s.472 of Criminal Procedure Code, 1973. The Court held that non-payment of the employer's contribution to the Provident Fund before the due date is a '*continuing offence*' and therefore, the period of limitation prescribed by s.468 of the Code cannot have any application. The offence will be governed by s.472 of the Code, according to which, a fresh period of limitation begins to run at every moment of the time during which the offence continues. The Court further observed that "the concept of 'continuing offence' does not wipe out the original guilt. It keeps the contravention alive, day by day."

In the above context, the Supreme Court made a pertinent observation that 'the hair-splitting argument as to whether the offence alleged against the appellants is of a continuing or non-continuing nature, could have been averted by holding that, considering the object and purpose of the Act, the learned Magistrate ought to take cognizance of the offence after the expiry of the period of limitation, if any such period is applicable, because the interest of justice so requires.'

Offences relating to non-payment of EPF related contributions and administrative charges were held to be continuous offences and the limitation period prescribed under s.468 is not applicable were held by the Madras High Court in *Meenakshi Industries v G. Guruswamy*.[877] In *Provident Fund Inspector v Harjit Singh, Secretary and another*.[878] the Punjab and Haryana High Court held that the failure to pay the employer's contribution or administrative charges before the due date is an offence of continuous nature and, therefore, the period of limitation prescribed under Section 468 of the Code of Criminal Procedure cannot have any application.

Non-payment of administrative charges – continuing offence

In *Provident Fund Inspector v Harjit Singh*,[879] a Division Bench of the Punjab and Haryana High Court held that the failure to pay administrative charges, which are payable under Para 38 of the Employees' Provident Funds Scheme, 1952, is an offence of a continuous nature and, therefore, the period of limitation prescribed under s.468 of the CrPC, 1973 cannot have any application in such a case, which is instead covered by Section 472 of the Code according to which a fresh period of limitation begins to run every moment of the time during which the offence continues.

---

[876] 1984 AIR 1688, 1985 SCR (1)626
[877] 1992 CriLJ 2115: 1999(sup3) LLJ 92
[878] Vol.C 1991(2) PLR 652: (1994) III LLJ 660 P H
[879] (1991) 2 LLN 1013: (1992) 1 Cur LR 198 (P & H) (DB)

Criminal Revision Petition under S.482 of Cr.P.C

In *Meenakshi Industries v G. Guruswamy*,[880] the Madras High Court held that the petition praying for quashing of criminal prosecution challenging the validity of the sanction granted by the Regional Provident Fund Commissioner, cannot be examined in a petition under s.482 of Cr.PC and the matter can be gone into only by the trial court. It is for the authority to be satisfied whether to give sanction for the making of the report or not, and the High Court will not go into the question as to whether that satisfaction was proper or not, or based on sufficient material or not unless it is shown that the sanction was given *mala fide*.[881]

In *Employees' State Insurance Corporation, Chandigarh v Gurdial Singh and others*[882] the Supreme Court held that the directors of the private limited company were not personally liable to pay contributions under the Employees' State Insurance Act, 1948 as the directors did not come within the definition of clause 1 of s.2(17) of the ESI Act. Relying on this case, the Bombay High Court, in *Sharad Mittersain Jain v State of Maharashtra*[883] quashed the prosecution in the exercise of jurisdiction under s.482 of Cr.PC, holding that the directors of the company are not 'employer' within the meaning of the term.

Question of Facts cannot be raised in Criminal Revision Petition

In *Aluminum Industries Ltd. and another v Enforcement Officer and another*,[884] the Kerala High Court held that resolution of disputed questions of fact is not an exercise which will be undertaken under the jurisdiction of the High Court under s.482 of Cr.PC. The parties will have the opportunity to raise all their contentions before the trial court. Whether the directors were in control and management of the factories' affairs is to be decided by the trial court and not by the High Court under s.482 of Cr.P.C.[885] A Court exercising writ jurisdiction under Article 226 or those under s.482 of the Criminal Procedure Code can interfere with ongoing prosecution proceedings or investigation only in cases where the complaint or the FIR, which constitutes the basis of such proceedings does not at the face of it disclose the commission of an offence or where there is some legal bar to the initiation or continuance of such proceedings.[886]

---

[880] 1992 CriLJ 2115: 1999(sup3) LLJ 92
[881] *Central Hindustran Orange & Cold Storage Co. Ltd. v Pratullachandra Ramchandra Oza* 1967 I LLJ 153 (Bom. HC)
[882] (1991) 24 LIC 52
[883] 2004(1) Mh.LJ 776: 2004 ALL MR(Cri) 75: 2004(101) FLR 410: 2004(2) LLJ 369
[884] 2003(2)LLJ 108: 2003(97) FLR 131: 2003(1) cLR 606 (Ker.HC)
[885] *Satish Kumar Modi v State of UP*, 1996 LIC 2506 (All.HC)
[886] *Orr Cee Electronics Ltd. v Judicial Magistrate, F.C. Mysore*, 2000 I LLJ 843 (Karn.HC)

Period of Limitation – a preliminary issue

In *Ram Kripal Prasad v State of Bihar*,[887] the Full Bench of the Patna High Court, referring to the Supreme Court order in *Nagawwa v Veeranna Shivalingappa*,[888] held that the failure of employer to deposit contribution in contravention of Para 38 and 76 of Scheme read with s.14 would be a continuing offence in view of s.472 of Cr.P.C. The court further held that the question of limitation should be raised and determined at the earlier stage before the trial court, and it cannot be raised directly in the High Court for quashing the proceedings under s.482 of Criminal Procedure Code.

Non-filing of statutory returns

In *Provident Fund Inspector, Chandigarh v Delhi Faridabad Textile Mills and others*,[889] the Supreme Court observed that "Section 468 CrPC can have no application to the facts and circumstances of the present case inasmuch as refusal to pay provident fund and to submit returns is a continuous offence and every day the breach continues a fresh cause of action arises." The Supreme Court relied upon the decision in *Bhagirath Kanoria v State of Madhya Pradesh*[890] in arriving at such conclusion. But in *C.B. Bhandari v Provident Fund Inspector, Bangalore*,[891] the question for consideration before the Karnataka High Court was whether non-filing of the statutory returns contemplated by Para 36(2) (a) and 2(b) and Para 38(2) of the EPF scheme would be a 'continuing offence' or would amount to an offence committed once and for all. The Karnataka High Court, again relying on the *Bhagirath* case, held that failure to file returns before the due date is not a continuing offence.

In *Premier Studs and Chaplets Company v State*,[892] a Division Bench of the Madras High Court held that the failure to pay the provident fund contributions and to submit the returns or statement continue from day to day and fresh offence is committed day to day so long as the employer continues in his failure to pay the contribution or to submit the returns. In *Provident Fund Inspector v Shama Beedi Factory and others*,[893] the High Court of Andhra Pradesh made a harmonious construction that if the failure to pay the contribution is a continuing offence as

---

[887] 1985(2) R.C.R.(Criminal) 69: 1985 CriLJ 1048: 1986 AIR (Patna) 254: 1986(2) Crimes 505: 1985 BLJ 422: 1986 LIC 571: 1985 PLJR 271: 1985(50) FLR 487: 1985 ECrC 397: 1985 BLJR 240: 1986(2) LabLN 578: 1985 BRLJ 71: 1985 BLT (Rep) 149: 1986(2) LLN 305
[888] AIR 1976 SC 1947: (1976 Cri LJ 1533)
[889] Crl. Appeal No. 372/1984 decided on September 17th, 1984 (SC)
[890] 1984 AIR 1688, 1985 SCR (1)626
[891] 1988 (1)CLR 296 (Kar. HC)
[892] 1980(56)FJR 611
[893] 2000 CriLJ 3427: 2000(1) Andh LD (Criminal) 369

held by the Supreme Court, the failure or refusal to submit any return, statement or other document required by the Scheme is also a continuing offence.

Non-payment of Administrative Charges – Prosecution valid

In *Andhra Sinters Ltd. v Provident Fund Inspector*,[894] the Andhra Pradesh High Court rejected the contention advanced by the counsel for petitioner that no prosecution can be launched for non-payment of administrative charges and that the liability to pay administrative charges arises only when the contributions are paid and held that such argument is contrary to the provisions of the Act.

COMMISSION OF OFFENCE AND PERSONS RESPONSIBLE

Director of a private limited company – Liable for prosecution under Section 14

The question as to whether a director of a private company who is neither an occupier nor a manager can be prosecuted under s.14A of the Act was considered by the Supreme Court in *Srikanta Datta Narasimharaja Wodiyar v Enforcement Officer, Mysore*.[895] The Court held that the expression 'was in charge of and was responsible to the company for the conduct of the business' are extensive in their import. It could not, therefore, be confined to the employer only. Sub-sections (1) and (2) of s.14A extend the liability for any offence by any person including a partner by an explanation if he was in-charge or was responsible to the company at the time of committing the offence. A director of a company may be concerned only with the policy to be followed and might not have any hand in the management of its day to day affairs. Such persons must necessarily be immune from such prosecutions.[896] The offence, if committed by the company, must have been committed with the consent or connivance of or is attributable to the neglect on the part of any Director etc., of the company.[897]

Managing Director need be necessarily the person-in-charge

The admittance made by the accused in his statement under s.313 Cr.P.C. that he was the Managing Director cannot lead to the presumption that it is he who was in charge of and was responsible to the company in the matter of the conduct of its business.[898]

---

[894] 1993 LIC 2346: 1994(3) CompL.J. 67: 1994(1) LLJ 1171
[895] 1993 AIR 1656, 1993 SCR (3) 508
[896] *Mahalderam Tea Estate Pvt. Ltd. v Prodan D.N.*, 38 FLR 13: II LLN 107: 52 FJR 392 1978 LIC (Cal.DB)
[897] *Bhagchand Jain v. Provident Fund Inspector*, 1999(82) FLR 608: 1999 LLR 912: 2000 II LLJ 599 (Cal.HC)
[898] *Rajagopalachari S. v Bellary Spinning & Weaving Co. Pvt. Ltd.* 1998 I LLJ 329 (Karn.HC)

Column 11 in Returns of Ownership (Form 5A)

In *Kailash Kumar Radhakrishna Kanoria v State of Gujarat*,[899] the Gujarat High Court observed that if all the persons who were the directors etc., of the establishment, namely, the limited company were to be made liable for the offence punishable under s.14 of the Act of 1952, then there was no necessity of insertion of Column 11 in Form 5A (Returns of ownership). The very fact that a particular column, namely, Column 11 has been inserted in the Form-5A would go to show that only those persons would be liable who were in-charge of and liable for the conduct of the business of the establishment. The Court further observed that impleadment of those directors who were not in-charge of and responsible for the conduct of the business of the establishment as accused persons under s.14-A would be nothing but 'a travesty of justice.'

In *Sampat Mal Lodha v State of Rajasthan*,[900] the High Court of Rajasthan held that the nomination of a person as the occupier of a factory by the provisions of s.2(e)(i) does not bar the prosecution of another person who is vicariously liable under s.14. In *State of U.P v Lala Ram Gopal Gupta*,[901] a Division Bench of the Allahabad High Court held that the cancellation of the exemption in accordance with s.17(4) of the Act *per se* does not amount to a penalty within the meaning of s.14(2-A) and hence, does not bar punishment thereunder.

Accused ought to have been in charge of the affairs of the company

In *Mahaldaram Tea Estate (P) Ltd. V D.N. Prodhan*,[902] a Division Bench of the Calcutta High Court observed that in the petition filed before the Magistrate, apart from the statement that the persons against whom the complaint was lodged were directors of the company concerned and hence responsible for the conduct of its business and management, there was no further material from which the Magistrate could have satisfied himself that those persons had taken some part in the running of the business of the company. In the absence of such averments in the petitions complaint, the cognizance taken by the Magistrate was bad in law. In *K.N. Genda Singh v State and another*,[903] Division Bench of the Calcutta High Court held that a mere statement in the complaint that the accused at all material time was the persons-in-charge of the establishment and were responsible to it for the conduct of its business, was not sufficient to connect the accused with the

---

[899] (1991)63 FLR 749(Guj).
[900] (1988) 72 FJR 111 (Raj)
[901] 1974 Lab IC 963 (All) (DB): 1973 All LJ 355
[902] 1978 Lab IC 898: (1978) 2 LLN 107 (Cal) (DB)
[903] 1982 LAB IC 1777

alleged offence of omission to deposit the amounts of contribution deducted from the wages of the employees. The prosecution has to prove that the accused were in the direct management of the affairs of the company. Mere proof that he was the director of the company would not satisfy the requirements of s.14-A(1) of the Act.[904]

In *Dwijendra Nath Singhhav v State*,[905] a single Judge of the Calcutta High Court held that it was not necessary that in the petition of complaint itself, it must be stated as to how and in what manner each of the accused was in charge of and were responsible to the company for the conduct of the business. That would be a matter of evidence. The averments in the complaint that the accused were partners of the defaulting firm and, as partners, they were in charge of and responsible to the firm for the conduct of its business is sufficient for the issue of the process.

In *Hind Tin Industries v State*,[906] a Single Judge of the Calcutta High Court held that at the stage of issuing process, the magistrate had only to see whether the essential averments regarding the accused being 'in charge' and also 'responsible for the conduct of the business' were present in the complaint. Whether the said averments were correct or not, or how far evidence might establish them, were different matters. The question of establishing the essential averments did not arise at the issuing process stage. In *State (PF Inspector) v Srinibas Paikray*,[907] the Orissa High Court held that in the absence of any evidence that the works manager of an establishment was in charge of, or responsible to the company, no prosecution could be launched against him.

In *Provident Fund Inspector v Harjit Singh*,[908] a Division Bench of the High Court of Punjab and Haryana held that prosecution of a person alleged to be in-charge of the establishment and responsible for the conduct of its business, without adducing evidence in support of such allegation, for committing offences under the provisions of the Employees' Provident Funds Scheme, 1952 and the Act is not maintainable.

In *Bihar Cotton Mills v State of Bihar*,[909] the Patna High Court observed that the requirements of s.14-A had been adequately complied with since at this stage the Magistrate was merely concerned with making out a *prima facie* case and not with the correctness of the said averment. It was for the trial court to find out whether or

---

[904] *Regional P.F. Commissioner v Kejriwal C.K.*, 1985 II CLR 388 (Del.DB)
[905] 1978 Lab IC 1420 (Cal)
[906] 53 FJR 185 (Cal).
[907] 1983 Lab IC (NOC)132 (Ori.)
[908] (1991) 2 LLN 1013: (1992) 1 Cur LR 198 (P & H) (DB)
[909] (1990) 1 LLN 151 (Pat.)

not the allegations in the complaint were correct. In *Bhuban Mohan Bose v State*,[910] the Calcutta High Court held that to make the directors vicariously liable for the offence committed by the company, it has to be shown that not only such persons were in-charge of the company but that they were responsible to the company in the conduct of its day to day business. In the absence of such evidence conviction of a director is unsustainable. In *Bajrang Mica Co v State of Bihar*,[911] the Patna High Court held that in case of commission of an offence by a company, unless there were specific evidence to the effect that the director being prosecuted for the offence was responsible for carrying on the business of the society, conviction of such a director would be wrong.

In *Momtaz Begam v The State*,[912] the Calcutta High Court held that sub-section (1) of s.14A makes it quite clear that it is incumbent upon the prosecution to prove that the Director concerned was in charge of, and was responsible to, the company for the conduct of the business of the company. It is only when the Prosecution discharges that initial onus that there is an onus upon the person concerned to prove that the offence was committed without his knowledge or that he exercised all due diligence to prevent the commission of such offence. In *State v S.P Bhadani*[913] held that the first sub-section of s.14-A would be confined only to officers in the immediate charge of the management of the company. It is, therefore, manifest that all the officers of the company not in direct charge of the management of the business are immune from the liability for the offence unless they have contributed to its commission by consent, connivance or neglect."

Drawing Adverse Inference

An adverse inference against the prosecution can be drawn only if it withholds specific evidence and not merely on account of its failure to obtain specific evidence. When no such evidence has been obtained, it cannot be said what that evidence would have been and therefore no question of presuming that the evidence would have been against the prosecution under s.114, illustration (g) of the Evidence Act can arise.

Remittance of the arrears before lodging prosecution – Effect of

In *Provident Fund Inspector, Faridabad v Jaipur Textile and another*,[914] the Supreme Court held that whenever payment of arrears of Provident Fund in respect of the

---

[910] (1991) 2 LLN 100: (1991) 1 LLJ 11: (1991) 1 Cur LR 313(Cal).
[911] (1991) 1 Cur LR 919: (1991) 2 LLN 196: 62 FLR 395 (Pat).
[912] AIR 1962 Cal 202, (1962) II LLJ 443 Cal
[913] AIR 1959 Pat 9
[914] AIR 1987 SC 1738, 1987 LabIC 1597, 1987 (1) SCALE 61, 1986 Supp (1) SCC 678

prosecution was paid within the time prescribed by the Court, the prosecution against them shall come to an end. The judgment was following by a Division Bench of the Calcutta High Court in *Regional Provident Fund Commissioner v Raj Kumar Nemani and others*,[915] where it was held that when the entire arrears of provident fund having been deposited before the lodging of the complaint the prosecution could not proceed.

Payment of dues after filing prosecution

In *Kishan Lal v Provident Fund Inspector*,[916] the Delhi High Court held that the deposit of amount after the filing of the complaint does not wipe out the offence and the complaint cannot be quashed by invoking powers under s.482 of Cr.P.C.

Offences under the Act is Economic Offences

In *H.V. Thimmegowda and others v State of Karnataka*,[917] the High Court held that failure to pay the contributions under the Employees' Provident Funds and Miscellaneous Provisions Act, 1952 is an 'economic offence' punishable under the Economic Offences Act, 1974. The High Court of Karnataka ruled that though the Employees' Provident Funds and Miscellaneous Provisions Act, 1952, is not included in the Schedule of the Economic Offences (Inapplicability of Limitation) Act, 1974, the offences do come within the definition of economic offences."

Acquittal for want of evidence

In *G.D. Singh, Enforcement officer v Koshi Refinery*,[918] the Patna High Court held that the cases in which no evidence at all is led in support of the allegations of the prosecution side are bound to be ended in acquittal of the persons, against whom cases are filed, observing that no court of law can take the allegations as gospel truth.

Company includes Partnership Firm also

In *K. Pandurangan v Abdul Shukoor Co.*,[919] the Madras High Court held that the explanation to s.14A of the Act makes it clear that the term 'Company' includes a partnership firm and the Direction of a firm means a partner of the firm. Thus, whenever the word 'company' is used in s.14A(1) and 14A(2) of the Act, the word 'firm' has to be read in its place. Therefore, the reason that the partnership firm is

---

[915] 1995 (1) CHN 115
[916] Crl.M.C. Nos.3728, 3737 to 3755, 4310, 4315, 4319, 4320 to 4341/2014, decided on November 12, 2014 (Del.HC)
[917] 2001 (4) LLN 354: 2002 (100) FJR.363)
[918] 2003(2) LLJ 671: 2003(1) ECrC 443: 2003(97) FLR 289
[919] 2003(2) LLJ 318: 2003(1) CTC 641: 2003(98) FLR 681

not a legal person or a separate entity under the Partnership Act and hence cannot be held guilty of the offence under the Act is contrary to law.

Proprietary concerns – Individual proprietor should be prosecuted

The Explanation to s.14-A states what a company means and this is analogous to s.11 of the Indian Penal Code. There can, therefore, be no prosecution against an establishment if it is not a Company or a firm contemplated in s.14-A of the EPF Act, but is only a sole proprietary concern. Thus, in case an establishment is owned by an individual owner and not by a Company or partnership firm, the individual proprietor should be prosecuted in his name and not by the name of his concern.[920]

Stereotyped complaints – Not maintainable

In *G.I.O. Johnson and others v L.B. Roy, Provident Fund Inspector*, a Division Bench of the Calcutta High Court held that where the complaint was made on a printed form even without striking off the inapplicable words printed therein and merely certain words of s.14-A was quoted to make the person concerned liable; such a complaint was not maintainable. In *Md. Reyazuddin and others v. The State of Bihar and another*,[921] the complaints were dismissed as the allegations made in the complaint were vague, and in fact, the complaint had been filed in a format which had also not been filled up correctly. The department was, therefore, directed to ensure that the time of the court is not wasted with complaints of such a type and the requisite ingredients of law are set out when such complaints are presented to the courts.[922]

Prosecution of the Company is a must

To fix criminal liability on an officer of a company, one of the essential conditions is that the company must be found first guilty of the commission of that offence.[923] However, in *K.P. Sundarson V D.K. Bhattacharjee*,[924] Calcutta High Court held that prosecution of a Director or a Chief Executive of a company under s.14-A even without prosecuting the company is maintainable. A complaint against an individual filed under s.14(1-A) read with s.14-A(1) is inconsistent and hence, not maintainable. The same person cannot be simultaneously liable for a default as an employer as well as in vicarious capacity.

---

[920] *Handbook of Legal Clarifications, 1963*
[921] 1998 (1) PLJR839
[922] *State of Maharashtra v Shivprakash Seth and others*, 1993 Lab.IC1979 (Bom.)
[923] *Jaipur Udyog Ltd. v Inspector of Provident Fund*, 1979 II LLN 207 (Raj.HC)
[924] (1988) 1 LLN 133: 56 FLR 328 (Cal).

Mens Rea – Not an essential element

In *Provident Fund Inspector v Ram Kumar*, the Punjab and Haryana High Court held that for an offence under s.14(1-A), *mens rea* is not an essential element.

Accused pleading guilty

In *Bajrang Mica Co. v State of Bihar*,[925] the facts of the case were that the persons accused of the offence under s.14(1-A) of the Act, on the substance of accusation being stated to them, pleaded not guilty. However, subsequently, they filed a petition, expressing their intention to plead guilty. Therefore, the Magistrate examined them under s.313 of the Cr.P.C, and when they pleaded guilty, convicted and sentenced them exclusively on that basis. It was held that Chapter XX of the CrPC did not provide for pleading guilty at a stage other than provided under s.251. Hence, the conviction recorded by the Magistrate was held illegal. The Patna High Court observed as follows:

"The procedure for regular trial of a summon case is provided under Chapter XX of the Code of Criminal Procedure. The Chapter shows that first of all when the accused appears or is brought before the Magistrate, the substance of the accusation is to be explained to him and then he shall be asked as to whether he pleads guilty or has any defence to make out. In case, he pleads guilty, he can be convicted, but in case he does not plead guilty, the Magistrate will proceed to examine the witnesses, and on taking such evidence, as provided under Section 273 of the Code of Criminal Procedure. If "he finds him guilty, he shall convict him, and if he finds him not guilty, he shall record an order of acquittal. Therefore, in the whole of this chapter, only one stage has been prescribed for the accused either to plead his guilt or not to plead his guilt as provided under Section 251 Cr.P.C. No stage has been prescribed under this Chapter that the accused at any stage of the trial, can again plead guilty and he can be convicted. Therefore, the procedure adopted in this case by the trial court is against the express provisions made under this Chapter."

It was observed that the Magistrate ought to have examined the witnesses and then to find the accused guilty or not guilty by evidence so recorded by him. As the Magistrate has not adopted the procedure laid down under the law, the conviction of the petitioners cannot be sustained.

Subsequent payment does not debar prosecution

In *Pranati Textiles v State of West Bengal*,[926] a Division Bench of the Calcutta High Court held that when there was failure to pay the amount of contribution and

---

[925] (1991) 2 LLN 196: (1991) 1 Cur LR 919: 62 FLR 395 (Pat.)
[926] (1989) 1 LLN 661: (1989) 2 Cur LR 824: 58 FLR 895

administrative charges in time, any later payment, even though made before initiation of prosecution, could be a mitigating circumstance, or a relevant factor to be taken into consideration in determining the sentence, but not one to forestall prosecution and conviction. In *Mathew Jose v State of Kerala*,[927] the High Court of Kerala refused to accept the contention that criminal proceedings for a violation under s.14 of the EPF Act will not survive in the light of the payment of amounts after initiation of the prosecution. However, payment can be a mitigating circumstance which the trial court can take into consideration while moulding the sentence if it ultimately concludes guilt of the accused. In *Provident Fund Inspector v Rajkumar Mills Ltd.*,[928] the accused, on conviction, pleaded that they had deposited the Provident Fund contributions and hence a lenient view should be taken. Rejecting this plea, the Madhya Pradesh High Court observed, "The liability of an employer cannot be lightly evaded. The insertion of sub-section (1-A) after sub-section (1) of Section 14 of the Act clearly indicates that the defaulting employer is to be dealt with severely. Imprisonment is a rule and mere imposition of a fine, an exception." The Court further held that non-deposit of his contribution and that of the employee by the employer should not be lightly viewed. Such white-collar crimes pose a threat not only regarding its impact on thousands of its victims that are defrauded of their hard earned money but also regarding what an average citizen thinks of our system of justice. Such frauds flourish today and must be curbed, and any leniency in the matter would be misplaced.

Though the fact that the petitioners pursuance had entirely discharged the obligations and liabilities for payment of the EPF contributions and other dues to the agreement or arrangement entered into by them with the Provident Fund Commissioner, may not itself exonerate them from the personal consequences flowing from the tentacles of s.14 of the EPF Act, yet it cannot be stated that such a circumstance cannot at all be construed as a mitigating or ameliorating circumstance to be taken into consideration by the court.[929] In *Hooghly Docking and Engineering Co Ltd. v Inspector, Employees' Provident Funds*,[930] the Calcutta High Court took a different view and observed that when the petitioners have acted on the basis an instalment scheme allowing time for payment of instalments, it is not open to the provident fund authorities later on to fall back upon the criminal prosecutions against the employer.

In *Adoni Cotton Mills Limited and others v. Regional Provident Fund Commissioner and others*,[931] the Supreme Court directed quashing of the

---

[927] 2017(1) Ker L.J. 914: 2017(1) KLT 1005: 2017 LabLR 454
[928] (1989) 58 FLR 262 (MP)
[929] *Hackbridge Hewitic and Easun Ltd. and others v. Provident Fund Inspector*, 1992CriLJ303
[930] (1980) 2 LLN 511
[931] 1995 Supp. 4 SCC 580

proceedings under s.14 and 14A of the EPF Act, considering the special circumstances of the case. In the case there was a default for a period of four months following which notices were given under the Act and on receipt of the notices the appellants therein filed writ petitions which were dismissed by the High Court and then during hearing of the civil appeal in the Supreme Court it transpired that the offences were committed some 15 years ago and two of the appellants died, and during the pendency of the appeal the appellants deposited money along with furnishing bank guarantee. Taking a cue from the decision of the Supreme Court, a Division Bench of the Calcutta High Court, in *Jasoda Glass & Silicate and others v. Regional Provident Fund Commissioner and others*,[932] made a similar order of dropping of the proceedings initiated under s.14 of the EPF Act. In *Howrah Motor Company Limited and others v. Samir Kumar Das*,[933] an extraordinary circumstance emerged. There was an order of injunction restraining the employer from withdrawing money from bank followed by order of an appointment of a special officer which prevented the petitioner from operating the banking transaction for deposit of dues and placing reliance on *Adoni Cotton Mills* case (supra), the Calcutta High Court ordered dropping of prosecution proceedings. In *Hotel Dock Palace Pvt. Ltd. and another v. State of West Bengal and another*,[934] Calcutta High Court held that the dropping of the criminal prosecutions in the aforecited cases are on consideration of special circumstances of each case, and therefore, it cannot be universally held that subsequent payment of the provident fund dues after the institution of prosecution will absolve the criminal liability.

Prosecution not maintainable when applicability is under challenge

In *Jagdish Prasad Choudhary v State of Bihar*,[935] the Patna High Court held that where the very applicability of the Act is disputed by the employer unless the authority under the Act records a contrary finding, prosecution of the employer would be illegal and not maintainable.

Executive Circulars are of no avail against statutory prosecution

In *Andhra Sinters Ltd. v Provident Fund Inspector*,[936] the Petitioner produced a copy of the circular issued by the Central Provident Fund Commissioner that the question of granting instalment facilities to the sick industrial companies was under

---

[932] 2002(2) Cr LJ 407
[933] 2004(4) CHN 291
[934] (2007)2CALLT259(HC),[2007(113)FLR692]
[935] 1986 Pat LJR 1133
[936] 1993 LIC 2346: 1994(3) CompL.J. 67: 1994(1) LLJ 1171

consideration by the Central Board of Trustees etc., and prayed for relief against the prosecution complaints filed against them. Rejecting the plea, the Andhra Pradesh High Court held that the administrative circulars could not be used as a shield in the prosecutions that have been launched against the petitioners. What is granted by the circular is an executive favour which the executive authorities can only give, and the Courts cannot grant any relief by the circular.

Sick Industry – Prosecution no bar

In *Andhra Sinters Ltd. v Provident Fund Inspector*,[937] the Andhra Pradesh High Court held that the protection provided under Section 22 of the Sick Industrial Companies (Special Provision) Act, 1985 for suspension of legal proceedings, etc. is limited and does not extend to prosecution launched under the EPF Act.

Onus of Proof in prosecution cases

It is for the prosecution to establish contravention of the provisions of the Act by the accused by the production of acceptable evidence. It is not for the employer to establish that he had not contravened any provisions of the Act. It is no doubt true that duty is cast on the employer to remit his part of the contributions. However, if there is any contravention of the provisions of the Act, the Provident Fund authorities have to establish the same by the production of the relevant materials.[938] On a plain language of s.14(1), it is seen that there is an element of *mens rea* and therefore, the burden is on the authority prosecuting the person to prove the offence.[939]

Prosecution – Importance of evidence

In *G.D. Singh, Enforcement Officer v Koshi Refinery and others*,[940] the trial court acquitted the accused as the complainant failed to adduce any evidence in support of the allegations. In the appeal, the Patna High Court observed that the cases in which no evidence at all is led in support of the allegations are bounded to be ended in the acquittal of accused. No Court of law can take the allegations as gospel truth for want of evidence in support of the same. The Magistrate can neither examine the accused nor has any such jurisdiction been conferred upon him under s.313 Cr.P.C to examine any person without any evidence.[941]

---

[937] 1993 LIC 2346: 1994(3) CompL.J. 67: 1994(1) LLJ 1171
[938] *Provident Fund Inspector v Sivarama Krishna Industries and others* (1992) I LLN 248 (AP. HC)
[939] *Provident Fund Inspector v Ram Kumar*, 1983 Lab. IC 717 (P & H.)
[940] 2003 (97) FLR 289, (2003) II LLJ 671 Pat
[941] *Bajrang Mica Co Pvt. Ltd. v State of Bihar*, 1991 I LLN 196 (Pat.HC)

14-AB Cognizable offence

Section 14-AB provides that notwithstanding anything contained in the Code of Criminal Procedure, an offence relating to default in the payment of contribution by the employer punishable under the said Act shall be cognizable. However, offences under Sections 406 and 409 I.P.C. are also cognizable, and hence, there is absolutely no difference between the special law and general law so far as cognizability of the offences is concerned.[942]

COGNIZANCE AND TRIAL OF OFFENCES

If the complainant is absent when the case is called out and when no reason is shown to the Court for the absence of the complainant, naturally the Court would presume that the complainant is absent because he does not wish to go on with the case, and accordingly an order of acquittal under s.247 of the Cr.P.C is made whatever the nature of the case may be.[943] The Magistrate has no powers to recall his order of acquitting the accused under s.256 Cr.P.C. and in such cases, the High Court also will not exercise its revisional powers under s.401 Cr.P.C. to set aside the order of dismissal.

Lenient view should be avoided

The provident fund provides a measure of safety and security for the workers who have invested their entire lifetime in the service of the employer. A person who robs a poor man of even the rags on his person deserves a very deterrent punishment and, if the Courts take a lenient view of such offences, the administration of justice will lose the respect which it enjoys at the hands of the society at large.[944] When for the alleged offences under s.14(1-A) and 14(1-B) of the Provident Fund Act, the statutory minimum is provided for, the trial court has no power to convene the said provisions even if the accused pleads guilty.[945] The Court should point out to the accused that there is a minimum sentence prescribed by the statute and record that the accused is pleading guilty despite being aware of those provisions.[946]

Indeed the report in writing of the inspector about the facts constituting the offence and the previous sanction of the Provident Fund Commissioner are integrally connected. Prosecutions under the Act cannot be indiscriminately ordered by inspectors appointed under s.13, and it can be so done only after a

---

[942] *Sushil Kumar Bagla v State*: (2003) 3 CALLT 470 HC, 2004 CriLJ 171, (2003) IIILLJ 510 Cal
[943] *Inspector of Provident Fund v Coelho A.J.*, 1973 I LLN 127 (Mys.DB)
[944] *C.K. Shah, P.F. Inspector v Natson Manufacturing Company Pvt Ltd.* (1976) 17 GLR 419
[945] *Regional P.F. Commissioner v Continental Textile Mills Ltd.*, 1998 III LLJ 1016 (Guj.HC)
[946] *State of Maharashtra v Shivprakash Seth*, 1999 III LLJ 11 (Bom.HC)

full and detailed consideration of the matter at the highest level. The Provident Fund Commissioner has first to be satisfied that the allegations and facts disclose an offence under the Act and therefore whether it is expedient to order prosecution. The sanction is in the shape of a speaking order which, after referring to the requisites and the requirements of s.14AC, authorises the prosecution concerning the periods for which default is made and specifying the names of persons who are to be prosecuted.[947]

There is a specific bar against the court taking cognizance and proceedings with the trial of such offences under s.14AC of the Act, except on a report in writing of the facts constituting such offence, made with the previous sanction of the Central Provident Fund Commissioner or such other officer as may be authorised by the Central Government. Therefore, it is not enough to make a bald allegation in the complaint borrowing the language of the section, to attract the provisions of s.14A(2). The facts essential to constitute the offence attracting the provisions of s.14A(2) have to be stated. In the absence of necessary allegations of the facts attracting those provisions of s.14A(2), it cannot be said that the prosecution launched and cognizance taken by the Magistrate against the accused was proper.[948]

A petitioner of complaint against offences under s.14 of the EPF Act need not in terms plead every minuscule relevant fact nor the precise number of employees of the prosecuted establishment. Failure to do so does not vitiate the proceedings on such technical ground alone.[949]

Compounding of charges/offences of similar nature

In *Jodhpur Wollen Mills Ltd. v State of Rajasthan,*[950] the Rajasthan High Court was considering a criminal revision petitions, where offence committed by the accused-persons were of the same kind but committed on different occasions spread over between March 1984 and December 1986. The High Court held that in a series of complaints of offences alleged to have been committed on thirty-three different occasions, it is not permissible to hold a single trial and it is only permissible to try the charges in a group of three. The Court held that the criminal cases could not be consolidated and tried together like a civil suit except within the limitations laid down by the Code of Criminal Procedure. Every non-payment of the employer's contribution by the 15th day of the next month constitute a separate offence and, therefore, only three of such charges can be tried together, and the thirty-three

---

[947] *Ram Kripal Prasad and others v The State Of Bihar and others,* 1985 CriLJ 1048
[948] *Modi Alkalines and Chemicals Ltd. and others v. State of Rajasthan,* 2008 CriLJ 2879
[949] *Ram Kripal Prasad and others v The State Of Bihar and others,* 1985 CriLJ 1048
[950] 1995(2) R.C.R.(Criminal) 52: 1995 CriLJ 769

charges of non-payment of employer's contribution cannot be tried jointly in one trial. A joint trial for thirty-three, charges spread over for thirty-three months will not be justified under Section 218(1) and, therefore, these eleven cases for thirty-three charges cannot be consolidated.

Sanction obtained but not placed on the Court

In *State of Maharashtra v Pankaj.A*,[951] the Bombay High Court held that the mandate of section 14AC is that without any sanction order, no court shall take cognizance of any offence punishable under the Act. Though the sanction was duly granted unless the sanction order has been filed before the Court, it cannot take any cognizance of the offence and hence the order of the trial Magistrate dismissing the prosecution is legal, just and proper. The Court also dismissed the appeal petition filed under s.378(1) of Cr.P.C., stating that the appeal is admissible under the previous sanction only where an order of acquittal has been passed whereas in the present case, the state of recording evidence had not reached and dismissed in the preliminary stage itself.

Notification by the Appropriate Government is mandatory

In *Provident Fund Inspector v Harjit Singh, Secretary and another*,[952] the Punjab and Haryana High Court held that mere allegation in the complaint did not constitute legal evidence, it was obligatory for the prosecution to produce notification appointing complainant as Provident Fund Inspector and he was also to prove that he had been accorded sanction for launching the prosecution. In the absence of evidence to this effect, it could not be said that the complaint has been filed by a person competent to launch the prosecution. In the present case, the prosecution has placed sanction to prosecute the respondents, but there is nothing on record to show that the complainant, who has filed the complaint was authorised to prosecute the respondents and he has been appointed as an Inspector under s.13 of the Act. Hence complaint is defective, and the Court can not take its cognizance. In *Provident Fund Inspector v Sudha Sood*,[953] the Himachal Pradesh High Court upheld the acquittal of the accused under s.14-A observing that there was nothing on record to show that the complainant was authorised to prosecute the respondents and he has been appointed as an Inspector under s.13 of the Act and hence the complaint was defective. In *State v Jagannath Ram and others*,[954] the Orissa High Court held

---

[951] 1995(1) BCR 353: 1994(2) Mh.LJ 1661: 1995(1) Crimes 203: 1995 ISJ (Banking) 84: 1995(3) CCR 128: 1994(2) CLR 902: 1994(1) LLN 762: 1995(1) LLJ 780
[952] Vol.C 1991(2) PLR 652: (1994) III LLJ 660 P H
[953] 2008(3) LLJ 632: 2008(1) SimLC 367: 2008(118) FLR 145
[954] 1982 CriLJ 118

that though the Regional Provident Fund Commissioner has been authorized by the Central Government to accord sanction for prosecution for offences under the Act, he failed to produce any notification to prove that he is an Inspector appointed under s.13 of the Act by the appropriate Government and requirements of s.13 have not been fulfilled

The Madras High Court took a different view in *Meenakshi Industries v G. Guruswamy*,[955] where the complaints filed by the Enforcement Officer (without producing the notification of his appointment as Inspector) was allowed based on the description of the complainant in the cause title and the elaboration given in the first paragraph of each of the complaints, that the complainant was a person appointed under s.13 of the Act as Inspector.

Application of the provisions of the Code of Criminal Procedure

The EPF Act does not provide for the particular procedure to be followed in respect of the prosecution launched under Para 76(a) read with Sections 14, 14A and 14-AA of the Act. Hence, the Code of Criminal Procedure applies.[956]

CONVICTION AND AWARD OF PUNISHMENT

Trial Court not to take the cases in a light-hearted manner

The Parliament has stepped up the punishment for offences under this Act, mainly because they are welfare measures which require being considered and implemented with a degree of seriousness. Prosecuting authorities should attend to complaints with a greater sense of responsibility. The provisions of the Act are wholly frustrated by the imposition of ridiculously low fines and more particularly, by passing acquittal orders on all sorts of frivolous, technical and unsustainable grounds. The learned Magistrates trying these cases shall ensure that the disposals are time-bound and that they are strictly by law. They will mainly take note of the fact that unlike in other statutes, none of the grounds on which sympathy, difficulty or extenuating circumstances are pleased is available under this Act. The courts shall not be shy of awarding the requisite sentences merely because the accused before them are directors of companies or the like.[957]

Company cannot be ordered to undergo Imprisonment

In *Bajran Mica Co (P) Ltd. v State of Bihar*,[958] the petitioner company had been convicted and sentenced to rigorous imprisonment by the trial court. Setting aside

---

[955] 1992 CriLJ 2115: 1999(sup3) LLJ 92
[956] *EPF Organisation v Shalimar Biscuits*, (1979) 1 APLJ (HC) 173
[957] *State of Maharashtra v Shivprakash Seth and others*, 1993 Lab.IC1979 (Bom.)
[958] (1991) 2 LLN 196:P (1991) 1 Cur LR 919: 62 FLR 395

the sentence, the High Court of Patna observed, "the company cannot be physically sentenced to undergo rigorous imprisonment. It is the juristic person, no doubt, but such sentence of imprisonment, which is incapable of execution, cannot be imposed."

Relief under s.633 of Companies Act – Not available

In *Rabindra Chamria and others v The Registrar of Companies, West Bengal & others*,[959] the facts of the case were that the Directors of the appellant company defaulted in payment of the provident fund dues due to lock-out and strike in the Jute industry. They applied under s.633 of the Companies Act, 1956 for being relieved of liability for delayed as well as non-payment of the provident fund and other allied dues. A Single Judge of the High Court allowed the appellant to liquidate the arrears in monthly instalments, and also restrained the Provident Fund Commissioner from initiating any criminal proceedings against them. On appeal by the Regional Provident Fund Commissioner, the Division Bench held that any proceeding referred to in s.633 of the Companies Act would mean only under the provisions of the said Act, and it had no application in respect of any liability under any other Act. In Civil Appeal, the Supreme Court ruled that a company falling under the explanation to s.14-A of the Employees' Provident Funds and Miscellaneous Provisions Act, 1952 which does not come within the purview of the Companies Act, the liability of the persons would be governed only by s.14A(1)(2) of the EPF Act. They will not be entitled to any relief under s.633 of the Companies Act. The benefit available under a social-welfare legislation cannot be defeated by invoking s.633 of the Companies Act.' In *Jagannath Prasad Jhalani and others v Regional Provident Fund Commissioner and others*,[960] the High Court rightly pointed out that s.633 of the Companies Act cannot be a panacea for all the ills committed in respect of various other enactments those already in force and those who came on the statute book at a subsequent date. All companies covered by the Companies Act are companies within the meaning of s.14A read with the Explanation, but all companies within the meaning of s.14A read with the Explanation are not companies covered by the Companies Act.[961] Take the case of a partner in a partnership firm and a director of a company covered by Companies Act. Both of them are covered by and can be made liable under s.14A given the Explanation, but such a director is entitled to such protection of s.633 of the Act, whereas the partner is not. This will lead to a peculiar situation.

---

[959] 1992 AIR 398, 1991 SCR Supl. (2) 338
[960] 1987 62 CompCas 571 Delhi, 1987 168 ITR 341 Delhi
[961] *Momtaz Begam v The State*, AIR 1962 Cal 202, (1962) IIL LJ 443 Cal

Adequate and Special Reasons

In *State of Gujarat v Indequip Engineering Limited*,[962] the Gujarat High Court held that the discretion under the proviso to s.14(1-A) to impose a lesser term of imprisonment or a sentence of finding could be exercised only when there are adequate reasons therefor. In *Meet Singh v State of Punjab*,[963] the Supreme Court had to discuss 'special reasons' in the context of the prevention of Corruption Act, 1947. The Court observed that the words 'special reasons' in the context in which they are used could only mean special to the accused on whom the sentence is being imposed. The Court has to weigh reasons advanced in respect of each accused whose case is taken up for awarding sentence. The Supreme Court further observed that anything which is common to a large class governed by the same statute could not be said to be special to each of them. It would thus unquestionably appear that 'special reasons' in the context of the sentencing process must be special to the accused in the case or special to the facts and circumstances of the case in which the sentence is being awarded. In *Union of India v Mohd. Ahmed*,[964] the Delhi High Court held that merely stating that the respondent who was looking after the concern was 'old and infirm' but yet looking after the concern would not be the special and adequate reason to impose a penalty less than the minimum contemplated by the legislature. In *Provident Fund Inspector v Harjinder Singh*,[965] the facts of the case were that the accused-respondents, being the Director in-charge of a private limited company and the company itself were convicted under s.14(1)(A) of the Act. The trial court did not impose on the accused the minimum sentence required under the law. The High Court of Punjab and Haryana declined to interfere in disposing of the revision petition filed by the Provident Fund Inspector observing that 'it was special and adequate to the accused of the particular case and that the trial magistrate cannot be said to have exceeded his jurisdiction.'

CRIMINAL BREACH OF TRUST AND FILING OF COMPLAINTS UNDER S.405 OF IPC

Criminal Breach of Trust – Mens rea and the 'legal fiction'

The offence under s.405 IPC is non-cognizable, bailable, non-compoundable and triable by a First Class Magistrate. However, if the FIR is lodged under s.406 IPC, the same is cognizable, non-bailable, compoundable and triable by the Magistrate

---

[962]   (1979) 2 GLR 784
[963]   1980 C.L.J. (Criminal) 126
[964]   1978 Lab IC 1026 (Delhi) 1978 CriLJ 1280, ILR 1978 Delhi 225
[965]   (1984) 64 FJR 273

of First Class. In *S.W. Palanitkar and others v State of Bihar and another*,[966] the Supreme Court held that without *mens rea*, a breach of trust might not result in a criminal breach of trust. Every breach of trust may not result in the penal offence of criminal breach of trust unless there is evidence of a mental act of fraudulent misappropriation. An act of breach of trust involves a civil wrong, in respect of which the person wronged may seek his redress for damages in a civil court, but a breach of trust with *mens rea* gives rise to a criminal prosecution as well. In *Kailash Kumar Sanwatia v State of Bihar and another*,[967] the Supreme Court held that the following ingredients of the offence are to be treated as 'criminal breach of trust': (1) Entrusting any person with property, or with any dominion over property. (2) The person entrusted (a) dishonestly misappropriating or converting to his own use that property; or (b) dishonestly using or disposing of that property or willfully suffering any other person so as to do in violation – (i) of any direction of law prescribing the mode in which such trust is to be discharged; or (ii) of any legal contract made touching the discharge of trust.

The Explanation 1, as added by amendment of 1973 to section 405 of the Indian Penal Code (with effect from November 1st, 1973), states that: "A person, being an employer, who deducts the employee's contributions from the wages payable to the employee for credit to a Provident Fund or Family Pension Fund established by any law for the time being in force, shall be deemed to have been entrusted with the amount of the contribution so deducted by him and if he makes default in the payment of such contribution to the said Fund in violation of the said law, shall be deemed to have dishonestly used the amount of the said contribution in violation of a directions of law as aforesaid." Pertinently, Explanation I to s.405 creates a 'legal fiction' to the effect that an employer who had deducted the workers' share of provident fund contributions but failed to remit it *"shall be deemed to have dishonestly used"* the money.

In *Lakshmirattan Engineering Works Ltd. v Union of India and others*,[968] the High Court of Punjab and Haryana held that the 1973 amendment Act added an explanation to s.405 of IPC, shifting the onus on to the accused.

Entrustment under Para 32(3) is a 'legal fiction'

In *Ahmed Ramlan v Gertie Mathias and others*,[969] a Division Bench of the Karnataka High Court held that the contributions deducted by the employer from the wages

---

[966] 2002(1) JIC 232 (SC); 2002 SCC (Cri) 129
[967] (2003) 7 SCC 399
[968] 1983 PLR 685: 1984(1) ILR (Punjab) 149: 1984(1) LLN 781: 1984 LIC 213
[969] 1977 CriLJ 309

of the employees under the Employees' Provident Fund would not amount to entrustment within the meaning of s.405 of IPC.

In *Jaswantrai Manilal v State of Bombay*,[970] and *State of Gujarat v Jaswantlal Nathalal*,[971] the Supreme Court discussed the legal meaning of the term 'entrustment.' According to the said decisions, 'entrustment' contemplates the creation of a relationship whereby the owner of property makes it over to another person to be retained by him until a certain contingency arises or to be disposed of by him on the happening of a certain event. The person who transfers possession of the property to the second party remains the legal owner of the property, and the person in whose favour possession is so transferred has only the custody of the property to be kept or disposed of by him for the benefit of the other party. The expression 'entrustment' also carries with it the implication that the person handing over any property or on whose behalf that property is handed over to another continues to be its owner.

Deemed Misuse of Money – Legal Fiction

Once it is found that employer deducted amounts from wages of the employees for contribution to Provident Fund and retaining the same without depositing it with the fund, an automatic presumption is available against the employer that he dishonestly used the amount of the said contribution in violation of a direction of law.[972] The mere fact of telling the employees that it is their contribution to the Provident Fund Scheme and then making deduction or recovery and retaining it, constitutes the offence of criminal breach of trust.[973] In *Sushil Kumar Bagla v State of West Bengal*,[974] the Calcutta High Court held that once it is found that the employer deducted amounts from the wages of the employees for contributing to the Provident Fund and retaining the same without depositing it with the fund, an automatic presumption is available against the employer that he dishonestly used the amount of the said contribution in violation of a direction of law.

Criminal Breach of Trust – 405 IPC is a continuing offence

In *State of Punjab v Sarwan Singh*,[975] the Supreme Court upheld a finding that a prosecution for an offence under s.406 of IPC was barred by limitation. In *Balram*

---

[970] AIR 1956 SC 575: 1956
[971] AIR 1968 SC 700: 1968 CrLJ 803
[972] *Sushil Kumar Bagla v State*, (2003) 3 CALLT 470 HC, 2004 CriLJ 171, (2003) IIILLJ 510 Cal
[973] *Akharbhai Nazrali v Md. Hussain Bhai*, AIR 1961 Madhya Pradesh 37: (1961 (1) Cri LJ 266)
[974] 2004 CriLJ 171: 2004(2) AICLR 192: 2003(3) LLJ 510: 2003 CalCriLR 274: 2003(3) Cal. L.T. 470: 2003(2) Cal. H.C.N. 324
[975] 1981 SCALE (1)619

Singh v Sukhwant Kaur and another[976] a Division Bench of the Punjab-Haryana High Court held that the offence under s.406 is a continuing offence, observing further that the *Sarwan Singh's* case (supra) cannot be taken as a binding preceding as the question whether the offences under s.406 of IPC was continuing or non-continuing one was neither debated nor decided.

Director – Not liable under s.405 IPC

The employer is the occupier of the company, and he is a person who has ultimate control over the affairs of the company given the definition of employer. In view of explanation I to s.405 IPC, the employer is the person who deducts the employees' contribution under the Act from the wages payable to the employees for credit to Provident Fund and therefore, in no way the Directors of the company can be held liable for prosecution under s.406 to 409 IPC as there is no entrustment to them in terms of Explanation 1 to s.405 IPC.[977] In *S. Sampath Kumar v State of Maharashtra*,[978] the Bombay High Court quashed the criminal proceedings under s.405 of IPC against the present director who is not responsible or not in-charge of the company at the relevant time. The Court held that the fundamental principle of invoking the prosecution is not only against the company, or against all the officers or Manager or Directors of the Company, but mainly against the person who is/are in-charge at the relevant time or who is or are conducting the affairs of the company.

Directors are not 'agents'; offence covered under s.405/406 and not 409 IPC

The directors of the company may be acting as trustees or agents quo the company, but they cannot be termed as trustees or agents qua the workers. Since they do not fall into the category of such agents, the offence of criminal breach of trust would not be covered under s.409 IPC, but would be covered under s.405 read with s.406 of the IPC under Explanation No. 1 of s.405 of the Indian Penal Code. Therefore, it is deemed to have been dishonestly used because of violation of a direction of law. The directors of the company may be acting as trustees or agents quay the company, but they cannot be termed as trustees or agents quay the workers. Since they do not fall in the category of such agents in the present case, the offence of criminal breach of trust would not be covered under s.409 of the Indian Penal Code but would be covered under s.405 read with s.406 of the Indian Penal Code alone.[979]

---

[976] 1992 CriLJ 792
[977] *Gupta B.P. V State of Bihar* 2000 I LLJ 1138 (Pat. HC)
[978] 2005(1) ALL MR(Cri) 566: 2005(1) Mh.LJ 1166: 2006(8) SLR 332: 2005(105) FLR 308
[979] *Hargovind Gangabisan Bajaj v State of Maharashtra*, 1986 II LLN 119 (Bom. HC)

In *Balgopal Goenka v State of West Bengal and others*,[980] a Division Bench of the Calcutta High Court held that the explanation to s.405 is not an explanation but some addition to the section and that addition was added by the Amendment Act 40 of 1973 which has no retrospective operation. As the alleged acts have been committed before the date of the amendment, they cannot amount to the offence.

Non-Payment of Workers' share – Offence punishable under S.406 and not under S.409 IPC

In *Hargovind Gangabisan Bajaj v State of Maharashtra*,[981] the Bombay High Court held that the failure on the part of the director of a company to deposit with the Board of Trustees the money deducted from the wages of the employees for paying the Provident Fund contributions is an offence under Section 405 read with Section 406 of the Indian Penal Code, 1860 and not under Section 409 thereof.

Criminal Breach of Trust

In *Akharbhai Nazarali v Md. Hussain Bhai*,[982] Madhya Pradesh High Court held that 'the deduction and retention of the employees' contribution is a trust created by that very fact, or by a provision in statute or statutory rule. However, even apart from the latter, the mere fact of telling the employees that it is their contribution to the provident fund scheme and then making a deduction or recovery and retaining it, constitutes the offence of criminal breach of trust.' The Supreme Court approved this view in *Harihar Prasad Dubey v Tulsi Das Mundra*; It may be mentioned here that the judgement rendered by the Supreme Court was long before Explanation-I was inserted to s.405 of IPC by the Amendment in 1973.

In *Kanknarrah & Co Ltd. v Union of India*,[983] the Calcutta High Court held that the employer's failure to deposit with the Board of Trustees, the amounts deducted from the wages of the employees towards the employees' contribution to the fund and towards repayment of amounts borrowed from their provident fund accounts, not only constitutes offence under the Act but also amounts to 'criminal breach of trust' within the meaning of Section 405 of the Penal Code, 1860.

Not a Double Jeopardy

In *T.S. Baliah v T.S. Rangachari, ITO, Madras*,[984] the Supreme Court held that the question for determination was whether accused could be prosecuted both under

---

[980] 1983 CriLJ 570: 1982(1) Cal. H.C.N. 112: 1981(86) Cal. W.N. 540
[981] (1986) 2 LLN 119 (Bom)
[982] AIR 1961 MP 37, 1961 CriLJ 266
[983] (1989) 2 LLN 431: 59 FLR 350 (Cal.)
[984] AIR 1969 SC 701

S.177 Indian Penal Code and s.52 of the Income-tax Act, 1922. It was contended on behalf of the accused that given s.26 of the General Clauses Act, accused could be prosecuted either under s.177 Indian Penal Code or s.52 of the Income-tax Act, 1922 and not for both offences at the same time. While rejecting this contention, the Supreme Court held that a plain reading of s.26 of the General Clauses Act shows that there is no bar to the trial or conviction of the offender under both the enactments, but there is only a bar to the punishment of the offender twice for the same offence. In other words, Section provides that where an act or omission constitutes an offence under two or more enactments, the offender may be prosecuted and convicted under either or both the enactments but shall not be liable to punishment twice for the same offence.

In *Lakshmirattan Engineering Works Ltd. v Union of India and others*,[985] the High Court of Punjab and Haryana, referring to the judgement of the Calcutta High Court in *Hari Nath Poddar v The State*,[986] observed that the ingredients of the offences under s.14(1) of the Act were not the same as those of an offence under s.406, of the Indian Penal Code, in that under s.14(1A) of the Act, the offence consists in the default in making the payment of the contribution; while under s.406 of Indian Penal Code in misappropriating the money entrusted to the employer in violation of a direction of law, that is, the money deducted from the wages of the employees as contribution to the provident fund along with the contribution of the employer made under the Act. The High Court, therefore, held that as the ingredients of the offence under s.14(1) of the Act and s.406 of the Indian Penal Code were not the same; there was no violation of Article 20 of the Constitution of India.

In *Kailash Kumar Radhakrishna Kanoria v State of Gujarat*,[987] the Gujarat High Court held that only that person who deducted the employees' contribution from the wages payable to the worker for credit to the provident fund and not other persons would be liable for the offence punishable under s.405 IPC. In *Maidhan Gupta v State of U.P.*,[988] the High Court held that the offence under s.14 of the Act is not the same as contained in s.409 of the Penal Code, 1860. Hence, a mere conviction under s.14 is no bar under s.300(1) of the Cr.P.C, 1973, against the prosecution of the same person under s.409 of the Code.

---

[985] 1983 PLR 685: 1984(1) ILR (Punjab) 149: 1984(1) LLN 781: 1984 LIC 213
[986] 1978 Crl.L.J. 1018
[987] (1991) 63 FLR 749 (Guj)
[988] 1976 Cri LJ 868: 1975 AWC 630

No sanction is required for prosecution under s.406 IPC

No sanction is required for prosecution for an offence under s.409 of Indian Penal Code.[989] In *Employees' State Insurance Corporation v Hukuchand Mills Ltd.*,[990] the Madhya Pradesh High Court held that when the accused persons are prosecuted for an offence under s.406 of IPC, the other ground for dropping entire proceedings, i.e., non-sanction of the prosecution of the accused under s.86 of the Act does not survive. The Court further held that under s.86 of the Act sanction is required only in cases when the accused persons are prosecuted for an offence under the provisions of the Act. In *Sushil Kumar Bagla v State of West Bengal*,[991] the Calcutta High Court refused to accept the contention that no cognizance can be taken for the offences under the EPF & MP Act except with the sanction from the competent authorities under s.14AC. The Court held that no sanction is required for the offences under s.406/409 IPC.

Subsequent payment does not mitigate the offence

In *Kamala Tea Company Limited v State of West Bengal*,[992] a Division Bench of the Calcutta High Court refused to quash the criminal prosecution under s.405 of IPC stating that the subsequent deposit, though welcome, as it is better late than never, cannot and does not absolve the accused persons of the liability for the criminal offence. The Court further observed that the employees could not be left to the mercy of their masters and the legislation attempts to ensure that the future of the employees is not thrown into an ocean of uncertainty. In *Rajneesh Aggarwal v Amit J Bhalla*,[993] the Supreme Court held that so far as the criminal complaint is concerned, once the offence is committed, any payment made subsequent thereto will not absolve the accused of the liability of criminal offence, though in the matter of awarding of sentence, if any have some effect on the Court trying the offence. In the Criminal Revision Petition filed by *Jenson Nicholson (India) Ltd.*,[994] the Calcutta High Court held that the subsequent payment of defaulted money, even though accepted by the Provident Fund Commissioner, will not constitute condonation of the offence itself.

---

[989] *Maidhan Gupta v The State of Uttar Pradesh*, (1976) Cr.LJ 868
[990] 1995(1) Crimes 812: 1995(2) CCR 793: 1995(1) VIBHA 185
[991] 2004 CriLJ 171: 2004(2) AICLR 192: 2003(3) LLJ 510: 2003 CalCriLR 274: 2003(3) Cal. L.T. 470: 2003(2) Cal. H.C.N. 324
[992] 2007(4) AICLR 442: 2007(2) CalCriLR 377: 2007(2) CalLJ 124
[993] AIR 2001 SC 518
[994] 2013(127) AIC 472: 2013(2) CalLJ 192: 2013(138) FLR 348: 2014(8) R.C.R.(Civil) 755

Chapter XVII
EXEMPTION

Grant of Exemption – Objective of

In *Mohmedalli and others v Union of India and another,*[995] the Supreme Court held, "It would appear from the terms of the relevant portion of Section 17 that the exemption to be granted by the appropriate Government is not in the nature of completely absolving the establishments from all liability to provide the facilities contemplated by the Act. The exemptions are to be granted by the appropriate Government only if in its opinion the exempted establishment has provisions made for provident fund, in terms at least equal, if not more favourable, to its employees. In other words the exemption is with a view to avoiding duplication and permitting the employees concerned the benefit of the pre-existing scheme, which presumably has been working satisfactorily, so that the exemption is not meant to deprive the employees concerned of the benefit of a provident fund but to ensure to them the continuance of the benefit which at least is not in terms less favourable to them. As the whole scheme of provident fund is intended for the benefit of employees, section 17 only saves pre-existing schemes of provident fund pertaining to particular establishments.

Exemption – Gazette notification is necessary

In *Lawly Sen & Co. v Regional Provident Fund Commissioner, Bihar and another,*[996] a Division Bench of the Patna High Court, construing s.17(1) held that where there is no order of exemption by the appropriate government under s.17, the legal liability of a factory to make contribution with effect from the date of the application of the Scheme remains unaffected. The employer, which is covered by the provisions of the Act, in case makes an application for exemption, till any decision is taken on the application, the employer is bound to comply with the provisions of the Act and cannot take shelter behind the fact that it has made an application seeking exemption from the operation of the Act.[997] The use of the word 'may' and 'relax' in paragraph 28(7) of the Scheme indicates that it is not obligatory to relax the provisions of the Act.[998]

---

[995] 1963 Suppl. I SCR 993
[996] AIR 1959 Pat 271, 1958 (6) BLJR 722, (1959) ILLJ 272 Pat
[997] *H.P. Agro Industries Corporation v Regional P.F. Commissioner* (1999) III LLJ 469 HP
[998] *Bharat Heavy Electricals Ltd. v Regional P.F. Commissioner,* 1985 Lab IC 282 (Ker)

In *D. Rani v Indian Drugs and Pharmaceuticals Ltd,*[999] Madras High Court held that the communication from the Regional Provident Fund Commissioner could not be treated as a notification granting an exemption because, under s.17(2A) of the Act, it is only a notification published in the official Gazette by which exemption can be granted.

Pendency of application for exemption

When an establishment has applied for a grant of exemption, and relaxation order under Paragraph 79 of the EPF Scheme, 1952 is granted pending grant of exemption, the employer is required to comply with the provisions of the employer's own Provident Fund rules.[1000] The establishment, which is covered by the provisions of the Act, in case makes an application for exemption, is bound to comply with the provisions of the Act till any decision is taken on the application, and cannot take shelter behind the fact that it has made an application seeking exemption from the operation of the Act.[1001]

Liability of the Contractors of Exempted establishments

In case exemption from the operation of the Scheme is allowed to the principal employer, he is out of the net of the Scheme. He is then obliged to set up a trust and maintain the accounts of his employees. Such a literal construction, therefore, naturally leads to the conclusion that the contractors are within the mischief of the Scheme. Not having obtained an exemption within the meaning of s.17 of the Act, the contractors are still covered by the scheme and obliged to obtain separate code numbers under the Act and the Scheme and deposit the contributions with the authorities under the Act.[1002]

Cancellation of Exemption – Authority which granted it can only cancel it

In *R.K.L. Gupta v Ram Babu Lal,*[1003] the Allahabad High Court held that the power of cancelling exemption is confined to the authority which granted it. The Court further held that if the exemption was granted by the Central Provident Fund Commissioner by the authority conferred on him by the Central Government, the Government of Uttar Pradesh might also be empowered to exercise the power of

---

[999] (1990) 2 MLJ 1
[1000] *Usha Sales Ltd. v Regional P.F. Commissioner,* 1980 LIC 546: 56 FJR 287: 1980 I LLN 452: 40 FLR 331 (Del.DB)
[1001] *H.P. Agro Industries Corporation Ltd. v Regional P.F. Commissioner,* 1999 III LLJ 469 (HP.DB)
[1002] *Bata India Ltd. and others v Union of India and another,* 2001 (4) LLN 536
[1003] (1970) ILLJ 390 All

granting exemption in respect of the same establishment. Any cancellation made by the Government of Uttar Pradesh will, therefore, not have the effect of making the exemption inoperative.

S.17 makes it clear that the appropriate government is the authority to reject an application for grant of exemption and the order by the Assistant Provident /Fund Commissioner rejecting such application had to be set aside with the direction to forward the application to the Ministry concerned.[1004]

In *Madura Coats Employees' Union v Regional Provident Fund Commissioner and others*,[1005] the Bombay High Court observed that the benefit cannot be taken away by the employer without prior permission of the Central Government, observing that whatever benefits were available to the employees either in the nature of pension, gratuity or provident fund on the date when the exemption was granted, express or implied, that benefit is not to be reduced in any manner without the previous permission of the Central Government, and the Division Bench also approved it. In *Madura Coats case*, there was no contention that the relaxation/exemption was withdrawn at any time. This is the main distinguishing feature in both these cases – *Madura Coats* and *Marathwada Gramin Bank*.

Commissioner cannot assume the role of the Appropriate Government

In *Delta Limited v Regional P.F. Commissioner, West Bengal*, a Division Bench of the Calcutta High Court held that in the absence of any provision empowering the Regional Provident Fund Commissioner to exercise any jurisdiction in relation to s.17(4), he cannot assume jurisdiction to discharge any of the functions exercisable by the appropriate Government. At the same time, there is nothing to prevent him from reporting non-compliance to the Central Board, which may bring the same to the notice of the appropriate Government. This may be part of the internal administration, but it cannot employ any of these authorities to recommend cancellation of exemption granted under s.17.

Exemption does not bar additional benefits for the employees

In *Bharatkhand Textile Manufacturing Co. Ltd. v Textile Labour Association*,[1006] the Supreme Court held that s.17 of the EPF Act brings out two points clear. If the benefits provided by the employer are not less favourable than the statutory benefits,

---

[1004] *Birla Sun Life Insurance Co Ltd. v Subhask Kumar* 2012 (3) LLJ 655 (Bom)(DB)
[1005] (1999) ILLJ 928
[1006] 1960 AIR (SC) 833: 1960(3) SCR 329: 1960(1) FLR 89: 1960(18) FJR 198: 1960(2) LLJ 21: 1968(1) SCJ 290

he may apply for an exemption and the appropriate Government may grant him such exemption. If, on the other hand, the benefits conferred by him are less favourable than the statutory benefits, he may not be entitled to any exemption, in which case both the benefits would be available to the employees. These provisions indicate that the statutory benefits which in the opinion of the Legislature are the minimum to which the employees are entitled, cannot create a bar against the employees' claim for additional benefits from their employers.

Cancellation of Exemption is not a penalty

In *Provident Fund Inspector v Lala Ram Gopal Gupta and others*,[1007] a Division Bench of the Allahabad High Court held that the cancellation of exemption by s.17(4)(a) does not involve the imposition of a penalty within the meaning of s.14(2A) of the Act.

In *N.K. Jain v C.K. Shah*,[1008] the Supreme Court referring to the above judgement stated that the Division Bench of the Allahabad High Court has rightly held that cancellation under s.17(4)(a) is not an alternative penalty for failure to comply with the conditions subject to which the exemption was granted and if the Parliament had contemplated that the cancellation of the exemption amounted to penalty within the meaning of s.14(2A), it was purposeless to provide for any similar penalty under s.14(2A). The Supreme Court further clarified that s.14(2A) was introduced in the year 1953 by Act No.37 of 1953 whereas sub-section 4 of s.17 was introduced in the year 1963 by the Amendment Act No.28 of 1963, nearly ten years later. This only shows that the cancellation is not meant to be treated as one of the penalties and the reasonable inference is that the expression 'penalty' in the context in which it is used in s.14 (2A) only connotes imposition of imprisonment or fine. The cancellation as provided under s.17 (4) is only consequential and also somewhat procedural meant to be applied to the exemption granted under s.17(1) in case of noncompliance with the conditions subject to which such exemption was granted.

Interest cannot be less than statutory rate

In *Binny Limited, Bangalore v The Regional Provident Fund Commissioner*,[1009] it was contended that the rate of interest at par with the statutory rate of interest could not

---

[1007] 1973 Allahabad Law Journal 355
[1008] 1991(2) S.C.T. 626: 1991(2) R.C.R.(Criminal) 141: 1991 AIR (SC) 1289: 1991 CriLJ 1347: 1991(2) SCC 495: 1991(2) JT 52: 1991(1) SCR 938: 1991(1) Scale 519: 1991 LIC 1013: 1991 SCC(Cri) 328: 1995(3) LLJ 300: 1991(2) GLR 910: 1991(3) RSJ 161: 1991(2) LLN 443: 1991 SCC (L&S) 656: 1991(79) FJR 242: 1991(62) FLR 657: 1995(Sup3) LLJ 300: 1991 AIR (SCW) 960: 1991(2) Crimes 94: 1991 Cri. L.R. 363
[1009] ILR 1998 KAR 2709, 1998 (4) KarLJ 544, (1999) IILLJ 73 Kant

be paid due to the low yields on its investments. A Division Bench of the Karnataka High Court held that even if the investments made by the appellant company are by the directions issued by the Central Government, the benefits prescribed under the Scheme is minimum and that cannot be denied to its employees.

Exempted Trust is a 'state' within the meaning of Article 12

When an authority discharges its statutory liability and its activities are governed by statute, and it deals with a particular class of public, then it discharges a public duty. It is, therefore, an instrumentality and agency of the State. Since, unless an exemption was granted, the fund would have been governed by the Provident Fund Act. Given the exemption, the Trust steps into the shoes of the Provident Fund authority to discharge the same liability according to the approved scheme. Thus, the Trust while dealing with the fund exempted under s.17 is an instrumentality and agency of state within the meaning of Article 12 of the Constitution.[1010]

Commissioner's jurisdiction is broad enough to take appropriate steps

In *Krishna Kumar Agarwala and others v Kelvin June Company Limited*,[1011] the facts of the case where that Kelvin Jute Mills Company Ltd. had two units viz., Kelvin Jute Mills and Kelvin Broadloom Division. Hooghly Mills Company Limited took over Kelvin Broadloom Division which was rechristened as Waverly Jute Mills Company. Thus, the two units of Kelvin Jute Mills Co Ltd. become separated from each other. When the Provident Fund Commissioner ordered the transfer of the provident fund accumulations of the employees of Broadloom Division from the Kelvin Trust to Waverly Trust, it was challenged. The Calcutta High Court refused to accept the proposition that the Provident Fund Commissioner has no jurisdiction to direct transfer of the PF accumulation from one fund to the other regarding the statutory provisions of the Act. The Court held that if there is any violation of the statutory conditions, it is open to the Regional Provident Fund Commissioner to take appropriate steps, as are permitted under the Act.

In *Pfizer Employees' Union and other v Regional P.F. Commissioner and others*,[1012] the Bombay High Court held that in view of insertion of Para 27-AA with effect from 6-1-2011, there cannot be any doubt about the power of the Commissioner to impose conditions for grant of exemption under Para 27 and insistence on compliance with these conditions for continuance of the exemption already granted and the Commissioner does have powers to impose conditions which were mentioned in Appendix A to Paragraph 27-AA.

[1010] *Krishna Kumar Agarwala and others v Kelvin June Company Limited* (2003) I LLJ 564 Cal
[1011] (2003) I LLJ 564 Cal
[1012] 2003 (5) BomCR 536, (2003) III LLJ 259 Bom, 2003 (4) MhLj 667

It has been stated in Para 31 of the relaxation order that the relaxation is liable for withdrawal for breach of any of the conditions and other sufficient cause. The term 'other sufficient cause' essentially covers the future contingencies.[1013] The Commissioner is empowered to impose any condition while granting the order of relaxation and he is at liberty to impose such conditions including the conditions found in Appendix –A either by revising the order of relaxation or imposing such of those conditions as he considers necessary. He is at liberty to issue show cause notice to the petitioner establishment for violation of any of the conditions found in the relaxation order and proceed to pass orders on merits and by law.[1014]

Employment strength – Not a criterion for grant of exemption

In *Cholamandalam Software Ltd. Regional P.F Commissioner,*[1015] the Assistant Provident Fund Commissioner rejected the application for grant of exemption merely on the ground that as per the orders of the Central Provident Fund Commissioner, the exemption should not be granted to establishments having employment strength of less than 200. The Madras High Court held such condition to be *ultra vires* of s.17(1)(a) and directed the Provident Fund Commissioner to dispose of the application on merits. There is no such condition in s.17(1)(a) of the Act and so long as the Acts remains un-amended, it is not open to the Central Provident Fund Commissioner to say that the establishment having employment strength of less than 200 will not be entitled to invoke s.17(1)(a) of the Act.[1016]

Exemption should be sought from appropriate government

In *Gulshan Khandsari Udyog v Union of India,*[1017] the petitioner contended that they provide manifold amenities like free drink of juice, free substantial quantity of *Gur*, provision for free fuel, clothes, etc and that these amenities taken as a whole are in no case less favourable than the benefits to be accrued under the Provident Fund Act and for this reason the petitioner ought to have been exempted under s.17 of the Act. The Allahabad High Court held that the petitioner ought to have raised his grievance before the appropriate government, which is authorised to grant an exemption, rather than before the High Court.

[1013] *Mahanagar Telephone Nigam Ltd. V Union of India and others* W.P.(C)No.4309/2013 Decision dated December 16, 2014 (Del.)
[1014] *Shell India Markets Pvt Ltd. v Central P.F. Commissioner,* 2012(1) CLR 983; 2012(3) LLJ 686
[1015] (1989) 2 LLN 1030 (Mad.)
[1016] *Honorary Secretary, CMS Matriculation Hr. Sec. School v Regional P.F. Commissioner* 1999 I LLN 469 (Mad. HC)
[1017] AIR 1968 All 75, 1968 (17) FLR 172, (1969) II LLJ 477 All

The appropriate government should notify revised conditions

In *Jiyajeerao Cotton Mills v Dev Kumar Holani*,[1018] the Supreme Court held that the revised terms and conditions did not and could not have become applicable automatically, and in order to make them applicable they were required to be incorporated by the appropriate Government in the notification granting exemption under s.17(1)(a).

Exemption – No extra liabilities can be saddled

In *Marathwada Gramin Bank K.S v Management of Marathwada Gramin Bank*,[1019] the facts were that the Marathwada Gramin Bank was exempted from complying with the provisions of the Employees' Provident Fund Scheme, on the framing of its Scheme by the Bank to pay provident fund to its employees more than the statutory obligations. After that, the exemption granted to the establishment was cancelled/withdrawn, and the bank issued a notice of the change to its employees expressing its intention to discontinue the excess payment of Provident Fund being paid to the employees, owing to massive accumulated losses. The Supreme Court held that the Respondent bank could not be compelled to pay the amount more than its statutory liability for all times to come, just because it formed its trust and started paying Provident Fund more than its statutory liability.

Exemption to individual employee

Item (1) of Schedule II to the EPF Act shows that individual employee or a class of employees can seek exemption only as a matter of privilege and not as of right and, therefore, the Commissioner is entitled to impose such conditions as he deems fit.[1020]

EXCLUSION TO CERTAIN CLASSES OF ESTABLISHMENTS

Cooperatives – Special status

The Supreme Court, in the case of *Mohmedalli and others v Union of India and another*,[1021] held that the exemption granted to the establishments registered under the Cooperative Societies Act does not result in discrimination because it is the settled policy of the Government to foster cooperative societies with a view to their development and growth in the interest of the community. Cooperative Societies stand on a special footing which distinguishes them from other establishments or corporations.

[1018] 1998 SCC (L & S): 1998 (2) LLJ 612
[1019] 2011 AIR (SCW) 5143: 2011(4) LLJ 305: 2011(9) SCC 620
[1020] *Rhone-Poulenc Employees' Union v Regional P.F. Commissioner and others*, 1996 (3)LLN 709 (Bom.HC.)
[1021] 1964 AIR 980, 1963 SCR Supl. (1) 993

Cooperative Societies – 'with the aid of power' meaning of

In a cooperative society, the condition for applicability of the Act is that the number of workers should exceed fifty and they are required to work with the aid of power. Only if both conditions are satisfied, then the provisions of the Act apply.[1022]

Merely because electricity is used in the premises of the society for providing light and other amenities at the workplace, it cannot be said that the establishment works with the aid of power. Working with the aid of power implies that there must be some work or process carried on in the establishment with the use of power. Such use must be direct and proximate as regards the activity carried on by the establishment. An indirect application such as the use of electric bulbs for providing light or electric fans for providing the comfortable working environment does not amount to working with the aid of power.[1023]

'Working with the aid of power' – Meaning of

In *Kalpana Kala Kendra, Kanpur v ESI Corporation*,[1024] the Allahabad High Court was concerned with an establishment making handmade greeting cards with manual labour without using power. The Court held that the use of electricity merely for light or fans only cannot be treated to be an aid in the manufacturing process. The Court was however concerned in that case with the definition of the term 'factory' under the Employees' State Insurance Act and not with a case under the provisions of the EPF Act.

In *New Taj Mahal Café Ltd. v Inspector of Factories, Mangalore*,[1025] the Madras High Court was concerned with a similar question under the Factories Act. The restaurant was using the refrigerator. The question was whether the restaurant was carrying on any manufacturing process with the aid of power. The Court held that the restaurant was engaged in the business of making snacks without the aid of power and that having a refrigerator for storage of food was not a part of the manufacturing process and, therefore, the use of electricity for running the refrigerator did not amount to the establishment carrying on manufacturing process with the aid of power. The Court further held that if however, the refrigerator is used for treating and adopting any article to its sale, then the test of the manufacturing process with the aid of power would be satisfied, but not otherwise.

[1022] *Pubali Housing Cooperative Society Ltd. v Union of India and others* – 2006(2) LLJ 936 (Guwahati HC)
[1023] *Central Board of Trustees, EPF v Nutan Pushpak Premises Co-op. Society Ltd.* 2016 LLR 1019
[1024] 1985 Lab I.C. 763 (Allahabad)
[1025] AIR 1956 Madras 600

S.16(1)(a) – Exemption is not meant for sizeable commercial establishment like a bank

In *Mansa Nagrik Sahakari Bank Ltd. v Regional Provident Fund Commissioner*,[1026] a Division Bench of the Gujarat High Court observed that clause (a) of s.16(1) contemplates a cooperative society with less than 50 employees and carrying on the manufacturing process without the aid of power. Since large-scale manufacturing operations would ordinarily not be possible without the aid of power, an establishment run by a cooperative society with fewer than 50 employees and without the aid of power would, therefore, be an establishment working on a small scale like a cooperative society running a handloom industry manufacturing without the aid of power. Clause (a) was not intended to grant an exemption to a commercial establishment run by a cooperative society with a large-scale business like banking business or other business with a turnover of crores of rupees merely because it uses power only for lighting or cooling.

Belonging to v Control of – Meaning of

In *Regional Provident Fund Commissioner v Sanatan Dharam Girls Secondary School and others*,[1027] the Supreme Court has clarified that there is a difference between the expressions 'belonging to' and 'under the control of' as appearing in s.16(1)(b) of the EPF Act. The Court held, the words "belonging to" signifies ownership, i.e. the Government owned institutions would be covered under the said part and the words "under the control of" signifies control other than ownership since ownership has already been covered under the words "belonging to." It must also be noted that the two words are separated by the word "*or*" and therefore these two words refer to two mutually exclusive categories of institutions. While interpreting s.16(1)(b) of the Act, held that the private schools which are governed and controlled by the state Acts of Education would be 'under the control of' the State as per the meaning of the expression as found in s.16(1)(b) of the EPF Act, 1952.

Entitlement to Contributory Provident Fund/Old-Age Pension Fund is mandatory

The question of exclusion under s.16(1)(b) or s.16(1)(c) was considered by the Himachal Pradesh High Court in *Himachal Pradesh Vikas Pradhikaran v Regional Provident Fund Commissioner*.[1028] The Court observed that there is specific mention under these provisions that the employees belonging to or under the control of the Central government or State government are entitled to the benefit of contributory

---

[1026] (2005) 2 GLR 1592, (2005) III LLJ 669 Guj
[1027] (2007) 1 SCC 268
[1028] (1998) II LLJ 267 HP

Provident Fund or Old-Age Pension in accordance to any scheme or rule framed by such government. In the absence of both the requirements being fulfilled, the exclusion clause cannot be given. As the petitioner does not have any scheme or rule by which the daily-wages employees are entitled to the benefit of the contributory provident fund, the petitioner cannot claim the benefit of exclusion under s.16(1)(b) or 16(1)(c).

Infancy Protection – Effect of repeal

S.16(1)(d) provided for protection from coverage of the newly set-up establishments for an initial period of 3 years, as a breathing time. S.16 was amended by the Amendment Act, 1998, omitting clause (d) with effect from 22.9.1997. The said omission was initially carried out by Ordinance No.17/1997 promulgated on 22.9.1997. In *S.L. Srinivasa Jute Twine Mills Pvt. Ltd. v Union of India and another*,[1029] the Supreme Court held that the appellant should continue to enjoy the infancy protection of 3 years already accrued to them, before the amendment in 1997 irrespective of the repeal of the provision for such infancy protection. Similarly, in *Sangam Spinners v Regional P.F. Commissioner*,[1030] the Supreme Court citing the legal maxim – *nova constitution futuris forman imponere debet non praeteritis* (a new law ought to be construed to interfere as little as possible with vested rights) held that the appellant shall be entitled to the protection for the period of 3 years starting from the date of setting up, irrespective of the repeal of the provision for such infancy protection.

Exclusion under s.16(2) – Not applicable to single establishment

In *Aravindadevi.J v Union of India and others*,[1031] petitioner sought for grant of exclusion under s.16(2) for the individual establishment and contended that when the Provident Fund Act applies to every establishment, why exemption should not be granted to an individual establishments invoking the powers of the Central Government under s.16(2) of the Act. Refuting the argument, the Madras High Court observed, "the expression, "any class of establishments" in s.16(2) clearly shows that the exemption is intended to be conferred only to a class of establishments and the use of the expression "any" before the expression "class of establishments" in s.16(2), and the emphasis given to the expression, "class of establishments" in s.16(2) show that exemption is intended to be conferred only to a class of establishments. If the intention of the Legislature is otherwise, the

---

[1029] 2006(3) ALL MR(SC) 219: 2006(3) J.C.R. 235: 2006(1) S.C.T. 692: 2006(2) JT 397: 2006(2) SCC 740: 2007(2) SLR 139
[1030] 2008(1) S.C.T.148: 2007(6) R.A.J 604: 2008(1)SCC 391, 2008(1) LLJ 661
[1031] 2000 (87) FLR 73, (2000) IILLJ 1264 Mad

Legislature would have used the expression "any establishment" instead of "any class of establishments." The financial position of an establishment is not the only criterion which entitles an establishment to an exemption under s.16(2) of the Act; other circumstances may also be considered.[1032]

The Calcutta High Court, in *Bharat Board Mills Ltd. v The Regional P.F. Commissioner*,[1033] observed, if Section 16(2) of the Act had empowered the Government to grant exemption in case of any individual factory, then it appears that such a provision would become more exposed to challenge or attack on the ground that it enabled the Government to single out an individual at their own sweet-will and pleasure and exempt it from the operation of the Act.

Meaning of 'other circumstances of the case'

The provision has been enacted for the benefit of the factories. It enables the Government to grant, temporary reliefs to a particular class of factories carrying on a particular industry. The business of a particular industry mentioned in the Schedule may for some reason become dull or the said business may suffer financial loss or stringency for a particular period. In such a case the Government may be approached for granting temporary reliefs to this class of industry and the Government may upon a consideration of all the circumstances of the case grant exemption to the group of factories engaged in the particular industry. How can such a provision be regarded as unreasonable, it is difficult to follow. It is true that the words "other circumstances of the case" do vest a wide discretion in the Government but there is no reason to presume that this power conferred on the Government will be abused by the Government while exercising this power. If it can be established that the Government has acted arbitrarily in any case, such arbitrary act can be challenged in a court of law inasmuch as an arbitrary exercise of discretion is no exercise at all.

BOTH THE CENTRE AND THE STATES CAN LEGISLATE ON PROVIDENT FUNDS

Entry 24 of the Concurrent List (List III in the VII Schedule to the Constitution) provides for the welfare of labour, including provident funds. Thus, the subject matter of provident funds can be legislated upon both by the State Legislature as well as by the Parliament.[1034]

[1032] *Visva Bharati v Regional Provident Fund Commissioner*, 1983 I LLJ 332: 1983 I LLN 653 (Cal.HC)
[1033] AIR 1957 Cal 702, 61 CWN 694
[1034] *Zila Sahkari Federation Ltd.v Regional P.F. Commissioner*, 44 FJR 254: 1974 I LLJ 1: 28 FLR 37 (All.HC)

Supremacy of State Act – Article 254 of the Constitution

In the case of an inconsistency between the laws made by the Parliament and the State Legislature, a solution is provided by Article 254. The general rule is that in the case of an inconsistency the law made by the State Legislature has to give way to the law made by the Parliament. However, Sub-Article (2) of Article 254 gives primacy to the law made by the State Legislature over that made by the Parliament if the former has been reserved for the consideration of the President and has received his assent.

In *Security Guards Board for Greater Bombay and Thane District and others v Regional P.F. Commissioner*,[1035] the Bombay High Court held that the Maharashtra Private Security Guards (Regulation of Employment and Welfare) Act, 1981, having been reserved for the assent of the President and having received his assent, has primacy over the EPF Act. That being the case, the EPF Act and the Schemes framed thereunder will not apply to the Security Guards Board constituted under the 1981 Act.

The Kerala Motor Transport Workers' Welfare Fund Act, 1985 is not repugnant to the EPF Act, 1952. The Kerala Act (state Act) had received the assent of the President of India, and the same would prevail over the Central Act even if the same is deemed to have occupied the field. The Kerala Act applies only to those establishments which the Central Act does not apply. Both the State Act and the Central Act can therefore simultaneously apply in their respective areas of operation. There is, therefore, no repugnancy as envisaged by Article 254(1) of the Constitution of India.[1036]

Trustees continue in office even if the union is bifurcated

The bifurcation of union, or other union having majority is not a ground to remove trustees duly appointed under the scheme, having statutory force of law.[1037]

Exemption is revoked on change in status

Paragraph 27-AA of the EPF Scheme, 1952 clearly stipulates that in case of change of legal status, the exemption will stand revoked.[1038]

[1035] 1991 (62) FLR 986, (1993) IIILLJ 381 Bom
[1036] *Unni Mammu Haji v State of Kerala* (1989) 2 LLJ 493 (Ker.)
[1037] *P. Gengaiyan and others v General Manager, Neyveli Lignite Corp Ltd., and another*, 2011(2) LLN 818(Mad.)
[1038] *Sundaram Motors Ltd. and another v The Employees Provident Fund Organisation*, W.P.Nos.6763 and 16443 of 2008, decision dated 7-6-2011 (Mad. HC)

Chapter XVIII
TRANSFEROR-TRANSFEREE LIABILITIES

TRANSFER OF LIABILITY

Section 17-B speaks that the liability on the employer would not cease because of the transfer, but would continue to exist and would also be fastened upon the transferee, though limited to the value of the assets obtained by the transferee by such transfer. The transfer by the employer of the establishment contemplated under s.17-B is an act by the employer.

By a Court sale or otherwise, a transfer takes place by operation of law and not by any transaction *inter vivos*. In that sense, it is an involuntary sale against the wishes of the person whose property is sold. That can hardly be called a transfer, as ordinarily understood, which connotes a voluntary transaction entered into between two parties. In this connection it has also to be remembered that the provisions of the transfer of property act generally dealing kinds of transfers do not affect transfer by operation of law, or by or in execution of a decree or order of a Court of competent jurisdiction under section 2(d) of the Transfer of Property Act.[1039,1040]

Agreement cannot save the skin of transferee

In *McLeod Russel India Limited v Regional Provident Fund Commissioner, Jalpaiguri and others*,[1041] the question before the Supreme Court for consideration were whether the transferee could escape the liability under s.17-B by way of an explicit agreement with the transferor. The Supreme Court observed that since EPF Act is a beneficial legislation, it needs to be construed in the best interest of the employees and held that *inter se* covenants between the two entities would not insulate the new employer from the rigours of damages imposed by the EPF Act. It also clarified that even though the transferor entity made the default in the payment of dues, the transferee shall not stand absolved of the liabilities even if such liabilities are specifically assigned to the former by an express agreement.

[1039] *Suburban Ply And Panels (P) Ltd. v Regional Provident Fund Commissioner*, 2004 LLJ Ori. 2 1069
[1040] *Shri Angappa Spinning Mills v. Regional Commissioner, Employees' Provident Fund*, (1986) 1 MLJ 386
[1041] 2014 (8) SCALE 272

Lessee – Lessor Liabilities

In *R.K. Trading and Rice Mills v Regional Provident Fund Commissioner*,[1042] the High Court of Punjab and Haryana, placing reliance on the Madras High Court order in *Neyveli Lignite Corporation Ltd. v Regional Provident Fund Commissioner, Madras and another*,[1043] held that the petitioner-lessor, being owner of the premises cannot be fastened with any liability arising out of the acts of omission and commission, if any, by the lessee during the period when the premises were leased out to the lessee. When the ultimate control like the power of dismissal of employees was vested in the lessor's hands, the lessee was not to be liable as an employer.[1044] An occupier need not be the owner or director and the owner need not necessarily be an occupier.[1045]

Transfer due to death of the employer

In *General Beedi Works v Provident Fund Inspector*,[1046] the Karnataka High Court dismissed the criminal revision petitions declining to accept the contention that the accused are not the transferees under s.17-B of the Act. In this case, the transfer was due to the death of the father and husband of the petitioners and therefore though it is not a case of succession as such, the assumption of management of the factory by forming the partnership is sufficient compliance of s.17-B of the Act, as transfer of establishment includes sale, gift, lease or licence or in any other manner whatsoever.

Transferee cannot insist recovery from the transferor first

In *Radhamani v Enforcement Officer, Kollam*,[1047] the High Court of Kerala held that the liability of the transferor and the transferee is joint and several. The transferee also would be liable in respect of the contribution or other sums due from the employer for the period up to the date of transfer. However, the liability of the transferee is limited to the value of the assets obtained by him by the transfer. Given the specific provision under s.17-B of the Act, the transferee cannot contend that the dues before the date of transfer should be recovered from the transferor or that the transferee could be proceeded against only on failure to recover the amount from the transferor. There is no liability on the part of the Employees' Provident Fund authorities to proceed against the transferor first, nor there is a right vested in the transferee to insist for such a course being adopted.

[1042] 2017 LabLR 36: 2017(152) FLR 910: 2017(1) LLN 796
[1043] 1998 (11) LLJ 159
[1044] *Inspector of Provident Funds v Mani PS*, 1967 II LLJ 647 (Ker.HC)
[1045] *Jyothi Switchgears Ltd. v Chief Inspector of Factories*, 34 FLR 354 (Guj. HC)
[1046] 1998(1) CLR 840: 1998(2) KantLJ 19: 1998(1) LLJ 983
[1047] 2011 LIC 2965: 2011(4) S.C.T. 554: 2011(1) Ker L.J. 9

In *Radhamani v Enforcement Officer, Kollam*,[1048] the High Court of Kerala observed that a reading of the proviso to s.8B(1) along with s.17-B makes the position clear on the following aspects: (1) The liability of the transferor and the transferee is joint and several; (2) The liability of the transferor is only up to the date of transfer; (3) The transferee would be liable to pay even the arrears which fell due before the date of transfer; (4) The liability of the transferee is limited to the extent of the value of the assets obtained by such transfer; (5) The attachment and sale by the Recovery Officer shall first be effected against the properties of the establishment; (6) If the attachment and sale of the properties of the establishment is insufficient for recovering the amount due, the Recovery Officer may proceed against the property of the employer.

Transferee's Liability under S.17-B

In *Employees' Provident Fund Organisation v Jai Corporation Limited*,[1049] the Gujarat High Court held that the provisions of s.17-B could be invoked when the employer does the voluntary transfer of establishment. The Court observed that the words 'transfers that establishment in whole or in part" is qualified and prefixed by the words "where an employer." Thus, the obligation of joint and several liabilities cast by this provision will come in play when an 'establishment is transferred by the employer of that establishment,' by sale, gift, lease or licence or in any other manner. It is clear that the legislature has intended to keep 'enforced sale' or 'auction sale/purchase' or a 'sale by operation of law' or 'involuntary sale' out of the purview of this provision, otherwise there was no purpose of using, at the outset of the Section, the words 'where an employer.'

Transferee has to ascertain all statutory liabilities before transfer

In *Dalgaon Agro Industries Ltd. v Union of India and others*,[1050] the Calcutta High Court observed that transfer is an agreement between the transferor and the transferee. It binds neither the employees nor the Provident Fund Authorities, which were not parties to the transfer. Therefore the transferee cannot claim immunity from the liability accrued under any provision of the Act on the date of transfer. It is not dependant on the ascertainment or determination. Once the liability accrues, it is only a matter for quantification. S.17-B is a caution to the transferee to include all such liabilities within the consideration for transfer. If he does not do so, he does so at his peril.

[1048] 2011 LIC 2965: 2011(4) S.C.T. 554: 2011(1) Ker L.J. 9
[1049] 2009 LIC 670: 2009(1) GCD 402: 2009(121) FLR 265: 2009(1) GLR 123
[1050] 2006) 1 CALLT 32 HC, 2005 (3) CHN 428, (2005) III LLJ 356 Cal

Penal Damages cannot be levied against the transferee

In *Darjeeling Dooars Plantation Ltd. and another v Regional P.F. Commissioner, West Bengal and others*,[1051] a Division Bench of the Calcutta High Court made a distinction between 'transferor' and 'employer' and 'the other person." The Court observed: "A plain reading of Sections 14-B, 15(2), 17(5) indicates that the said sections contemplate a period and stage before any transfer of the establishment. Section 17-B of the Act, on the other hand, contemplates a stage post transfer. The same will be evident from the use of the expression 'the employer, and the person to whom the establishment is so transferred shall jointly and severally be liable to contribute and' other sums due 'from the employer.' So that expression 'the employer and other persons to whom the establishment is transferred,' clearly indicates that the transferee does not come within the meaning of the employer as in Section 2(e) of the Act. Under Section 17-B of the Act, the transferee is 'the other person.' So there is a distinction between 'employer' and 'the other person.' The other person' comes only after transfer of the establishment either in whole or in part. Transfer of the establishment is contemplated under Section 17-B of the Act. The sections are prior that in the Act does not contemplate either the transfer of the establishment or 'the other person.' Section 17-B does not contemplate any hearing of 'the employer' and 'the other person' or either of them. However, Section 14-B contemplates a hearing of 'the employer.' The absence of the expression 'the other person' in Section 14-B shows that it is a stage before the transfer of the establishment. In other words Section 14-B contemplates in its proviso notice upon 'the employer,' and not upon 'the other person.'

However, in the case of *Dalgaon Agro Industries Ltd. v Union of India and others*,[1052] another Division Bench of the Calcutta High Courted did not subscribe to the above view, and held as follows: "Though the word "employer" and "other person" connote two different identities, yet in the context of Section 17-B on transfer of the establishment notionally and legally the transferor ceases to be the employer and the transferee steps into the shoes of the employer. However, a legal fiction has been created in respect of the liability arising under any provisions of the 1952 Act to continue the liability to facilitate recovery even in respect of the dues that had accrued before the date of transfer making both the transferor and the transferee liable jointly and severally. The legislature had intended to identify the other person, the transferee as employer liable along with the transferor by the creation of fiction in Section 17-B. The expression "other person" also connotes the transferee who is stepping into the shoes of the employer. As soon the transferee

---

[1051] 1995 (1) LLJ 939
[1052] 2006) 1 CALLT 32 HC, 2005 (3) CHN 428, (2005) III LLJ 356 Cal

steps into the shoes of the employer the continuity of liability is not affected by the transfer and both the transferor and transferee, as employer past and present remain liable jointly and severally. Therefore the other person even if connotes a different meaning but in the context in which it has been used it cannot be construed to divide the liability to pre-transfer and post-transfer period being recoverable from one and not from the other. When the legislature creates a joint liability even being other person becomes liable for the dues of the pre-transfer period."

The Calcutta High Court, in *Dalgaon Agro Industries Ltd. v Union of India*,[1053] laid down certain principles for attributing liability for employer's statutory dues under the EPF Act as under. (i) Liability for payment of due amount remains unaffected by transfer of establishment (ii) Transferee entity is jointly and severally liable for payment of such dues, (iii) Outstanding due is first charge on the asset transferred (iv) Such due can be recovered as damages (v) Acquirer's liability is limited to the value of the asset transferred; and (vi) No personal liability attaches to the acquirer or any other asset of the acquirer.

In *Regional Provident Fund Commissioner v Karnataka Forest Plantations Corporation Ltd.*[1054] held that the concept of penalty would arise only when there is guilt. While interpreting Section 17-B, it was held that the transferee employer would be liable to contribute for the period preceding the transfer. Section 17-B cannot be interpreted to mean that the transferee employer would be liable also to pay the penalty for the default committed by the previous employer during the period anterior to the transfer. The penalty as correctly interpreted cannot be treated as either contribution or as other sums due from the employer. Such an interpretation would be opposed to the principle of natural justice. The penalty cannot be saddled on somebody who is not guilty.

But the law is now well settled in *McLeod Russel India Limited v Regional Provident Fund Commissioner, Jalpaiguri and others*,[1055] where the Supreme Court affirmed the decision of the Regional Provident Fund Commissioner, and held that the transferee company could be made liable for 'damages' as the language in s.17-B speaks explicitly of "contributions and other sums due from the employer."

Hearing the transferee is essential when delay was committed by him

Even if the transferee is given hearing, by no stretch of imagination he could be able to explain the reason for default committed by the transferor, a knowledge personal to the transferor. The determination of the liability under Section 14-B only upon

---

[1053] (2006) 1 CALLT32(HC)
[1054] 2000-I-LLJ-1134 (Kant)
[1055] 2014 (8) SCALE 272

hearing the transferee would render the proviso futile and ineffective. Therefore, the transferee cannot be treated at par with the employer in respect of damages contemplated under Section 14-B.[1056]

Reconstruction Company cannot be deemed as 'occupier'

In *Employees' Provident Fund Organisation v Jai Corporation Limited*,[1057] the facts for consideration before the Gujarat High Court were that Santogen Spinning Mills Ltd. was a sick undertaking under the provisions of the Sick Industrial Companies (Special Provisions) Act, 1985 and proceedings were initiated under the Securitisation And Reconstruction of Financial Assets and Enforcement of Security Interest Act, 2002. The Assets Reconstruction Company (India) Ltd. (ARCIL) took over the possession of the secured assets of the said company. The EPFO contended that since ARCIL has taken over the establishment, it should be deemed as the transferee employer under s.17-B of the Act and ARCIL should pay the outstanding dues payable by Santogen Spinning Mills Ltd. Refuting such contention, the High Court observed that ARCIL is a 'reconstruction company' defined under s.2(v) of the SARFAESI Act, and it can take-over only 'secured assets' and that too only for the specific purpose, it cannot be deemed as the 'occupier.' The Court further held that s.17-B does not take in its sweep auction sale, enforced sale, sale by operation of law or involuntary sale.

[1056] *Dalgaon Agro Industries Ltd v Union of India* (2006) 1 CALLT32(HC)
[1057] [2009(121)FLR265]; (2009)1GLR123

Chapter XIX
PUBLIC SERVANTS AND THEIR PROTECTION

S.18A declares the Presiding Officer of a Tribunal and certain other officers (viz., the authorities referred to in s.7-A and every Inspector) shall be deemed public servants within the meaning of s.21 of IPC.

Provident Fund Commissioner – Public Officer

In *Coal Mines Provident Fund Commissioner v Ramesh Chandra Jha*,[1058] the Supreme Court held that the Coal Mines Provident Fund Commissioner is a *'public officer'* within the meaning of s.2(17) of the Code of Civil Procedure, 1908 and that the Union of India is a necessary party against suits if any filed against the Coal Mines Provident Fund Commissioner, in view of Order 27 Rule 5A of the Code of Civil Procedure, which reads, "where a suit is instituted against a public officer for damages or other relief in respect of any act alleged to have been done by him in his official capacity, the Government shall be joined as a party to the suit."

A contrary view was taken by the Supreme Court in *Regional Provident Fund Commissioner v Shiv Kumar Joshi*[1059] and *Steel Authority of India Ltd. & others v National Union Waterfront Workers and others*[1060] where it had been held that the Regional Provident Fund Commissioner under the Employees' Provident Funds and Miscellaneous Provisions Act, 1952 is not a public officer, though he discharges statutory functions for running the Scheme. It was also observed that the Board of Trustees had not in any way been delegated the sovereign powers of the State even if it is held that the administrative charges were payable by the Central Government.

Removal of Public Servants from Office

In the case of *R. Balakrishna Pillai v State of Kerala*,[1061] the Supreme Court has held that in the case of a person who is or was a public servant not removable from his office save by or with the sanction of the Government and who is accused of any offence alleged to have been committed by him while acting or purporting to act

---

[1058] AIR 1990 SC 648: 1990(1) SCC 589
[1059] AIR 2000 SC 331
[1060] 2001 (7) SCC 1
[1061] AIR 1996 SC 901 at pp. 902–03: (1996) 1 SCC 478

in the discharge of his official duty, sanction under s.197 of Cr.P.C. is required for the prosecution of a public servant even after his retirement. S.197 of the Criminal Procedure Code, 1973 provides that when any person who is or was a Judge or Magistrate or a public servant not removable from office save by or with the sanction of the Government is accused of any offence alleged to have been committed by him while acting or purporting to act in the discharge of his official duty, no court shall take cognizance of such offence except with the previous sanction of the appropriate authority.

PROTECTION OF ACTION TAKEN IN GOOD FAITH

Good Faith clause covers not only officers but also 'any person'

The language of s.18-A is broad enough to cover not only officers or government servants but also 'any person.' Managers and occupiers of factories who have specific duties cast upon them by the Act are also protected.[1062] The protection of action taken in good faith is available subject to the condition that the act complained of should have been necessitated by a statutory duty, and the person should have acted in good faith to give effect to the provisions of the Act. There must be a compliance or an intended compliance with a provision of the Act before the protection can be claimed. The section cannot cover a case of a breach or an intended breach of the Act however honest the conduct otherwise.[1063]

Willful Negligence sacks protection

The Supreme Court of *Kailas Sizing Works v Municipality of Bhivandi and Nizampur*[1064] made a detailed discussion of the 'good faith' clause. 'Good faith' therefore implies, not only an upright mental attitude, and clear conscience of a person, but also the doing of an act, showing that ordinary prudence has been exercised according to the standards of a reasonable person. 'Good faith' contemplates an honest effort to ascertain the facts upon which exercise of the power must rest. It must, therefore, be summed up as 'an honest determination from ascertained facts.' 'Good faith' precludes pretence or deceit and also negligence and recklessness. A lack of diligence, which an honest man of ordinary prudence is accustomed to exercise, is, in law, a want of good faith. Once this is shown, good faith does not require a sound judgment." The definition of the term in the General Clauses act lays stress on the one aspect of honesty only irrespective of negligence, but that in the Indian Penal Code lays stress on two

---

[1062] *Public Prosecutor v Mangaldas V Thakker* 1958 CriLJ 150 [relating to Factories Act, 1947]
[1063] *State of Gujarat v Kansara Manilal Bhikhalal* AIR 1964 SC 1893 (1964) II LLJ 456 SC, 1964 7 SCR 656
[1064] AIR 1969 Bom 127, (1968) 70 BOMLR 554, ILR 1969 Bom 564

aspects, viz., the honesty of intention along with due care and attention. Both the definitions retain the real essence of good faith, which is honesty. This is a feature common to both the definitions.

Good faith precludes willful negligence under the General Clauses Act

S.3(22) of the General Clauses Act defines the term 'good faith' as 'a thing shall be deemed to be done in good faith where it is in fact done honestly, whether it is done negligently or not.' On the other hand, s.52 of the Indian Penal Code defines it as 'nothing is said to be done or believed in good faith which is done or believed without due care and attention.' The definition of the term in the General Clauses Act lays stress on one aspect only, but, that in the Penal Code emphasises two aspects, namely, the honesty of intention along with due care and attention. In *Public Prosecutor v Vattam Venkataramayya*,[1065] held, the definition of s.3(22) of the General Clauses Act, and not the IPC, applies under the EPF Act. This section only restricts the filing of suits against acts done in good faith but not otherwise.[1066]

SECTION 19 – DELEGATION OF POWERS

As the Supreme Court of India has observed, it is now well settled that the power of delegation is a constituent element of the legislative power as a whole, and in modern times when the legislatures enact laws to meet the challenge of the complex socio-economic policies, they often find it necessary and convenient to delegate subsidiary or ancillary powers to delegates of their choice for carrying out the policy of the legislation.[1067] In *Northern India Press Works v Regional Provident Fund Commissioner*,[1068] a Division Bench of the High Court of the Allahabad High Court held that the delegation of power under the Act has got to be done strictly by the provisions of the statute and any departure from it would be unwarranted and void in law. 'A perusal of sub-section (b) of Section 19 indicates that the State Government can delegate its powers to any officer or authority subordinate to the State Government which may be specified in the notification and not to an officer or authority subordinate to the Central Government. Hence, the State Government can validly delegate the powers exercisable by it under s.14-B to an officer, who is an employee of the State Government and not of the Central Government.

[1065] 1962 II LLJ 21 (AP.HC)
[1066] *Union of India v Sir Shadi Lal Sugar & General Mills Ltd.*, AIR 1980 All 379 (FB)
[1067] *VM. Sanjawalla v The State of Hombay*, AIR 1961 SC4; *Makhan Singh v The State of Punjab*, AIR 1964 SC 281; *Mohamedali v The Union of India*; AIR 1964 SC 980 (a case under the Employees' Provident Funds Act, 1952).
[1068] 1983 Lab IC 1314 (All).

Provident Fund Commissioner acts as a ministerial officer

As regards the exempted establishments for which the State Government is the appropriate government, the Regional Provident Fund Commissioner merely acts as a ministerial officer who sends a proposal to the State Government. He is not a delegate of the State Government and cannot exercise the function of the State Government, which are of judicial nature, and as such cannot be delegated.[1069]

ADVICE BY CENTRAL GOVERNMENT

In *Bankimchandra v Regional Provident Fund Commissioner*,[1070] a Division Bench of the Patna High Court ruled that the Central Government could issue a direction only when any difficulty arose in giving effect to the provisions of the Act and when any doubt arose as to any of the matters referred in that Section in the mind of the authority which had to deal with the subject and that if the authority did not entertain any doubt to be given by the Central Government at the instance of a private party who might raise a dispute on any issue envisaged by the Section. The Court added that the question of any dispute being raised by the party concerned was foreign to the section.

Power to remove difficulties

S.20 to 22 have been substituted for s.19-A by s.25 of the EPF & MP (Amendment) Act, 1988 with effect from a date to be notified by the Central Government. In *I.T.C. Ltd. v Regional Provident Fund Commissioner*,[1071] a Division Bench of the Punjab and Haryana High Court interpreted s.19-A and held that it did not provide for any enquiry by the Central Government. The parties affected are not required to be heard nor any decision rendered. There is only an administrative or a ministerial order and not a judicial or quasi-judicial order. Therefore, the remedy envisaged in section 19-A of the Act cannot be a remedy to bar a writ petition.

The proviso to s.22(1) stipulates that the Central Government can pass the no order after the expiry of a period of 3 years from the date on which the said amendment Act receives the assent of the President. As the amendment received the assent of the President in the year 1988 itself, the time limit for exercise of powers by the Central Government has since expired, and the provision would remain a mere dead letter.

[1069] *Lakshmiji Sugar Mills Co. Ltd. v Union of India*, 30 FLR 122 (All. HC)
[1070] AIR 1958 Pat 314, 1958 (6) BLJR 239, (1958) IILLJ 444 Pat
[1071] 1988(1)ILR (Punjab)73: 1987(2)LLN 932 (P&H) (DB)

Rules cannot contravene the Act

A rule cannot exceed the four corners of the authority conferred by the Act itself under which the rule is framed in particular and the law in general.[1072] The validity of an Act of a competent Legislature cannot be made to depend upon what some subordinate authority chooses to do or not to do.[1073] Where rules are to be framed for carrying out the purpose of the Act, such rules cannot travel beyond the four corners of the Act itself.[1074] Rules cannot take away what is given by the Act.[1075] If a rule goes beyond the scope of the authority conferred by the statute, then the rule would obviously be bad and the rule cannot extend the authority of an officer not conferred upon him by the legislature.[1076] Rules cannot enlarge the scope of the statutory provision.[1077] The rules framed under a statute cannot govern or control the words of the statute.[1078] If a statutory instrument contains words identical to those under the Act under which it is made, those words must be construed in the same way as they are construed in the Act.[1079] Statutory rules, if validly made within the powers conferred by the Act, must be regarded as part of the Act itself and made with the full authority of the Legislature.[1080]

A delegated power to legislate by making rules for carrying out the purposes of the Act is a general delegation without laying down any guidelines; it cannot be so exercised as to bring into existence substantive rights or obligations or disabilities not contemplated by the provisions of the Act itself.[1081]

[1072] *Munnalal v Nazim*, AIR 1950 Hyd 5
[1073] *State of Bombay v United Motors Ltd*, AIR 1953 SC 252
[1074] *Huzrat Syed v Commissioner of Wakf*, AIR 1954 Cal 436
[1075] AIR 1954 All 202.
[1076] *Pramod C. Bhat v Kanwar Raj Nath*, AIR 1954 Bom 518
[1077] *K. Muthuvadivelu v R.T. Officer*, AIR 1956 Mad 143
[1078] *Madan Singh v Collector*, AIR 1954 Raj 104
[1079] *Ram Piare v Municipal Committee*, AIR 1955 Pat 125.
[1080] *Saligram Singh v Emperor*, 23 Pat 22
[1081] *Kunj Behari Lal Butail and others v State of H.P and others*, (2000) 3 SCC 40 2000 Indlaw SC 160

Chapter XX
SCHEDULE HEAD ENTRIES

Liberal Construction of Schedule Head entries

The word 'lantern' is a case enclosing a light whereas a 'lamp' is a vessel with oil and wick for giving light. The term 'hurricane lanterns' used in item 16 of the Explanation of Schedule I of the Act includes 'incandescent lamps.'[1082]

Trading and Commercial establishments

In *Canara Bank Financial Services Ltd. v Regional Provident Fund Commissioner*,[1083] the Karnataka High Court held that the words 'purchase, sale or storage' are disjunctively placed, and therefore it is not necessary that an establishment must be engaged in all the three activities simultaneously, namely, purchase, sale and storage, for being treated as 'trading and commercial establishment.'

In *Christian Association for Radio and Audio Visual Service v Regional PF Commissioner*,[1084] the Madhya Pradesh High Court were considering whether the petitioner society, which is a religious organisation running on the no-profit-no-loss basis, would come under the purview of the Act. The activity of the society was to render specialised service to Christian churches and institutions in the field of audio-visual aids and in lieu of the service, it was being aided by the churches and charitable institutions. The Court held that there was an organised cooperation between the petitioner society and its employees in production and distribution of goods and services and merely because the churches aided it, it did not cease to be a trading and commercial establishment.

Electrical, Mechanical or General Engineering Products

In *The Regional Provident Fund Commissioner, Punjab v Shibu Metal Works*[1085] the Supreme Court, construing the entry, 'Electrical, Mechanical or General Engineering Products,' held that in construing the material provisions of such an Act, if two views are reasonably possible, the court should prefer the view which helps the achievement of the object. If the words used in the entry are capable of

---

[1082] *East India Industries (Madras) Private Ltd. v Regional Provident Fund Commissioner*, 1964(1)LLJ 706: 26 FJR 42: 1964(1) MLJ 441
[1083] 1995(71)FLR446
[1084] 1979 Lab IC 283
[1085] 1965(1) LLJ 473: AIR 1965 SC 1076: 1965(2) SCR 72 (SC – 3 M)

narrow or broad construction, both of which are reasonably possible, and it appears that the broad construction would help the furtherance of the object, then it would be necessary to prefer the said construction.

The use of the word 'includes' shows that the 25 items listed in the Explanation do not exhaust the scope of the expression 'Electrical, mechanical or general engineering products," but either illustrate the scope or extend it. Further, the words "without prejudice to the ordinary meaning of the expressions used therein" bring out two more important features which help the proper construction of the meaning of the entry "electrical, mechanical or general engineering products, viz., it has to be given its 'ordinary meaning' and the expression is a general one.[1086] In *Great Eastern Electroplaters Ltd. v Regional Provident Fund Commissioner,*[1087] it was held that the scope of the words 'electrical and mechanical products' is not to cover all products which are made by means of mechanical or electrical process but it means products which are utilised for the purpose of producing electricity or implements and other apparatus and machinery or goods like fans, radio and battery shells. A Division Bench of the Bombay High Court in *Nagpur Glass Works Ltd., Nagpur v Regional Provident Fund Commissioner, Bombay,*[1088] dissented from the decision of the Allahabad Court mentioned above and held that the expression 'electrical, mechanical or general engineering products' means engineering products relating to or connected with electricity, or engineering products acting or worked or produced by a machine or mechanism, or products produced by a craftsman employing a certain design or invention. The Court held that burners and metal lamps fall within the meaning of the expression above. Reiterating the above view, the High Court of Punjab and Haryana, in *Hindustan Electric Co Ltd. v Regional Provident Fund Commissioner,*[1089] held that the words 'electrical, mechanical or general engineering" is used in an extensive sense and even though specific articles are mentioned in the explanation, that cannot cut down the generality of the expressions employed.

Products manufactured by students – not covered

The expression 'engaged' in s.1(3)(a) indicates commercial production as a primary concern, and by no stretch of the imagination, an educational institution can be treated as engaged in the production of electrical, mechanical and general engineering productions. The products manufactured by the students are not sold, nor the Institute derives any monetary benefits out of such production. As the

---

[1086] *Wire Netting Stores v Regional Provident Fund Commissioner and others,* A.I.R. 1970 Delhi 143
[1087] AIR 1956 All 495 (T)
[1088] AIR 1957 Bom 152 (L)
[1089] AIR 1959 P H 27, (1960) ILLJ 640 P H

sole intention of producing such goods is to impart training to the students of the institution, it is impossible to hold that the institution is engaged in the production of such goods.[1090]

Bodybuilding for buses and trucks

The word 'automobiles' in schedule I, Explanation (a), item (12) of the EPF Act, 1952, includes a bus and a truck. As there cannot be a bus or truck without a body thereon, the body is a necessary part of the same. Hence, the body of a bus or truck must be considered as its part or accessories within the meaning of item (25) of the said Explanation. Thus, a factory in which more than 20 persons are engaged in the process of building of bodies on the chassis of buses and trucks is a factory engaged in 'electrical, mechanical or general engineering products.'[1091]

Manufacturing of musical instruments

In *Haji Nadir Ali Khan and others v The Union of India and others*,[1092] the Punjab-Haryana High Court observed that the items generally from No.10 onwards in the explanation to the expression 'electrical, mechanical or general engineering products' are intended to be covered by the heading 'mechanical products' though some of them such as hurricane lanterns, drums and containers and cutlery and surgical instruments may not appear on the face of it to be very obviously mechanical and in this context the word 'mechanical' would seem to be intended to cover all manufactured objects which are put to some use as opposed to articles of food and drink which are intended for consumption. The Court further held that the musical instruments which are intended to be played by their ultimate owners fall within the category of 'mechanical products.'

Manufacture of micanite sheets and mica folium,[1093] manufacture of burners and accessories of hurricane lanterns,[1094] manufacture of stoves,[1095] domestic stoves,[1096] wire netting rolls, wire-netting, wire gauze, wire cloth and 'jail' from galvanized iron wires,[1097] manufacture of brass utensils,[1098] shuttles, wire-heads and reeds,[1099]

[1090] *Victoria Jubilee Technical Institute v K.S. Naik, Regional P.F. Commissioner* (1980) ILLJ 254 Bom
[1091] *Regional P.F. Commissioner, Punjab v Free India Industries* (1964) I LLJ 662
[1092] AIR 1958 P H 177
[1093] *Indian Mica & Micanite Industries Ltd. v Union of India* 1969 I LLJ 436
[1094] *National Hurricane Works v Union of India* 44 FJR 401: 1973 II LLN 450(Del.HC)
[1095] *Hindustan Electric Co. Ltd. v Regional P.F. Commissioner* 16 FJR 235: 1960 I LLJ 640
[1096] *Regional P.F. Commissioner v Lakshmi Ratan Engineering Works Ltd.* 22 FJR 278: 1962 II LLJ 604
[1097] *Wire Netting Stores v Regional P.F. Commissioner* 59 FJR 24: 1982 I LLJ 7 (Del. DB)
[1098] *Regional P.F. Commissioner v Shibu Metal Works* 1965 I LLJ 473
[1099] *Swastic Textile Trading Co. Ltd. v Union of India* 1965 II LLJ 254

chromium plated household and sanitary fittings,[1100] metal lamps and burners,[1101] making of vessels out of metal sheets and circles,[1102] manufacture of perambulators and tricycles,[1103] electric torches,[1104] incandescent lamps,[1105] artificial limbs for disables,[1106] cycle parts,[1107] clinical thermometer,[1108] come within the meaning of 'electrical, mechanical or engineering products.'

Medical Practitioners and Specialists

In *Employees' Provident Fund Inspector v Poly Clinic (P) Ltd,*[1109] the Kerala High Court observed, "to make an establishment a hospital or a clinic, it is immaterial as to who owns, controls or manages it. What is material is only the operation and activities there. We are aware of hospitals, dispensaries, clinics and other establishments owned, controlled and managed by people not qualified in the medical field, but employing qualified men. To make it an establishment of medical practitioners and specialists, it is not the ownership, control or management that counts. It is the business transacted that is material otherwise the beneficent provision could be easily defeated by keeping ownership, management and control in somebody else."

Hospital – Inpatient Facility not mandatory for coverage

In *Kottayam District Cooperative Hospital Society v Regional Provident Fund Commissioner,*[1110] the appellant 'hospital society' contended that it is not offering any provision for hospitalization or admitting inpatients, and it is not offering any treatment facility to patients and that its activity is related to diagnosis of diseases by running the whole body scan unit, clinical laboratory, pathological laboratory and it runs a medical store. A Division Bench of the Kerala High Court held that the facility of hospitalization is not a condition precedent to making an institution a 'hospital,' if it satisfies the requirement as a centre for study of diseases or as a place where there is 'practice of medicine,' as understood in the larger sense of the term.

[1100] *Evershine Metals v Regional P.F. Commissioner* 1962 II LLJ 479
[1101] *Nagpur Glass Works Ltd. v Regional P.F. Commissioner* 1958 I LLJ 281
[1102] *T.R. Raghava Iyengar & Company v Regional P.F. Commissioner* 1963 I LLJ 32
[1103] *Gopalan M.V v State of Madras* 1963 I LLJ 52 (Mad. HC)
[1104] *Regional P.F. Commissioner v Great Eastern Electroplaters Ltd* 1958 II LLJ 676 (All. DB)
[1105] *Bankim Chandra Chakravarty v Regional P.F. Commissioner* 1958 II LLJ 444
[1106] *Navedic Prosthetic Centre, Daulatsinghwala v Regional P.F. Commissioner* 1998 III LLJ 1163
[1107] *Deep Cycle Industries v Union of India* (1971) 39 FJR 407
[1108] *Jintan Clinical Thermometer Co. Pvt Ltd. v Union of India,* 46 FJR 371: 1975 LIC 303: 1975 I LLJ 169: 1974 II LLN 266 (Guj. FB)
[1109] 1989 Lab IC 969: (1989) 2 LLJ 562: (1988) 2 Cur LR 212
[1110] 2015(1) CLR 714: 2015(146) FLR 143: 2015(1) LLN 719: 2015 LabLR 540: 2014(25) S.C.T. 868

Similarly, in a previous case *EPF Inspector, Thrichur v The Poly Clinic (P) Ltd.*,[1111] the Kerala High Court observed, "The word 'Hospital' itself may have its origin from the words 'hospitable' or 'hospitality' which includes giving or affording a general welcome and entertainment to guests or strangers received. It is not necessary that reception or entertainment must be for the stay even though stay could also be contemplated."

Newspaper Employees

By a notification of the Government of India, Ministry of Labour SRO/2981 c dated 4th December 1956, a special provision in the case of newspaper establishment and newspaper employees had been inserted as Para 80 of Chapter X of the Employees' Provident Funds Scheme, 1952.

Cinema Theatres

It is by s.24 of the Cine-Workers and Cinema Theatre Workers (Regulation of Employment) Act, 1981, which was brought into force from December 24, 1981, that the Employees' Provident Funds Act became applicable to cinemas. For this purpose, the Central Government issued a notification G.S.R.347 on April 30, 1986, making it effective from October 1, 1984. Before that date, the Act did not apply to cinemas.[1112] S.5(2) and 7(1) both confer express powers of making the Scheme applicable retrospectively.[1113]

Applicability to Messes

In *Indian Institute of Technology, Madras v R.P.F.C, Madras*,[1114] the Madras High Court observed: "The test to be applied is, does the establishment sought to be covered under this Act has the avowed purpose of running messes? If it is so, then the establishment would be covered by Notification No.299 dated 24.03.1973 which applies the Act to the messes other than military messes." In '*R.N. Shah and others v Regional Provident Fund Commissioner*,[1115] it was held that the Notification dated 15.03.1973 specifying that every mess, not being a military mess, employing 20 or more persons, as the class of establishment to which the Act would apply with effect from 31.03.1973 would not apply to a mess run by a residential school. The mess run by a residential school cannot be termed as a separate and distinctive unit from that of the school itself.

[1111] 1989 (II) LLJ 562
[1112] Majestic Trading House v. Union of India, (1990) 2 LLN 626: 60 FLR 793 (All)(DB)
[1113] District Exhibitors Association v Union of India, (1991) 3 SCC 119: (1991) 2 LLJ 115
[1114] 1979 -54 FJR 429
[1115] 1991 (1) LLN 774

Textiles

In *Porritts & Spencer (Asia) Ltd. v State of Haryana*,[1116] the Supreme Court held that the concept of 'textiles' is not a static concept. It has, having regard to newly developing materials, methods techniques and processes, a continually expanding content and new kinds of fabric may be invented which may legitimately without doing any violence to the language be regarded as textiles. The word 'textiles' is derived from Latin *'texere'* which means 'to weave,' and it means woven fabric. When yarn, whether cotton, silk, woollen, rayon, nylon or of any other description made out of any other material is woven into fabric what comes into being is a 'textile' and is known as such.[1117]

A person who purchases cloth or other textile and then alters ornaments, finishes or otherwise treats or adapts the article to its use, sale, transport, delivery or disposal is said to manufacture. Therefore the Company which buys various types of cloth and then treats them and alters them to convert them into bandages, gatizes, lints, etc., is precisely manufacturing textiles.[1118]

Oriental Carpet

The process of weaving is an essential factor in the making of an oriental carpet as in any other woven textile. The process of knotting which also goes into the making of an oriental carpet is in addition to weaving. By using both the processes, the craftsman produces an oriental carpet which combines the advantages of a woven textile with those of an animal fleece. Oriental carpet is also, therefore, the product of weaving yarn, and in that sense, it is 'textile' within the ambit of the entry in Schedule I. The word textile, in its ordinary meaning, is broad enough to include carpets, both hand-woven as well as machine-made.[1119] The Supreme Court upheld this decision of the Rajasthan High Court in *Ess Dee Carpet Enterprises v Union of India and others*.[1120]

Durries

The only material that is used in the manufacture of durries is yarn, cotton, and woollen and the process is by weaving or spinning yarn into durries. Durries, therefore, squarely fall within the term 'textiles.'[1121]

[1116] [1979]1 S.C.R. 545
[1117] *Ess Dee Carpet Enterprises v Union fo India and others*, 1990 AIR 455, 1989 SCR Supl. (2) 417
[1118] *Surgical Dressing Mfg. Co. Ltd. v Regional P.F. Commissioner* 17 April, 1956 in Civil Writ No. 368 of 1955 (Punj.HC)
[1119] *Ess Dee Carpet Enterprises v Union of India*, 1985 LIC 1116 (Raj.HC)
[1120] 1990 AIR 455, 1989 SCR Supl. (2) 417
[1121] *Hindustran Durree Factory v Regional P.F. Commissioner* 1975 LAB.I.C. 950 (P & H DB).

Bleaching, dyeing, finishing and processing are all part of the textile industry.[1122] If a factory where, apart from weaving, bleaching, dyeing and printing are also done, would fall within this definition of the expression 'any industry engaged in the manufacture or production of textiles.'[1123]

Carpets come within the meaning of 'textile'

In *Ess Dee Carpet Enterprises v Union of India*,[1124] the question was whether the carpets would come within the meaning of the expression 'textiles' described in Schedule 1 to the EPF Act. The Supreme Court, referring to the case of *Porritts and Spencer (Asia) Ltd. v State of Haryana*,[1125] where it was held that the concept of 'textile' is not a static one and having regard to newly developing materials, methods, techniques and process, a continually expanding content and new kinds of fabric may be invented which may legitimately without doing any violence to the language be regarded as textiles, held that the carpet comes under the head 'textiles.'

Textile includes 'khadi'

In *Saharsa Zila Khadi Gramodyog Sangh v Union of India*,[1126] a Division Bench of the Patna High Court held that being a beneficial legislation, the Act has to be construed liberally with the view to see that the object of the Act was achieved by providing maximum benefit to the employees engaged in industry and similar establishments. Keeping this in view, the Court interpreted the word 'textile' occurring in Schedule I widely to cover 'khadi' within its meaning.

Dyeing wool on job-work basis – a textile industry

In *Standard Dyeing and Finishing Mills v Union of India*, the High Court of Punjab and Haryana held that an establishment engaged in the business of dyeing wool brought to the establishment by third parties which are returned to the owners after collecting charges for the job done, is engaged in the manufacture of 'textiles' under schedule I.[1127] Manufacturing tapes, wicks, braided cords, sewing thread rolls is an industry engaged in 'textiles.'[1128]

[1122] *Central P.F. Commissioner v Ganesh Dyeing & Printing Works* 13 FJR 197 (Bom. DB)
[1123] *Kapur Textile Finishing Mills v Regional P.F. Commissioner*
[1124] 1990 AIR (SC) 455: 1990(1) CurLJ 247: 1990(1) SCC 461: 1989(Sup2) SCR 417
[1125] (1979)1 SCR 545
[1126] 1996(72) FLR279
[1127] (1970) 38 FJR 360
[1128] *K.R. Subbaier v Regional P.F. Commissioner* AIR1963Mad112; (1963) I LLJ 23

Manufacturing of tarpaulin – Textiles

In East *India Industries, Madras (Private), Ltd. v Regional Provident Fund Commissioner, Madras*,[1129] held, an establishment manufacturing "water-proof paper" and also "tarpaulin" was a factory which came under Schedule I to the Act under the items of the paper industry and textile industry.

Multi-State Cooperative Bank

In *The Ratnakar Bank Ltd. v The Regional P.F. Commissioner*,[1130] the Bombay High Court was considering the question whether the EPF Act applies to a Multi-State Cooperative Bank. A Division Bench of the Bombay High Court in *The United Western Bank Ltd. v Central Provident Fund and others*[1131] held that the provisions of the EPF Act are not applicable to the Multi-State Cooperative Bank. After the judgement of the Division Bench in the aforesaid case, a notification was issued on 25th February 2000, under s.5 read with s.7(1) of the Act whereby the words 'Banks doing business in one State or Union Territory and having no departments or branches outside that State or Union Territory" found in Para 1(3)(b) Item III were deleted and substituted by the words "Banks other than the Nationalized Banks established under any Central or State Act." The notification was challenged in Civil Writ Petition No.314 of 2001 by a Bank on the ground that an arbitrary distinction was drawn between the Nationalized Banks and other Banks and therefore the amendment violated Art.14 and 21 of the Constitution. By the order dated 13th August 2009, the Division Bench of Bombay High Court quashed the above notification dated 25th February 2000, being violative of Article 21 of the Constitution.

Engineering Contractors

To discharge its functions efficiently as engineers and engineering contractors engaged in building and construction industry, an establishment has to maintain workshop or workshops where the work of smithy, welding, cutting, carpentry etc. are carried on. In the instant case, the work carried on at the appellant company's workshop at Bombay was the work of maintaining and repairing of the equipment belonging to the appellant only. The appellant was not earning any income or profit by carrying on the work of any other establishment at the said workshop. It is wrong to treat the workshop in question as a separate unit of the business of the appellant forming a separate establishment for purposes of determining whether the Act applies to the appellant or not. All the business operations carried on by the appellant in their totality

---

[1129] 1964 – I L.L.J. 706
[1130] 2010 LLR 1152 (Bom. HC)
[1131] 1984 LAB.I.C. 1504.

should be taken into consideration to ascertain whether the appellant was engaged exclusively in building and construction industry or not. Such a workshop in which works connected with the business of building and construction industry of the owner were being carried on cannot be construed as a separate establishment for the Act.[1132]

Automobile Industry – Painting is part of repair

The word 'and' has to be read as 'or' in the entry *automobile repairing and servicing industry* in Schedule I.[1133] Painting is covering or coating in the reconditioning or rectifying process of repair and defects, necessary for the efficient operating condition of an automobile. Hence, painting is part of repair and establishment engaged in spray painting of automobiles falls under the schedule entry automobile repairing and servicing.[1134] Like a motor-car, a bus or truck is also a self-propelled vehicle, and hence the term 'automobile' includes trucks, buses and tractors.[1135]

Heavy and Fine Chemicals

Lime industry comes within the expression "heavy and fine chemicals.[1136]

Crushing of bones

In *Nazeena Traders Pvt. Ltd. v Regional P.F. Commissioner*,[1137] the facts for consideration before a Division Bench of the Andhra Pradesh High Court were that the petitioner was doing the business of crushing bones and exporting them to foreign countries. The Provident Fund Commissioner sought to cover the establishment under the schedule head entry 'Heavy and Fine Chemicals' including fertilisers. The High Court held that there was no manufacturing process involved and crushing of bones into small pieces without further process of conversion and consequently, it will not come under the 'Heady and Fine chemicals' including fertilisers (as it could be used for purposes other than fertilisers).

Ayurvedic preparations

In *Gangatharan Vaidyan v Regional Provident Fund Commissioner, Kerala*,[1138] the Kerala High Court had to consider the item 'Heavy and fine chemicals' including medical and pharmaceutical preparations and the Court held that the manufacture

---

[1132] *Cemindia Company Ltd. v Bachu Bhai N. Rawel* 1988 (1) LLJ 138
[1133] *Parameswaran Nair G. v Regional P.F. Commissioner* 1987 I LLN 724: 1987 CLR 104 (Ker. DB)
[1134] *Parameswaran Nair G. v Regional P.F. Commissioner* 1987 I LLN 724: 1987 CLR 104 (Ker. DB)
[1135] *Regional P.F. Commissioner v Free India Industries*, 1964 I LLJ 662: 25 FJR 382: 8 FLR 144 (Pun.DB)
[1136] *Brijbasi Lime Works v Assistant P.F. Commissioner*(2001) IILLJ 1665 MP
[1137] AIR 1965 AP 200
[1138] 1996-II LLJ 216

of ayurvedic preparations would fall within the entry "medical and pharmaceutical preparations." This view was endorsed by the Madras High Court in *The Venkataramana Dispensary and Ayurvedic College v Union of India*.[1139]

Saw mills

The meaning of the entry 'saw mills' (Notification GSR 1232 dated 1.5.1962) cannot be restricted to mills engaged in the cutting of wood. It has to be given a wide meaning to include the dictionary meaning of the term 'saw mill' which includes cutting of stone or metal as well.[1140]

Stone quarries

In *Lakshmani Stone Products v Union of India*,[1141] the Supreme Court held that the appellants being lessee under the State Government under the provisions of Mines and Minerals (Regulation and Development) Act, 1952 to quarry and to crush stones, are engaged in the manufacturing process, and the dominant activity is to quarry the stones and to cut or chipping the stones is only a subsidiary or incidental activity.

Cold Storage vis-à-vis Preservation Industry

The Explanation to the entry 'Fruit and Vegetable preservation industry' reads that it should be engaged in the preparation or production of (iii) frozen fruits and vegetables (ix) any other unspecified items relating to the preservation or canning of fruits or vegetables. The difference between cooling and freezing in that the articles are cooled in cold storage for a transitional period for quick marketing. When the articles are to be required to be preserved for a very long time, then, in that case, those articles are frozen below the freezing point so that they become nearly dormant and can be used after a long time.[1142]

Cold storage of potatoes

The cold storage means to bring the potatoes into the cold storage, keep them in the cold storage at a certain degree of temperature and then whenever they are needed outside, to take them out. There is no preparation as such, neither production of the potatoes and as such, this would not fall under the head of 'Fruit and Vegetable

---

[1139] 1987 (54) FLR 128, (1986) IILLJ 411 Mad
[1140] *Raghunand Prasad & Company v Union of India* 2011(2) CLR 1018: 2011 LLR 989: 011 (130) FLR 1054 (Mad.)
[1141] 2001(1) S.C.T. 1124: 2001 AIR (SC) 783: 2001(2) SCC 496: 2001(1) Scale 434: 2001(2) JT 240: 2001 LIC 722: 2001(1) LLJ 738: 2001(1) SCR 689
[1142] *Central Hindustran Orange & Cold Storage Co. Ltd. v Pratullachandra Ramchandra Oza* 1967 I LLJ 153 (Bom. HC)

preservation' industry.[1143] But the word 'storage' used in the notification dated 7 March, 1962 (Trading and Commercial establishments engaged in the purchase, sale or storage of any goods including establishments of exporters, importers, advertisers, etc) is of a large amplitude and covers all kinds of storages, maintained under different conditions for different purposes.

Educational Institutions

In *Welham Girls High School v Union of India and others*,[1144] the Supreme Court held that the provisions of the EPF Act apply to the educational institutions with effect from 1.3.1982.

Khandsari and confectionary come under Sugar

Khandsari is sugar within the meaning of Schedule I.[1145] Sugar cubes are made of sugar, and they are an altered form of sugar. Consequently, the confectionary shall be deemed to be an industry engaged in the manufacture of sugar.[1146]

Milk and Milk Product Industry

Milk is being converted in the premises into curds, butter, buttermilk and ghee. Such process of conversion of milk into milk products would undoubtedly constitute a manufacturing process. The process of bottling of the milk procured from the members of the Milk Producers' cooperative society amounts to 'manufacture' or 'manufacturing process.'[1147]

Coir Industry

Coir industry has to mean not only the industry of converting coir (coconut fibre) into coir yarn but to the industry of making products out of coir yarn.[1148]

[1143] *Central Hindustran Orange & Cold Storage Co. Ltd. v Pratullachandra Ramchandra Oza* 1967 I LLJ 153 (Bom. HC)
[1144] 1988(1) JT 349: 1988(2) SLR 172: 1988 FLR 453: 1988 BLJR 367
[1145] *Gulshan Khandsari Udyog v Union of India*, 38 FJR 149, 17 FLR 172, AIR 1969 All HC 432 (All. DB)
[1146] *Delhi Cloth & General Mills Co Ltd., v Regional P.F. Commissioner*, 20 FJR 410: 1961 II LLJ 444 (All.HC)
[1147] *Ernakulam Coop. Milk Supply Union Ltd. v Government of India* 1969 LIC 223: 1968 II LLJ 666 (Ker. HC)
[1148] *Kerala Coir Works v Regional Provident Fund Commissioner*, 41 FJR 138: 1972 LIC 1241: 1972 II lLJ 82: 1973 I LLN 168 (Ker.DB)

Chapter XXI
NATURE AND SCOPE OF WRIT JURISDICTION

POWER OF THE HIGH COURT UNDER ARTICLE 227

The power of superintendence conferred by Article 227 is to be exercised most sparingly and only in appropriate cases to keep the subordinate courts within the bounds of their authority and not for correcting mere errors.[1149] The High Court can set aside the orders passed by the trial courts or tribunals only on limited grounds, namely illegality, irrationality and procedural impropriety.[1150] The High Court under Article 227 cannot assume unlimited prerogative to correct all species of hardship or wrong decisions. It must be restricted to cases of grave dereliction of duty and flagrant abuse of fundamental principles of law or justice, where grave injustice would be done unless the High Court interferes.[1151]

Alternative remedy should be exhausted first

It is well-accepted principle of law that while exercising power under Article 226 of the Constitution of India, the High Court does not act as an appellate authority, of course, its jurisdiction is circumscribed and confined to correct an error of law or procedural error, if any, resulting in manifest miscarriage of justice or violation of principle of natural justice. The Supreme Court in numerous cases has observed that where the alternative remedy is available, the court must move at a very slow pace in entertaining the writ petition under Article 226 of the Constitution of India.

In *Rashid Ahmed v Municipal Board Kairana,*[1152] the Supreme Court has held that existence of an adequate legal remedy was a factor to be taken into consideration in the matter of granting writs. This was followed by another decision, namely *K.S. Rashid and Son v Income Tax Investigation Commission,*[1153] where the Supreme Court reiterated the proposition and held that where alternative remedy existed, it would be a sound exercise of discretion to refuse to entertain a petition under Article 226 of the Constitution of India. This proposition was again considered

---

[1149] *Dalmia Jain Airways Ltd. v Sukumar Mukherjee* AIR 1951 CAL 193
[1150] *Mohammed Yusuf v Faij Mohammad and others* 2009 (1) SCALE 71
[1151] *Laxmikant Revchand Bhojwani and another v Pratapsing Mohansing Pardeshi*, JT 1995(7) SC 400
[1152] AIR 1959 SC 163
[1153] AIR 1954 SC 207

by a Constitution Bench of the Supreme Court in *A.V. Venkateswaran, Collector of Customs v Ramchand Sobhraj Wadhwani*,[1154] and another Constitution Bench decision in *Calcutta Discount Co Ltd. v ITO, Companies Dist.*[1155]

In *Whirlpool Corporation v Registrar of Trade Marks, Mumbai and others*,[1156] the Supreme Court indicated a guideline for the hearing of the matters under Article 226 of the Constitution by the High Courts. It held that the restriction of the High Court is self-imposed. If an adequate and efficacious remedy is available, the High Court would not ordinarily exercise its jurisdiction. There are four exceptions, firstly, where the writ petition has been filed for the enforcement of any of the fundamental rights, secondly, where there has been a violation of the principle of natural justice, thirdly, where the order or proceedings are wholly without jurisdiction and fourthly, where the *vires* of an Act is challenged.[1157] Referring to the above judgement, the Supreme Court, in *Godrej Sara Lee Ltd. v Assistant Commissioner and another*,[1158] said, 'it is well known that when an order of a statutory authority is questioned on the ground that the same suffers from lack of jurisdiction, alternative remedy may not be a bar. In the face of the remedy available to the appellants under the provisions of the Act itself, the writ petition is absolutely misconceived,[1159] not maintainable.[1160]

Re-appreciation of evidence – Outside the domain of Writ Jurisdiction

In *Professional Assistance for Development Action v Presiding Officer, EPFAT (Delhi)*,[1161] the Delhi High Court held that the question whether a particular notification covers the establishment or not is a mixed question of law and fact. "The scope of the writ petition against the concurrent findings of the RPFC and the Appellate Authority is limited. This Court can only examine whether any material evidence has not been considered or whether any evidence which ought not to have been read has been considered. Re-appreciation of evidence is outside the domain of scrutiny in the Writ jurisdiction." In *Lakshmi Metal Industries v Assistant Provident Fund Commissioner*,[1162] the Madras High Court held that when law creates a statutory

---

[1154] AIR 1961 SC 1506
[1155] AIR 1961 SC 372
[1156] (1998) 8 SCC 1
[1157] *Eveready Industries (India) Ltd. and others v Regional Provident Fund Commissioner*, (2003) 3 CALLT 113 HC, 2003 (97) FLR 580
[1158] (2009) 14 SCC 338
[1159] *Committee of Management, Mahavir Singh Inter College v Union of India and another* 2010(2) LLJ 427 (All) (DB)
[1160] *Arun Dua and others v Union of India and others* 104 (2007) CLT 475, (2008) I LLJ 148 Ori
[1161] 2011 LIC 767: 2011(3) LLJ 119: 2010(168) DLT 555: 2010(115) DRJ 605: 2010(125) FLR 961: 2010(6) S.C.T. 890
[1162] 2011(2) LLJ 36: 2011(128) FLR 432: 2010(25) S.C.T. 921

forum for redressal of grievance and that too in a fiscal statute, a writ petition should not be entertained ignoring the statutory dispensation. The High Court is a statutory forum of appeal on a question of law, and that should not abdicate and given a go-by a litigant for invoking the forum of judicial review of the High Court under writ jurisdiction.

In *George Issac v The Assistant Provident Fund Commissioner*,[1163] the petitioner filed a Public Interest Litigation (PIL) seeking direction to the Central Government to make the provisions of the Act applicable to all the establishments, irrespective of the number of workers, even if it is fewer than 20. A Division Bench of the Kerala High Court held that whether a particular class of establishment can be included or excluded from the applicability of the Act is exclusively a legislative function, and the question cannot be considered by the Writ Court.

Writ Jurisdiction – Certiorari

In *Harbans Lal v Jagmohan Saran*,[1164] the Supreme Court held that the limitations on the jurisdiction of the High Court under Article 226 of the Constitution are well settled. The writ petition before the High Court prayed for a writ in the nature of certiorari, and it is well known that a writ in the nature of certiorari may be issued only if the order of the inferior tribunal or subordinate court suffers from an error of jurisdiction, or from a breach of the principles of natural justice or is vitiated by a manifest or apparent error of law. There is no sanction enabling the High Court to reappraise the evidence without sufficient reason in law and reach findings of fact contrary to those rendered by an inferior court or subordinate court. When a High Court proceeds to do so, it acts plainly more than its powers. In *Grand Chemical Works v The Presiding Officer, Employees' Provident Fund Appellate Tribunal and another*,[1165] the Delhi High Court held, "there is no dispute as regards the legal position that the Regional PF Commissioner and Employees' Provident Fund Appellate Tribunal are the final fact-finding authorities and this court normally would not re-appreciate and reassess the finding of facts. It is equally well known that a writ like certiorari may be issued only if the order of the inferior tribunal or subordinate court suffers from an error of jurisdiction, or from a breach of the principles of natural justice or is vitiated by a manifest or apparent error of law." It is not every error either of law or fact which can be corrected by a Superior Court. Mere formal or technical error even though of law, would not be sufficient to attract the extraordinary jurisdiction of High Court of Certiorari.[1166]

[1163] 2015(145) FLR 871: 2015 LabLR 844: 2015(1) CLR 1028: 2015(9) S.C.T. 331
[1164] (1985) 4 SCC 333
[1165] 2010 (2) SCT 160
[1166] *Nagendra Nath Bora and another v Commissioner of Hills Division and Appeals, Assam and others*

Writ Petition is premature when inquiry is pending

The jurisdiction under Article 226 of the Constitution is to be exercised against final order and not against the interim order. Whenever any record was required to concluding the applicability of the Act, the petitioner must have been candid enough to furnish details of all documents so that a correct decision may arrive.[1167]

Fresh Reasons cannot be considered for Writ Petition

In *Cannanore Shop v Regional P.F. Commissioner*,[1168] the High Court of Kerala placing reliance on the Supreme Court decisions in *Mohinder Singh Gil and another v The Chief Election Commissioner, New Delhi*[1169] and in *N.P. Ponnuswami v Returning Officer, Namakkal and others*,[1170] held that the reasons mentioned in the levy order could not be allowed to be supplemented by new reasons by way of affidavit. If that is permitted the order which is invalid at the admission of the Writ Petition for lack of reasons will become valid at the time of final hearing.

Misleading affidavits – Abuse of process of law

In *V. Chandrashekaran and another v Administrative Officer and others*,[1171] the Supreme Court observed that a petition or affidavit containing misleading or inaccurate statement amounts to an abuse of process of Court. The judicial process cannot become an instrument of oppression or abuse, or a means in the process of the court to subvert justice, for the reason that the court exercises its jurisdiction, only in furtherance of justice. The petition or an affidavit containing a misleading and an inaccurate statement, only to achieve an ulterior purpose amounts to an abuse of process of the court.

Suppression of facts – Writ Petition not maintainable

It is settled position of law that litigant who is approaching the writ jurisdiction conferred under Art.226 of the Constitution of India is supposed to come out with a clean hand and without suppression of material facts. The Supreme Court, in *Prestige Lights Ltd. v State Bank of India*,[1172] and *K.D. Sharma v Steel Authority*

AIR 1958 SC 398
[1167] *Midlands (Pvt.) Ltd. v Regional P.F. Commissioner*, (1994) I LLJ 1230 (All.)
[1168] (1995) IIILLJ 134 Ker
[1169] 1978 SC 851
[1170] 1952 SC 64
[1171] (2012) 12 SCC 133
[1172] (2007) 8 SCC 449

*of India and others,*¹¹⁷³ has held that writ petition cannot be entertained in case of suppression of material facts.¹¹⁷⁴

Question of Facts cannot be raised for the first time in Writ Appeal

The question as to whether notice under s.7-A was issued was a question of fact, and a plea that no notice was given ought to have been raised in the writ petition itself. It could not be permitted for the first time in appeal.¹¹⁷⁵

Interim Stay orders should be avoided against recovery of State dues

The Supreme Court has repeatedly emphasised the inadvisability of making interim orders which have the effect of depriving the State (the people of the State) of the revenues legitimately due to it. The Court should not take upon itself the responsibility of staying the recovery of amounts due to State unless a clear case of illegality is made out and the balance of convenience is duly considered. Otherwise, the odium of unlawfully depriving the State, or the people of the monies lawfully due to them would lie upon the Court.¹¹⁷⁶

Party gets a stay from Court at its own risk

It is a settled principle of law that as and when a party applies and obtains a stay from the Court of law, it is always at a risk and responsibility of the party applying. Mere passing of an order of stay cannot be presumed to be conferment of any additional right upon the litigating party.¹¹⁷⁷ If the employer disputes his liability to make contributions and obtains an injunction against recovery from a court and subsequently his business is closed, he cannot be allowed to deny his liability on the ground of hardship ultimately it is held that the Act applied to his establishment.¹¹⁷⁸

Court cannot direct legislation

The Court cannot issue a writ directing the legislature or a subordinate legislating authority to enact a particular law or rule.¹¹⁷⁹

[1173] 2008 12 SCC 481
[1174] *Vinayaka Mission Lord Jagannath Institution of Dental Science and Research v Assistant Provident Fund Commissioner* 2016 (3) LLJ 506
[1175] *Central P.F. Commissioner v. S.K. Nasiruddin Beedi Merchant Ltd.,* (1999) I LLJ 360 (Pat-DB)
[1176] *State of Madhya Pradesh v M.VVyavsaya & Co,* 1997 (1) SCC 156
[1177] *Rajasthan Housing Board and others v Krishna Kumari* 2005(13) SCC 151
[1178] *Kokkalai Rice & Oil Mills v Regional P.F. Commissioner,* (1960) 2 LLJ 528
[1179] *Supreme Court Employees' Welfare Association v Union of India,* (1989) 4 SCC 187

Even a small fraction of cause of action attracts Writ

The Supreme Court, in *Kusum Ingots and Alloys Ltd. v The Union of India and another*,[1180] held that keeping in view the expression used in clause 2 of Article 226 of the Constitution of India, even if a small fraction of cause of action accrues within the jurisdiction of the High Court, the Court will have jurisdiction in the matter.[1181] The Court sitting under Article 226 of the Indian Constitution and in exercise of power of judicial review is only required to see whether the decision making process is proper or not.[1182]

Abstract Question of Fact not under Writ Jurisdiction

Resolution of disputed questions of fact is not an exercise which will be undertaken in Writ jurisdiction. The parties will have the opportunity to raise all their contentions before the appropriate forum and no interference is necessary or warranted under s.482 of the Criminal Procedure Code on the basis of any disputed question of fact.[1183]

[1180] 2004 (6) SCC 254

[1181] *Belal Biri Factory Pvt. Ltd. and another v. Regional P.F. Commissioner and another*, (2006) 2 CALLT 202 HC, 2006 (4) CHN 566, (2006) III LLJ 532 Cal

[1182] *Orissa Hydro Power Corporation Ltd. v Assistant Provident Fund Commissioner and others*, 2016(2) CLR 216: 2016 LLR 772 (Ori.)

[1183] *Aluminum Industries Ltd. and others v Enforcement Officer and another*, 2003 (97) FLR 131, (2003) II LLJ 108 Ker

Chapter XXII
SCHEMES FRAMED UNDER THE ACT

EMPLOYEES' PROVIDENT FUNDS SCHEME, 1952

The Act does not place any unreasonable restrictions on the business of the factory owners so as to offend Article 19 of the Constitution. The enactment is in public interest, and the restriction so called is in no manner unreasonable, for all it demands is that a certain contribution, the maximum limit of which is contained in the Act, should be made by the employers for the benefit of the employees. The legislation is essentially calculated to harmonise the relations between the employer and the employee in certain industries, and, in the modern context, this can in no sense be called unreasonable.[1184] The Act is full of carefully laid down principles to guide the Central Government, and s.5 of the Act does not in any manner offends Article 14 of the Constitution.[1185] Section 5 of the Employees' Provident Funds Act, 1952 does not infringe Article 14 or Article 19 (1) (f) of the Constitution.[1186]

Membership continues till full and final settlement of benefits

Withdrawal of a substantial portion of the amount accumulated in the Fund does not result in loss of membership of the Fund.[1187]

Family includes wife living separately

The definition of 'family' under Para 2(g) includes a wife living separately; so long as a wife is entitled to get maintenance allowance, she continues to be the member of the family. The status of such a Hindu wife is not, in any real sense, equivalent to the status of a wife judicially separated under the Divorce Ac.[1188]

Para 26B – Resolving the membership entitlement dispute

In *Glamour v Regional P.F. Commissioner*,[1189] the Delhi High Court clarified that the dispute envisaged by Paragraph 26B relates to one between the employer and the

---

[1184] *Regional P.F. Commissioner v. Lakshmi Ratan Engineering Works Ltd* (1962) 2 LLJ 604
[1185] *Regional P.F. Commissioner v Lakshmi Ratten Engineering Works Ltd* AIR 1962 P H 507, (1962) IILLJ 604 P & H (DB)
[1186] *Hindustan Electric Co. Ltd. v Regional P.F. Commissioner* AIR 1959 P H 27, (1960) ILLJ 640 P H
[1187] *Diocesan Press v Regional P.F. Commissioner*, 1990 Lab IC (NOC) 27 (Mad.)
[1188] *Subhadraammal v Kannammal*, AIR 1940 Mad 590
[1189] (975) I LLJ 514 Del

employee and in respect of particular employees of an establishment. This paragraph has no reference to the dispute arising between the Provident Fund Commissioner and the employer about the direction of the former to the latter to pay the amount due under the Act. This view finds support from the fact that under s.7-A, there is no express provision for hearing an employee (though there is no bar to the authorities hearing the employees). On the other hand, Para 26B, the dispute is to be resolved after hearing both the employer and the employees. The Act further accords a finality to the decision under s.7-A, but no such express provision is found in Para 26B. It is obligatory for the Commissioner to hear the employee.[1190] Simply because the employer happens to remain *ex parte* in a particular case, it cannot be said that no notice to the employee is necessary before taking a decision under paragraph 26-B.[1191]

S.5 – No conflict with paragraph 26B

Para 26-B is only a part of the Provident Fund Scheme framed under Section 5(1-B), and it only empowers the Regional Commissioner to decide some questions as provided, therefore. There is no conflict between Para 26-B and Section 5.[1192]

Migrant Workers

By a notification dated November 1, 1990, Para 26(2) of the Employees' Provident Fund Scheme, 1952 was amended to require every employee to become a member of the Fund right from the date of joining the establishment. Para 26(2) was amended by notification dated 1-11-1990 requiring that every employee, other than an excluded employee, should be enrolled as EPF member right from the date of joining the establishment and the Supreme Court in *J.P. Tobacco Products etc v Union of India*,[1193] upheld the constitutional validity of this amendment. The validity of the para 26(2) of the EPF Scheme came to be challenged before the Madhya Pradesh High Court in the case of *Khemchand Motilal Tobacco Products Ltd. v Union of India*.[1194] The Madhya Pradesh High court upheld the validity and the same was later confirmed by the Supreme Court in *J.P. Tobacco Products v Union of India and others*[1195] wherein the Supreme Court held that the amendment to para 26(2) of the Scheme was valid and compulsory contribution towards provident fund does not amount to denial of minimum wages. It was further held that the

---

[1190] *Mysore State Coop. Printing Works Ltd. v Regional P.F. Commissioner*, (1976) 49 FJR 288 (Kar).
[1191] *Sasidharan v Regional P.F. Commissoiner*, 1982 Lab IC 597 (Ker).
[1192] *South India Research Institute v Regional P.F. Commissioner*, 59 FJR 160: 1982 I LLN 53 (AP.DB)
[1193] 1995(II) C.L.R. 369
[1194] 1995 (II) CLR 360
[1195] (1996) ILLJ 822 SC

amendment is not impracticable and unworkable and it is not ultra-vires of the Act and Articles 14 and 19(1)(g) of the Constitution of India. As such, there is no distinction of temporary or permanent employees or contract and or casual employees employed by the contractor under the Act and there is no eligibility condition for enrolment of employees, since all employees or workmen who come under the definition of "employee" are bound to be enrolled as member, and the EPF Act and Schemes will have to be extended to such employees.

Liability to transfer – with the Trust

In *Express Newspaper Ltd. v Regional Provident Fund Commissioner*,[1196] the Madras High Court held that a combined effect of Section 15(2) and Paragraph 28 of the EPF Scheme, 1952 cast the liability to transfer the assets of the existing provident fund trust to the fund established under the Scheme, *not* on the employer but the trustees of the existing provident fund trust.

Employer to pay both shares 'on the first instance'

A reading of paragraph 30 shows that it is the employer who is to make contributions both with regard to his share and with regard to the share of the employees. He can, under paragraph 32, recover the amount from the employees. In case the employer does not carry out his duty to make the contributions, he has to blame himself, and he cannot be allowed to say later on that some of the employees have left service, he is unable to recover the employees' share of contributions.[1197]

Membership is compulsory

The government has no power to exempt the employees of any establishment from payment of their contribution by giving them an option. Neither s.6 of the Act nor paragraph 29 of the Scheme permits such an option to pay or not to pay.[1198] The employees of an establishment to which the Act applies have no option to opt out of the Scheme. It is a statutory mandate for the employer to require his employees to become members and for the employees to obey it.[1199]

Deduction of employees' share from future wages

In *District Exhibitors Association, Muzaffarnagar and others v Union of India and others*,[1200] the Supreme Court held that the third proviso to Para 32(1) of the

---

[1196] AIR 1961 Mad 226, 1961 (2) FLR 156, (1961) ILLJ 610 Mad, (1961) 1 MLJ 179
[1197] N.K. *Industries (P) Ltd. v Regional P.F. Commissioner*, (1958) 2 LLJ 19
[1198] *Aluminium Corporation of India v. Regional P.F. Commissioner*, (1959) 1 LLJ 249: AIR 1958 Cal 570
[1199] *Provident Fund Inspector v Ram Kumar*, 1983 Lab IC 717 (P & H).
[1200] 1991(2)LLJ 115(SC)

Employees' Provident Fund Scheme could be taken advantage of by the employer only where no deduction has been made from the wages of the employees due to accidental mistake or clerical error when the Scheme is operative. Such deduction which has not been made by accidental mistake or clerical error, could not be made from the subsequent wages with the consent in writing of the Inspector concerned.

Para 38 – Due date for payment of contributions should be reckoned based on wage month

As per s.4 of the Payment of Wages Act, 1936, every employer can fix a wage period and no such wage period shall exceed one month. In *Delhi Press Patra Prakashan Ltd. v The Regional P.F. Commissioner and others*,[1201] it was contended that the petitioner has adopted the wage month commencing from the 16th day of each English calendar month ending on the 15th day of the following month and hence 15 days' time should be allowed from the ending of wage month (not English or Gregorian Calendar month). Allowing the petition, the Delhi High Court held that the word 'actually drawn' appearing in Para 29(3) of the Scheme and the word 'whole month' refer to the wage month and not the British English Calendar month.

Para 68-B – Agency includes all Cooperative Societies

In *Jayakar Rao N. Shetty v Regional P.F. Commissioner and others*,[1202] the order of the Provident Fund Commissioner rejecting a claim for housing loan under Para 68-B of the EPF Scheme was challenged contending that the meaning of the term 'cooperative society' in sub-clause 1(a) of Para 68 cannot be restricted to a cooperative housing society, and it can be any cooperative society. The Patna High Court while allowing the petition, observed: "Had the Legislature intended to restrict the 'agency' to include only a cooperative housing society and not all cooperative societies, nothing was simpler than to specifically mentioning a cooperative housing society."

Para 68 – Misuse of Advance: No recovery without notice

Under Para 68-B of the EPF Scheme, if the amount advanced has not been utilised for the purpose for which it was sanctioned, the Commissioner is empowered to take steps forthwith to recover the amount. In *Periyar District Textiles Labour Union v Regional P.F. Commissioner*,[1203] the Madras High Court held that the employees must be heard on this question, and it is open to the employee to convince the Commissioner, not to order the recovery from his wages or that there is no case for recovery.

[1201] WP (C) Nos.3850/1992 & 3887/1993 decided on September 11, 2009
[1202] (1993) II LLJ 78 Bom, 1993 (1) MhLj 85
[1203] 2000(97)FJR 362: (Mad.HC)

Nomination can be made in favour members of family only

No nomination can be made under the Provident Fund Scheme in favour of a person who is not a member of the family as defined in Para 2(g) of the Employees' Provident Funds Scheme, 1952. Brother is not a member of the family within the meaning of the word 'family' as defined in the Scheme.[1204] In *Antonio Joao Fernandes v Assistant Provident Fund Commissioner and others*,[1205] the deceased member had named two nominees viz., his sister and his cousin, for his Provident Fund account. The Bombay High Court held that a nomination could not operate to the exclusion of legal heirs, and the nomination in favour of a cousin is not valid. Where the member has a family, he cannot leave his provident fund to anyone outside the family, and must leave it to one or more members of the family whether he likes them or not; but if he does not have a family, then he is not compelled to leave it to any individual or individuals with whom he has no interest. A nomination in favour of an association is a perfectly good nomination.[1206] As per Paragraph – 61(1) of the Employees' Provident Funds Scheme, 1952, the nomination shall effect to the extent that it is valid on the date on which the Commissioner receives it. In *Shibani Motha v Employees' Provident Fund Organization and others*,[1207] the Karnataka High Court held that if a member makes a valid nomination before his death, merely because the said nomination is communicated by the employer to the organisation, after the death of the member does not render the nomination invalid.

Illegitimate children shall be treated as legitimate for benefits under the Scheme

Section 16 of the Hindu Marriage Act, 1955 makes a rule of *fiction juris* that the children, though illegitimate, shall nevertheless be treated as legitimate notwithstanding that the marriage of their parents was void. The illegitimate children, for all practical purposes, including succession to the properties of their parents have to be treated as legitimate. The Jharkhand High Court, in *Bhimendra Kumar Kashyap v Manager (Personnel), SAIL and others*[1208] directed the provident fund commissioner to allow the children, though the legality of the marriage of their parents is under dispute, to be mentioned as nominees for the Provident Fund benefits of their father. In case of bigamous marriage by a Hindu employee, the

---

[1204] *Nozer Gustad Commissariat v Central Bank of India and others* – 1993 (2) LLJ 98: 1993 LLR 757: 1993(67) FLR 1056
[1205] 2010(3) LLN 712: 2010(4) LLJ 460
[1206] *Ellen Florence Rodriguez v Edith Mary Hannay*, AIR 1942 Rang 64
[1207] [2005(104)FLR630]; ILR2005KAR117; 2005(3)KarLJ381
[1208] 2009(2)LIC 2236 (Jhar. HC)

second wife would be entitled to family pension only if she was married on or before 18-5-1955, the date of enforcement of the Hindu Marriage Act, 1955.

Beneficiary in case of a deceased member

Where a valid nomination exists, no succession certificate is required for payment of provident fund accumulations to the nominee.[1209] Where the deceased member had made a valid nomination, a person other than the nominee could not claim the amount of his provident fund merely by a succession certificate issued under s.372 of the Succession Act, 1925.[1210]

Para 72 – Responsibility of the Commissioner to settle the benefits

In *S. Loganathan (Deceased) represented by L. Indirani v The Assistant Provident Fund Commissioner and another*,[1211] the Madras High Court held that if the member is unable to get his claims attested by his employer, he can send them to the Provident Fund Commissioner, who is empowered with substantial provision to enforce their order. In case of undue delay in settlement of the provident fund benefits, the member is entitled to get damages for the delayed payment, and the same may be deducted from the salary of the commissioner for deficiency in service.

In the strict interpretation of clause 72 of the Scheme, it is the liability of the Provident Fund Commissioner to pay the amount standing to the credit of the member and if the employer fails to pay his contribution towards the provident fund, then in that event there is no liability on the Provident Fund Commissioner to pay the amount which the employer has failed to pay.[1212]

Para 76(a) – Relief Undertakings – No relief from prosecution

In *Inderjit C. Parekh and others v VK. Bhatt and another*,[1213] the appellant-directors of Rajnagar Spinning and Weaving Manufacturing Co. Ltd. were prosecuted under the EPF Act, 1952 on the ground that they had failed to contribute to the provident fund and thereby committed an offence punishable under paragraph 76(a) of the EPF Scheme, 1952. Later, an investigation was made into the affairs of the company under s.15 of the Industries (Development and Regulation) Act, 1951, the Gujarat State Textile Corporation took over the management of the company and by a notification the State Government declared the company to be a 'relief undertaking' under s.4 (1)(a) (iv) of the Bombay Relief Undertakings (Special Provisions) Act,

---

[1209] *Imambhai Gulamhusain Shaikh v Regional P.F. Commissioner*, (1982) 45 FLR 166 (Guj)
[1210] *Brij Lal Singh v Regional P.F. Commissioner*, (1992) 64 FLR 206 (MP) (DB)
[1211] W.P. No.12213 of 2006 decided on 21st April, 2010
[1212] *Rashtriya Mill Mazdoor Sangh v Regional P.F. Commissioner*, 1991 Lab IC 1572 (Bom.)
[1213] 1974 AIR 1183, 1974 SCR (3) 50

1958. The Supreme Court held that the responsibility to pay the contributions to the provident fund was of the appellant-directors, and if they have defaulted in paying the amount, they are liable to be prosecuted under Para 76(a) of the Scheme. Such a personal liability cannot fall within the scope of s.4(1)(a)(iv) of the Bombay Relief Undertakings (Special Provisions) Act, 1958.

Para 76(b) – Falsity of statement is not necessarily a precondition

The culpability under s.14(1) of the Act which is entirely in different situation of the person liable to make payment under the Act evading it on the basis of false statement or false representation while the culpability under Sections 14(2), 14A and Paragraph 76 (b) of the Scheme is the outcome of failure to submit the return or documents supporting it within time. The falsity of the statement or representation made by the delinquent is not the *sine qua non* of the criminal liability envisaged in Clause (b) of paragraph 76 of the Employees' Provident Funds Scheme, 1952.[1214]

Newspaper Employees – Constitutional validity of Paragraph 80(2)

In *Express Publications (Madurai) Ltd. and another v Union of India and another*,[1215] the constitutional validity of Para 80(2) of the EPF Scheme, 1952 was challenged on the grounds that only in case of employees of newspaper industry, the test of income has been excluded, and the result is that the newspaper employees alone do not come in the category of 'excluded employee,' which is wholly discriminatory. The Supreme Court held that the provision under Para 80(2) of the EPF Scheme and the enacting of the Working Journalists Act, 1955 was part of a package deal treating the press industry as a class by itself. Hence, the Supreme Court refused to accept the contention that Para 80(2) is in violation of Article 14 of the Constitution.

Cine-Workers

The Cinema Theatre Workers Act received the assent of the President on 24-12-1981 and was published in the Gazette on the same day. The classification of cinema theatres as a separate class for coverage under the Employees' Provident Funds Act cannot be said to be discriminatory or violative of Article 14 of the Constitution. As is clear from the objects and reasons of the Act and its provisions, the Act is for the benefit of employees who form part of the economically weaker sections of the society and s.24 of the Cinema Theatre Workers Act, 1981 extending the coverage of the Employees' Provident Funds Act to cinema theatre employing five or more workmen cannot, therefore, be said to be in any way discriminatory or opposed to

---

[1214] *Provident Fund Inspector v New Janta Bus Service Co. Ltd*, (1999) III LLJ 190 P H, (1992) 101 PLR 16
[1215] 2004(2)LLJ 356:2004(2)LLN 748

Article 14 of the Constitution.[1216]

In *District Exhibitors Association, Muzaffarnagar and others v Union of India and others*,[1217] the Supreme Court held that by applying the scheme, the employer could not be asked to pay the employees' contribution for the period antecedent to the notification. The Act and the Scheme neither permit any such payment nor deduction. The employer cannot be saddled with the liability to pay the employee's contribution for the retrospective period since he has no right to deduct the same from the future wages payable to the employees. The employees of newspaper industry have always been treated as a class apart as such not treating them as 'excluded employees' under the Act and Scheme even when they are getting wages or salary more than the prescribed cap for coverage.[1218]

Trustees cannot be removed prematurely

Para 79(c) of the Employees' Provident Funds Scheme leaves no manner of doubt that the terms of the office of the Trustees are for five years from the date of election or nomination. The nominated person is also eligible for re-appointment to a maximum of two terms. In *P. Gengaiyan and others v The General Manager, Neyveli Lignite Corporation Ltd. and another*,[1219] the Madras High Court held that it is not open to the Respondent to change the board of trustees before expiry of statutory period of five years, and reasons like bifurcation of union, or other union having majority is not a ground to remove the trustees duly appointed under the scheme, having statutory force of law.

Artificial break-in service to avoid statutory liabilities not permissible

In *The Joint Commissioner/Executive Officer, Arulmigu Subramaniaswamy Thirukoil, Tiruttani v the EPF Appellate Tribunal and another*,[1220] the Madras High Court held that the scheme of the petitioner to give one day break-in-service on completion of every 90 days of work shows that artificial break was given only to prevent the workers from getting the benefit of regular employees, which is not permissible.

EPF-related services come under Consumer Protection Act

In *Regional Provident Fund Commissioner v Shiv Kumar Joshi*,[1221] the Supreme Court,

---

[1216] *Vishwanatha Pai and others v Regional P.F. Commissioner*, (1994) IIILLJ 1044 Ker
[1217] 1991(2)LLJ 115(SC)
[1218] *Express Publications (Madurai) Ltd. v Union of India*, 2004 LLR(SN)479(SC)
[1219] W.P. No.12132 of 2009 decided on February 10,2011
[1220] W.P. No.29158 of 2010 decided on June 7th, 2011 (Mad. HC)
[1221] 2000 (1) SCC 98

with reference to the operation of the Consumer Protection Act to the EPF Scheme, held, "'A perusal of the Scheme clearly and unambiguously indicates that it is a 'service' within the meaning of Section 2(1)(o) and the member a 'consumer' within the meaning of Section 2(1)(d) of the Act. "In *Regional P.F. Commissioner v Bhavani*,[1222] the Supreme Court held that the Regional Provident Fund Commissioner, who is the person responsible for the working of the Employees' Pension Scheme, 1995, is a 'service provider' and the Pension Scheme is a 'service' within the meaning of the s.2(1)(o) of the Consumer Protection Act.

EMPLOYEES' PENSION SCHEME, 1995

Permanent total disablement not related to percentage of medical disability

In *Satyabadi Patra v Regional P.F. Commissioner and another*,[1223] the Orissa High Court held that under Para 15 of the Employees' Pension Scheme, 1995, the term 'permanent total disablement' has been defined to mean such disablement of permanent nature as incapacitates an employee for all work which he was capable of performing at the time of disablement, and it is not necessarily connected with the percentage of medical disability. When the Medical Board has opined that the employee has suffered permanent total disablement, denial of pension to the employee who is a member of the Employees' Pension Scheme, is not justified.[1224]

Army pension is not a bar to receive EPS pension

The entitlement of a member or his family members to receive pension under the Army Regulations shall not stand in the way of the member or his family members receiving any other benefit under the family pension scheme introduced under the Employees' Provident Funds and Miscellaneous Provisions Act, 1952, which is based on such a definite understanding that deductions were made from the wages of employees.[1225]

Pensionable Salary – Option to contribute above the ceiling

Regarding clause 11(3) of the Employees' Pension Scheme, 1995, the maximum pensionable salary was limited to Rs.5,000/- which was subsequently enhanced to Rs.6,500/- per month with effect from October 8th, 2001. A proviso to clause 11(3) was added with effect from March 16th, 1996 permitting the option to the employer and an employee for contributing to salary exceeding the statutory ceiling

---

[1222] 2008(7)SCC 111: 2008(3)LLN 45
[1223] 2011(4) LIC. 3925(Ori. HC)
[1224] *Sudhakar Pani v Assistant Provident Fund Commissioner* ILR 2005 KAR 2792, 2005 (4) KarLJ 18, (2005) IIILLJ 239 Kant
[1225] *Union of India v Visalakshy*, 1998 IV LLN 749 (Ker.DB)

(Rs.5,000/- and Rs.6,500/- with effect from 8-10-2001). When the appellant employees took the pleas that the proviso brought in by the amendment of 1996 was not within their knowledge, and therefore, they may be given the benefit thereof, such request was rejected by the Provident Fund Commissioner, stating that the proviso visualised a cut-off date for exercise of option, namely, the date of commencement of Scheme or from the date the salary exceeded the ceiling amount of Rs.5,000/- or Rs.6,500 as the case may be. This plea was turned down by the Provident Fund Authority on the ground that the proviso visualised a cut-off date for exercise of the option, namely, the date of commencement of Scheme or from the date the salary exceeded the ceiling amount of Rs.5,000/- or 6,500/- per month, as may be. As the request of the appellant-employees was after either of the said dates, the same cannot be acceded to. The said dates are not cut-off dates to determine the eligibility of the employer-employee to indicate their option under the proviso to Clause 11(3) of the Pension Scheme.

The Supreme Court, while observing that the beneficial Scheme ought not to be allowed to be defeated by reference to a cut-off date, held that the option under Para 26 of the Employees' Provident Fund Scheme, 1952 cannot be construed to be estoppels against the employees from exercising a similar option under paragraph 11(3) of the Employees' Pension Scheme, 1995. Instead, the exercise of the option under paragraph 26(6) is a necessary precursor to the exercise of an option under Clause 11(3). The exercise of such option, therefore, would not foreclose the exercise of a further option under Clause 11(3) of the Pension Scheme unless the circumstances warranting such foreclosure are clearly indicated.[1226]

Nomination under the erstwhile scheme is valid under the new Scheme

The nomination made by a member under the erstwhile Employees' Family Pension Scheme, 1971, by force of Para 44(2) of the Employees' Pension Scheme, 1995, becomes the nomination made under the latter Scheme.[1227]

[1226] *R.C. Gupta and others v Regional P.F. Commissioner and others*, Civil Appeal Nos.10013–10014 of 2016 (Decision dated 4-10-2016)

[1227] *Rukminibai A. Khamkar v Regional P.F. Commissioner*, 1998 LLR 1065 (Karn.HC)

EMPLOYEES' DEPOSIT-LINKED INSURANCE SCHEME, 1976

Constitutional validity of the Scheme

In the year 1976, a deposit linked insurance scheme was introduced providing for lump sum insurance benefit linked to provident fund accumulation additionally upon the death of the member while in service with a ceiling limit initially at Rs.10,000/- and raised from time to time to Rs.6,00,000/-. In this scheme, there is no contribution by the employees. An additional contribution of the employer is to the extent of @ 0.5 percent and by the Central Government to the extent of 0.25 percent for financing the scheme. However, the Central Government contribution ceased with effect from November 1995. The validity of this Scheme was challenged before the Supreme Court in *Mafatlal Group Staff Association and others v Regional Commissioner Provident Fund and others*,[1228] on the ground that retiral benefits under the Scheme were very meagre and did not match the contribution of employees to the Fund. However, the challenge was rejected.

Non-payment of EDLI contributions is more severe in nature

Unless regarding Paragraph 8 of the Employees' Deposit Linked Insurance Scheme, 1976, if the employer's contribution is not remitted, then the employee in case of an accident will not be eligible to insurance coverage. The gravity of the offence in case of non-deposit of Deposit-Linked Insurance Fund appears to be more severe than non-deposit of employer's contribution to the provident fund scheme. If non-payment of provident funds dues is a continuing offence till payments are made, so also non-payment of employer's contribution to the Deposit-Linked Insurance Scheme is also a continuing offence.[1229]

[1228] 1994 (4) SCC 58
[1229] *Deepak Puri v State of West Bengal and others*, 2010(126)FLR 28: 2010 LLR (SN.143) p.1018 (Cal.HC)

Appendix
CONTROLLED INDUSTRY

Section 2 of the Industries (Development and Regulation) Act, 1951, declares that it is expedient in the public interest that the Union should take under its control the industries specified in the First Schedule.

1. **Metallurgical Industries:** A. Ferrous: (1) Iron and Steel (Metal). (2) Ferro-alloys. (3) Iron and Steel castings and forgings. (4) Iron and Steel structurals (5) Iron and Steel pipes. (6) Special steels. (7) Other products of iron and steel B. Non-Ferrous: (1) Precious metals, including gold and silver, and their alloys. (1A) Other non-ferrous metals and their alloys. (2) Semi-manufactures and manufacturers.

2. **Fuel:** (1) Coal, lignite, coke and their derivatives. (2) Mineral oil (crude oil), motor and aviation spirit, diesel oil, kerosene oil, fuel oil, diverse hydrocarbon oils and their blends including synthetic fuels, lubricating oils and the like. (3) Fuel gases – (coal gas, natural gas and the like).

3. **Boilers and Steam Generating Plants:** Boilers and steam generating plants.

4. **Prime Movers (Other than Electrical Generators):** (1) Steam engines and turbines. (2) Internal combustion engines.

5. **Electrical Equipment:** (1) Equipment for generation, transmission and distribution of electricity including transformers. (2) Electrical motors. (3) Electrical fans. (4) Electrical lamps. (5) Electrical furnaces. (6) Electrical cables and wires. (7) X-ray equipment. (8) Electronic equipment. (9) Household appliances such as electric irons, heaters and the like. (10) Storage batteries. (11) Dry cells.

6. **Telecommunications:** (1) Telephones. (2) Telegraph equipment. (3) Wireless communication apparatus. (4) Radio receivers, including amplifying and public address equipment. (5) Television sets. (6) Teleprinters.

7. **Transportation:** (1) Aircraft. (2) Ships and other vessels drawn by power. (3) Railway locomotives. (4) Railway rolling stock. (5) Automobiles (motor cars, buses, trucks, motor cycles, scooters and the like). (6) Bicycles. (7) others, such as fork lift trucks and the like.

8. **Industrial Machinery:** A. Major items of specialised equipment used in specific industries:— (1) Textile machinery (such as spinning frames, carding

machines, power looms and the like) including textile accessories. (2) Jute machinery. (3) Rayon machinery. (4) Sugar machinery. (5) Tea machinery. (6) Mining machinery. (7) Metallurgical machinery. (8) Cement machinery. (9) Chemical machinery. (10) Pharmaceuticals machinery. (11) Paper machinery. B. General items of machinery used in several industries, such as the equipment required for various 'unit processes': (1) Size reduction equipment—crushers, ball mills and the like. (2) Conveying equipment—bucket elevators, skip hoist, cranes, derricks and the like. (3) Size separation units—screens, classifiers and the like. (4) Mixers and reactors—kneading mills, turbo mixers and the like. (5) Filtration equipment—filter presses, rotary filters and the like. (6) Centrifugal machines. (7) Evaporators. (8) Distillation equipment. (9) Crystallisers. (10) Driers. (11) Power driven pumps—reciprocating, centrifugal and the like. (12) Air and gas compressors and vacuum pipes (excluding electrical furnaces). (13) Refrigeration plants for industrial use. (14) Fire-fighting equipment and appliances including fire engines. C. Other items of Industrial Machinery: (1) Ball, roller and tapered bearings. (2) Speed reduction units. (3) Grinding wheels and abrasives.

9. **Machine Tools:** Machine Tools.
10. **Agricultural Machinery**: (1) Tractors, harvesters and the like. (2) Agricultural implements.
11. **Earth-Moving Machinery**: Bulldozers, dumpers, scrapers, loaders, shovels, drag lines, bucket wheel excavators, road rollers and the like.
12. **Miscellaneous Mechanical and Engineering Industries:** (1) Plastic moulded goods. (2) Hand tools, small tools and the like. (3) Razor blades. (4) Pressure Cookers. (5) Cutlery. (6) Steel furniture.
13. **Commercial, Office and Household Equipment:** (1) Typewriters. (2) Calculating machines. (3) Air conditioners and refrigerators. (4) Vacuum cleaners. (5) Sewing and knitting machines. (6) Hurricane lanterns.
14. **Medical and Surgical Appliances:** Surgical instruments—sterilisers, incubators and the like.
15. **Industrial Instruments**: (1) Water meters, steam meters, electricity meters and the like. (2) Indicating, recording and regulating devices for pressure, temperature, rate of flow, weights, levels and the like. (3) Weighing machines.
16. **Scientific Instruments:** Scientific instruments.
17. **Mathematical, Surveying and Drawing Instruments:** Mathematical, surveying and drawing instruments.

18. **Fertilisers**: (1) Inorganic fertilisers. (2) Organic fertilisers. (3) Mixed fertilisers.

19. **Chemicals (Other than Fertilizers):** (1) Inorganic heavy chemicals. (2) Organic heavy chemicals. (3) Fine chemicals including photographic chemicals. (4) Synthetic resins and plastics. (5) Paints, varnishes and enamels. (6) Synthetic rubbers. (7) Man-made fibers including regenerated cellulose-rayon, nylon and the like. (8) Coke oven by-products. (9) Coal tar distillation products like naphthalene, anthracene and the like. (10) Explosives including gunpowder and safety fuses. (11) Insecticides, fungicides, weedicides and the like. (12) Textile auxiliaries. (13) Sizing materials including starch. (14) Miscellaneous chemicals.

20. **Photographic Raw Film and Paper**: (1) Cinema film. (2) Photographic amateur film. (3) Photographic printing paper.

21. **Dye-Stuffs**: Dye-stuffs.

22. **Drugs and Pharmaceuticals**: Drugs and Pharmaceuticals.

23. **Textiles (Including those Dyed, Printed or Otherwise Processed)**: (1) Made wholly or in part of cotton, including cotton yarn, hosiery and rope, (2) Made wholly or in part of jute, including jute twine and rope. (3) Made wholly or in part of wool, including wool tops, woollen yarn, hosiery, carpets and druggets; (4) Made wholly or in part of silk, including silk yarn and hosiery; (5) Made wholly or in part of synthetic, artificial (man-made) fibers, including yarn and hosiery of such fibers.

24. **Paper and Pulp including Paper Products**: (1) Paper—writing, printing and wrapping. (2) Newsprint. (3) Paper board and straw board. (4) Paper for packaging (corrugated paper, Kraft paper), bags, paper containers and the like. (5) Pulp—wood pulp, mechanical, chemical, including dissolving pulp.

25. **Sugar**: Sugar.

26. **Fermentation Industries (Other than Potable Alcohol):** (1) Alcohol. (2) Other products of fermentation industries

27. **Food Processing Industries**: (1) Canned fruits and fruit products. (2) Milk foods. (3) Malted foods. (4) Flour. (5) Other processed foods.

28. **Vegetable Oils and Vanaspati:** (1) Vegetable oils, including solvent extracted oils. (2) Vanaspati.

29. **Soaps, Cosmetics and Toilet Preparations**: (1) Soaps. (2) Glycerine. (3) Cosmetics. (4) Perfumery (5) Toilet preparations.

30. **Rubber Goods**: (1) Tyres and tubes. (2) Surgical and medicinal products including prophylactics. (3) Footwear. (4) Other rubber goods.1. Subs. by Act 27 of 2016, s.3, for "26. FERMENTATION INDUSTRIES:" (w.e.f. 14-5-2016).

31. **Leather, Leather Goods and Pickers**: Leather, leather goods and pickers.

32. **Glue and Gelatin**: Glue and gelatin.

33. **Glass**: (1) Hollow ware. (2) Sheet and plate glass. (3) Optical glass. (4) Glass wool. (5) Laboratory ware. (6) Miscellaneous ware.

34. **Ceramics**: (1) Fire bricks. (2) Refractories. (3) Furnace lining bricks—acidic, basic and neutral. (4) China ware and pottery. (5) Sanitary ware. (6) Insulators. (7) Tiles.1 [8] Graphite Crucibles.]

35. **Cement and Gypsum Products**: (1) Portland cement. (2) Asbestos cement. (3) Insulating boards. (4) Gypsum boards, wall boards and the like.

36. **Timber Products**: (1) Plywood. (2) Hardboard, including fiber-board, chip-board and the like. (3) Matches. (4) Miscellaneous (furniture components, bobbins, shutters and the like).

37. **Defence Industries:** Arms and ammunition.

38. **Miscellaneous Industries**: 2 [(1)] Cigarettes.3 [(2) Linoleum, whether felt based or jute based.] 1. Ins. by Act 17 of 1979, s.3 (w.e.f. 30-12-1978). 2. Item "Cigarettes" re-numbered as item (1) thereof by Act 67 of 1973, s.4 (w.e.f. 7-2-1974). 3. Ins. by s.4, ibid. (w.e.f. 7-2-1974). 36 1 [(3) Zip fasteners (metallic and non-metallic). (4) Oil Stoves. (5) Printing, including litho printing industry.]

Explanation 1.—The articles specified under each of the headings Nos.3, 4, 5, 6, 7, 8, 10, 11 and 13 shall include their component parts and accessories. Explanation 2.—The articles specified under each of the headings Nos.18, 19, 21, and 22 shall include the intermediates required for their manufacture.]

References

1. Das, R.K.(1941). *History of Indian Labour Legislation.* Calcutta: University of Calcutta
2. *Handbook of Legal Clarifications.* (1963). New Delhi: Employees' Provident Fund Organisation
3. Renton, Q.L. (1990) Current Drafting Practices and Problems in the United Kingdom. *Statute Law Review*, 11 (14).
4. *Savings in a Welfare State* by V.R. Mutalik Desai (1966) P.C. Manaktalas & Sons Pvt Ltd., Bombay
5. *Labour Investigation Report*, 1946 published by the Manager, Publication Dept., Government of India.
6. *Annual Report on the working of the EPF Scheme*, 1952 for period 1953–54
7. *Provident Fund for Workers,* D.G. Damle, Labour Officer, East India Cotton Association, Bombay
8. *Parliamentary Debates*, Official Report, Volume 41, Issue 1–10
9. B.S. Narula. (1963). *The Abolition of the Labour Appellate Tribunal.* New Delhi: The Indian Institute of Public Administration.
10. R.C. Saxena. (1952). *Labour Problems and Social Welfare.* Meerut: Jai Prakash Nath & Co.
11. S.K. Wadhawan. (1968, March). Employees' Provident Fund Scheme – Development and Future Plans. *Indian Labour Journal, IX* (3).

Index

Actionable Claim 249
actus reus 202, 203, 205, 207
Adhoc payment 68
adversary system 147
Advice by Central Government 394
aid of power' 373
Appellate Tribunal 93, 123, 141, 152, 157, 171, 174, 184, 186, 187, 190, 205, 207, 221, 229, 231, 288, 299, 313, 415, 428, 440
Appointment of Receiver 310
Apprentices 13, 89, 91
Appropriate Government 60
Arrest and Detention 294
Article 254 378
Assessment 148, 163, 169, 265
Attachment 240, 271, 274, 276, 277, 280, 281, 301, 308, 310
Automobile Industry 408

Basic Wages 60, 61
Beveridge Report 20
BIFR See Sick Industrial Companies
Burden of Proof 46, 159

Cancellation of Exemption 364, 368
Canteen Allowance 73
Casual Employees 80
Central Board of Trustees 64, 80, 102, 118, 141, 143, 190, 193, 228, 229, 234, 325, 344, 373
Central Government Industrial Tribunals 184
Certiorari 415

Cinema Theatres 51, 404
Civil Prison 294
civil process 272
Closure of Establishment 51
Cognizable offence 346
Companies Act 13, 102, 109, 138, 248, 251, 253, 257, 313, 351
Compounding of charges 347
Concurrent List 377
Confirmation of Sale 281
Constitutional Validity 39, 262
Consumer Protection Act 428, 430
Contingent Debt 275
Contractors' Liability 131
Controlled Industry 74, 435
Conviction 350
Cooperatives 372
Court attachment 241
Criminal Breach of Trust 353, 356, 359
Criminal Revision Petition 330, 362
Cross-Examination 159
Crown Debt 248

Deemed Misuse of Money See Criminal breach of trust
Delegation of Powers 392
Demand Notice 265
Double Punishment 200
Due process of law 297

Educational Institutions 411
Electrical, Mechanical or General Engineering Products 397

Index

Employees' Deposit-Linked Insurance Scheme, 1976 433
Employees' Pension Scheme, 1995 430
Employees' Provident Funds Scheme, 1952 420
Engineering Contractors 407
Escaped amount 182
Exclusion 376
Exempted Trust 370
Exemption 363
Exonerating Factors 221

Garnishee order 319
Gazette notification 363
General Clauses Act 57, 155, 198, 268, 361, 392
Good Faith clause 391

Heavy and Fine Chemicals 408
Holding Company 138
Homeworkers 78
Hospital 48, 136, 182, 402, 404

Income Tax (Certificate Proceedings) Rules, 1962 260, 320
Independent Contractor 97, 129
Infancy Protection 376
inquisitorial system 147
insolvency 253, 257
Insolvency and Bankruptcy Code 257
Inspector 323

Judges (Protection) Act, 1985 176
Judicial Proceedings 178
Jurisdiction 233, 273, 413, 415, 419

Leave Encashment 66
legal fiction 38, 353, 355, 384
Legal Representatives 269

Lessee 382
Liquidator 48, 102, 246, 248, 251, 255, 278, 313, 315

Maharashtra Private Security Guards (Regulation of Employment and Welfare) Act, 1981 378
Marsh Plan 20
Mens rea 202, 353
Migrant Workers 421
Minority institutions 48
Multi-State Cooperative Bank 407

Newspaper Employees 404, 427
Nominee 242
Non-obstante clause 37
Notice Pay 68
Notice period 155

Onus of Proof 344
Overtime Allowance 72

P.B. Gajendragadkar 260
Partition of the Establishment 53
Penal Damages 192, 197, 208
Pensionable Salary 430
Period of Limitation 182, 328, 332
Power to remove difficulties 394
preamble 23
Presumption of Service 155, 269
Principles of Natural Justice 153
Priority of Payment 246
Proclamation of Sale 283
Production Bonus 62
Prosecution 328
Protection against attachment 237
Public Servants 389

Question of Fact and Law 48

Ramanujam Committee 192, 194
Receiver See Appointment of Receiver
Reconstruction Company 387
Recovery Certificate 262
Rege Committee 20
Rules of Interpretation 29

Sale Certificate 281
SARFAESI Act 251, 387
Saw mills 410
Search and Seizure 326, 327
Service of Summons 153
Settlement allowance 70
SICA See Sick Industrial Companies
Sick Industrial Companies 14, 231, 255, 257, 315, 317, 344, 387
Speaking Order 166
Special Allowance 64
State Financial Corporation 246, 249, 251
Statement of Objects and Reasons 23, 26, 28, 30, 50
Stone quarries 410
Subsidiary Company 138

Subterfuge of wages 73
Suppression of facts 417

Testimonial compulsion 327
Textiles 207, 228, 287, 317, 339, 405, 407, 423, 438
The Cawnpore6 Labour Enquiry Committee 19
The Kerala Motor Transport Workers' Welfare Fund Act, 1985 378
Transfer of Liability 380
Trustees 141, 229, 359, 378, 389, 428

Unsecured Debts 246

Voluntary Coverage 55

Wagner-Murray-Dingell Bill 20
waiver 169, 197, 210, 229
Warrant of attachment 274
Whitely Commission 19
Willful Negligence 391
winding up 55, 253, 313, 317
Writ Jurisdiction 412

www.ingramcontent.com/pod-product-compliance
Lightning Source LLC
Chambersburg PA
CBHW020629220526
45464CB00001B/71